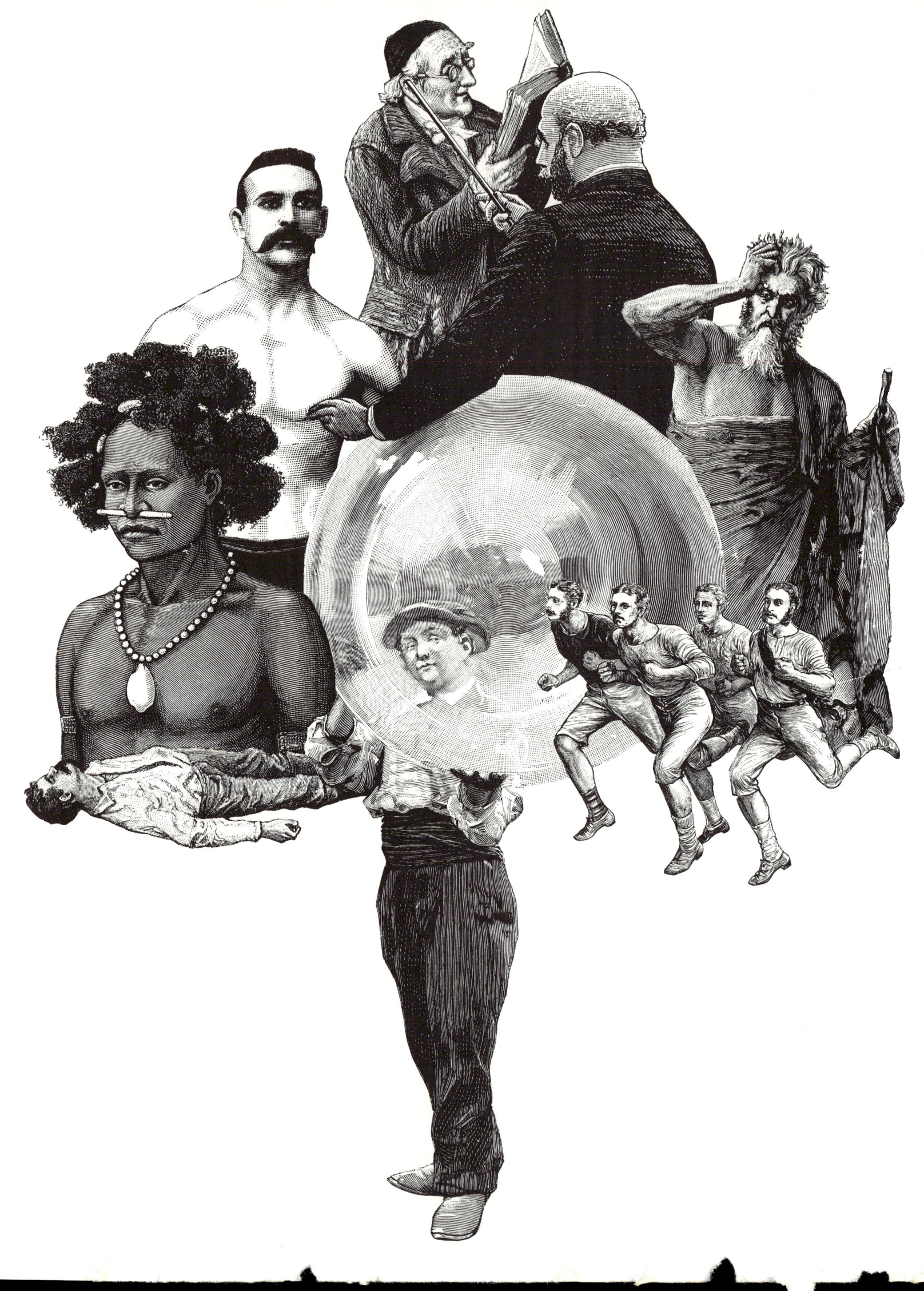

MEN

A PICTORIAL ARCHIVE FROM NINETEENTH-CENTURY SOURCES

412 Copyright-free Illustrations for Artists and Designers

Selected by
JIM HARTER

Dover Publications, Inc.
New York

Copyright © 1980 by Dover Publications, Inc.
All rights reserved under Pan American and International Copyright Conventions.

Published in Canada by General Publishing Company, Ltd., 30 Lesmill Road, Don Mills, Toronto, Ontario.

Men: A Pictorial Archive from Nineteenth-Century Sources is a new work, first published by Dover Publications, Inc., in 1980.

DOVER *Pictorial Archive* SERIES

This book belongs to the Dover Pictorial Archive Series. You may use the designs and illustrations for graphics and crafts applications, free and without special permission, provided that you include no more than ten in the same publication or project. (For permission for additional use, please write to Dover Publications, Inc., 31 East 2nd Street, Mineola, N.Y. 11501.)

However, republication or reproduction of any illustration by any other graphic service whether it be in a book or in any other design resource is strictly prohibited.

International Standard Book Number: 0-486-23952-7
Library of Congress Catalog Card Number: 79-56030

Manufactured in the United States of America
Dover Publications, Inc.
31 East 2nd Street
Mineola, N.Y. 11501

PUBLISHER'S NOTE

Wood engravings, with their crisp black-and-white lines, were popularized by Thomas Bewick at the end of the eighteenth century and quickly became the favored medium of mass reproduction of artwork in the nineteenth. While there were only about 20 wood engravers in the United States in 1838, by 1870 their number had swelled to about 400. Most of them earned their living by engraving illustrations for the great periodicals of the era, *Harper's Weekly* and *Leslie's Illustrated* foremost among them. With great skill the artists rendered sketches and photographs into precise illustrations. The medium admitted a wide variety of styles from simple, bold line drawings to those so carefully worked that the effect of gradation of tone was achieved, sometimes with an impressionistic feeling.

By the mid-1880s the means had become available for reproducing photographs as halftone illustrations, but they were both crude and expensive. It was not until the 1890s that the art of wood engraving began to be superseded by the new process. Ironically, now that the technique of the wood engraving has been largely lost, the popularity of these illustrations is reviving. Artists find the material widely adaptable to projects such as collage. Graphic designers are rediscovering how well the engravings complement typography.

Using his keen eye, artist Jim Harter has culled this selection from issues of *Harper's, Leslie's, Illustrated London News,* and more than twenty other sources. He has chosen the material to reflect both the diversity of the subject and the variety of styles of wood engraving. It has also been selected to be of maximum use to artists and designers.

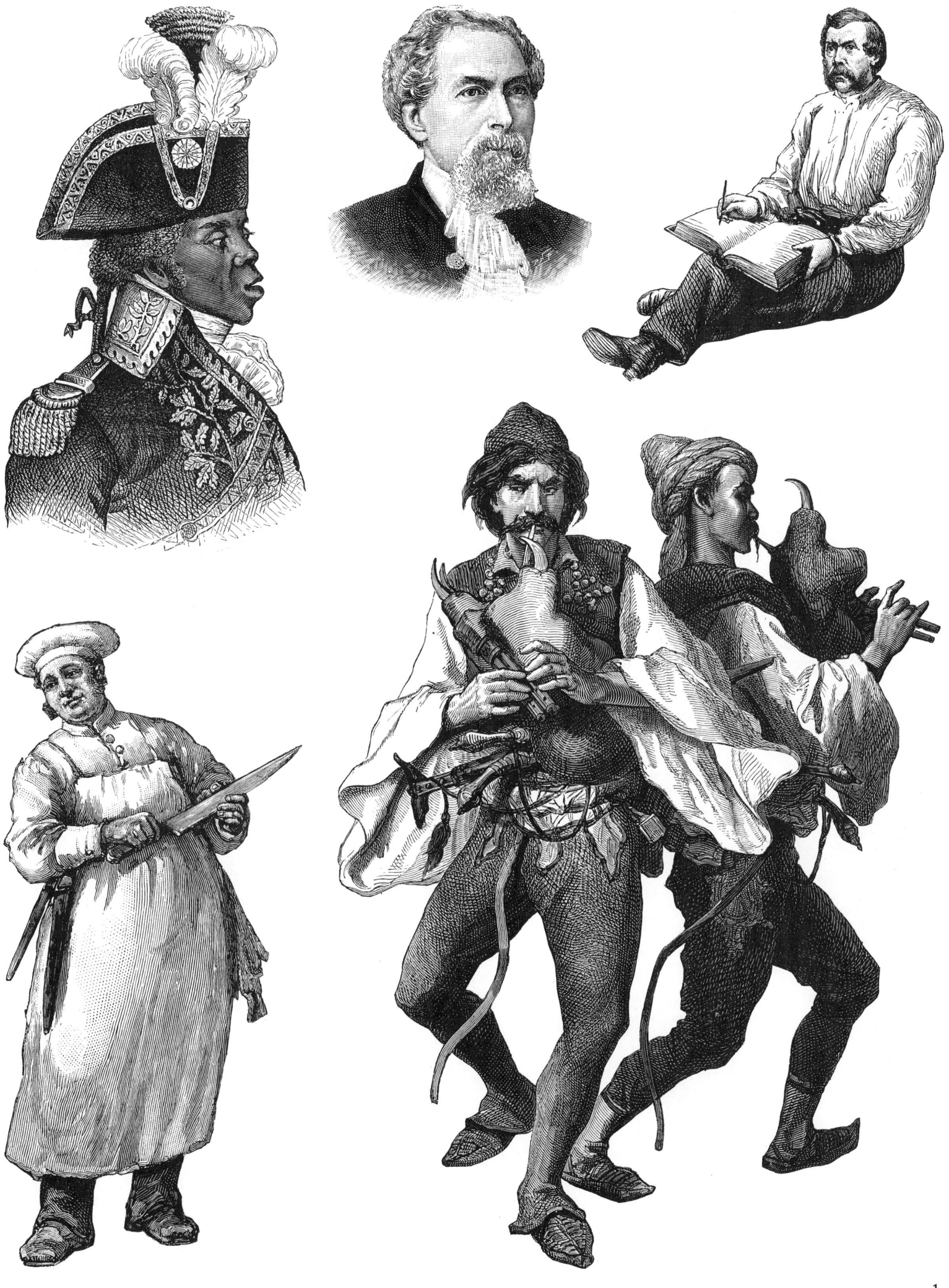

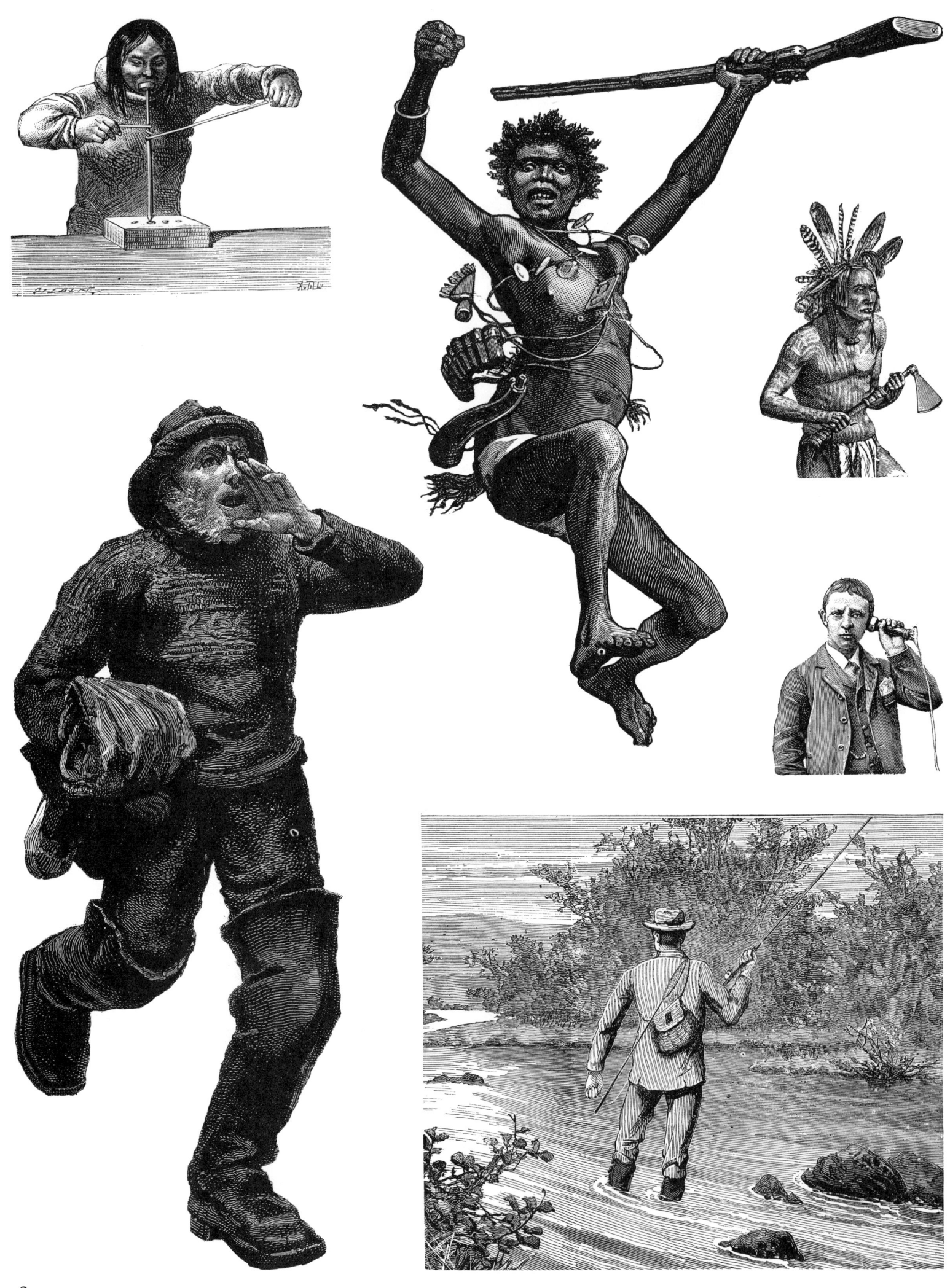

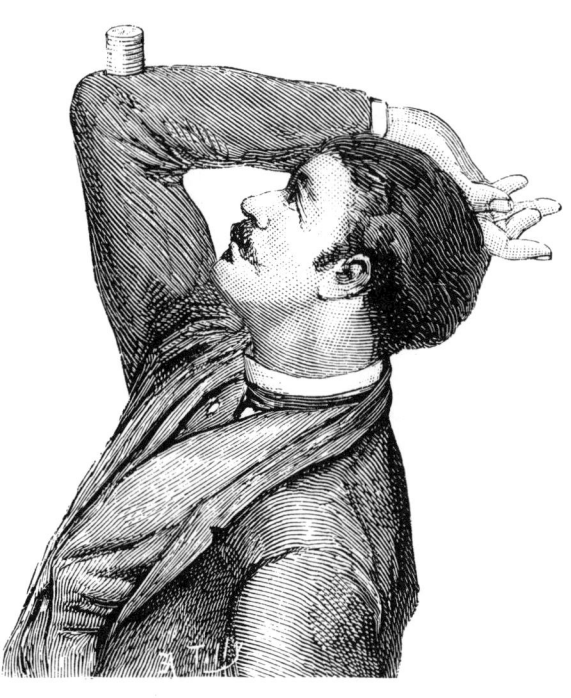
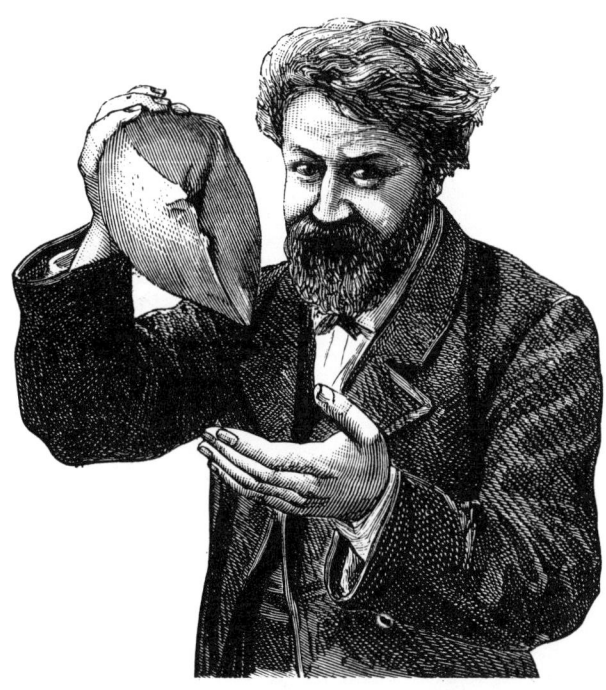
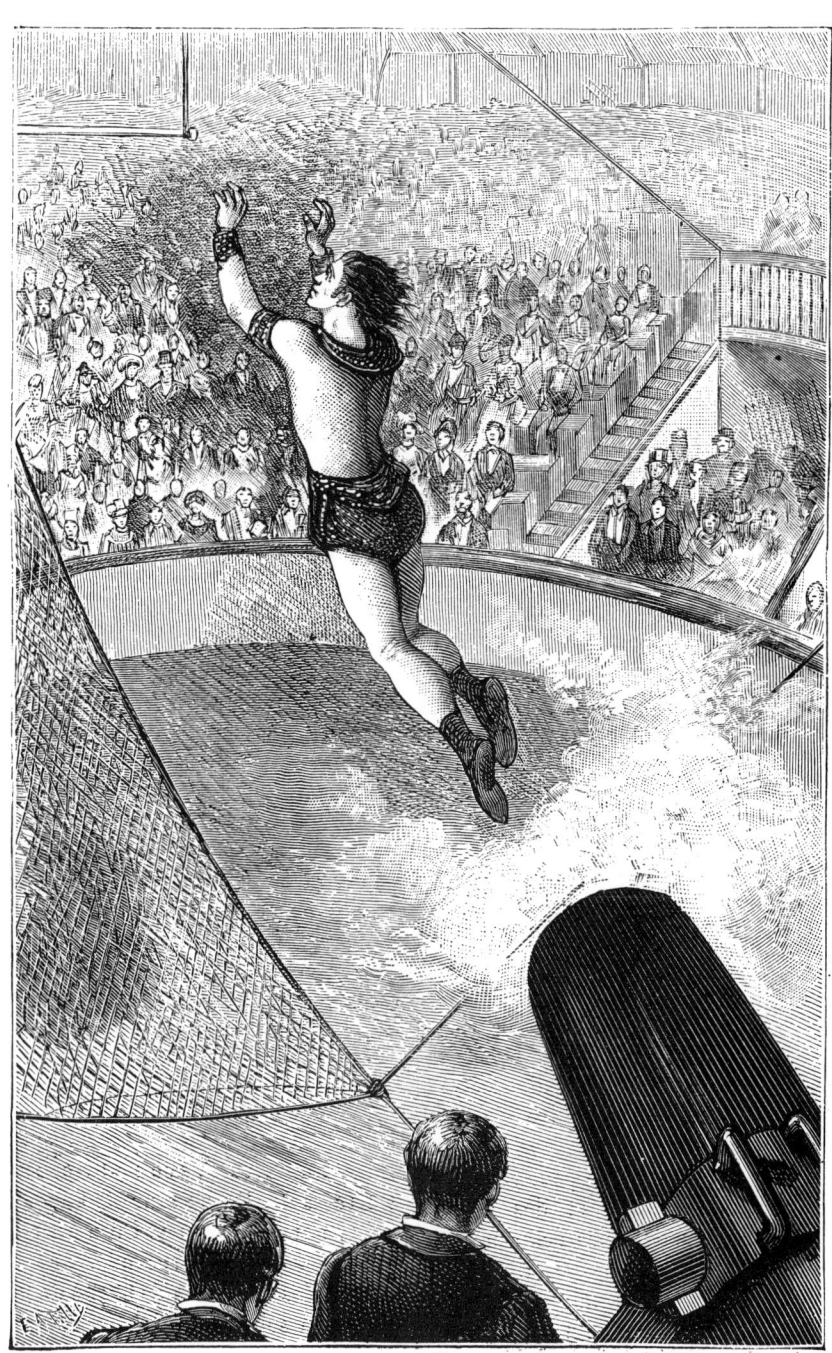
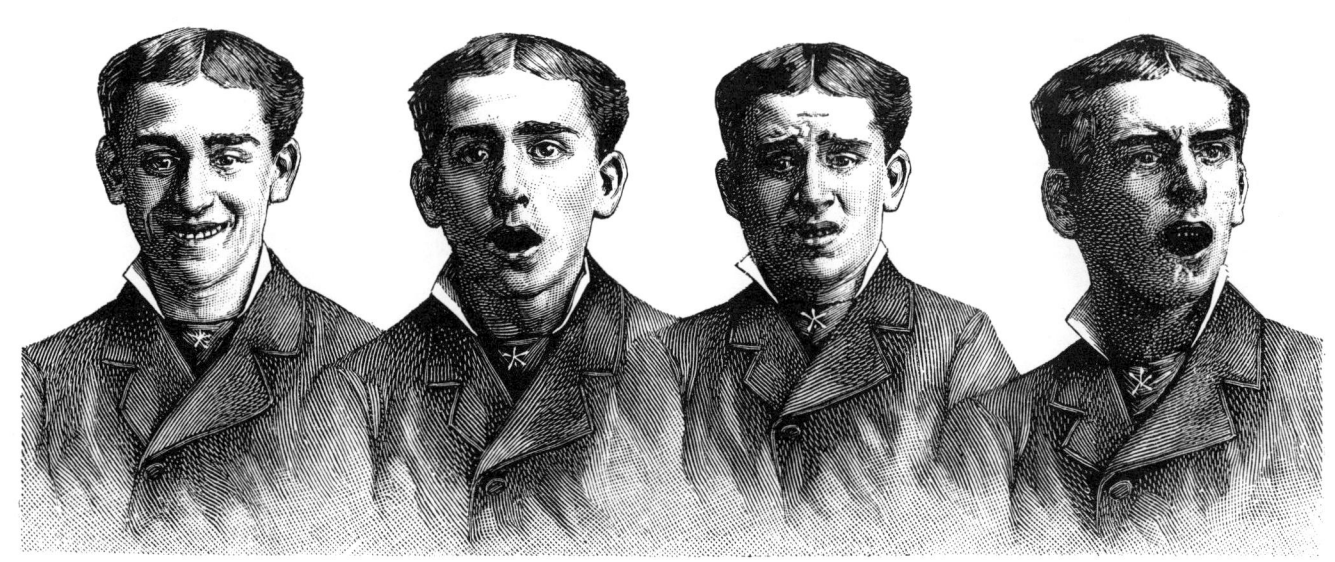

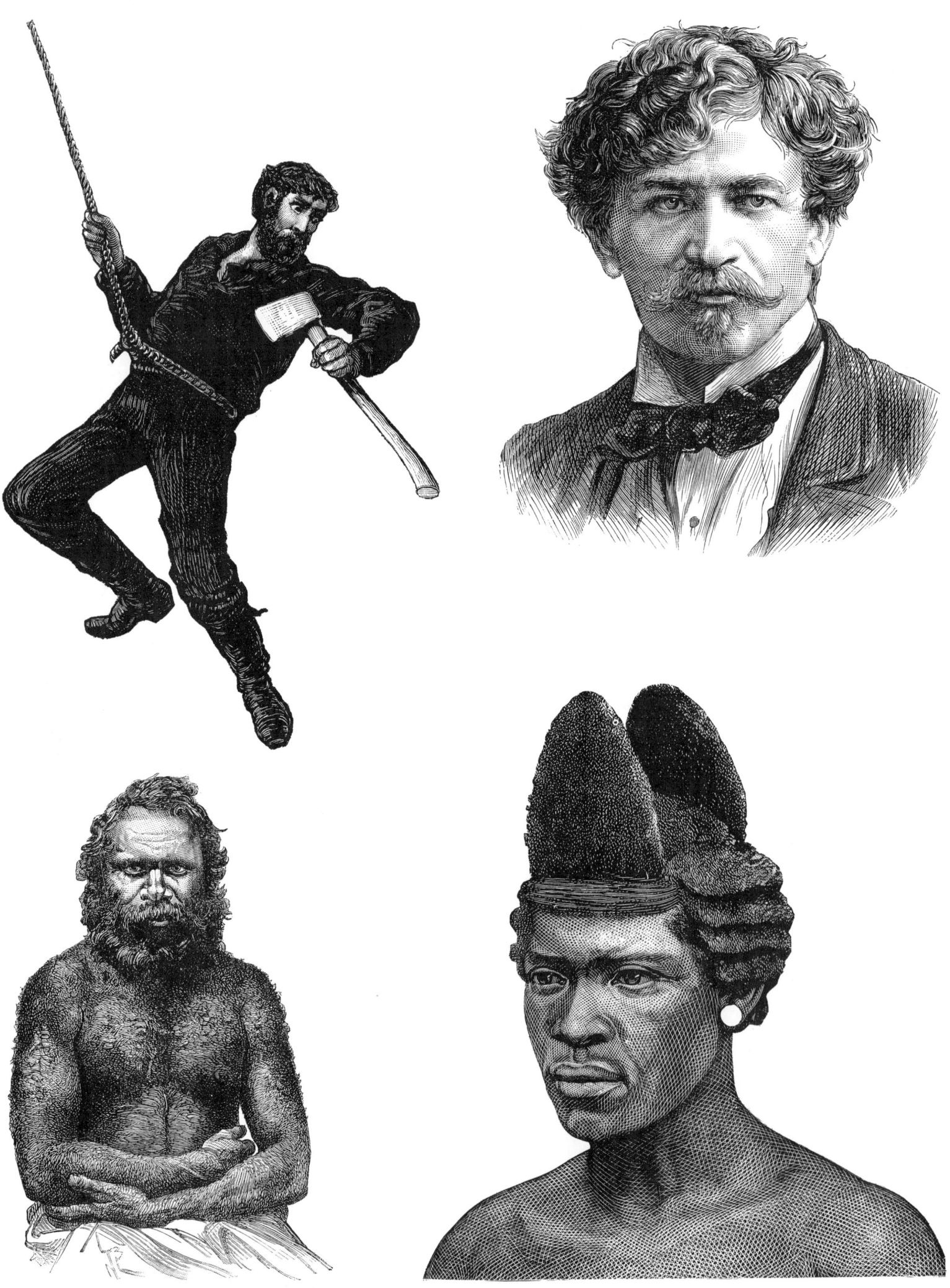

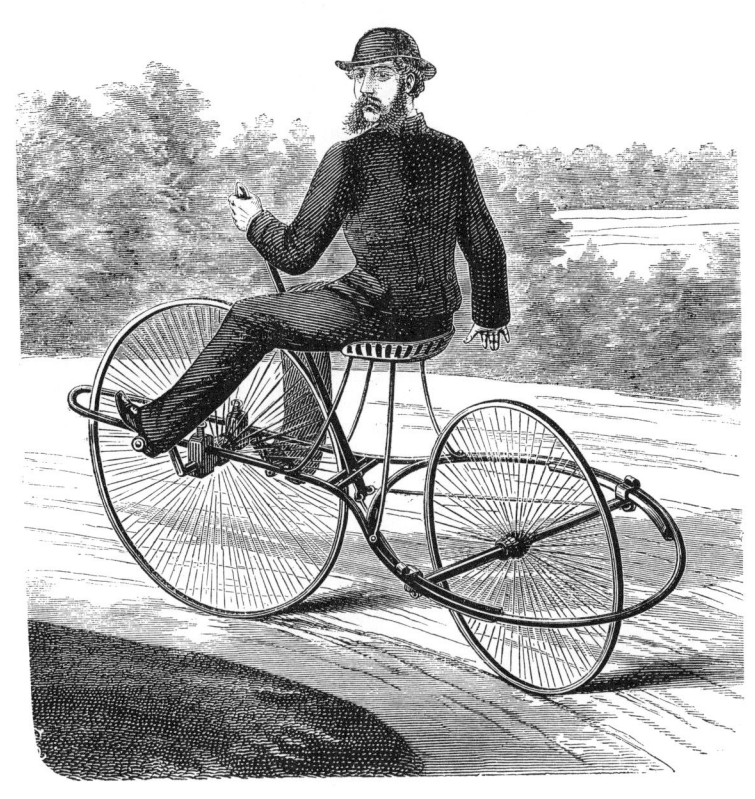
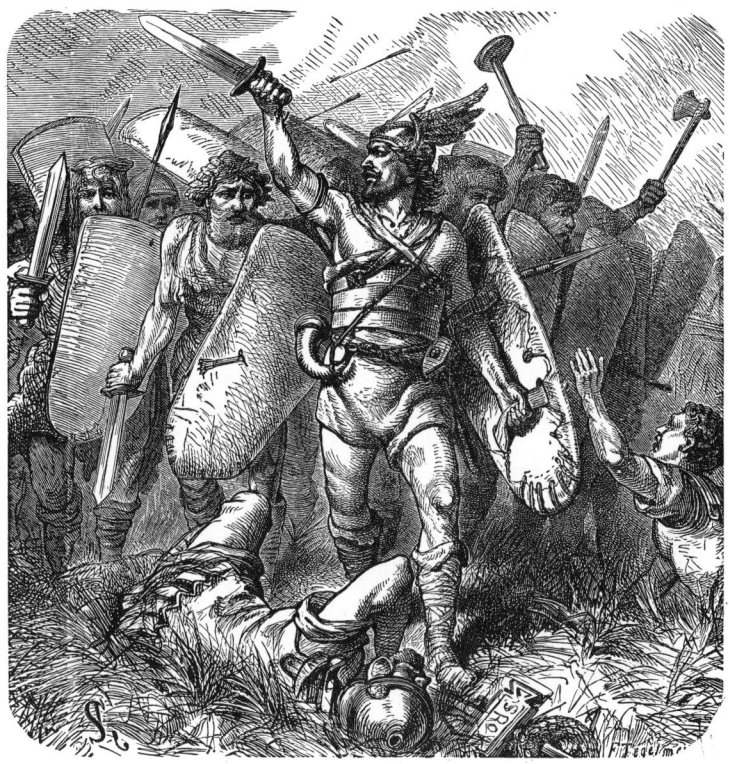

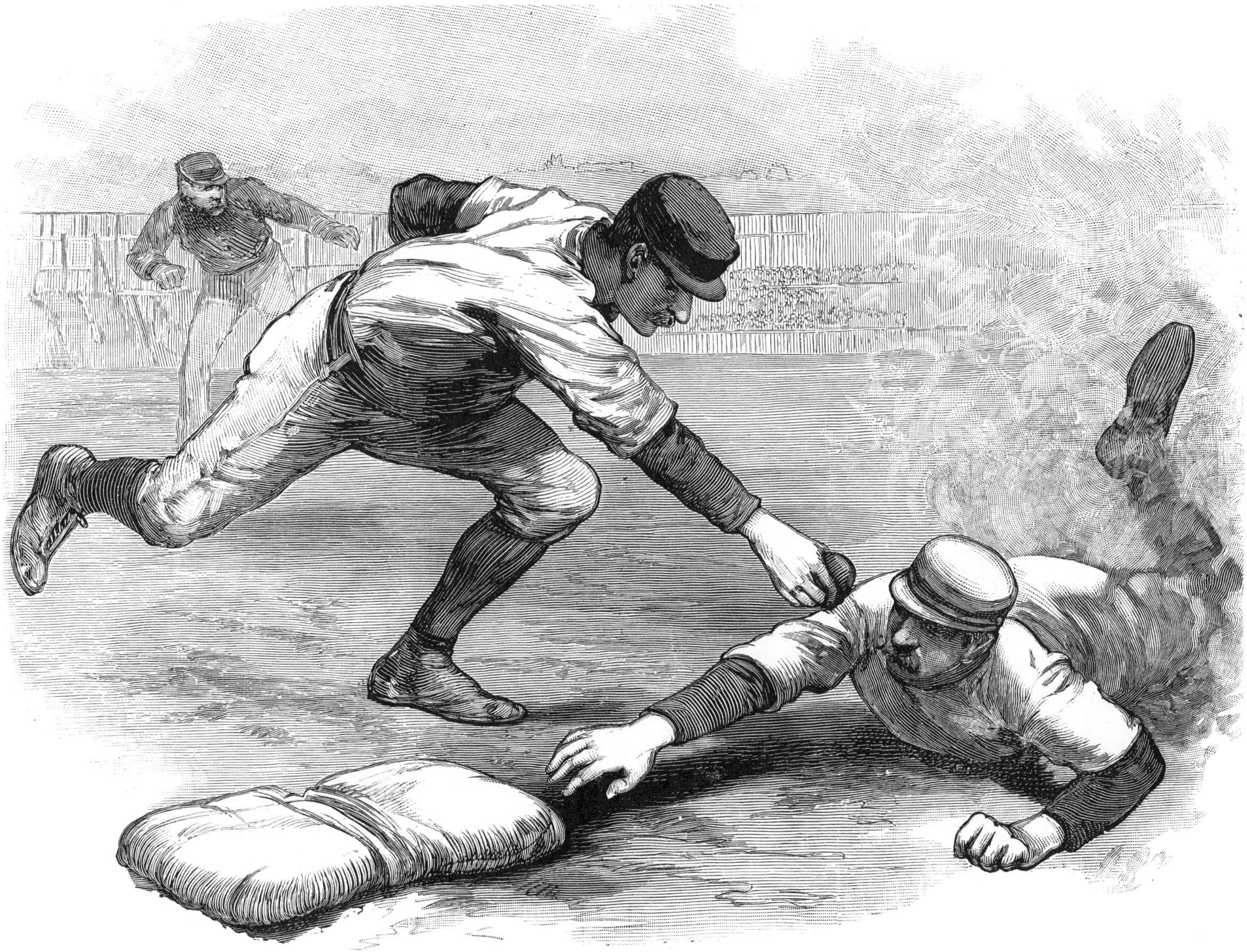

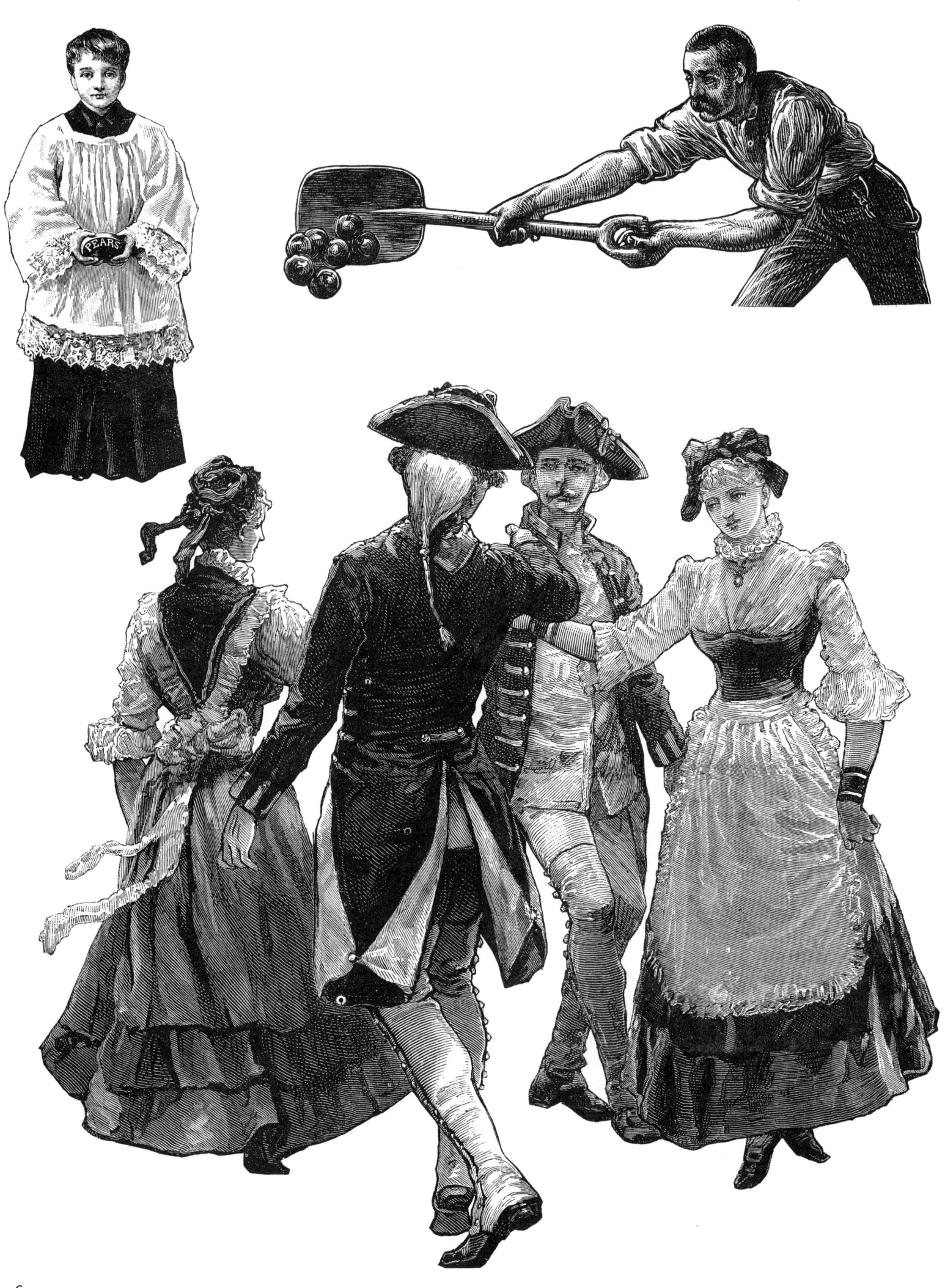

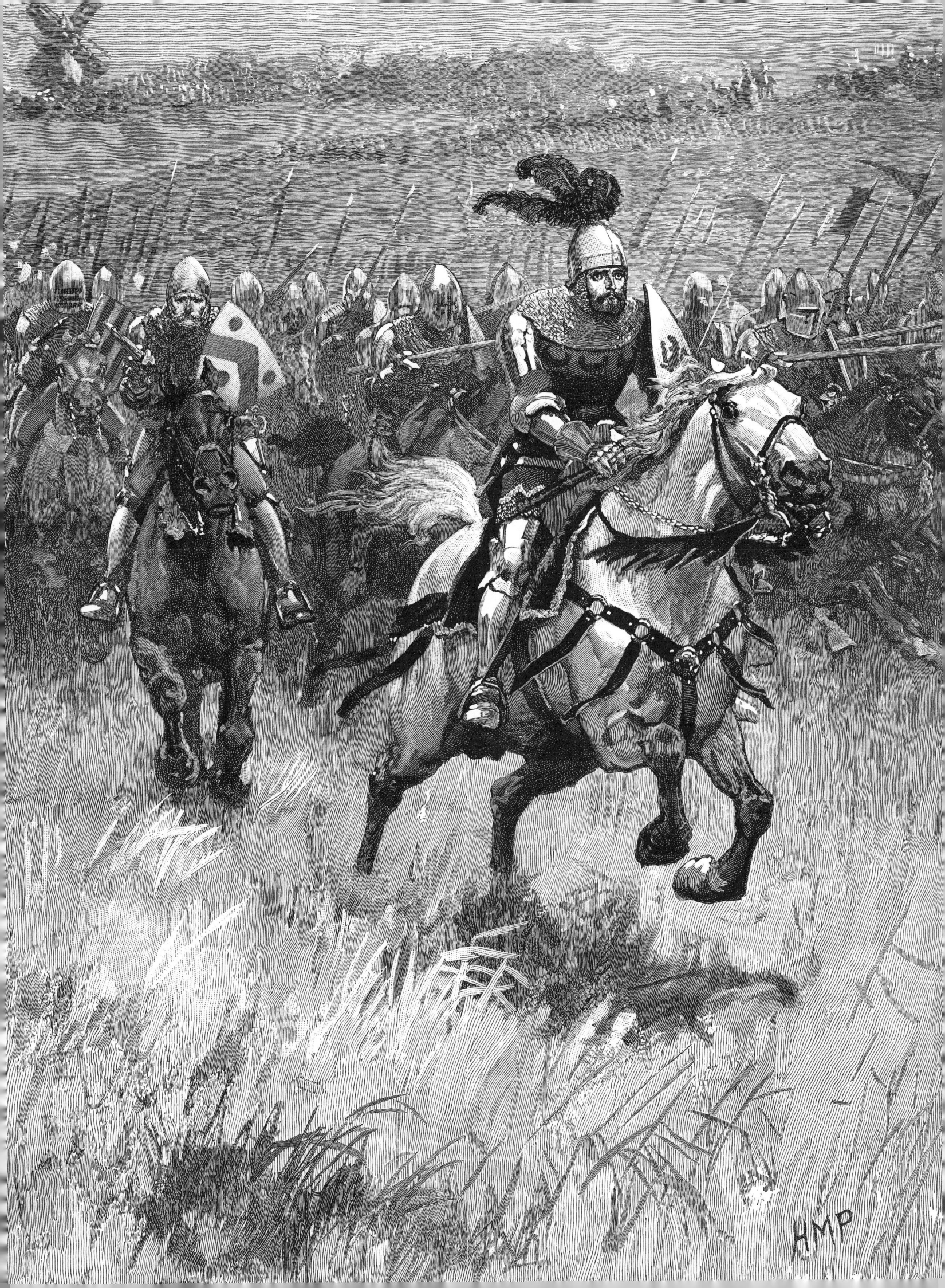

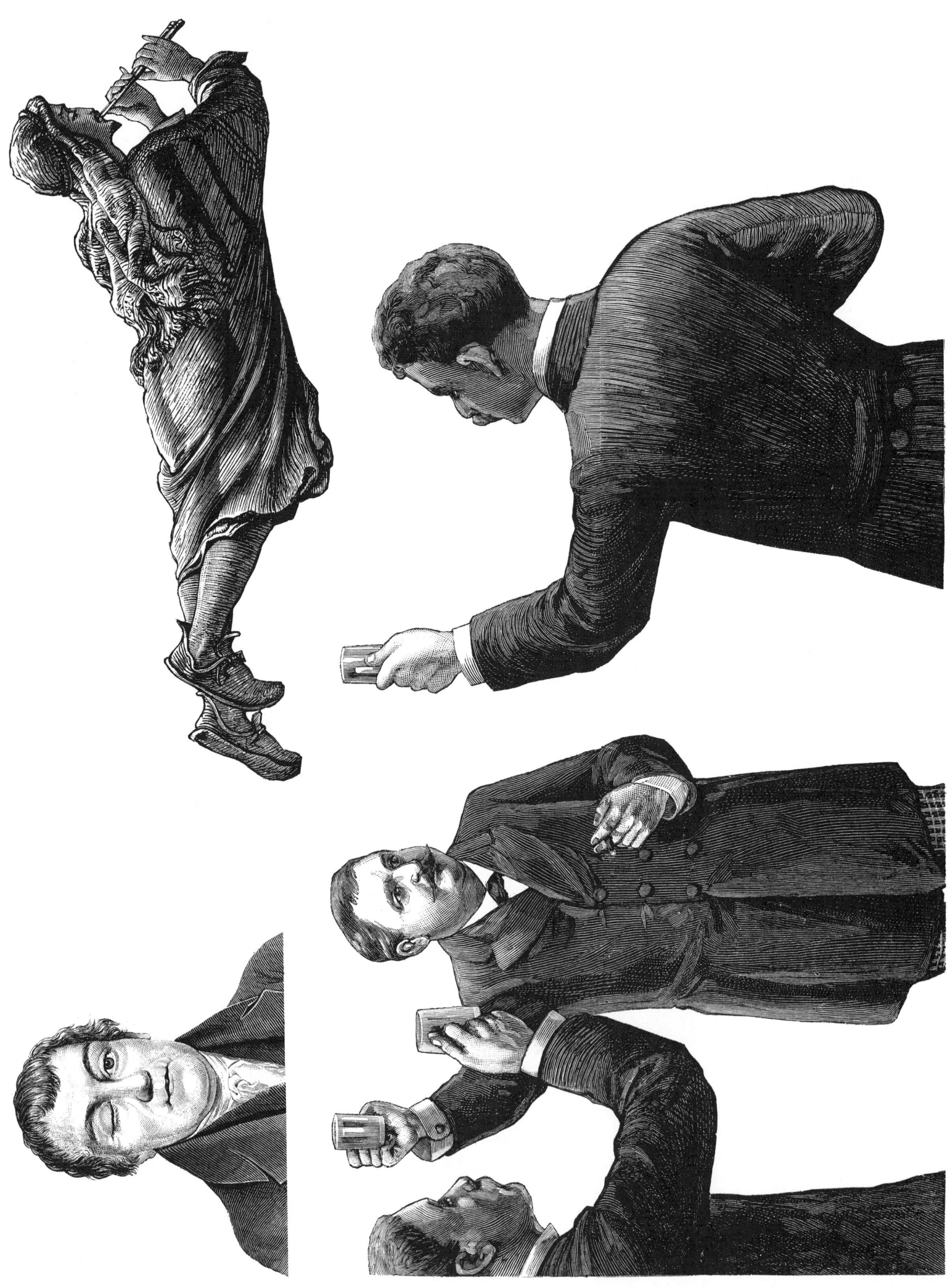

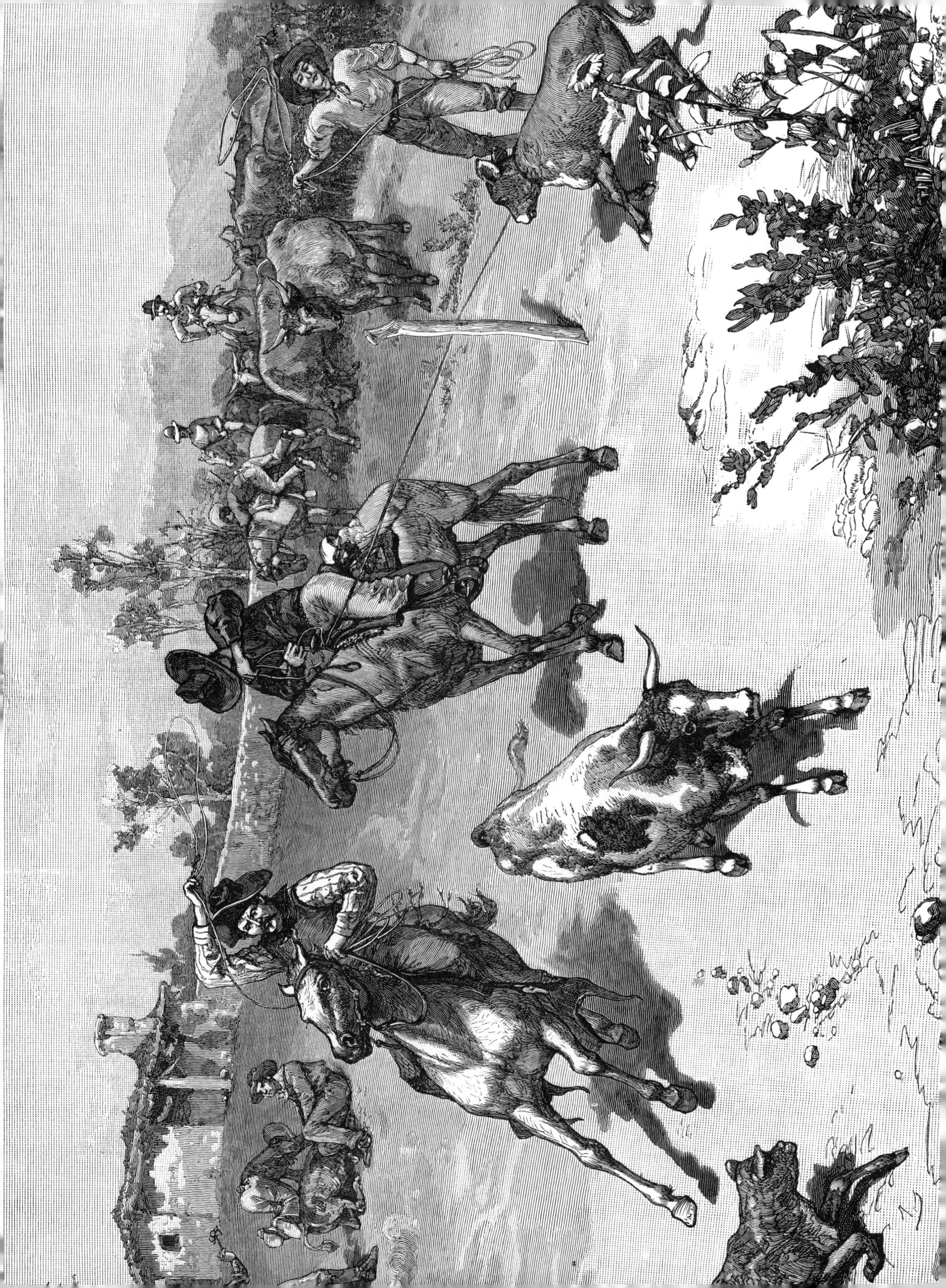

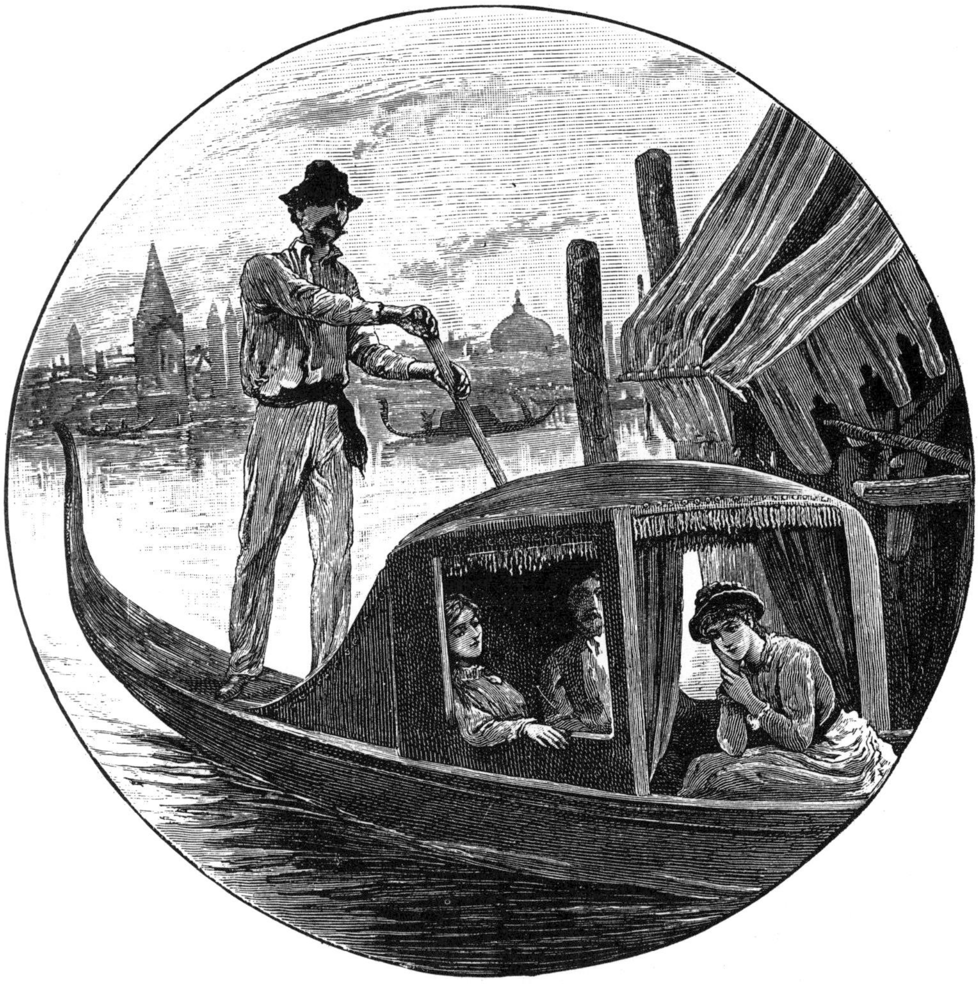

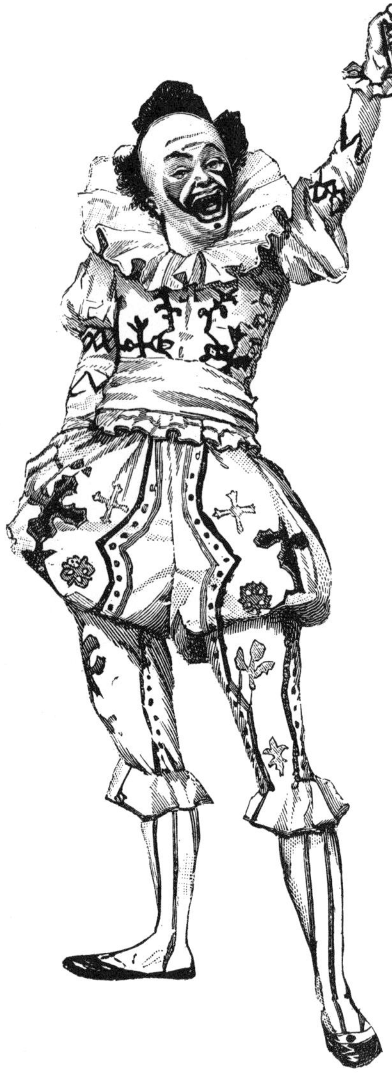

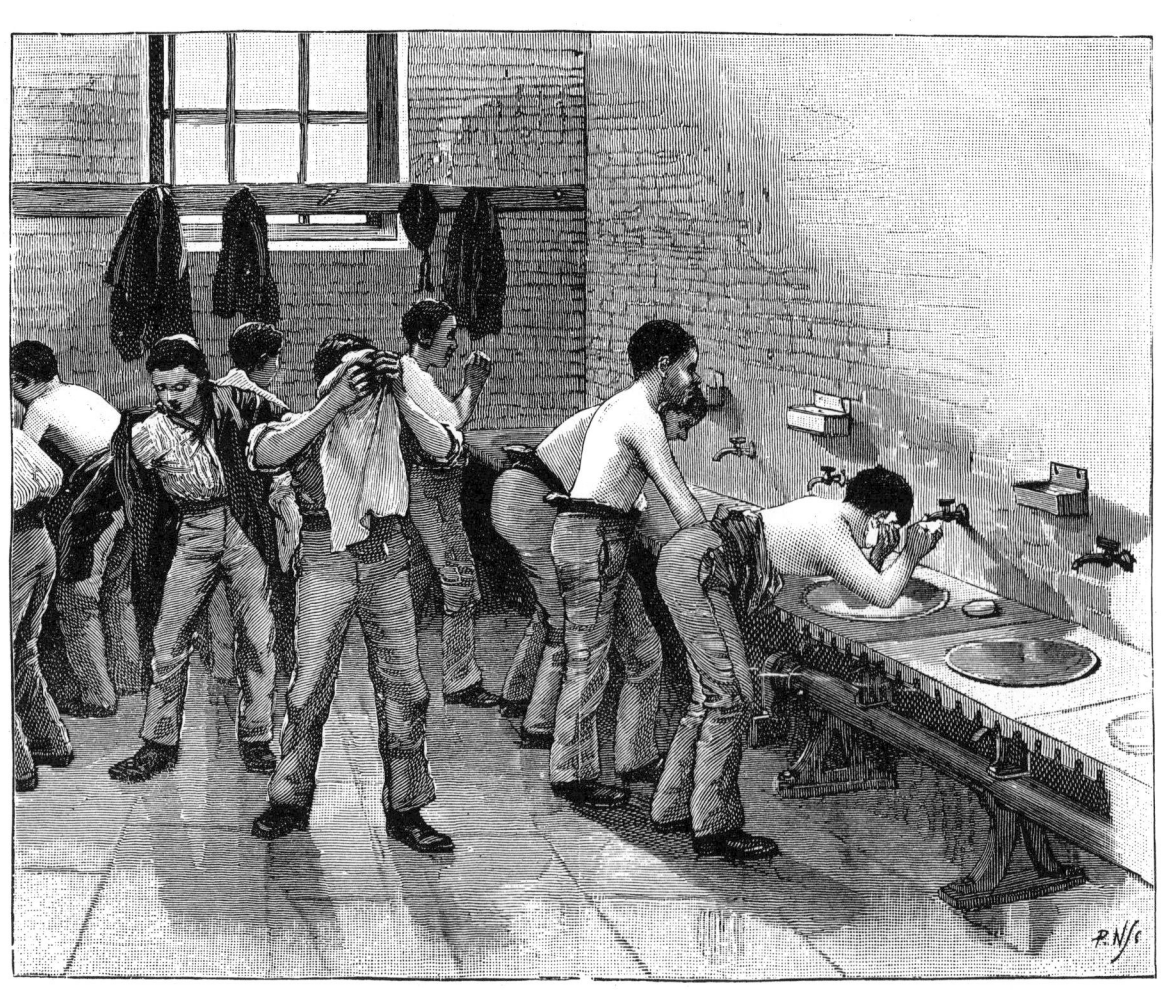

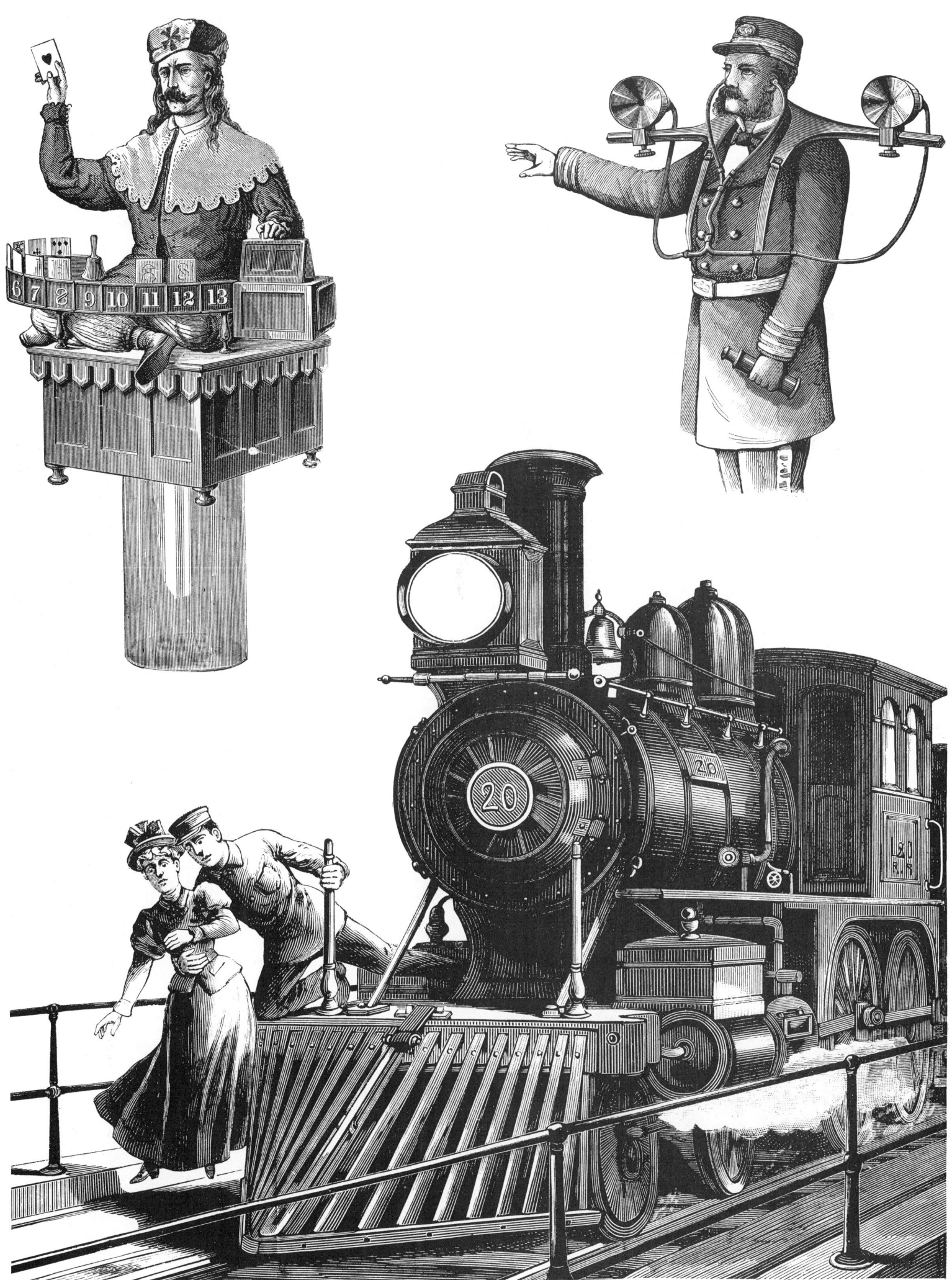

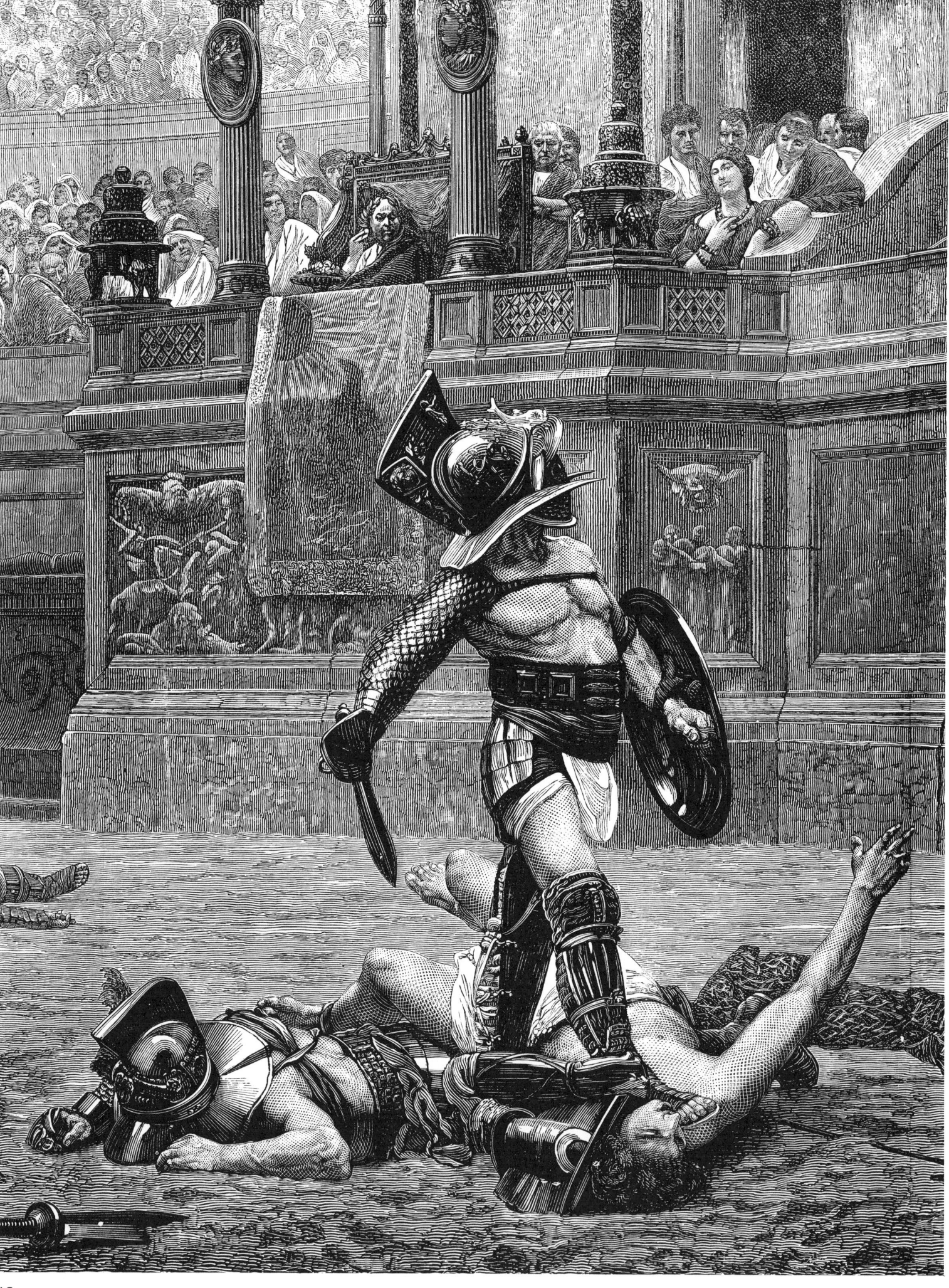

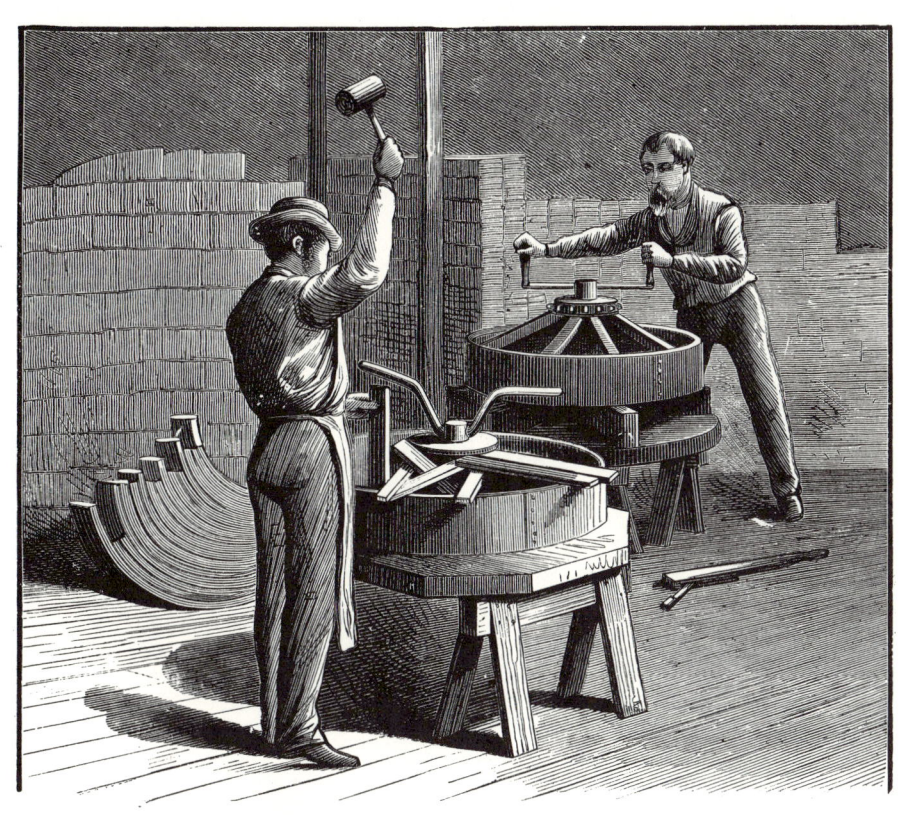
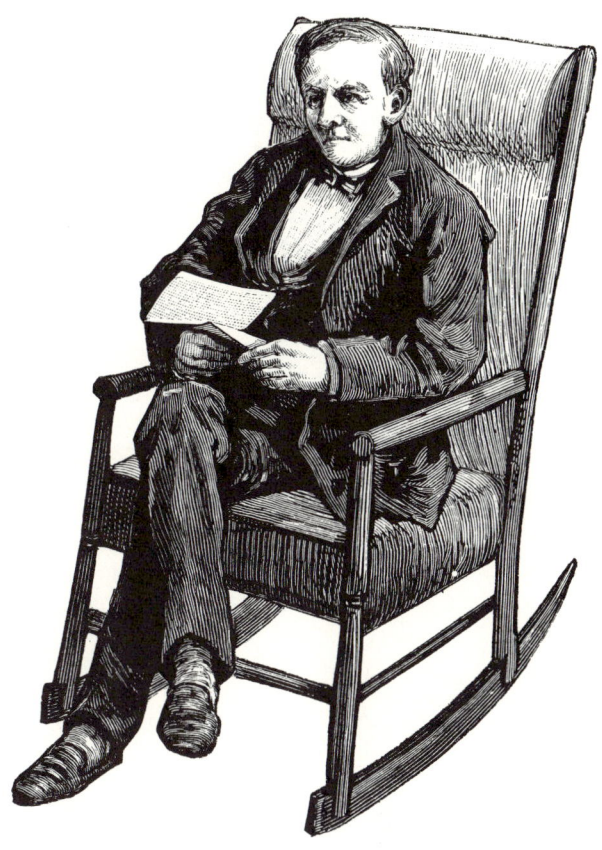
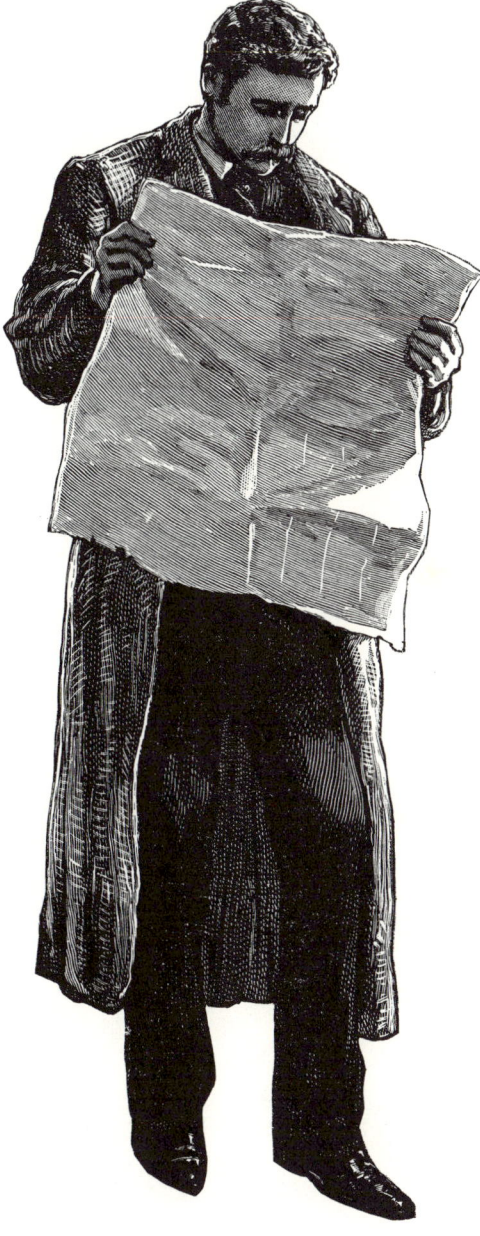
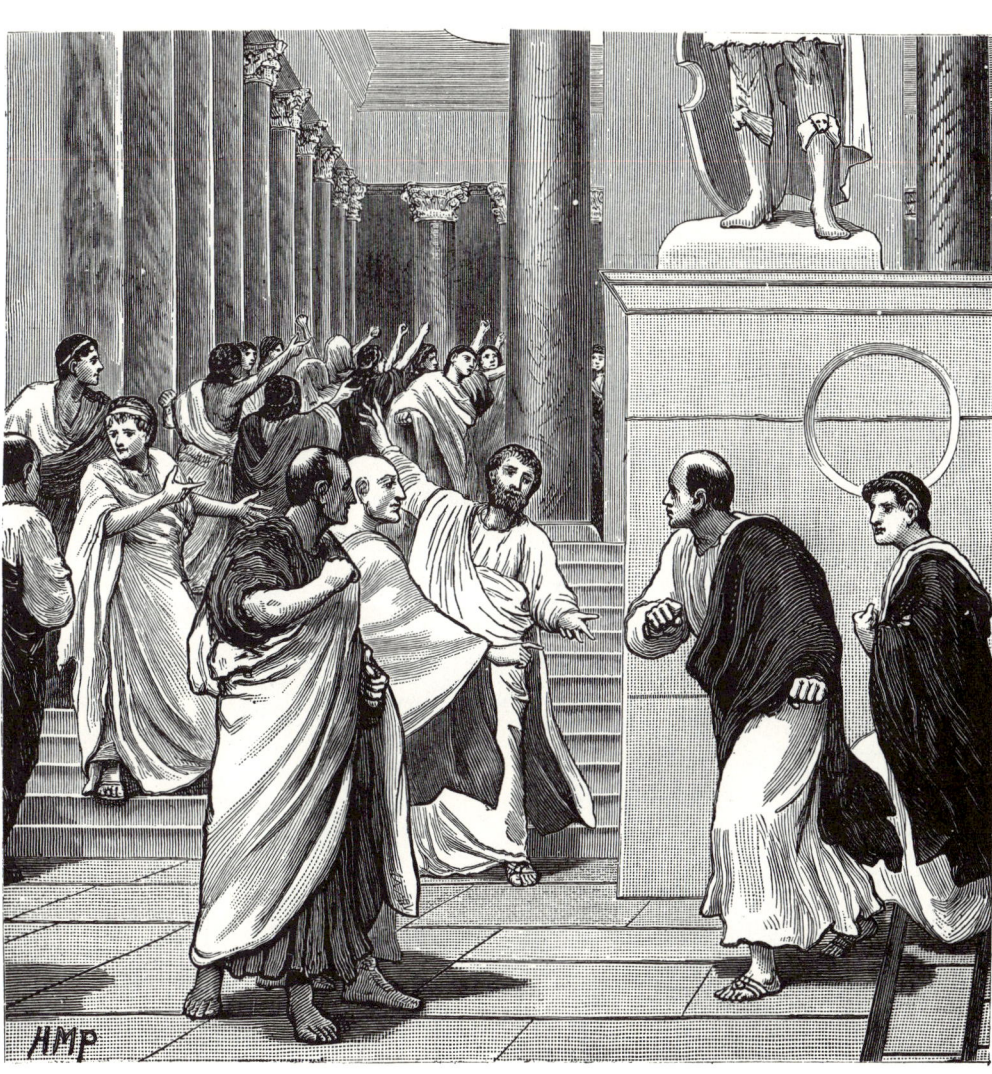

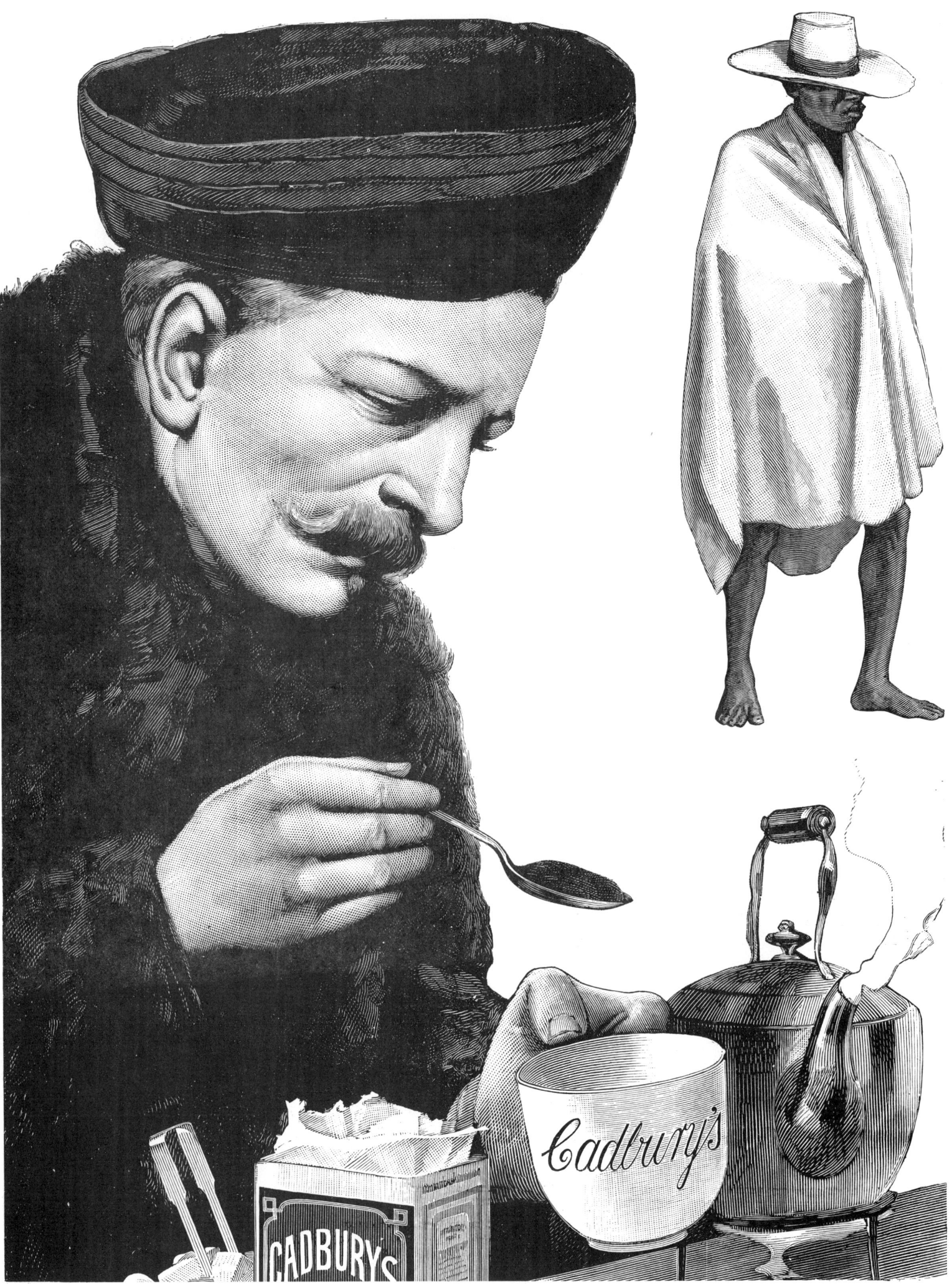

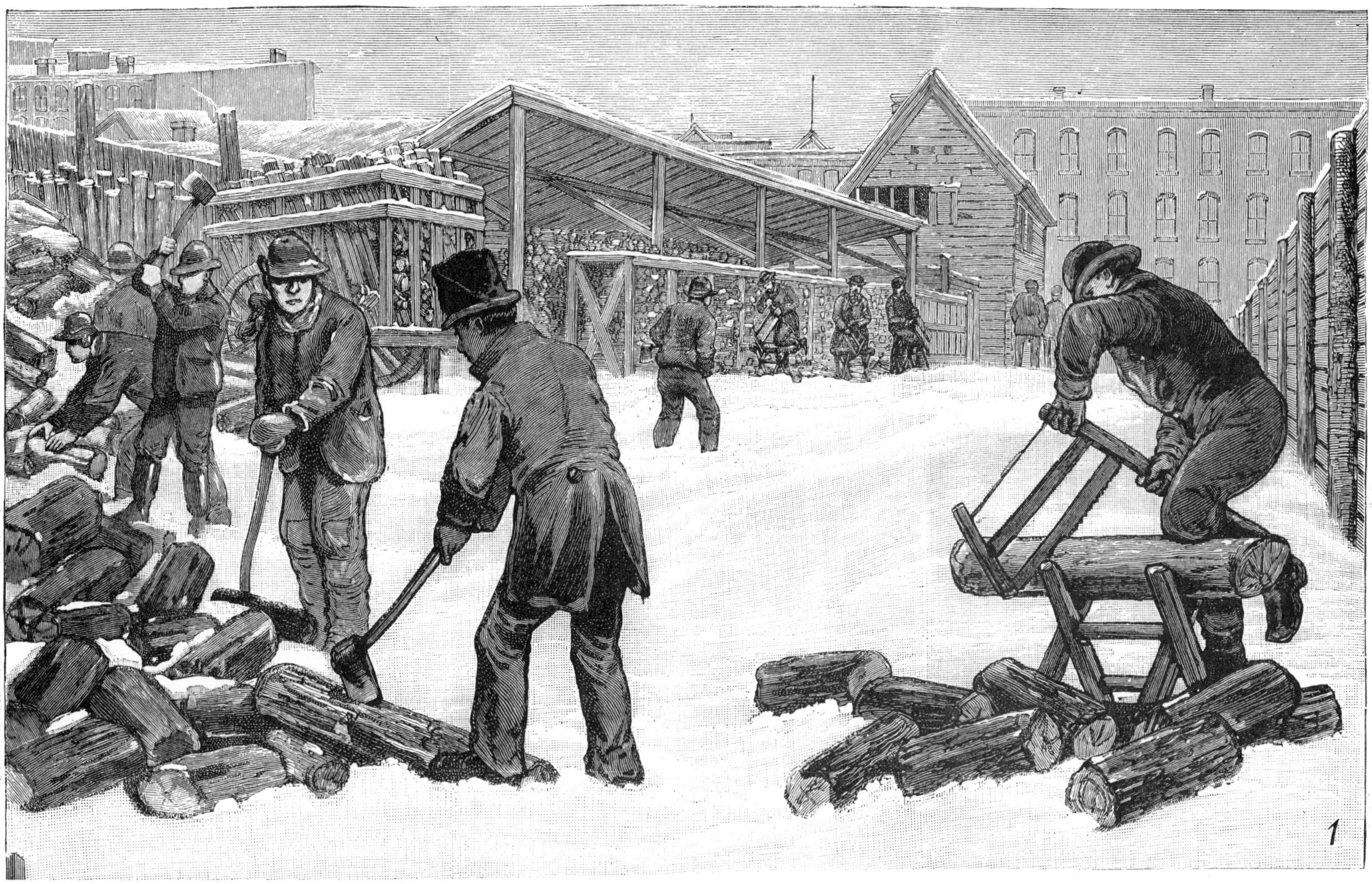

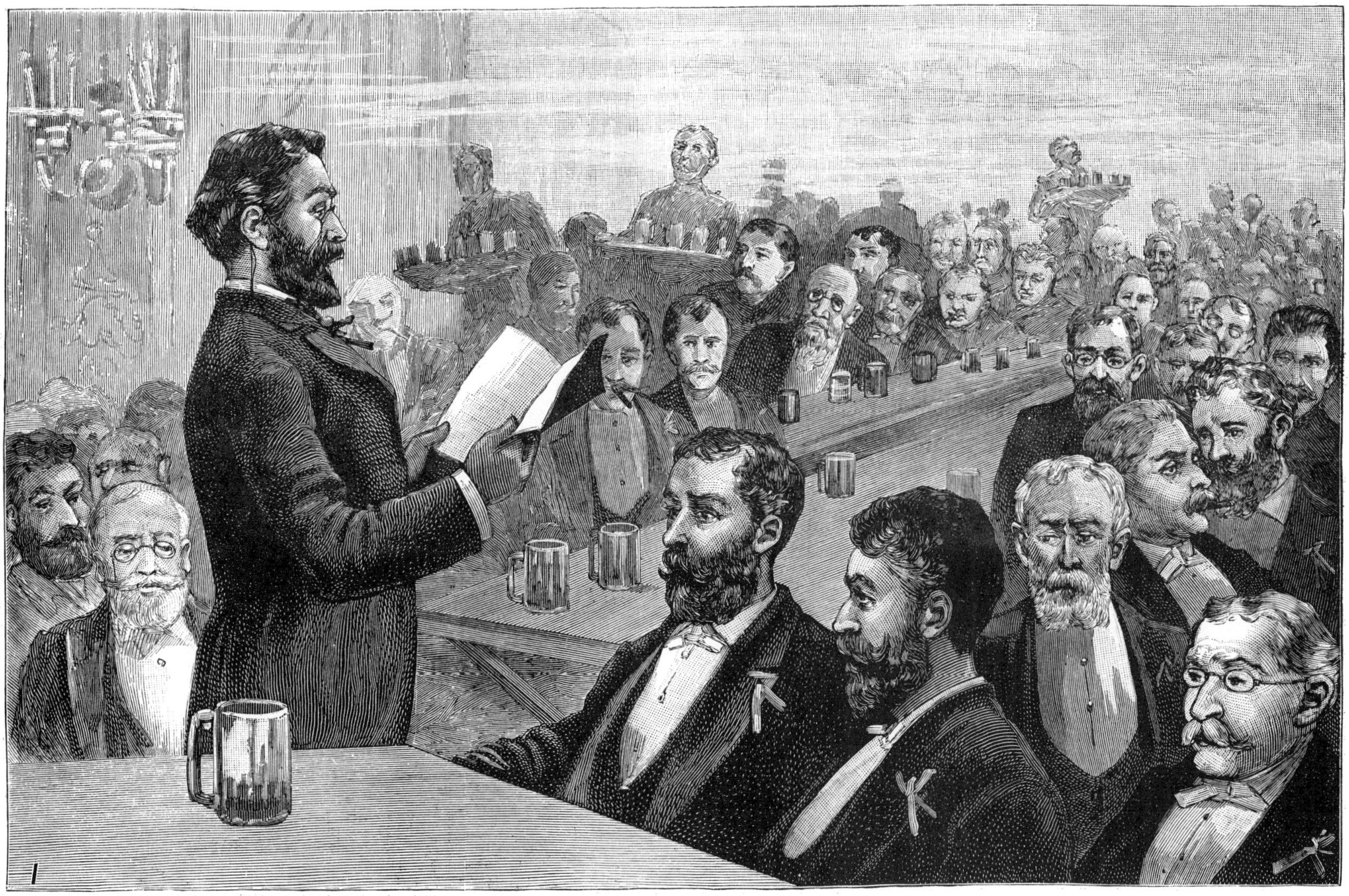

15

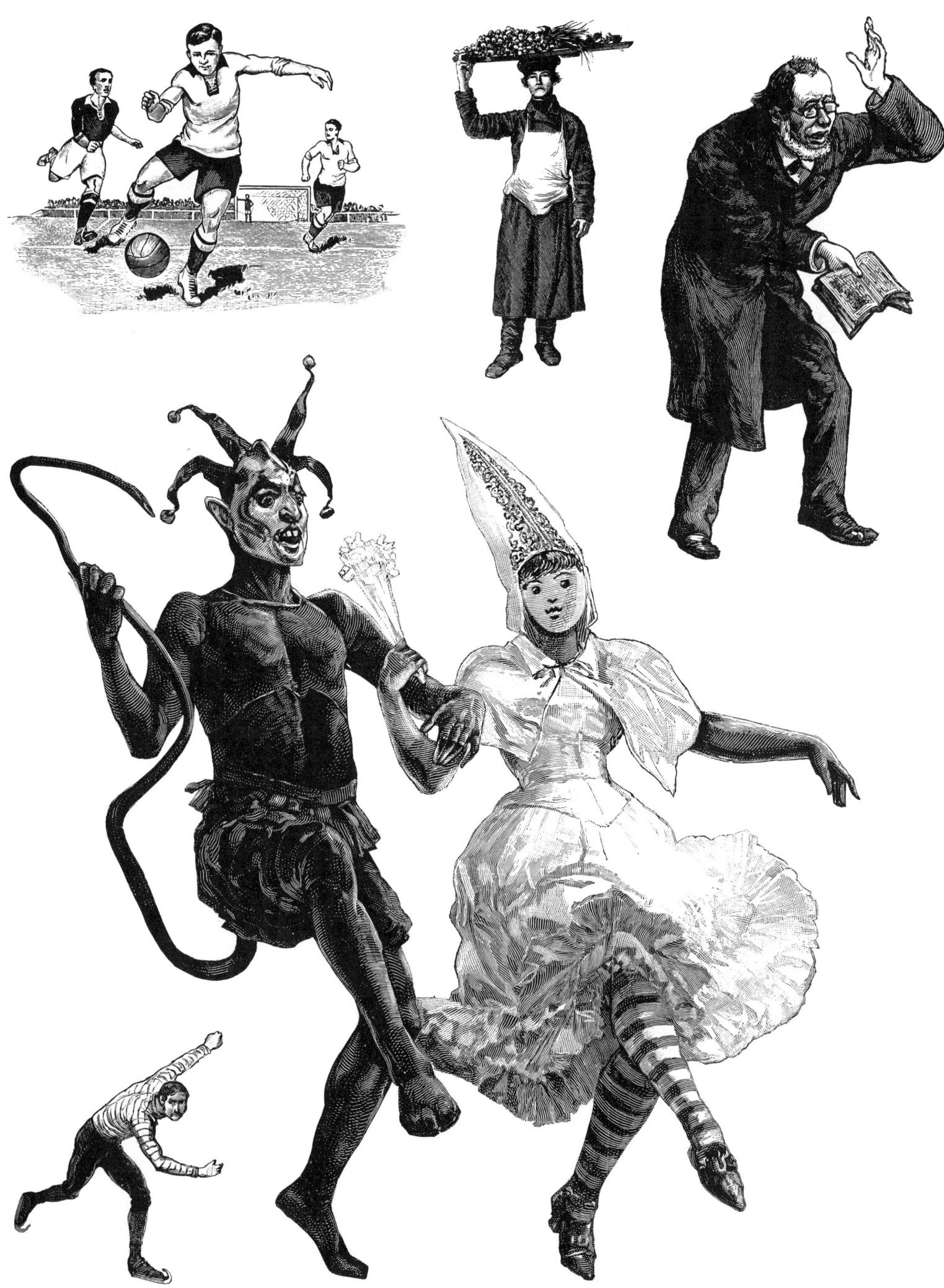

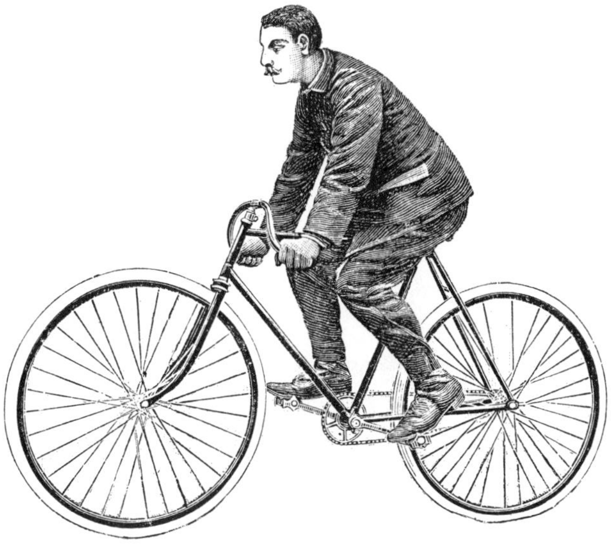

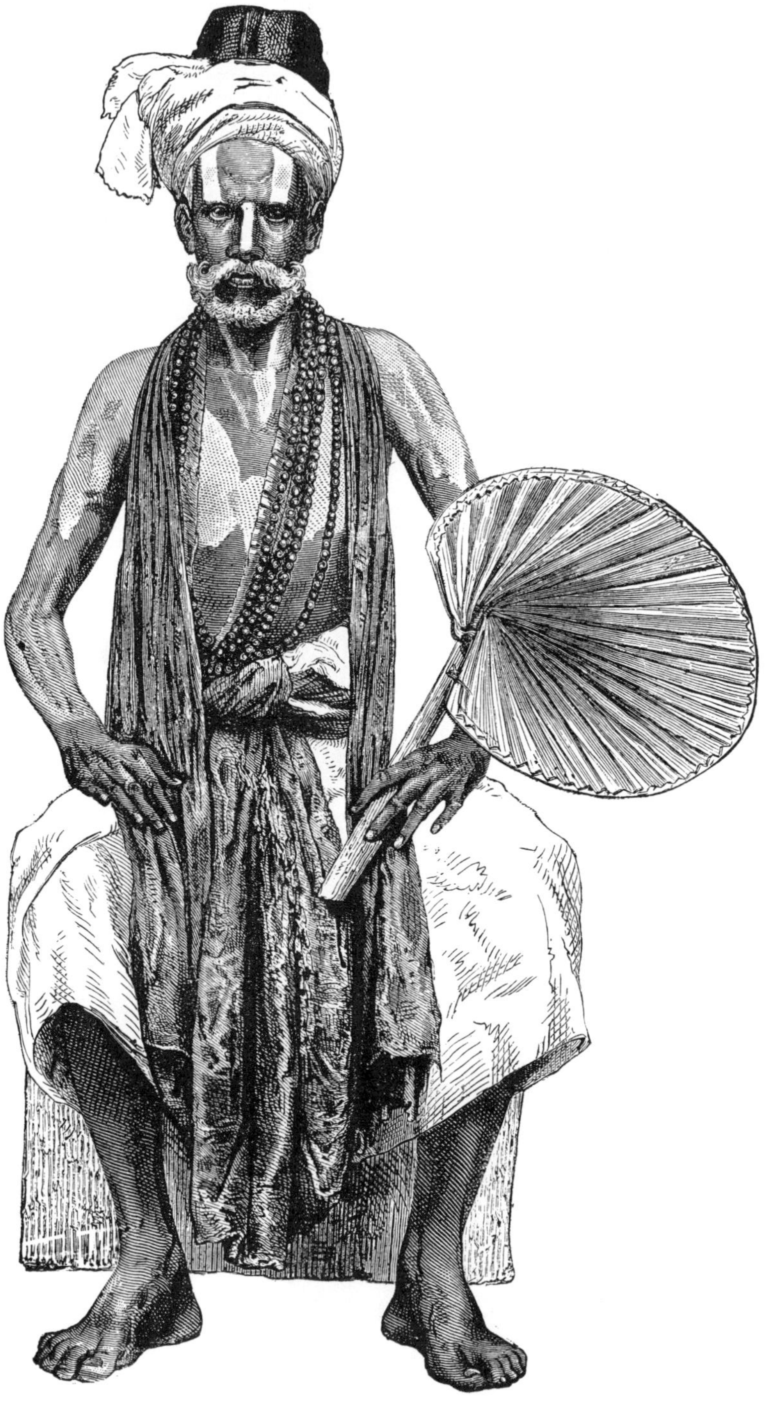

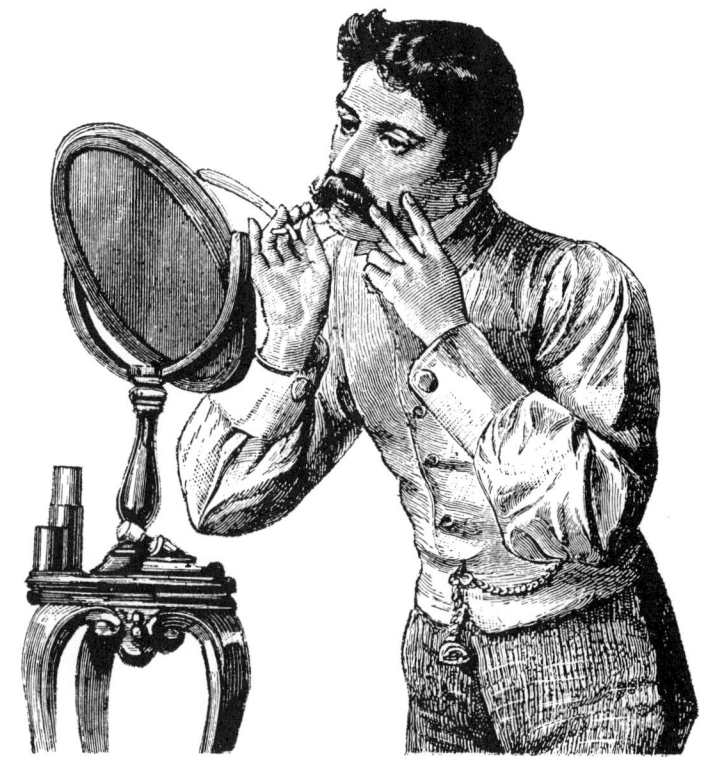
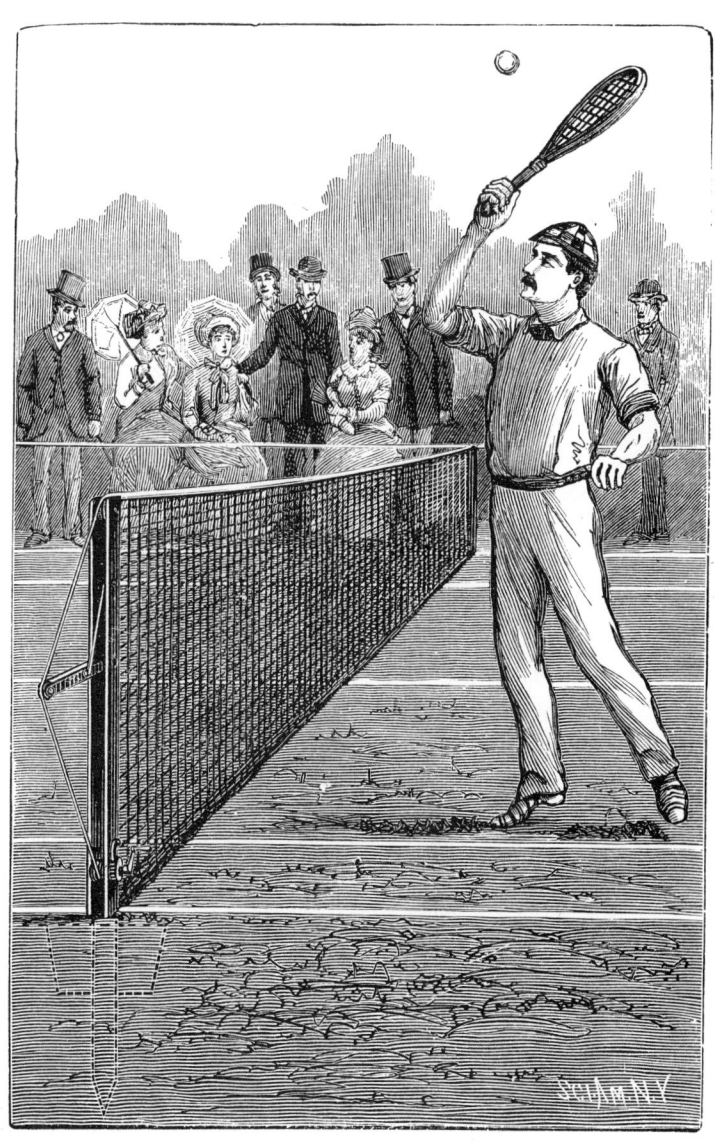

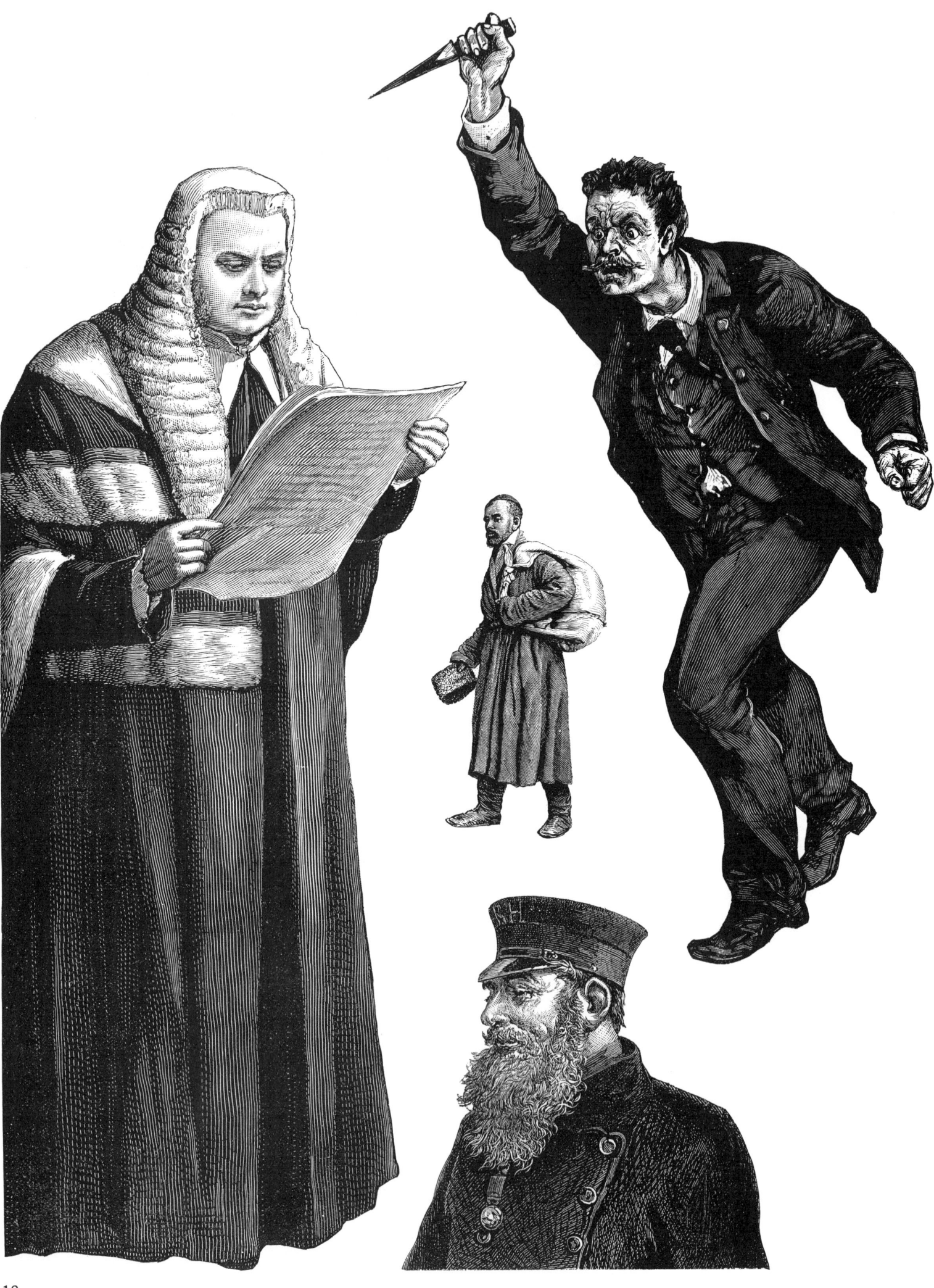

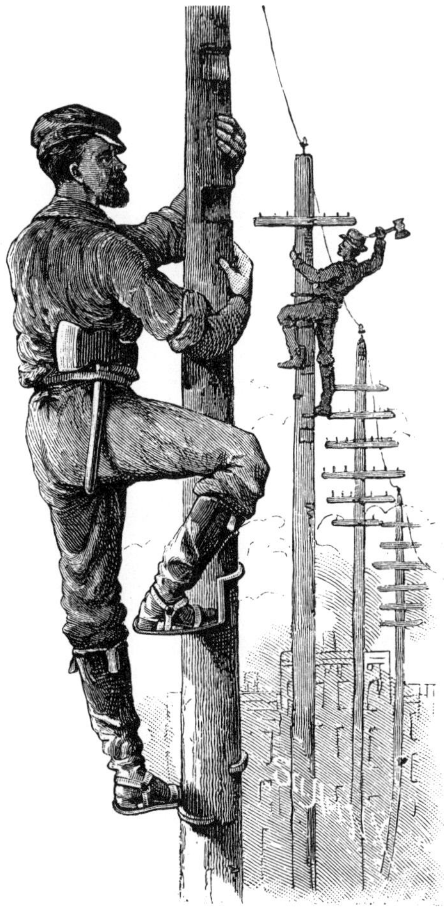

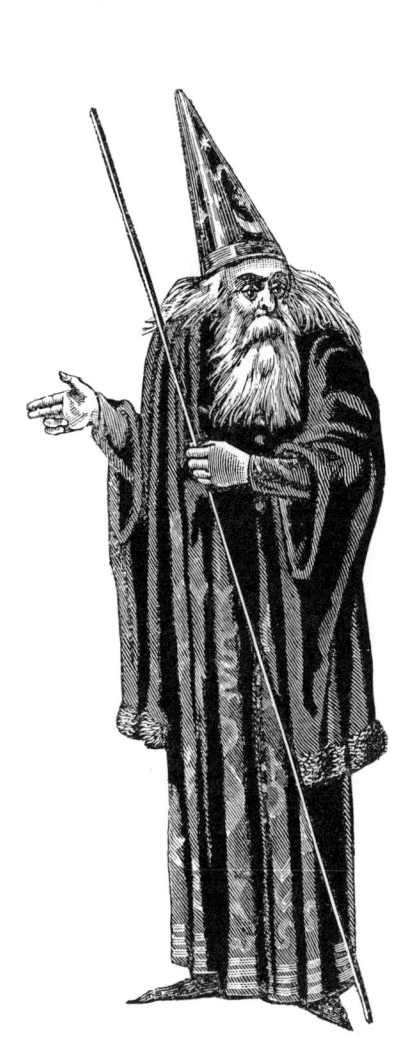
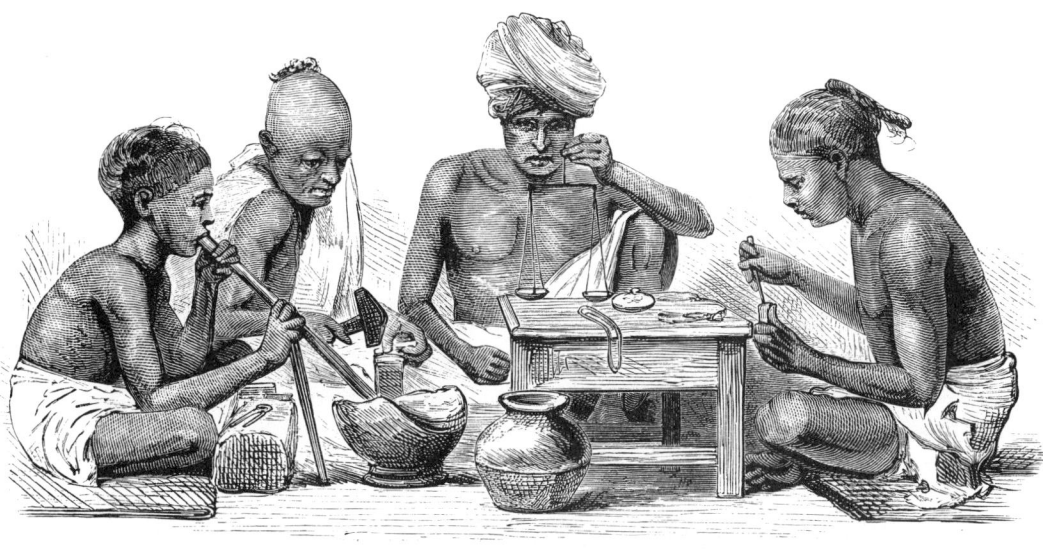
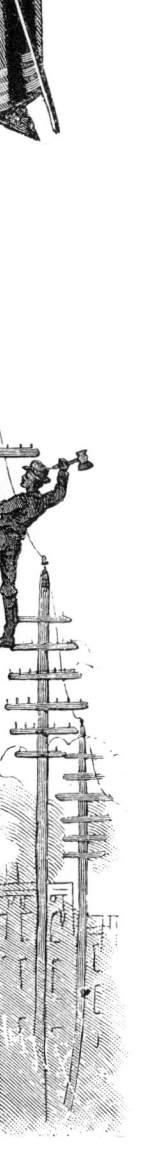

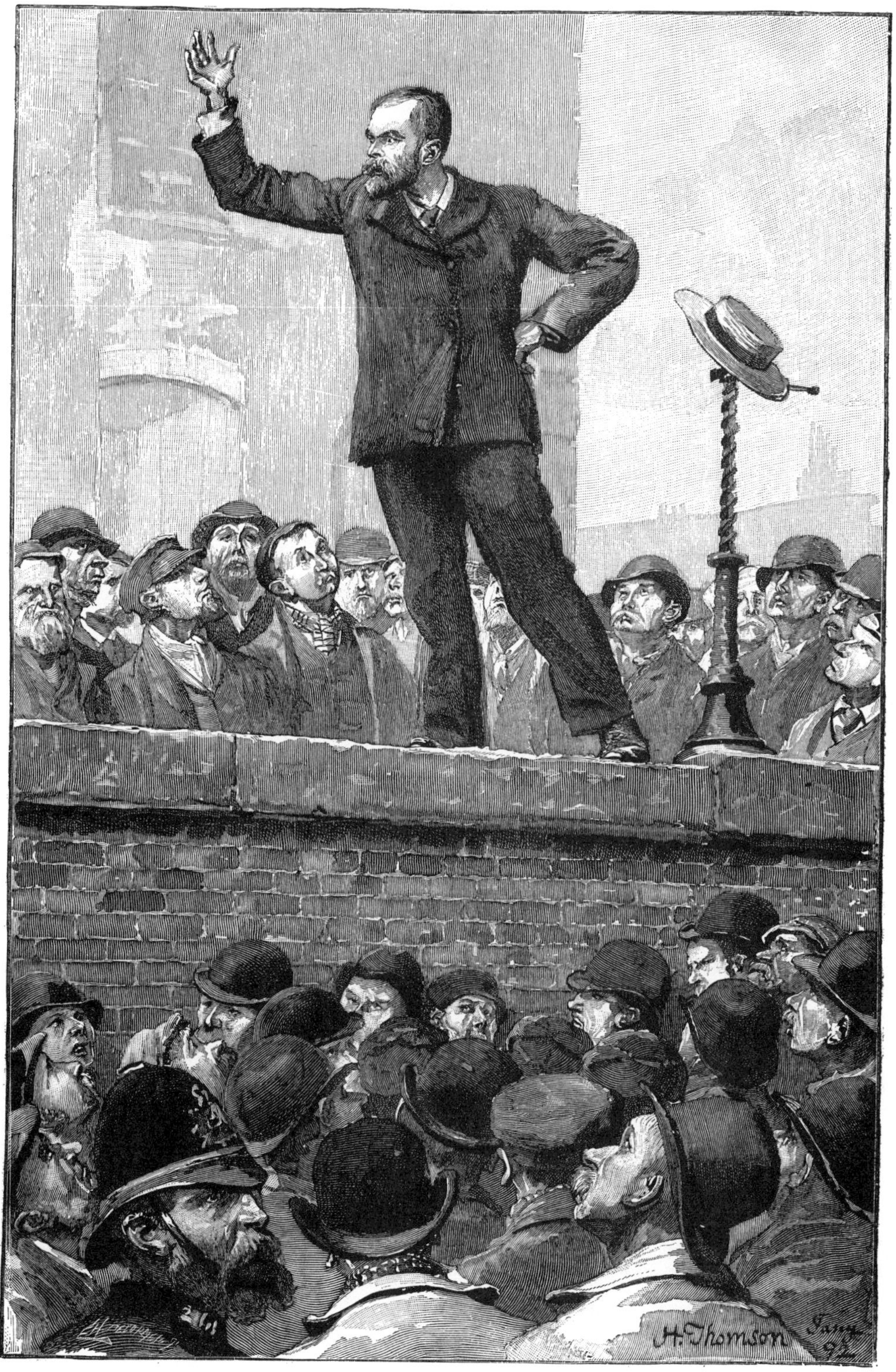

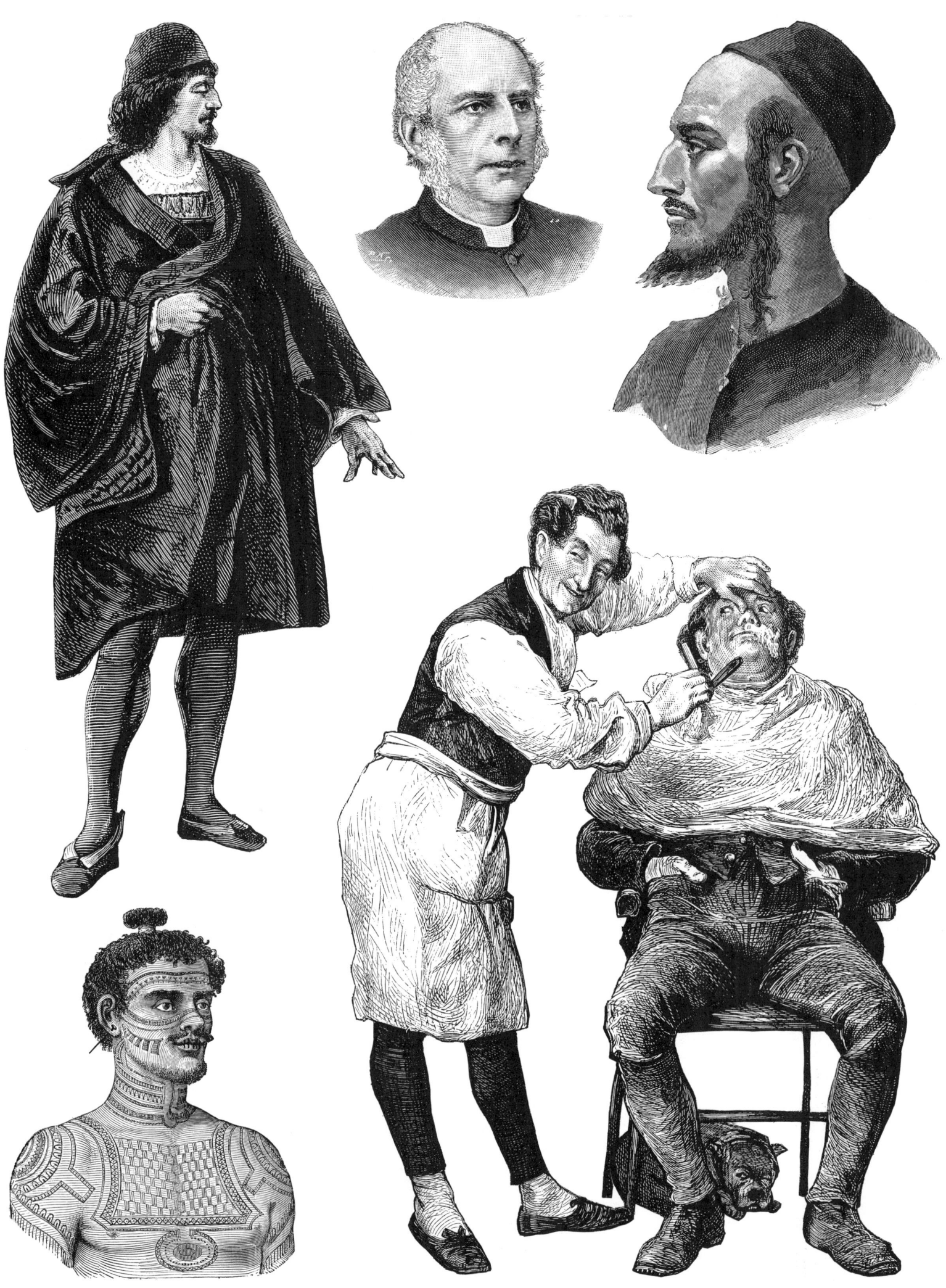

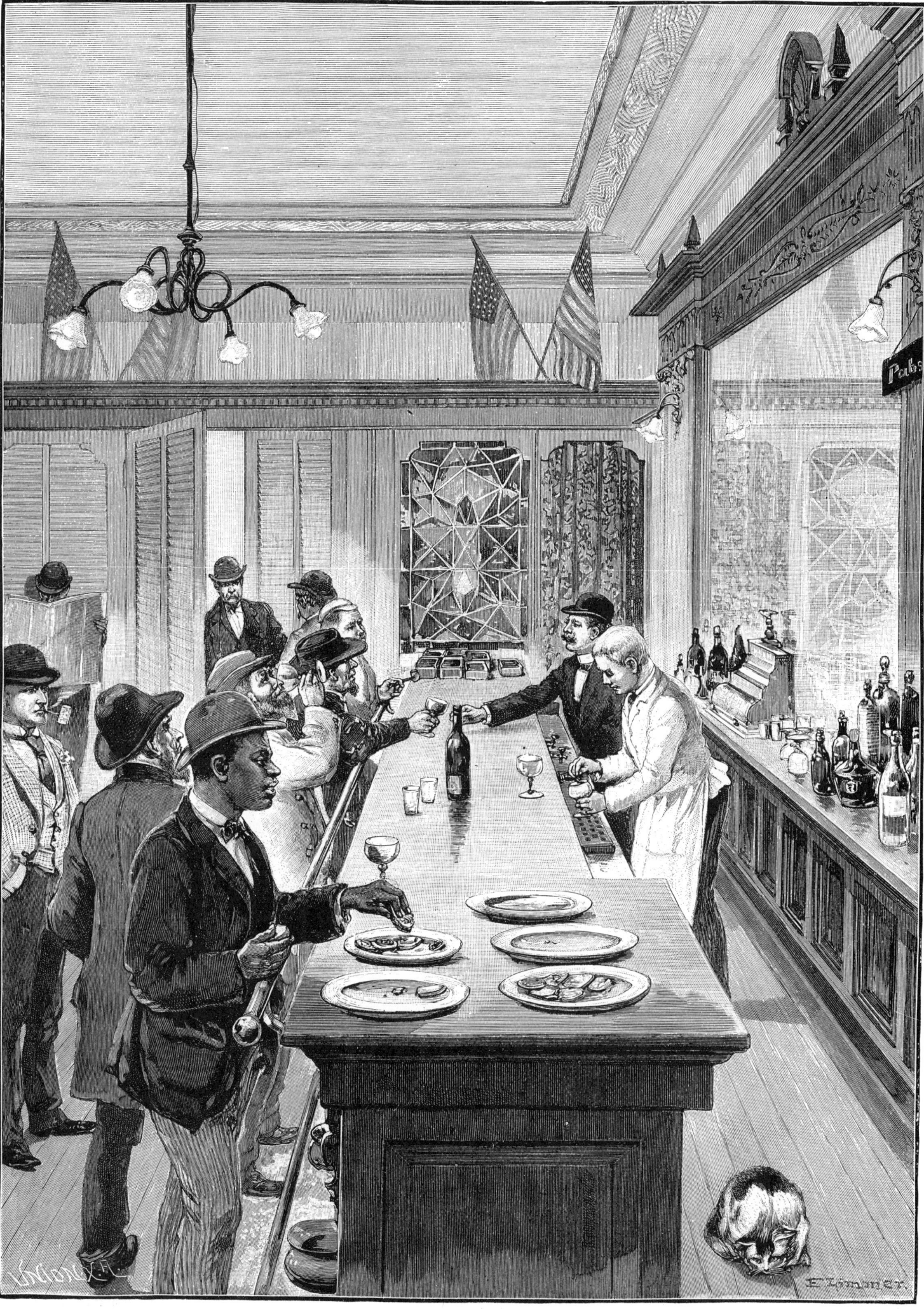

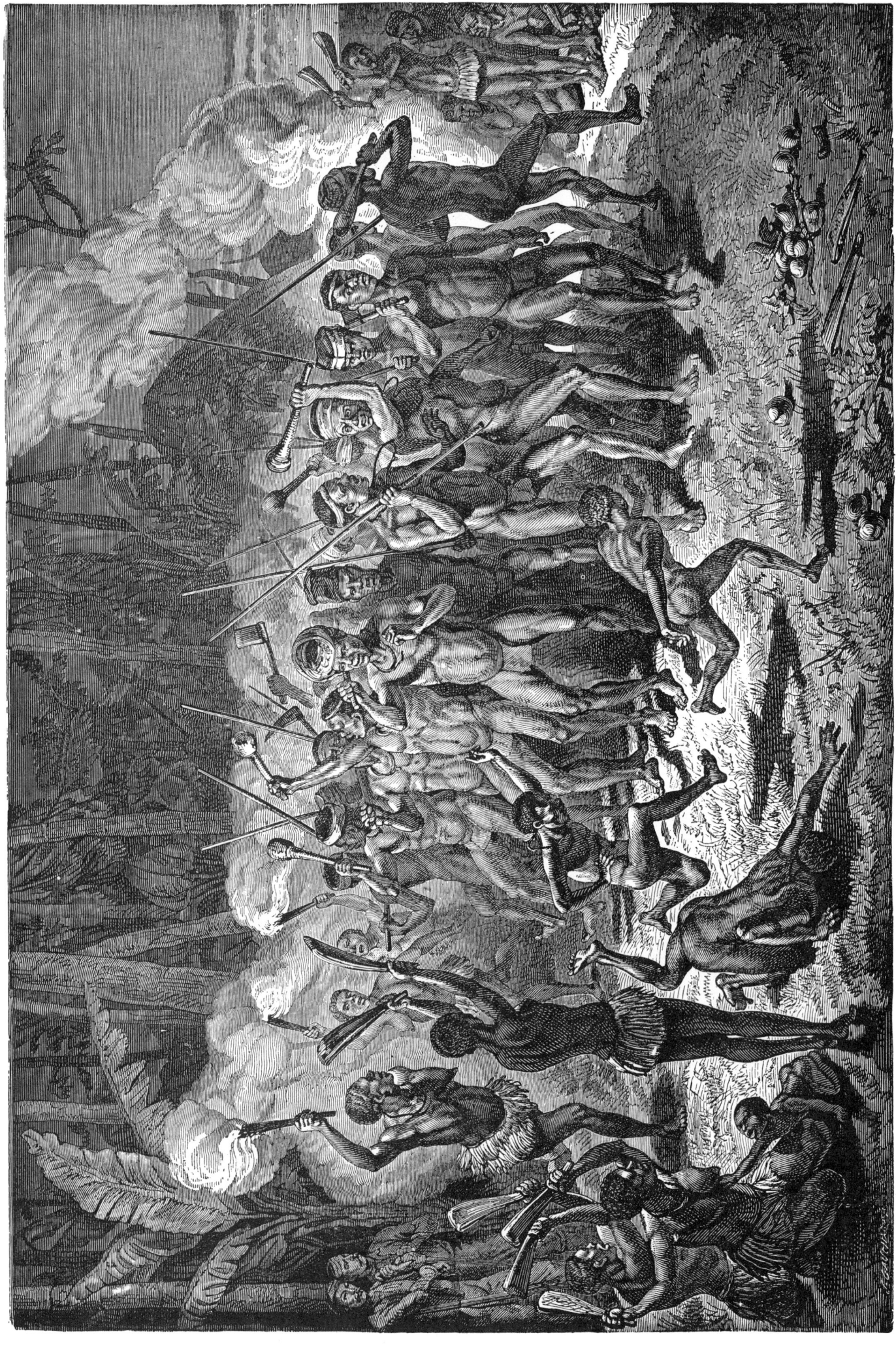

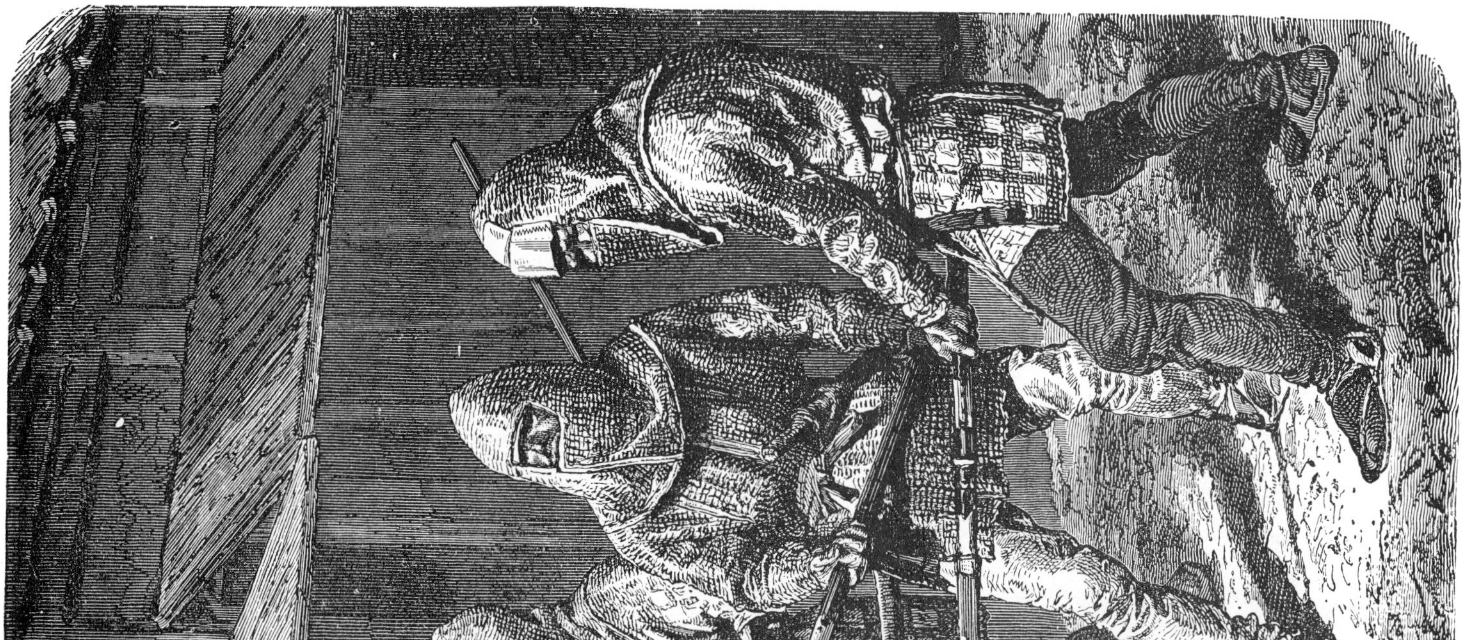

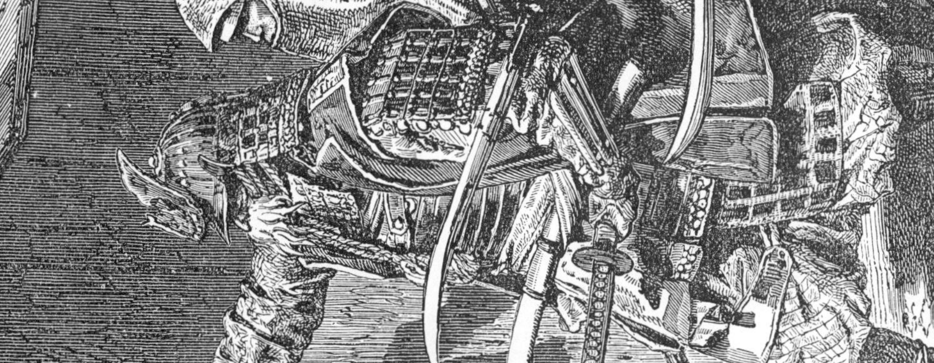

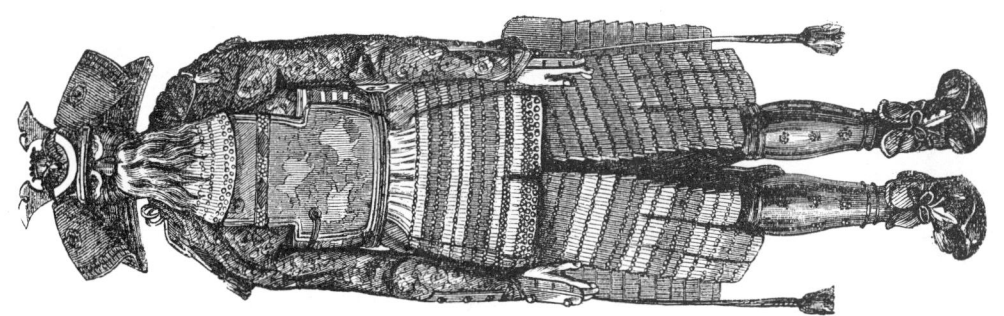
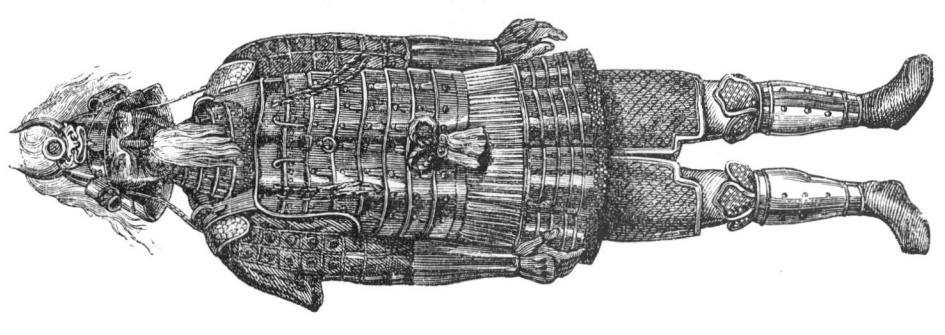

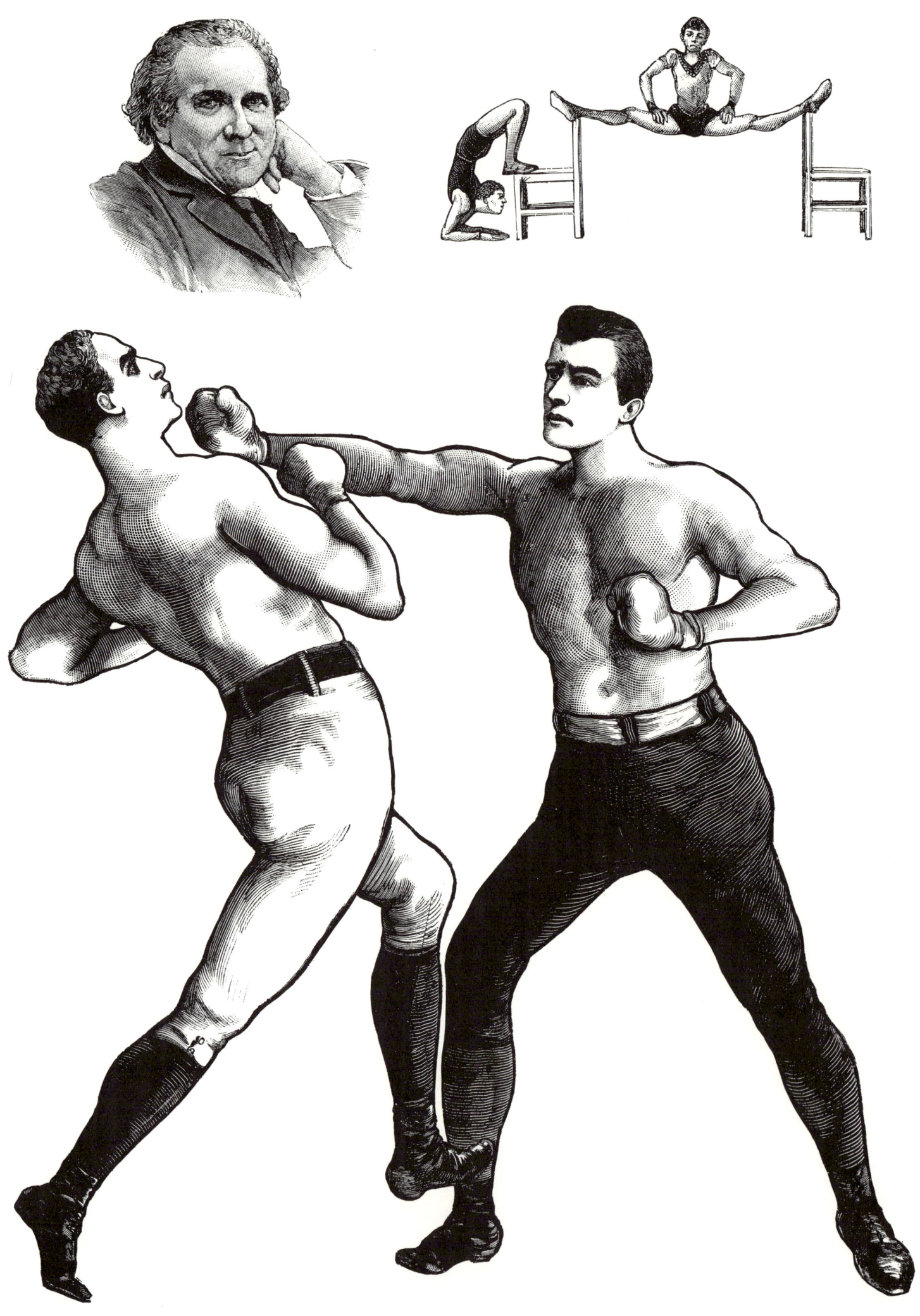

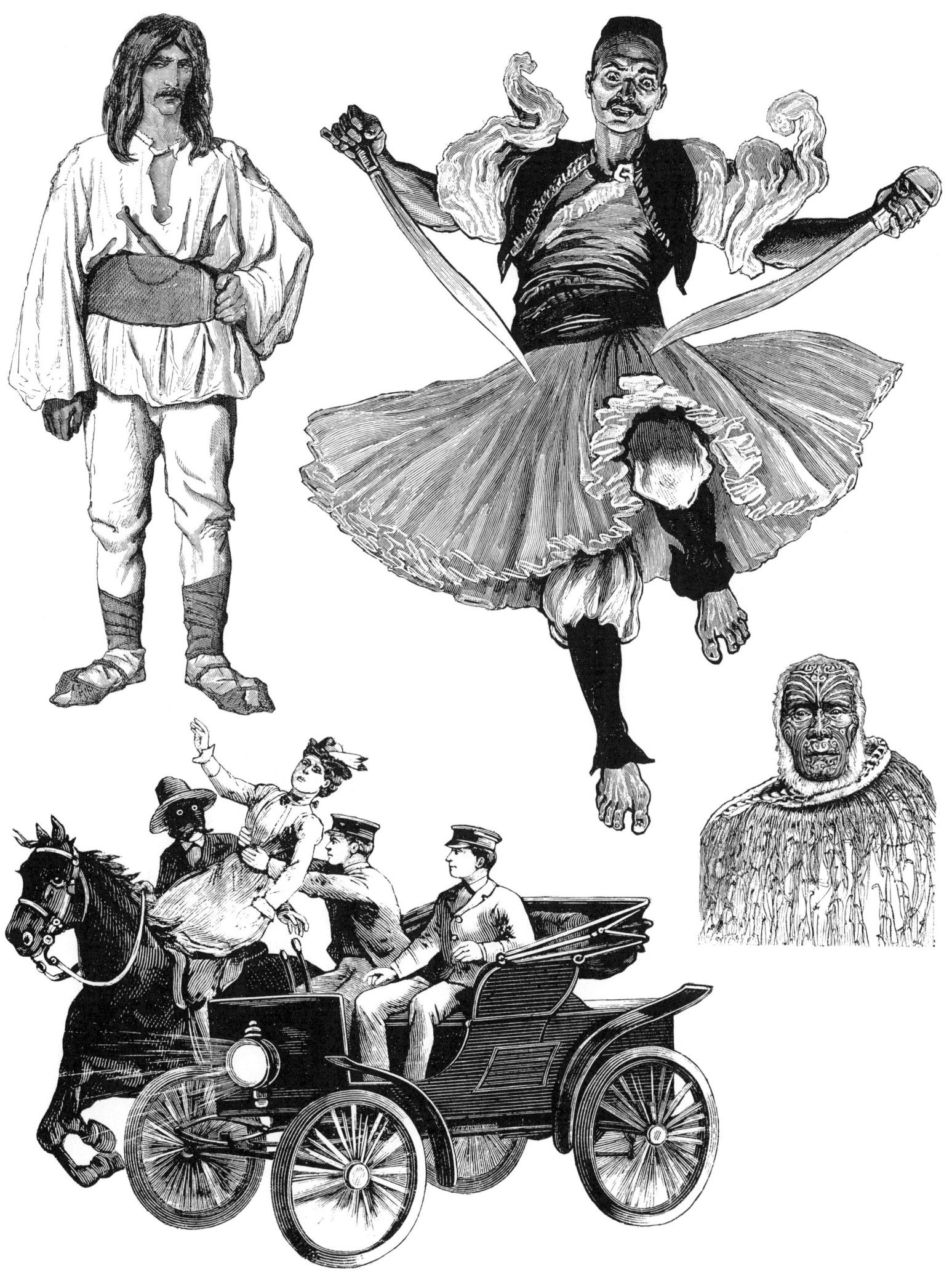

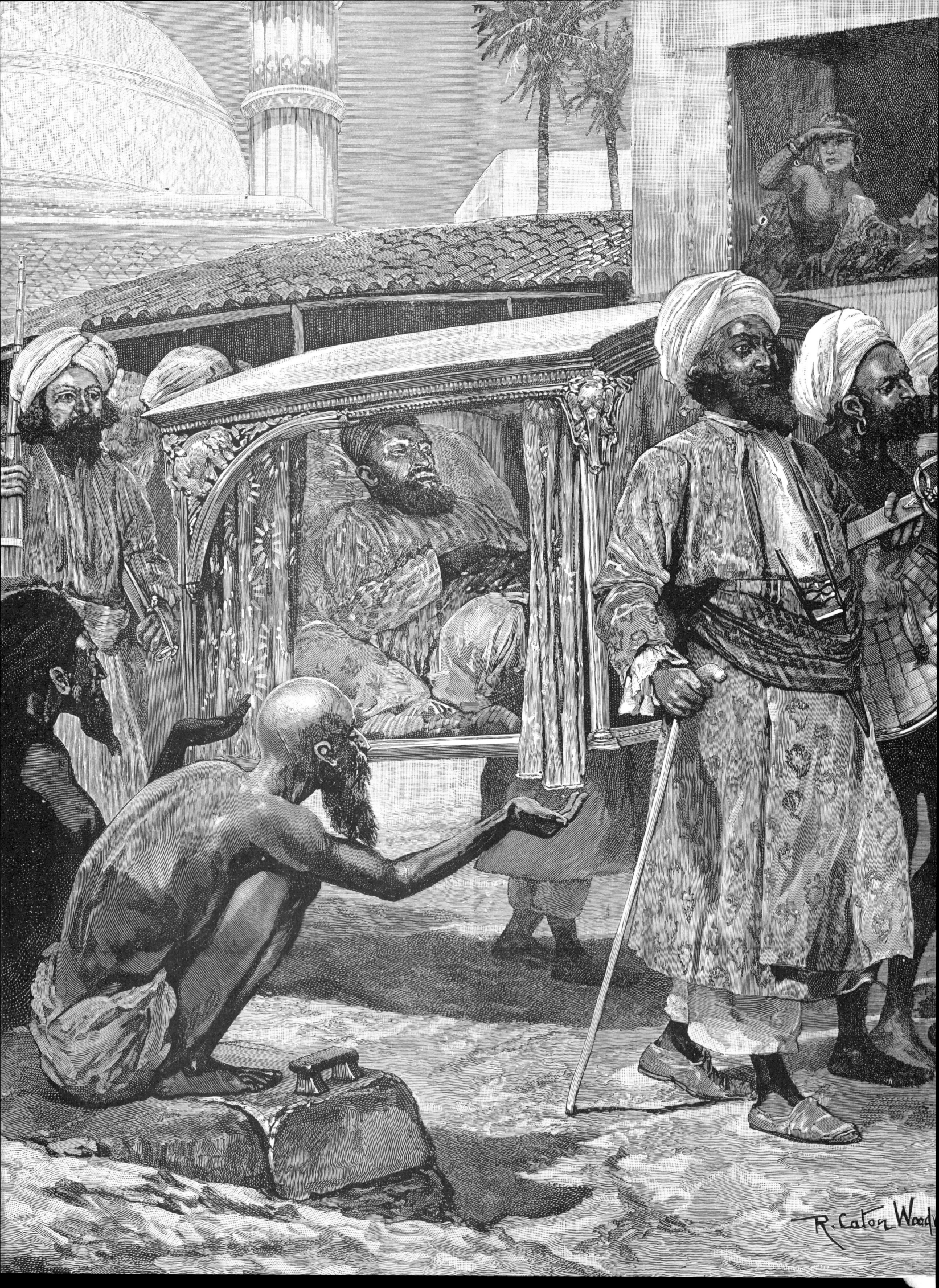

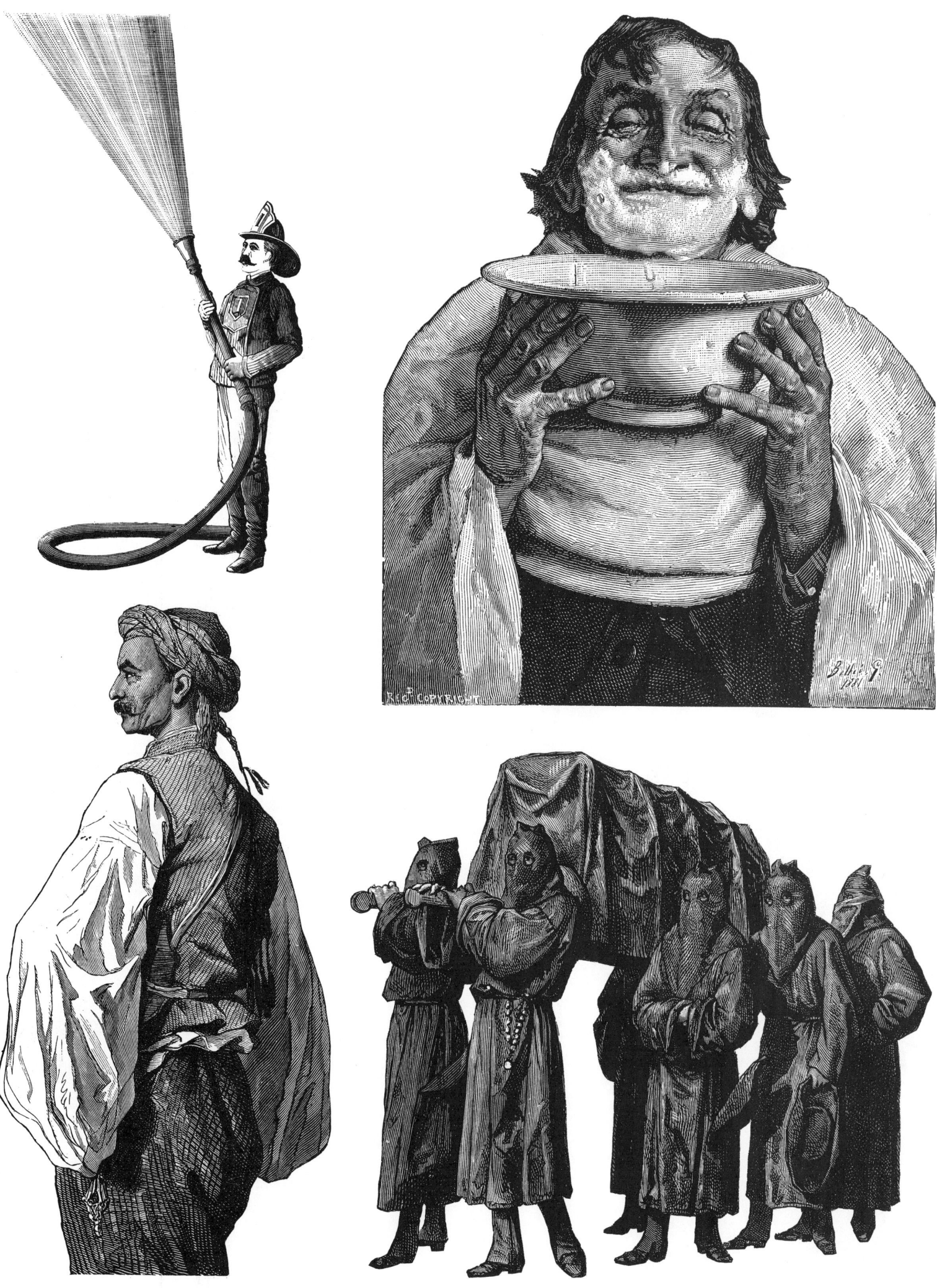

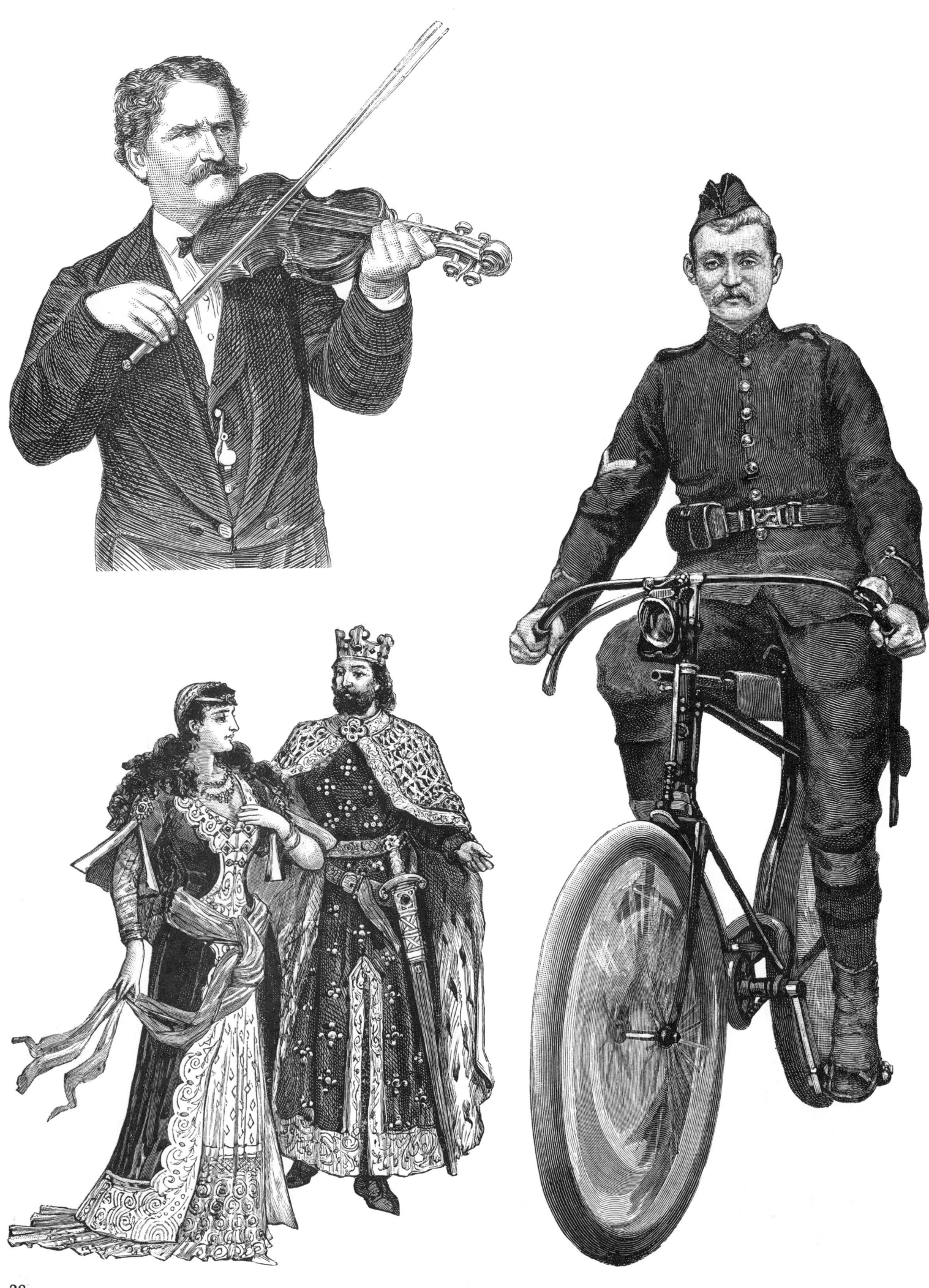

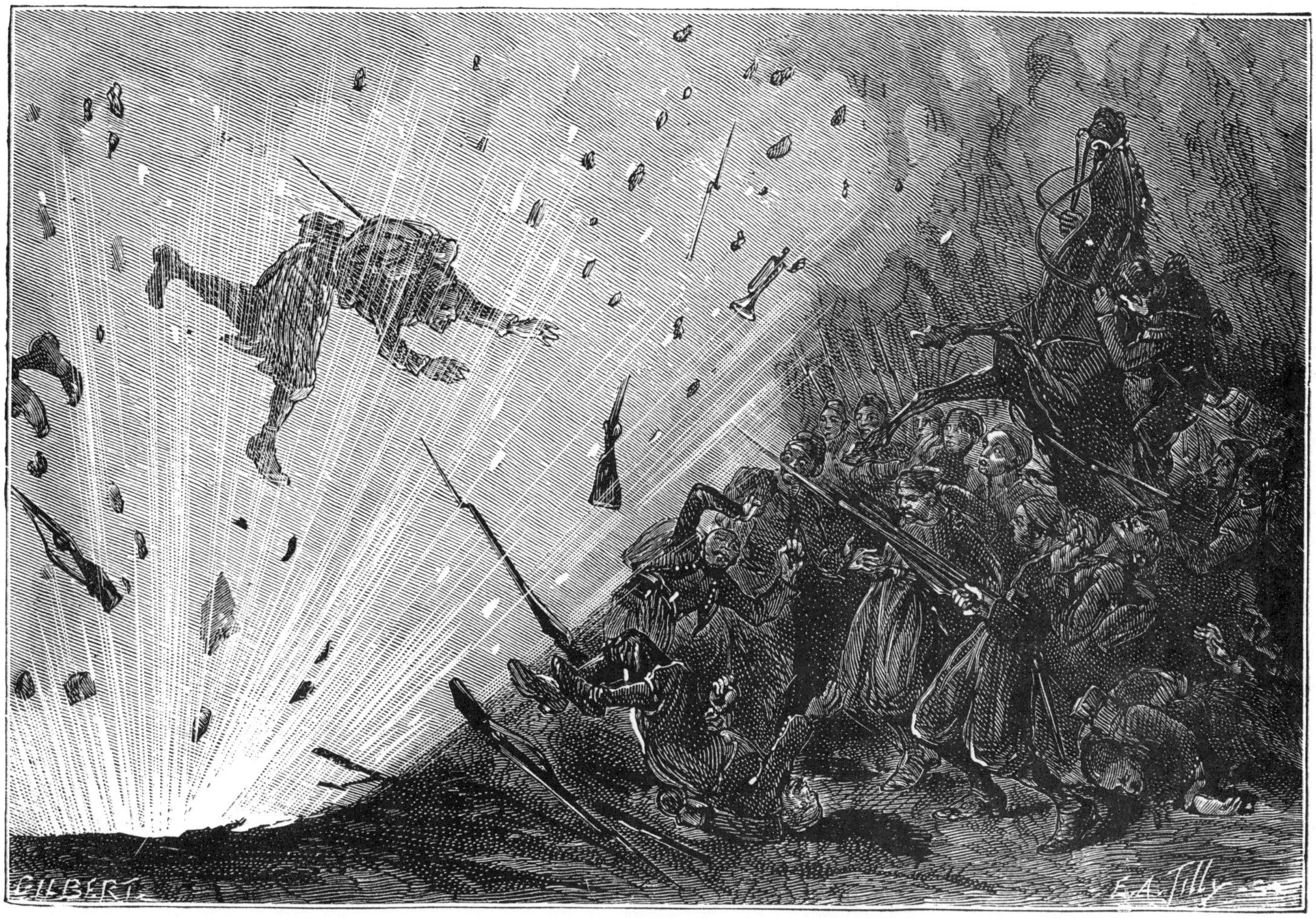

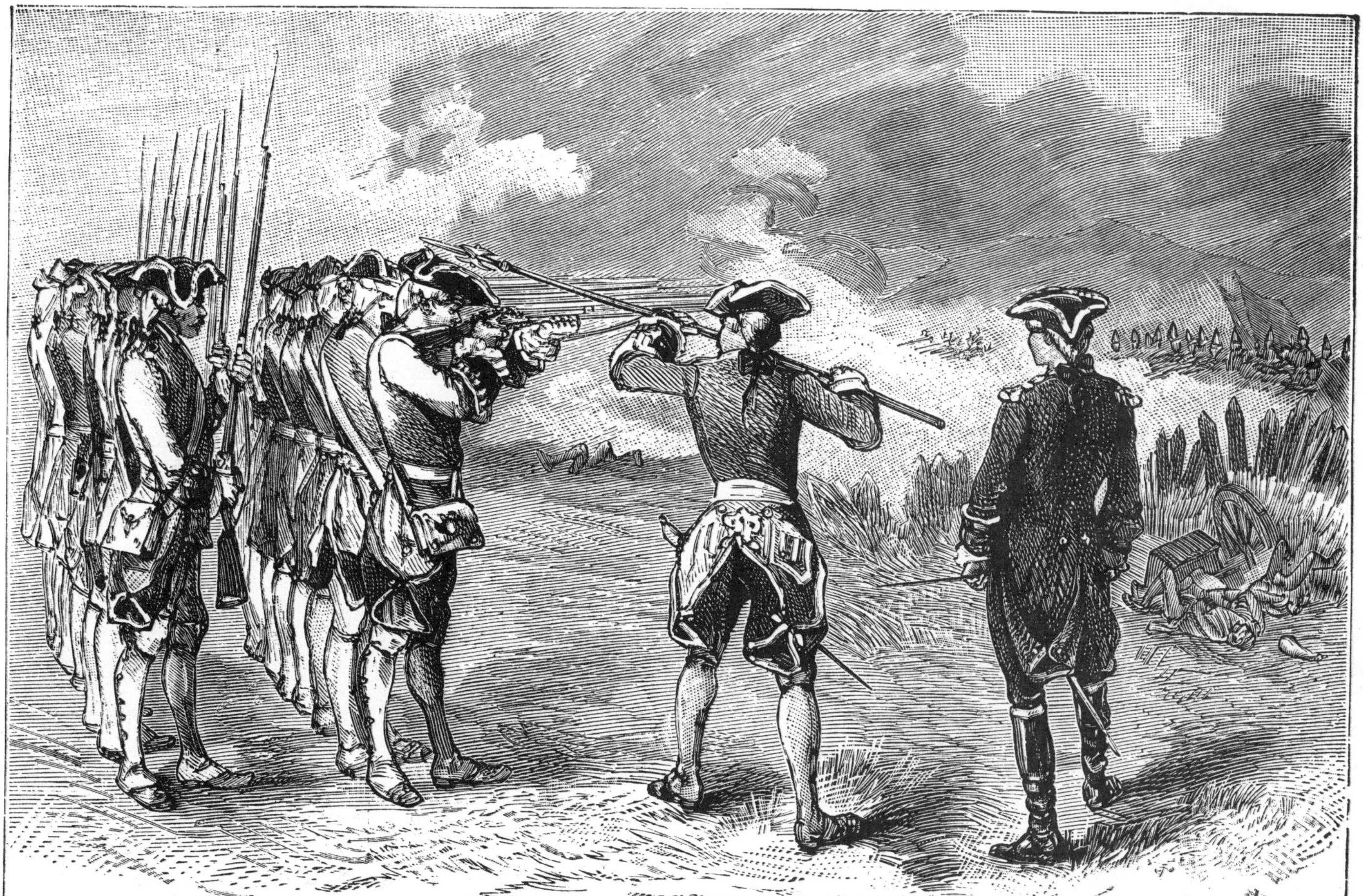

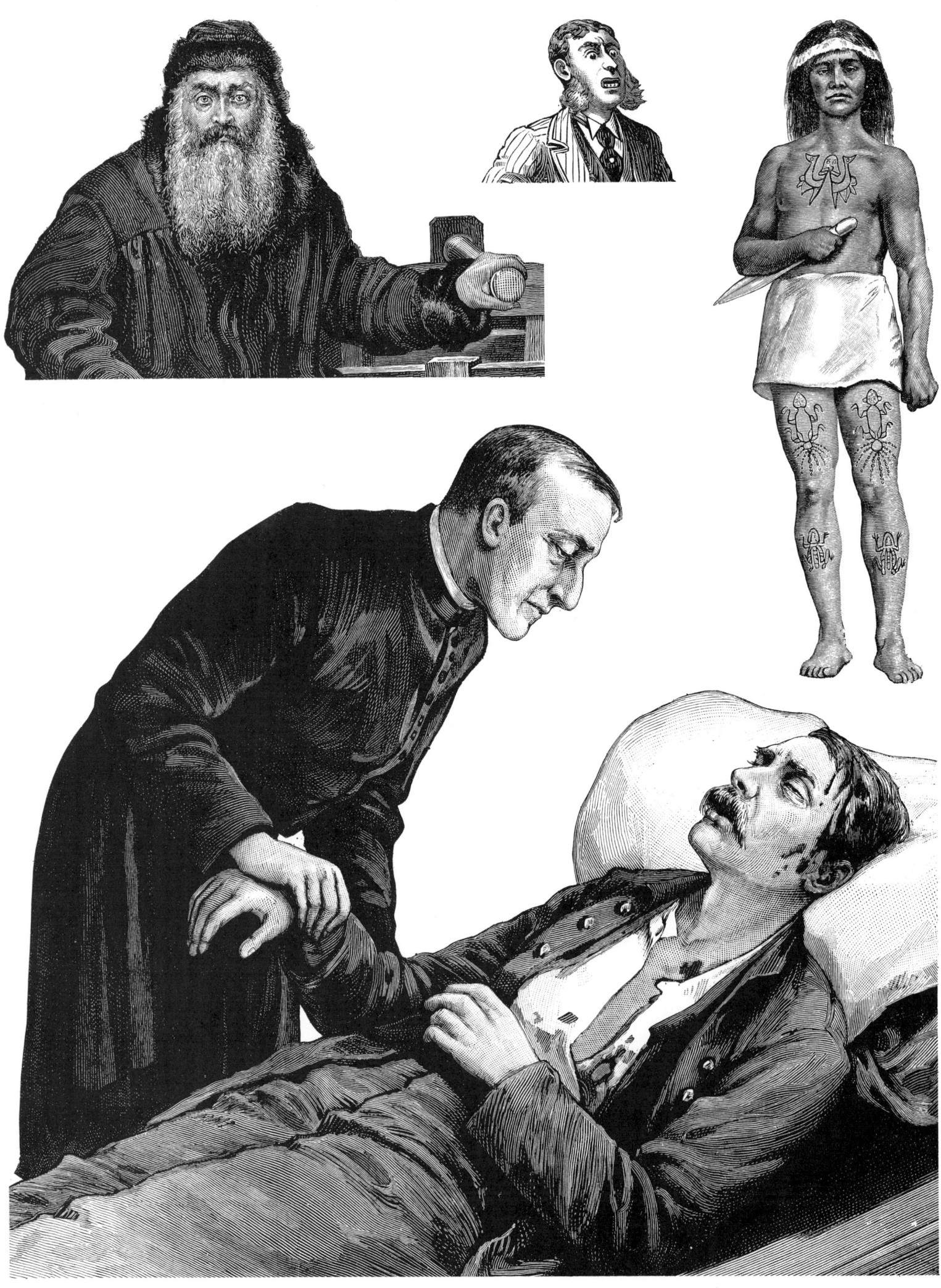

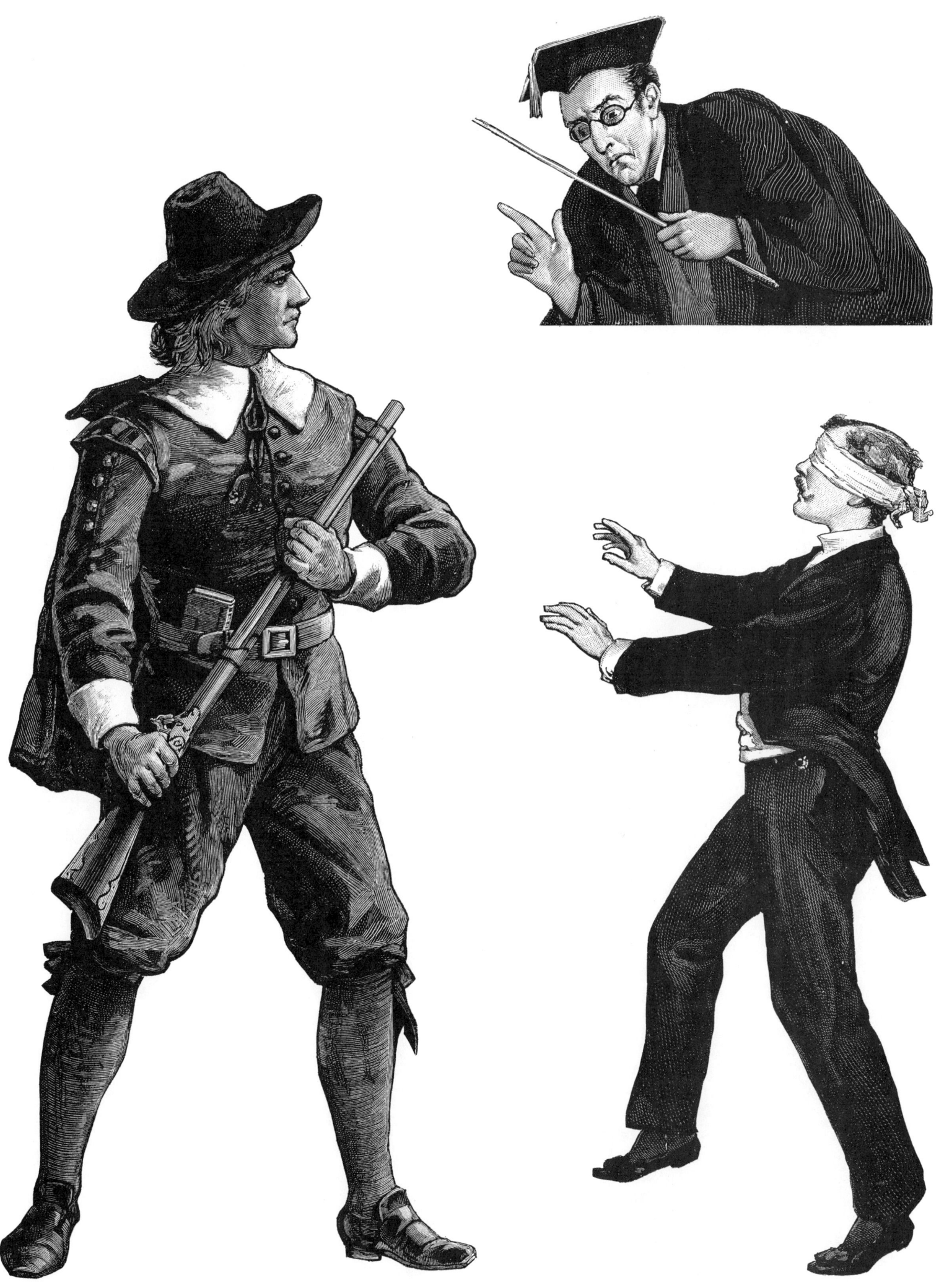

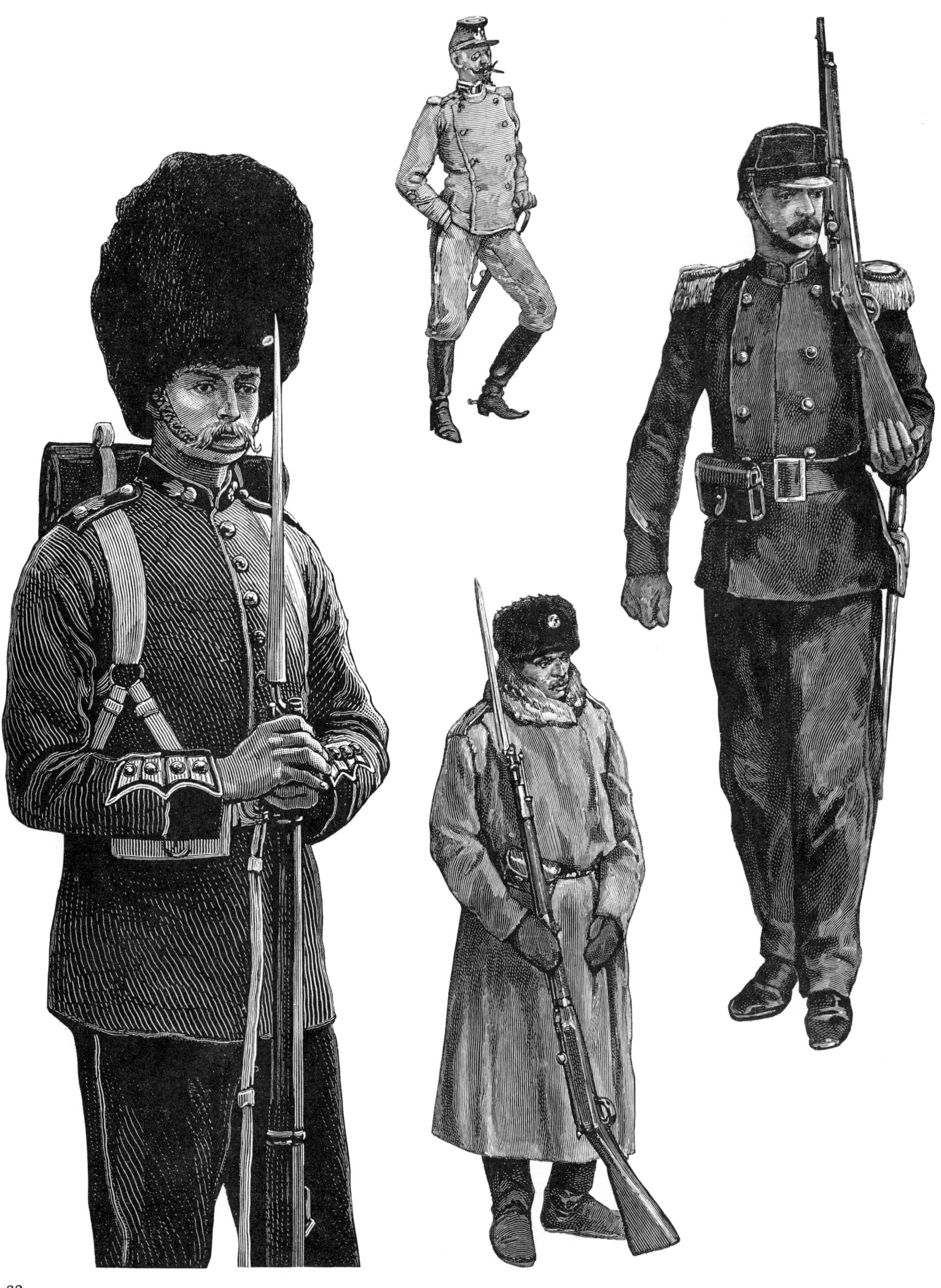

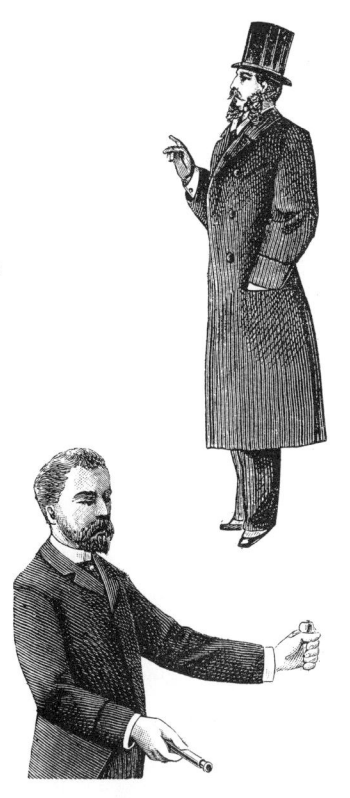
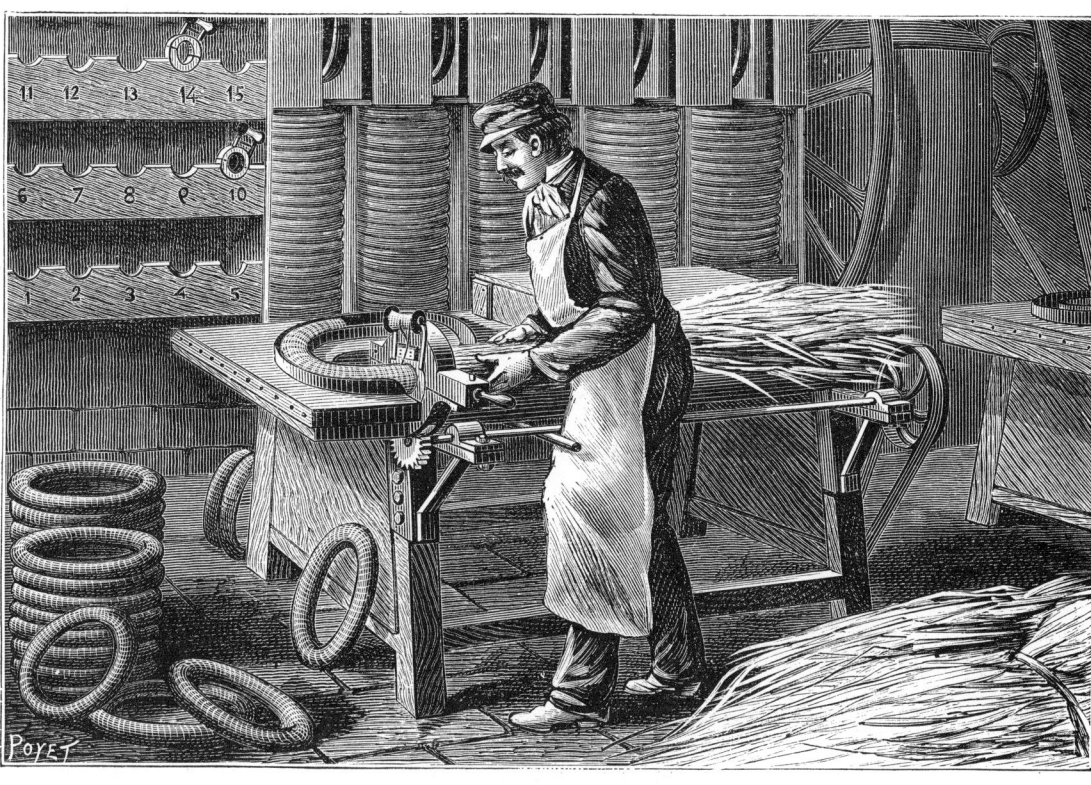

33

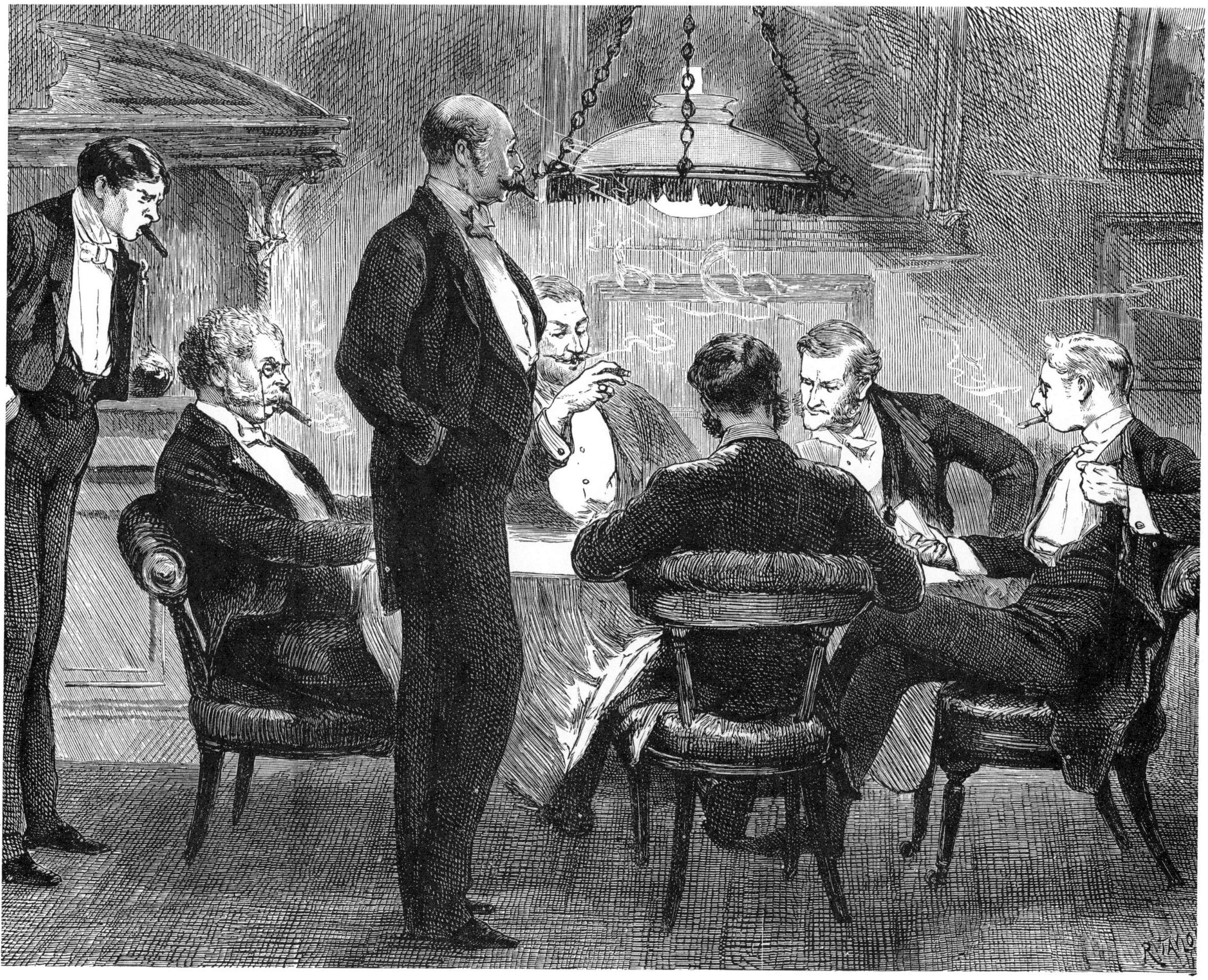

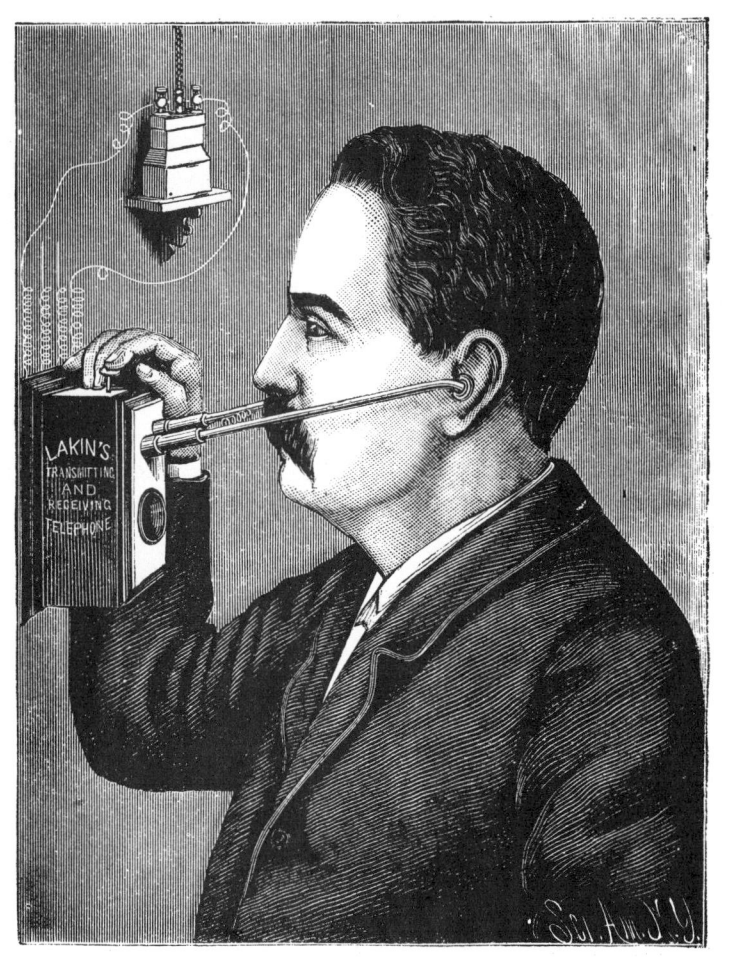
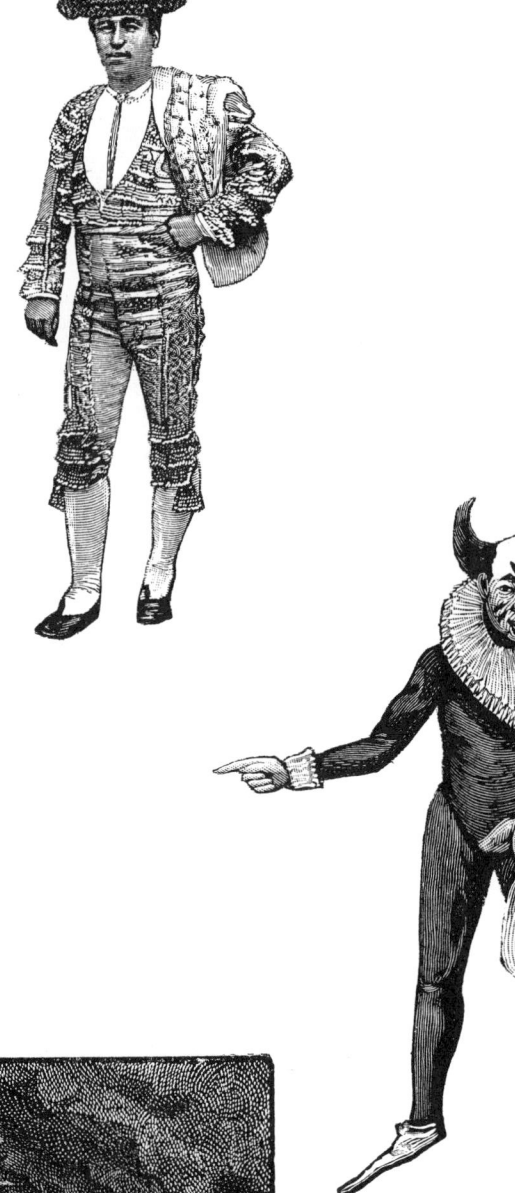
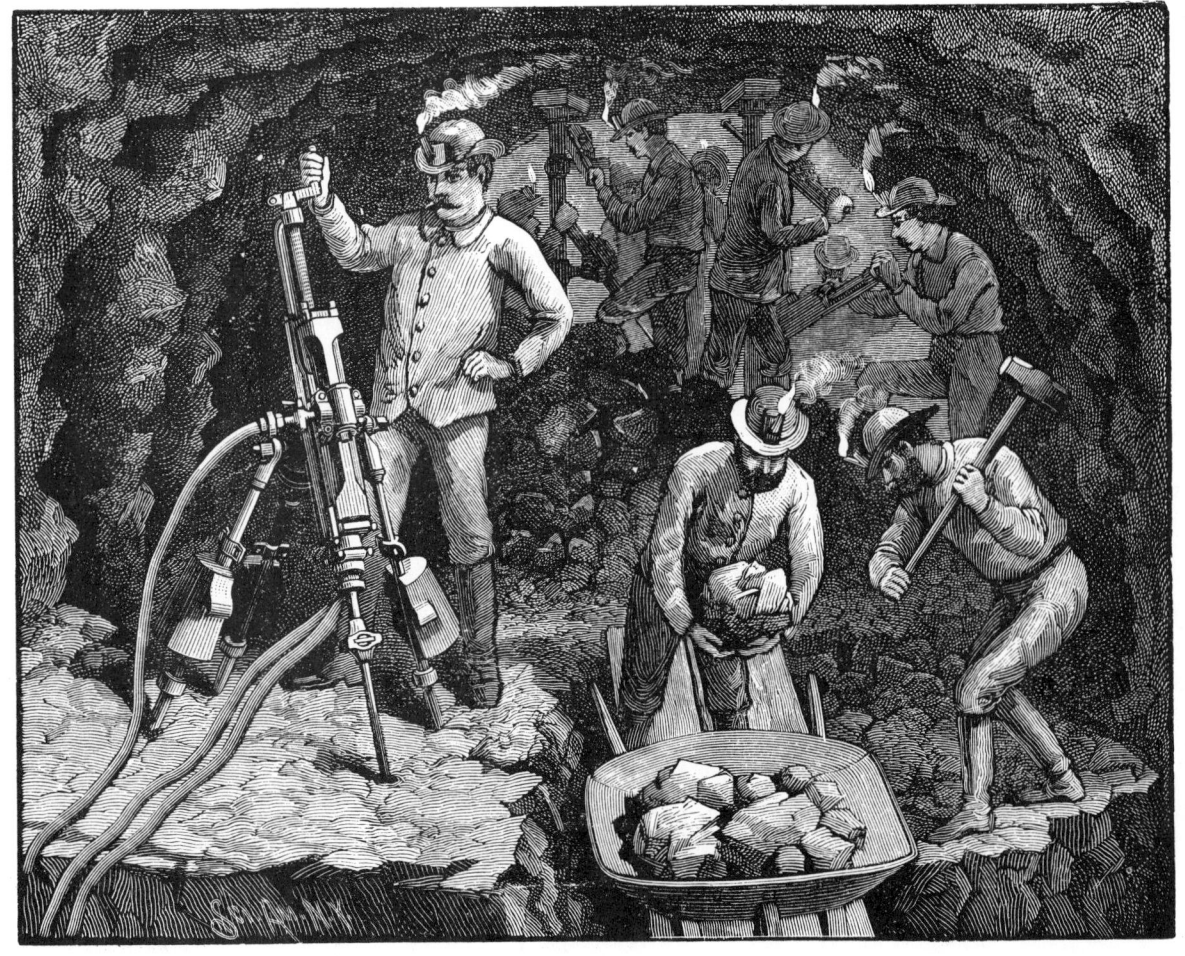
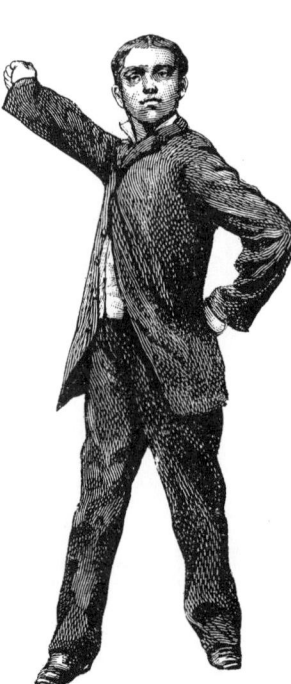

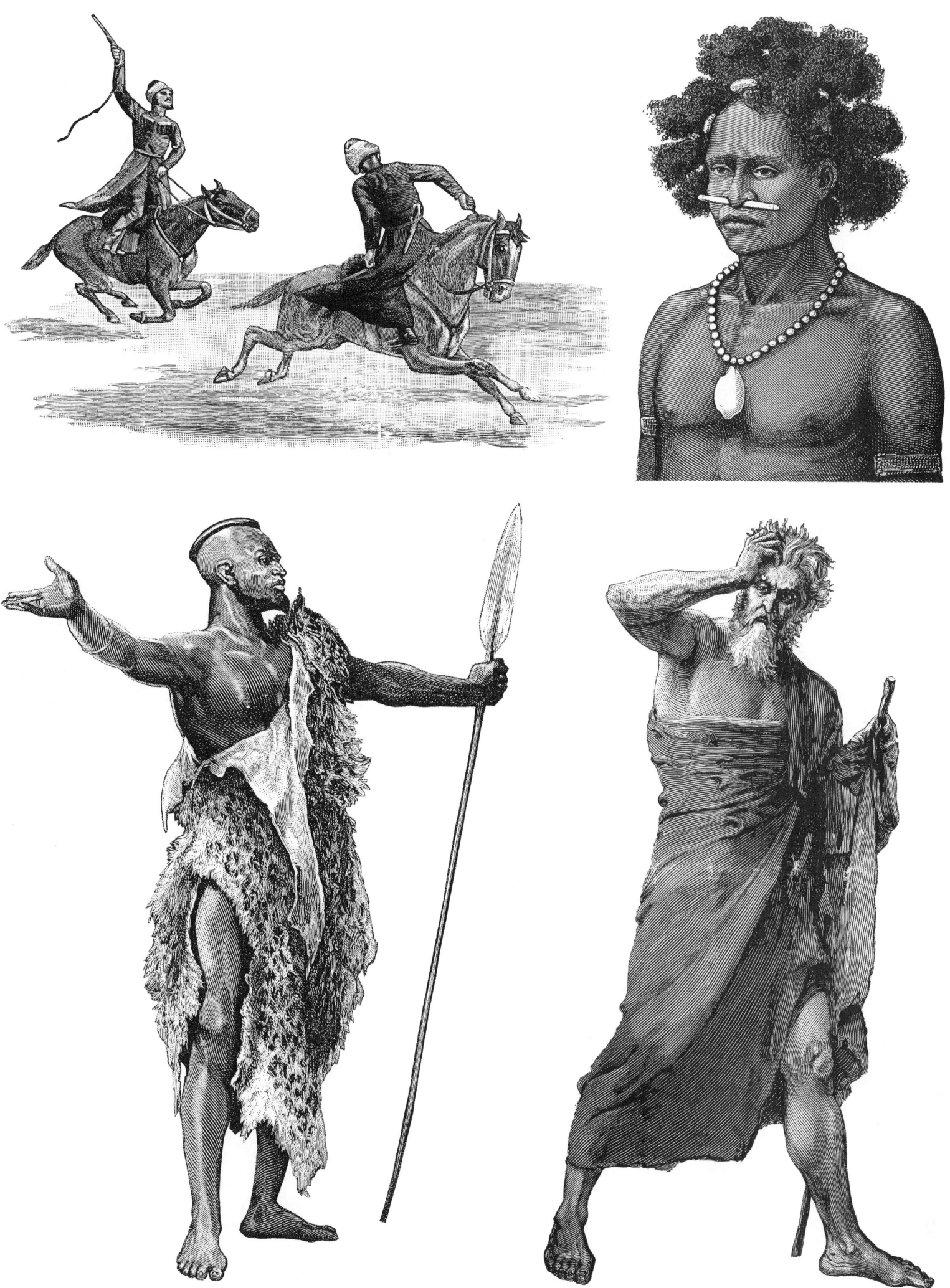

35

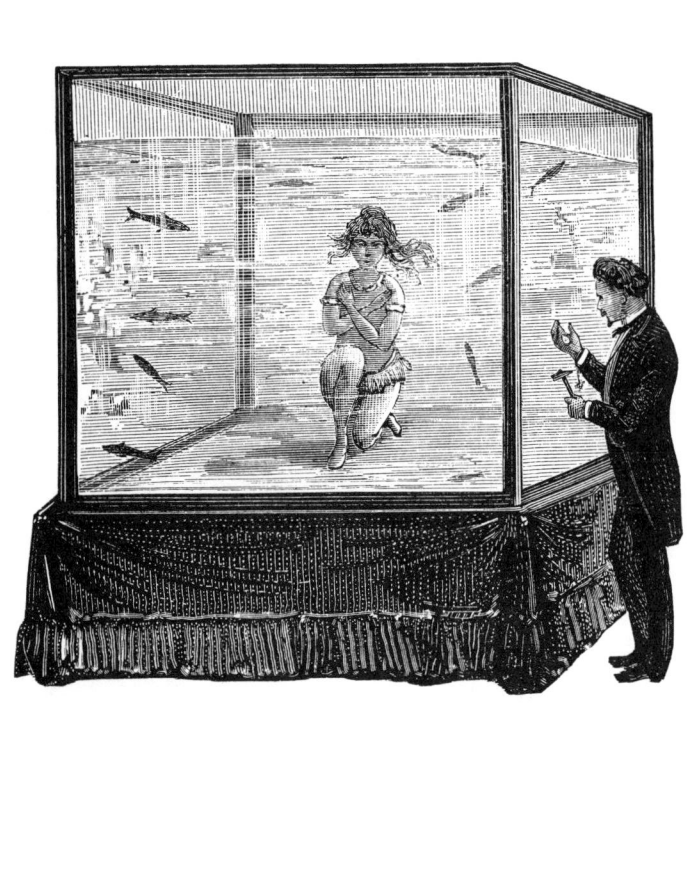
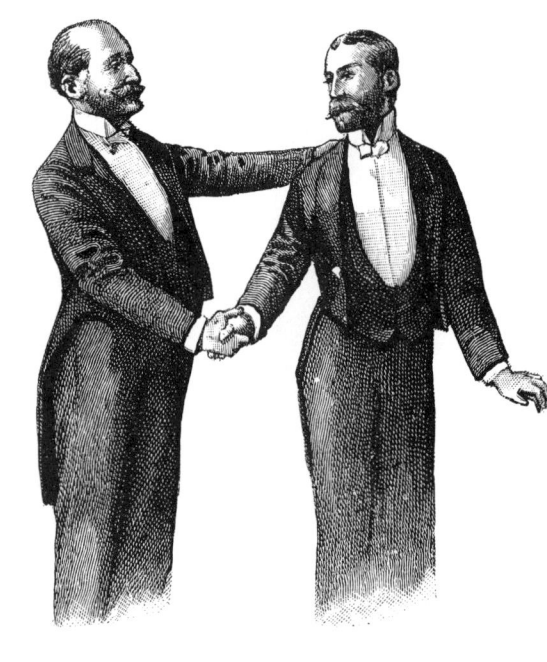
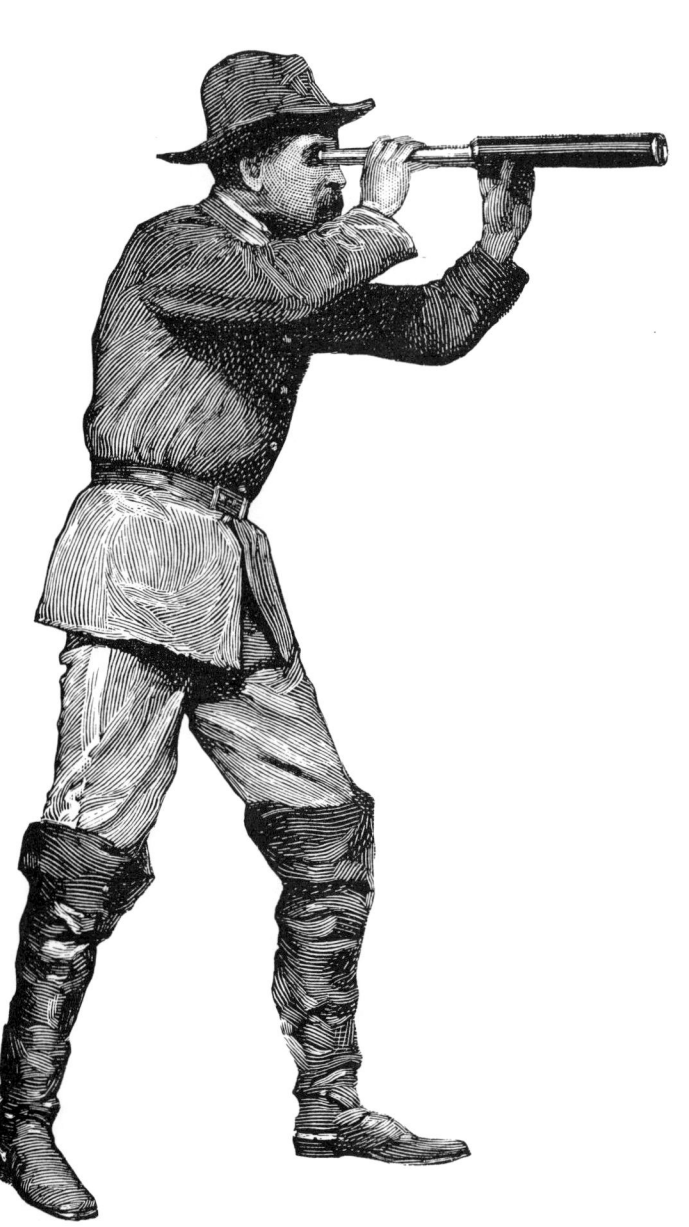
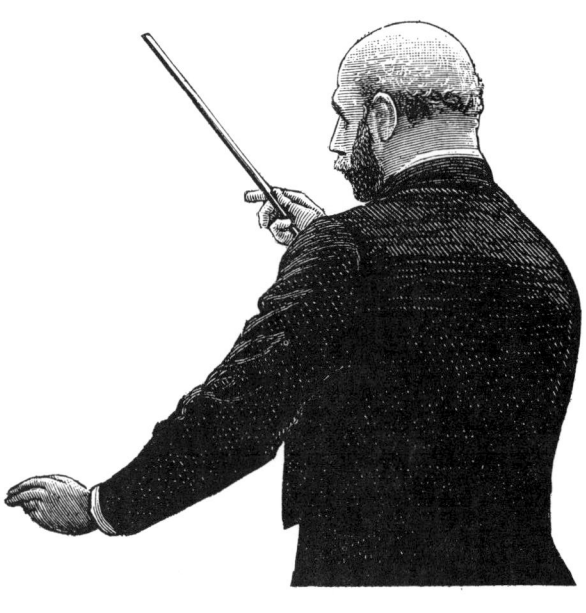
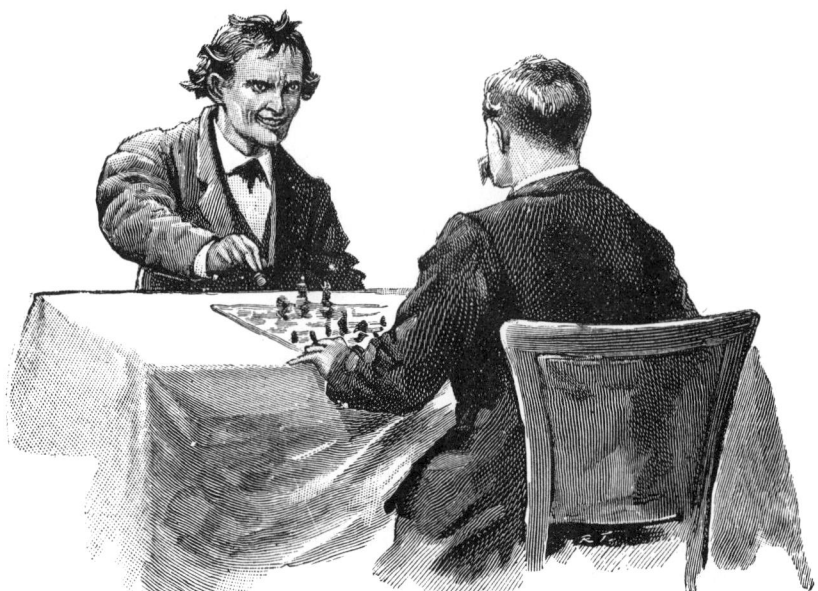

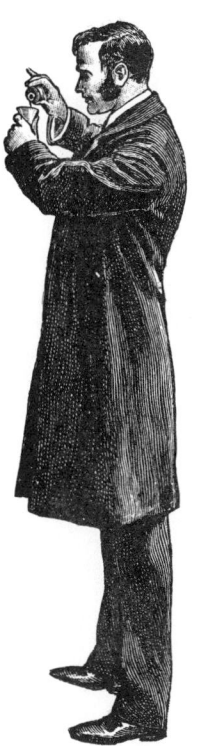
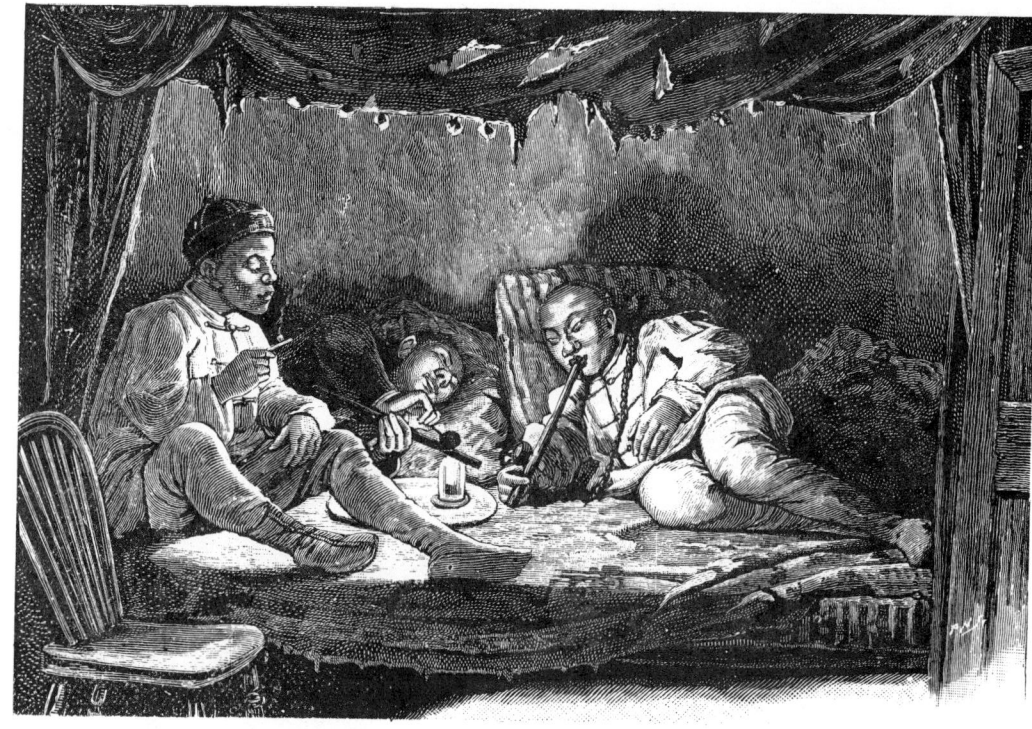
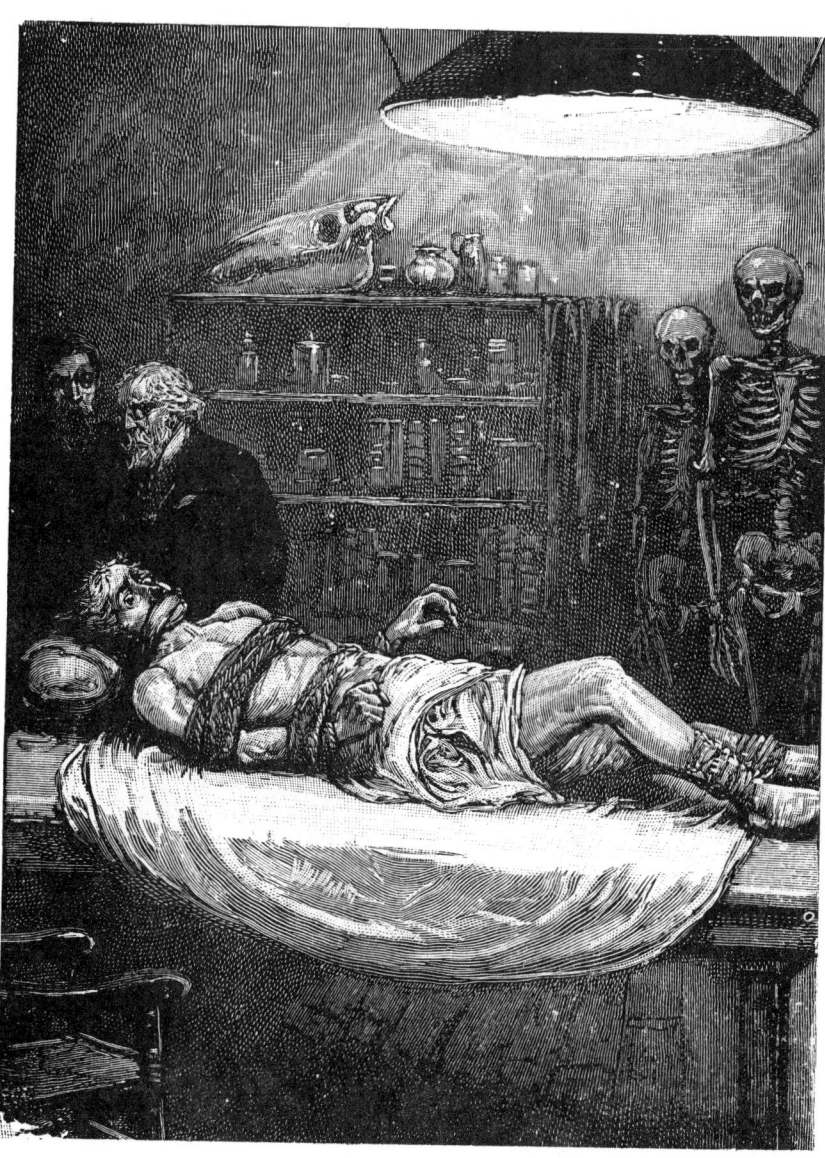
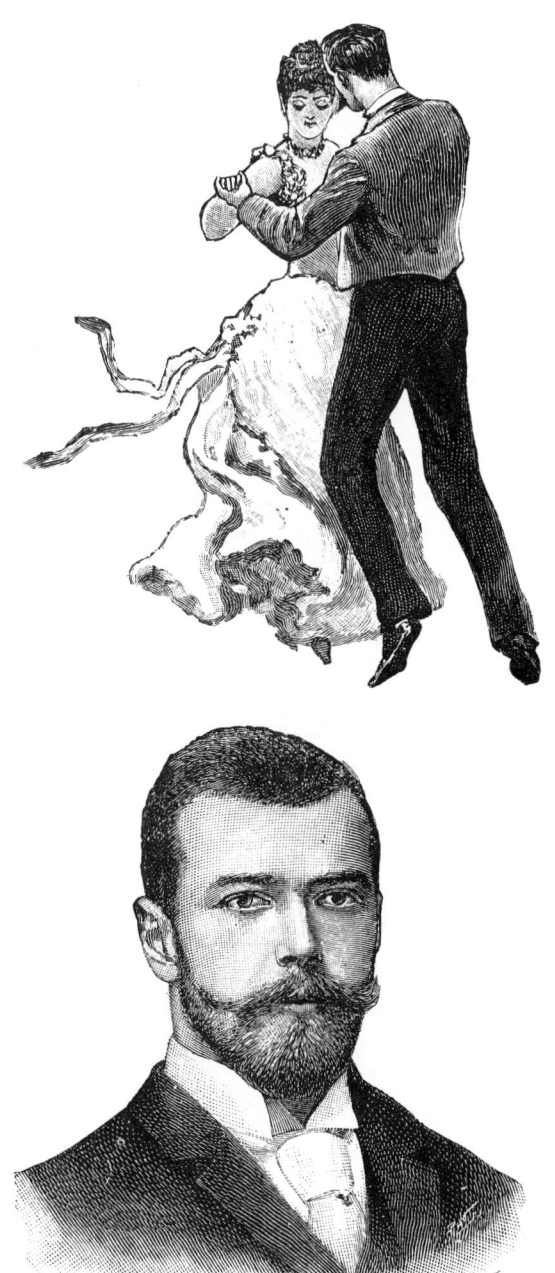

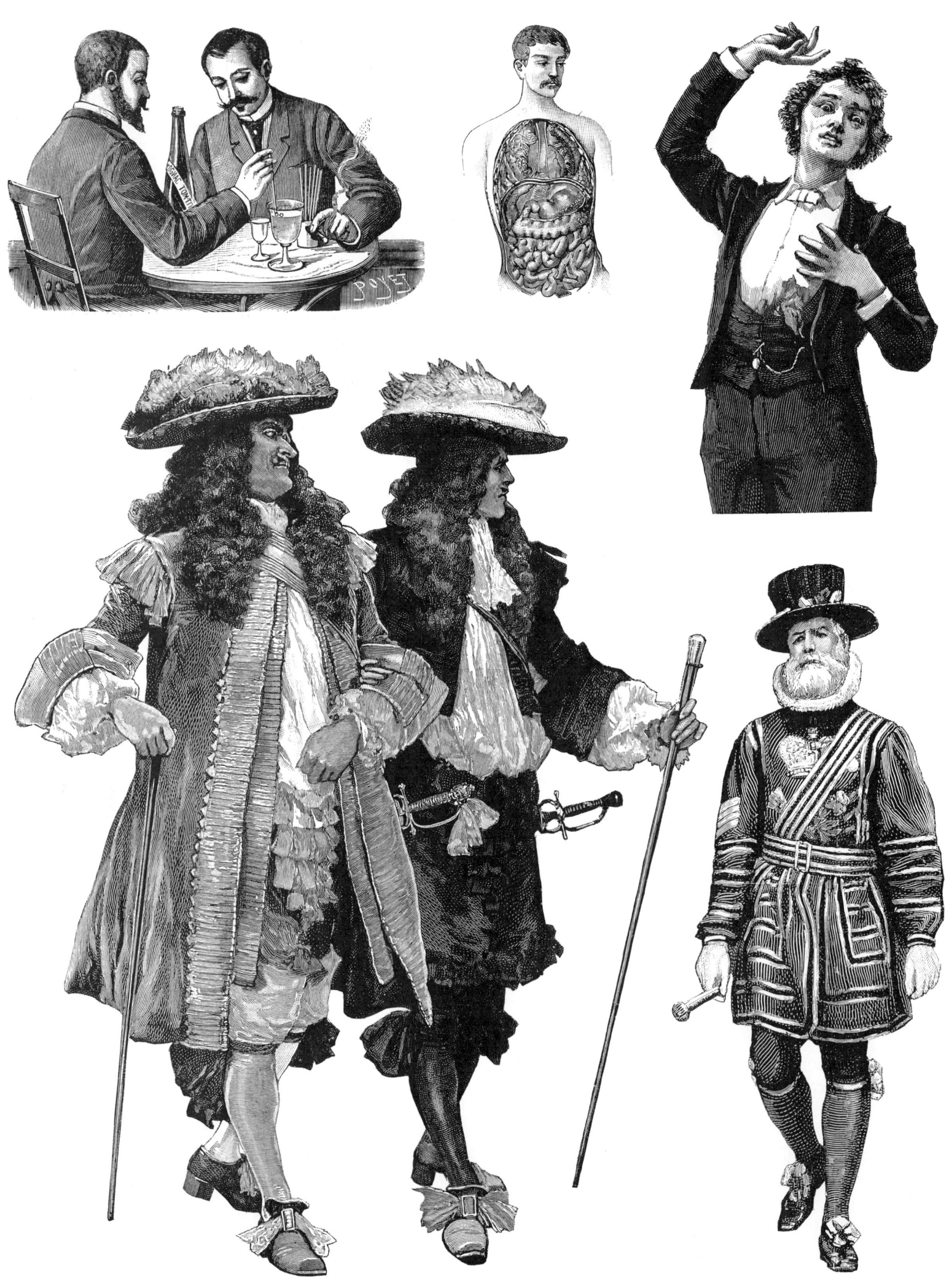

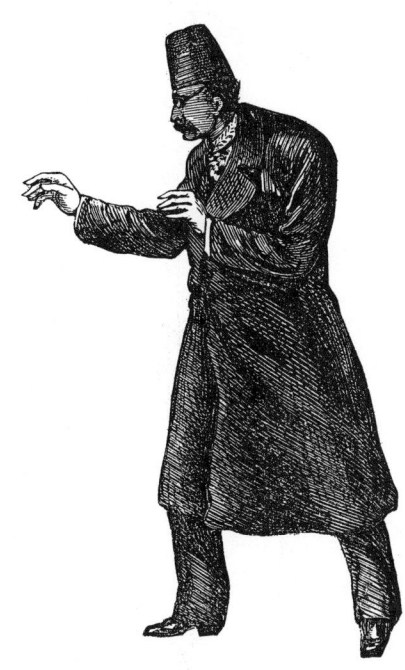
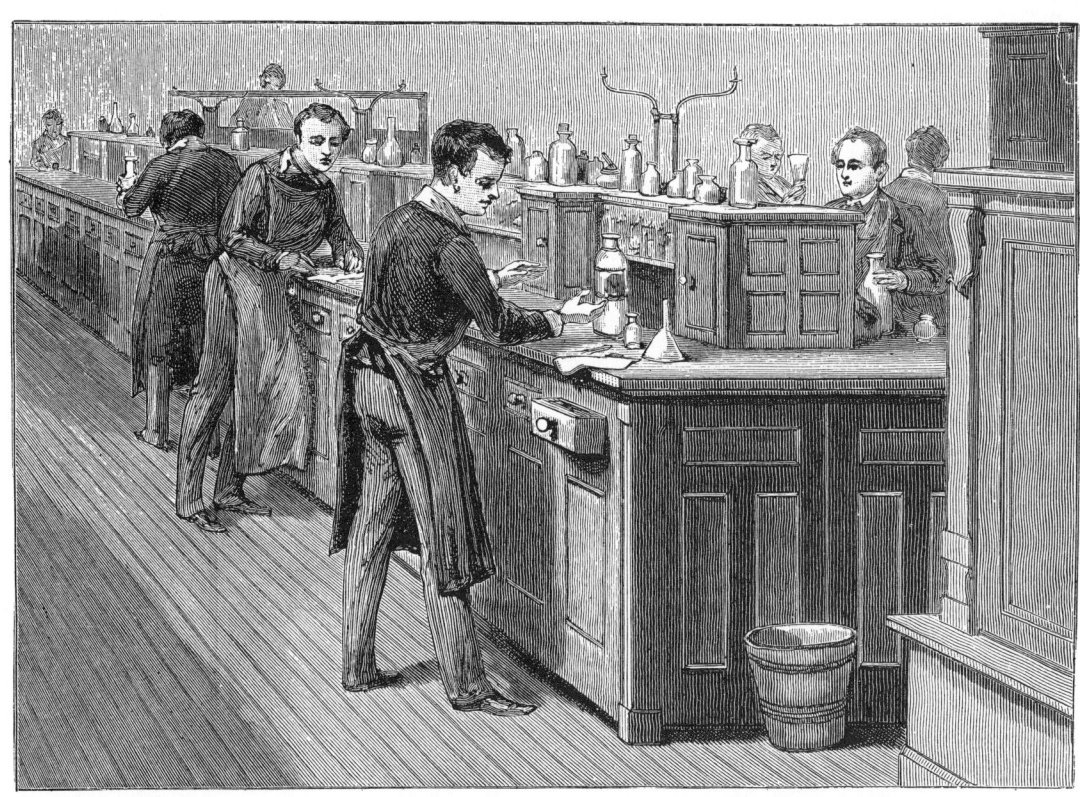

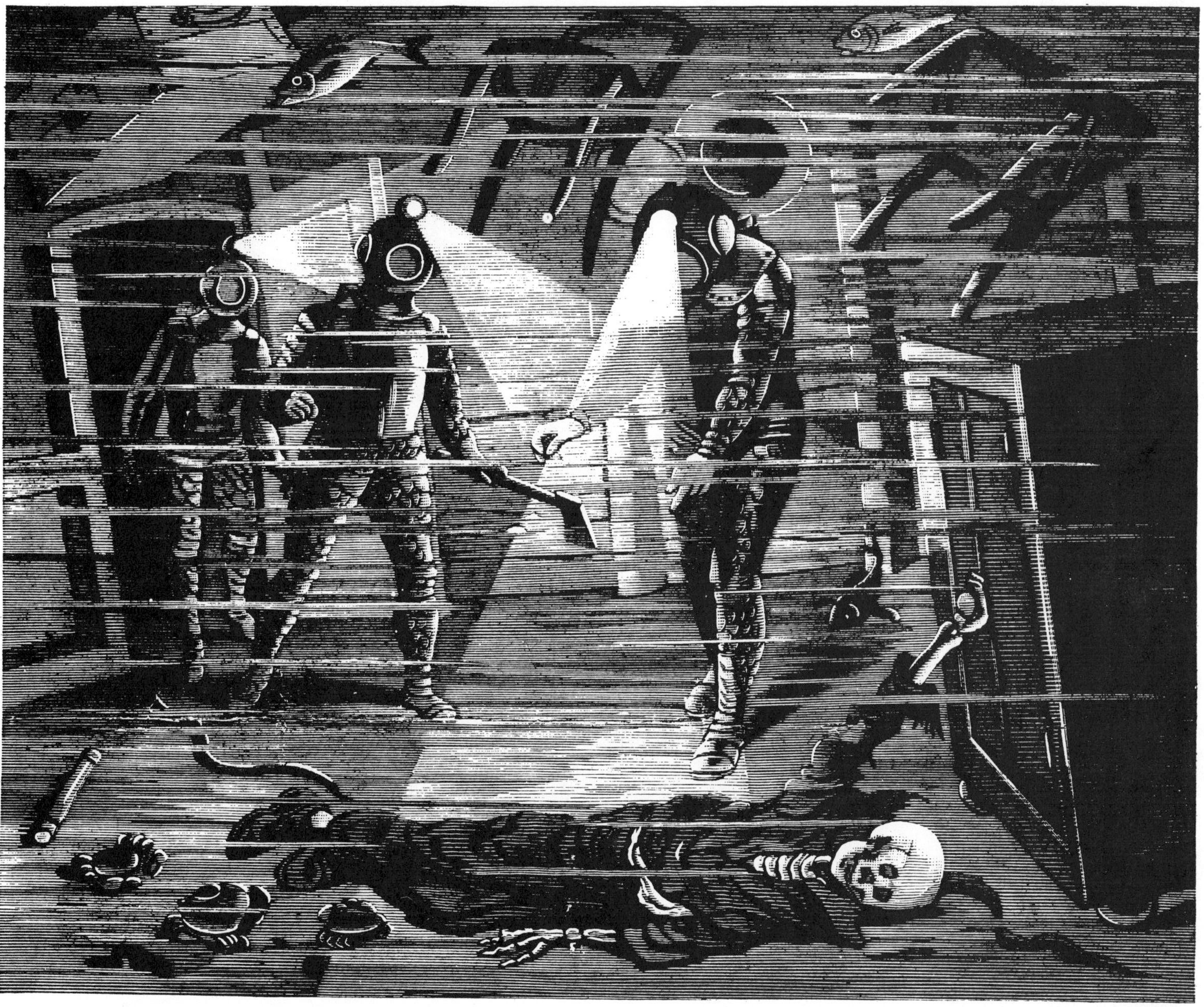

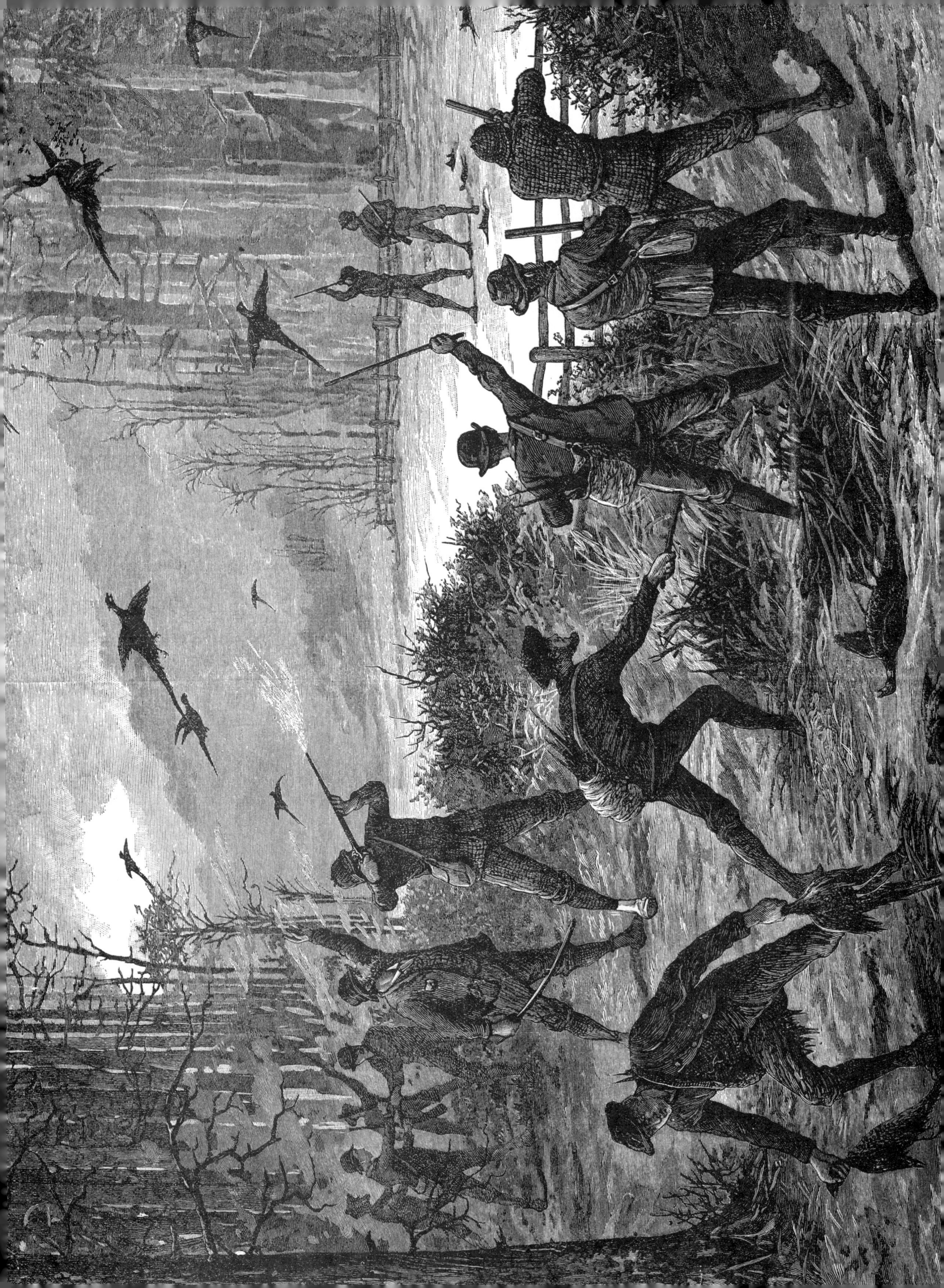

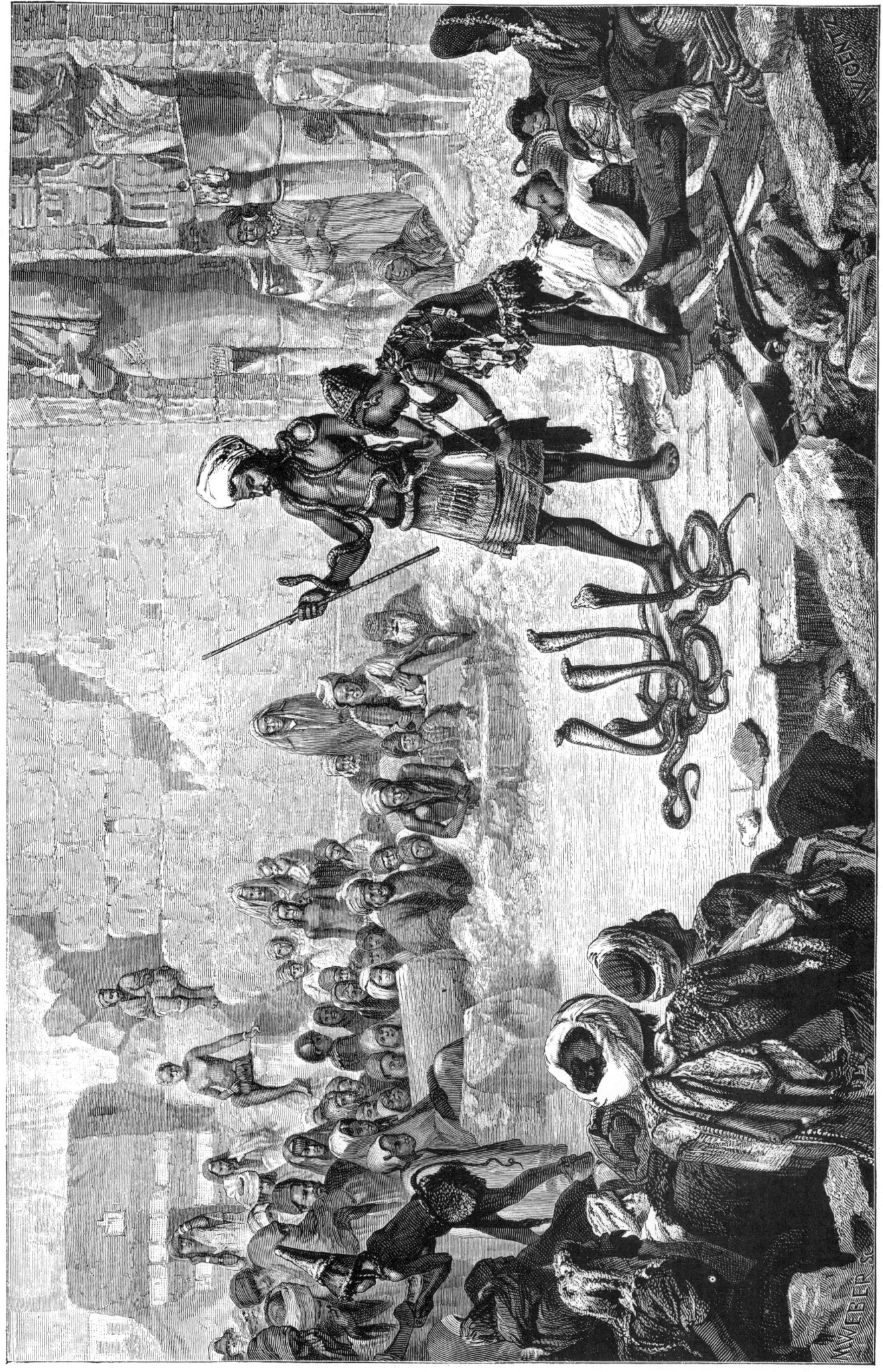

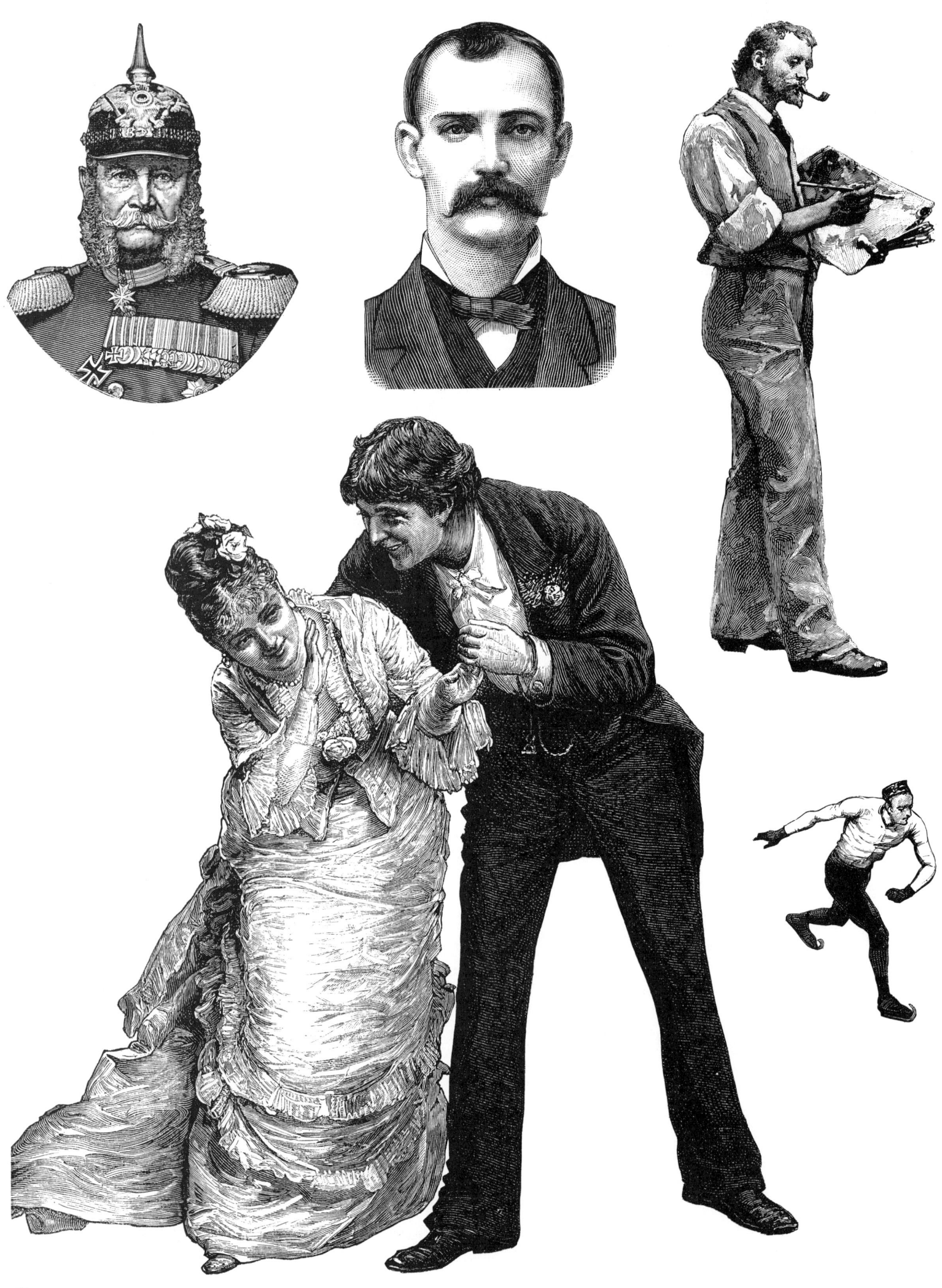

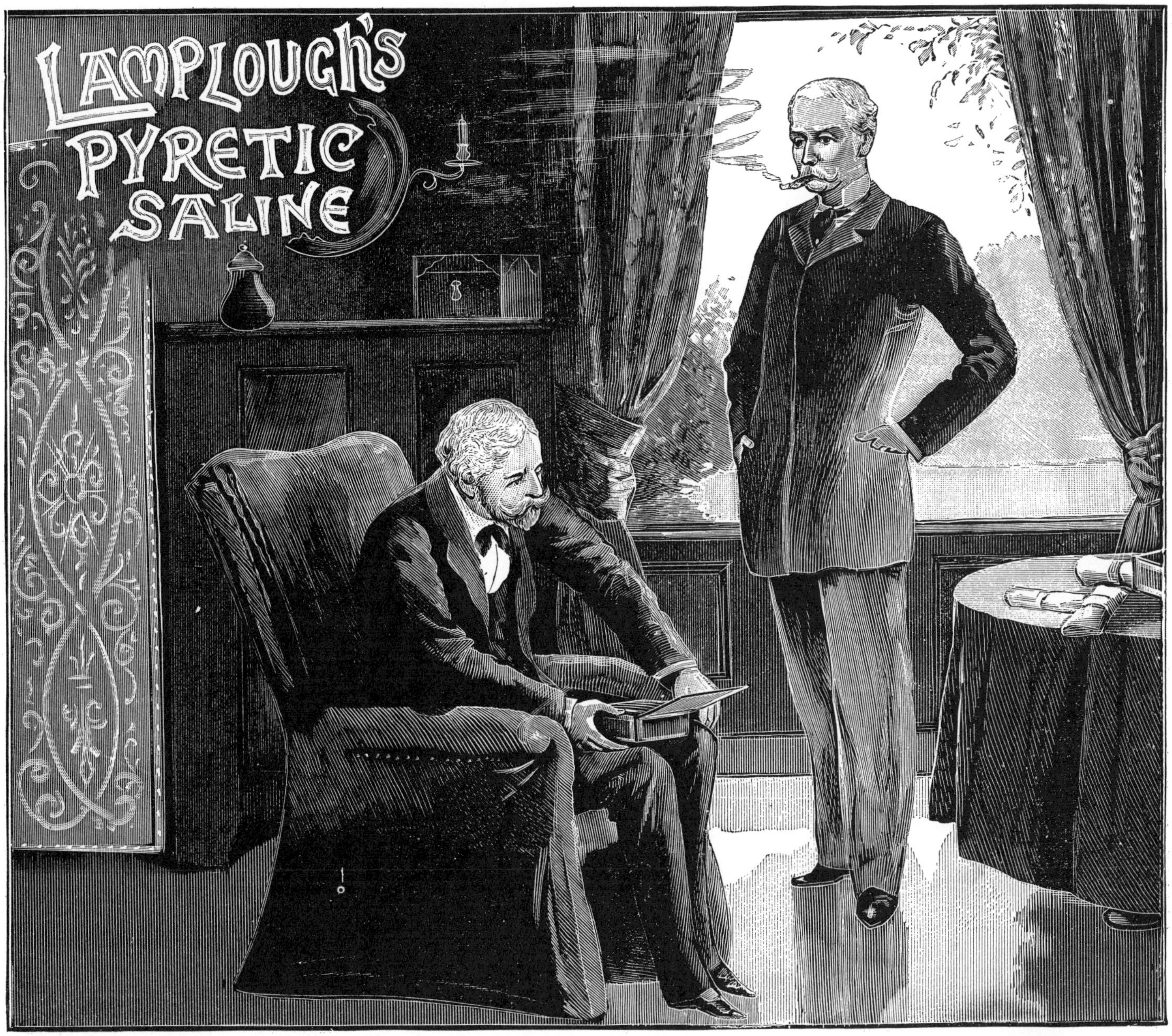

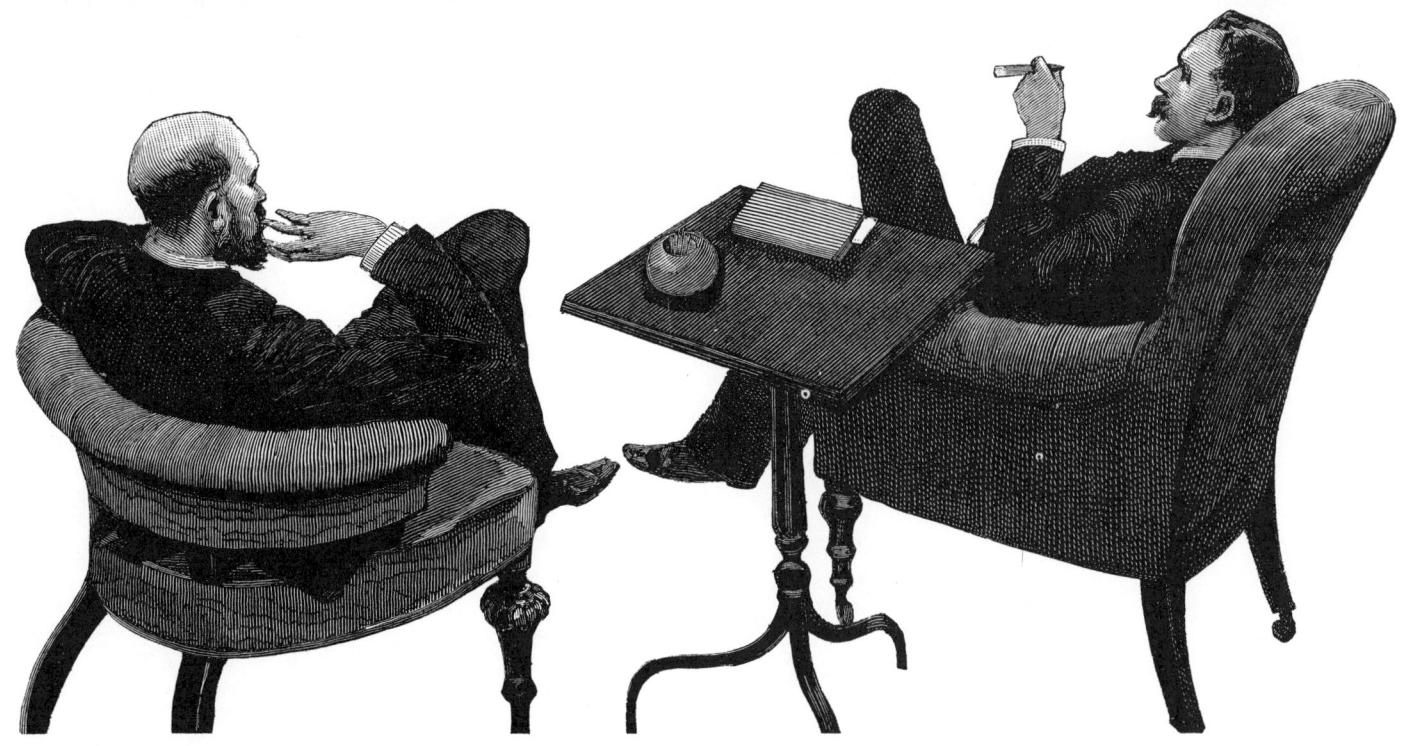

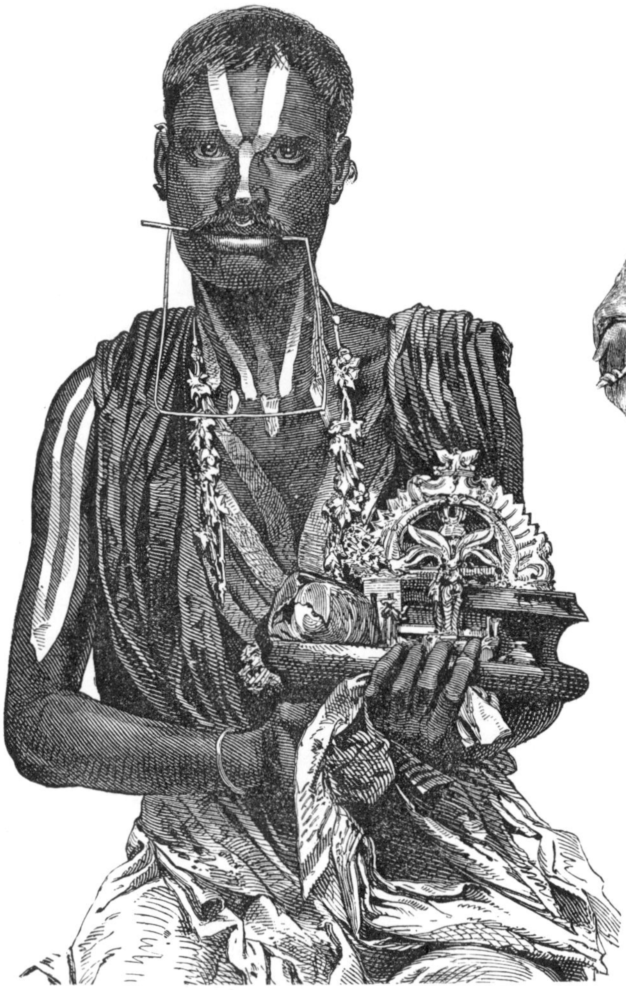

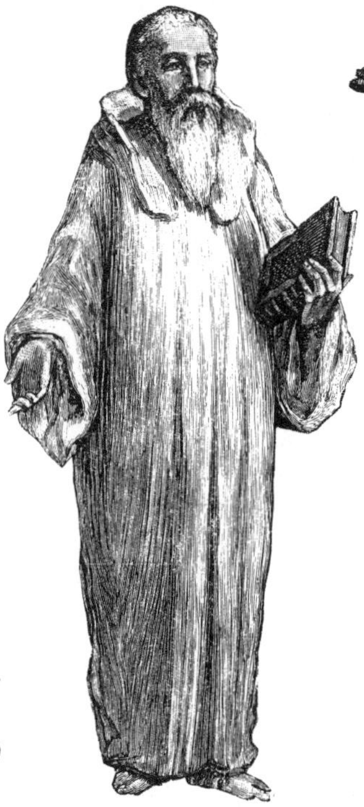

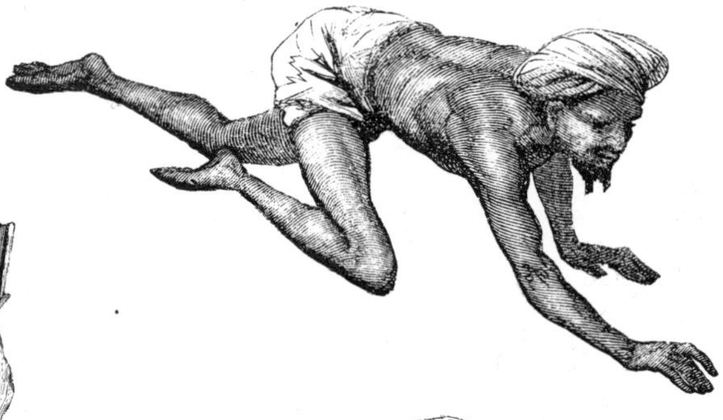

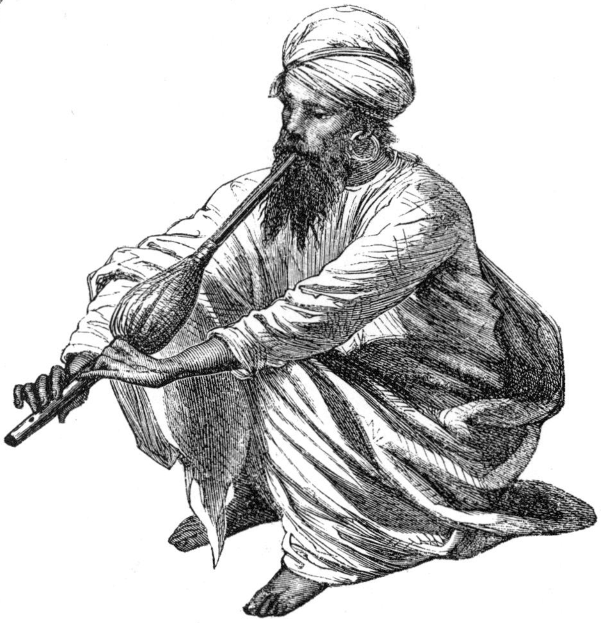

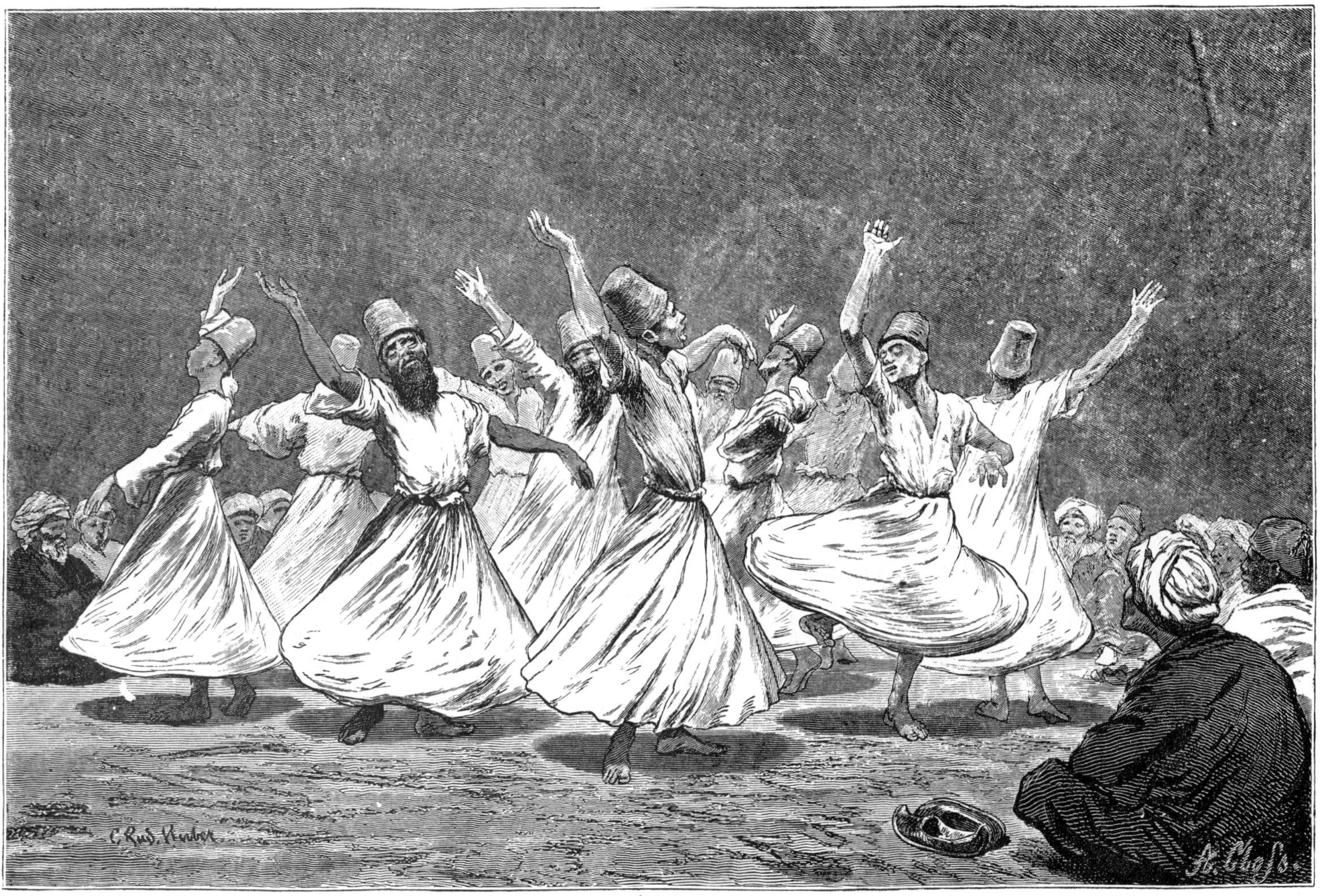

44

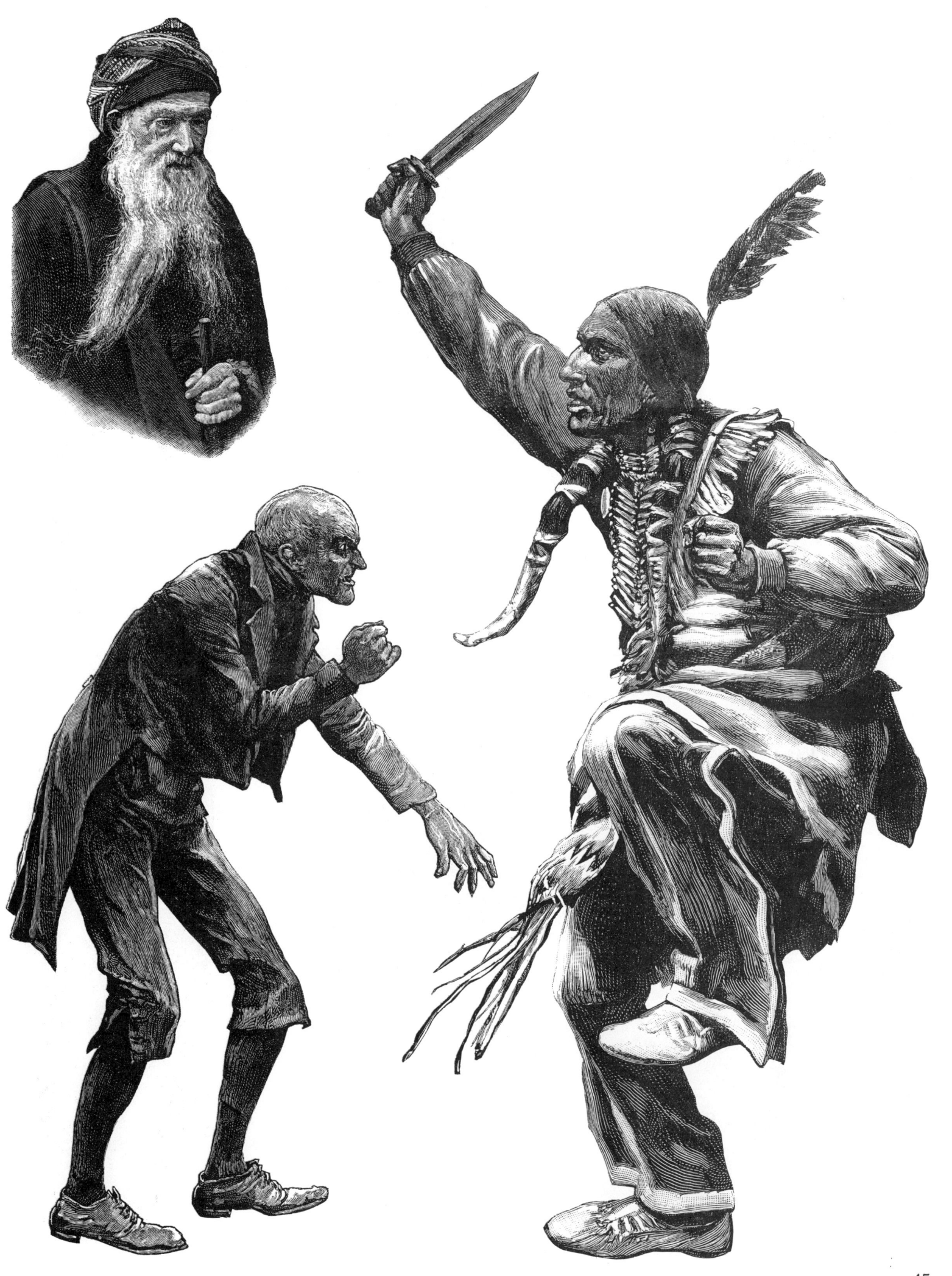

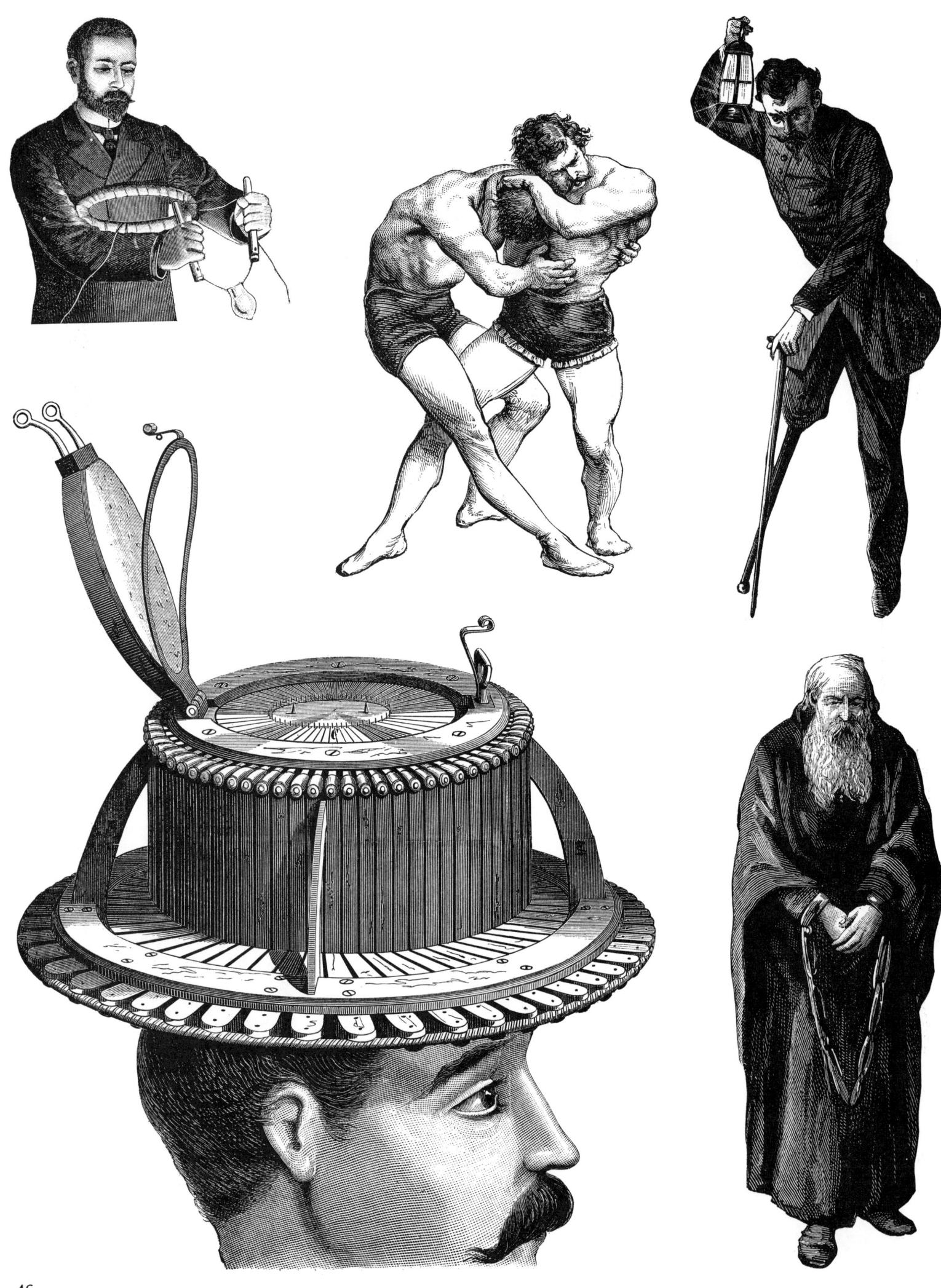

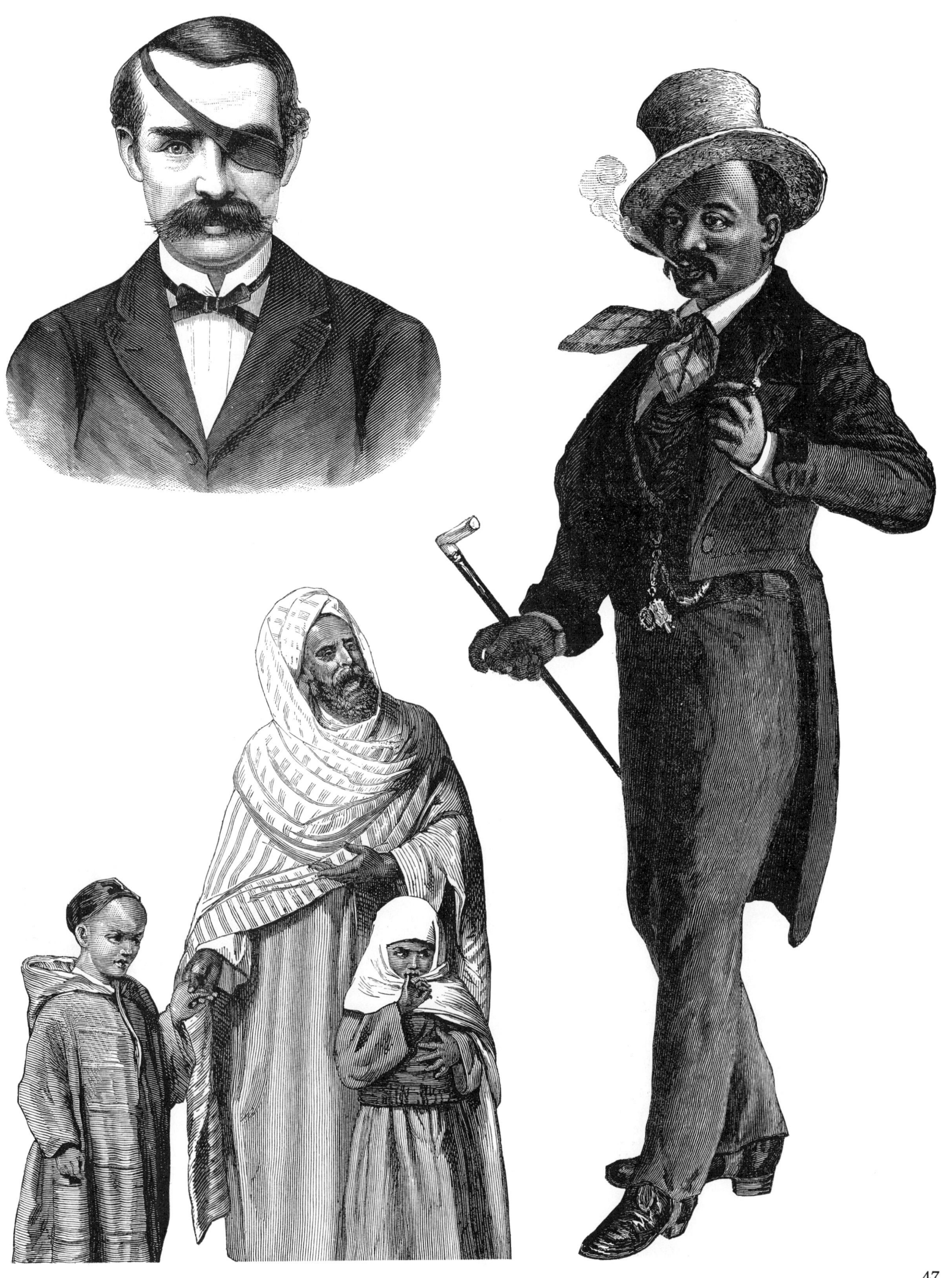

47

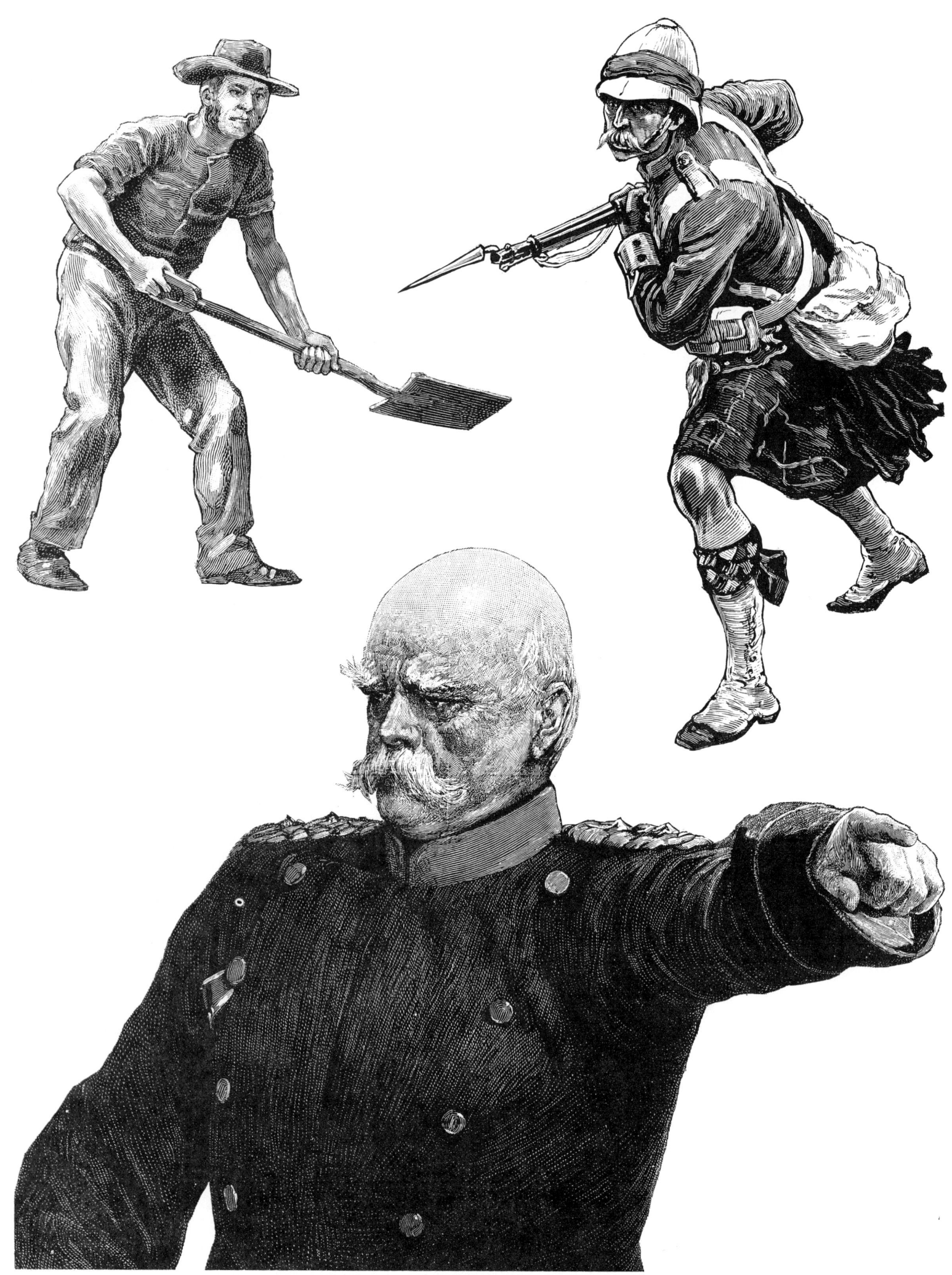

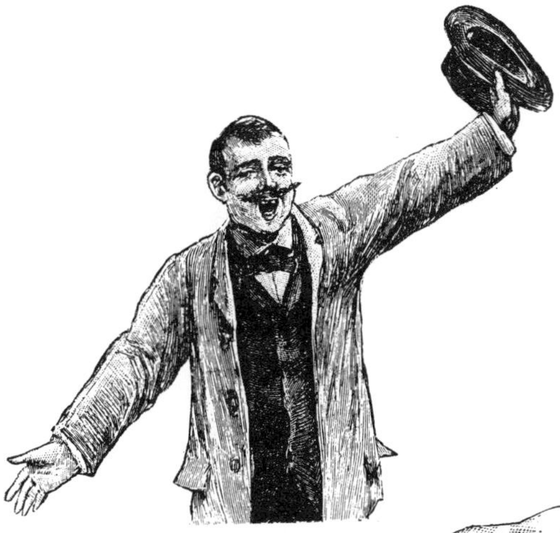

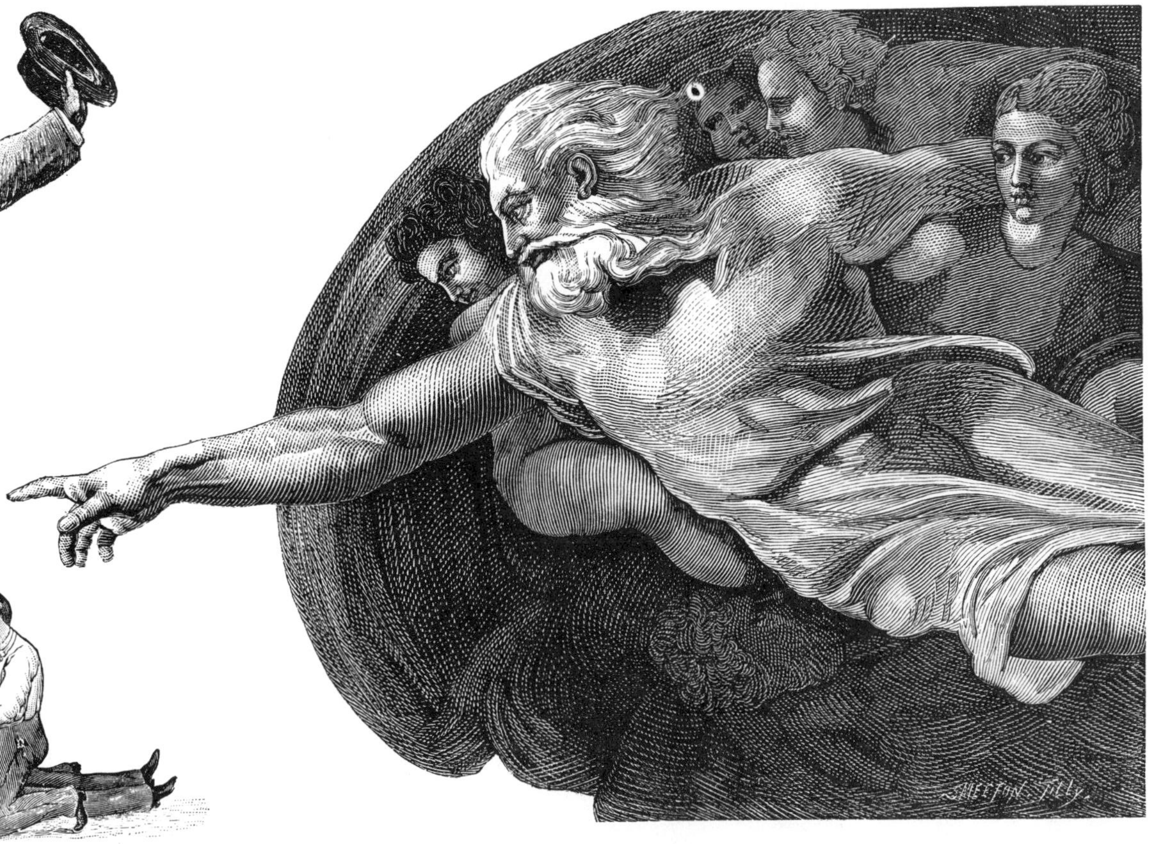

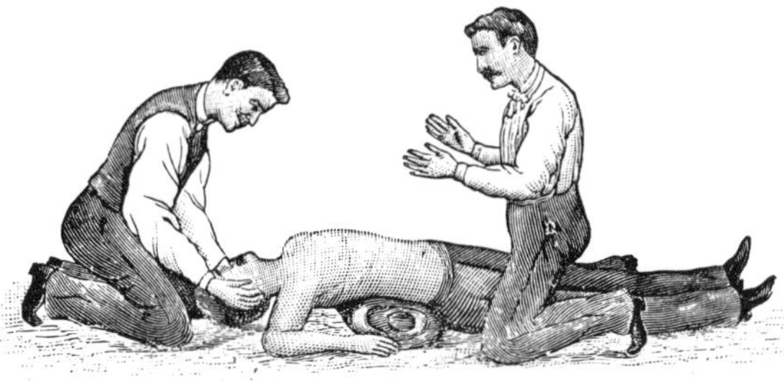

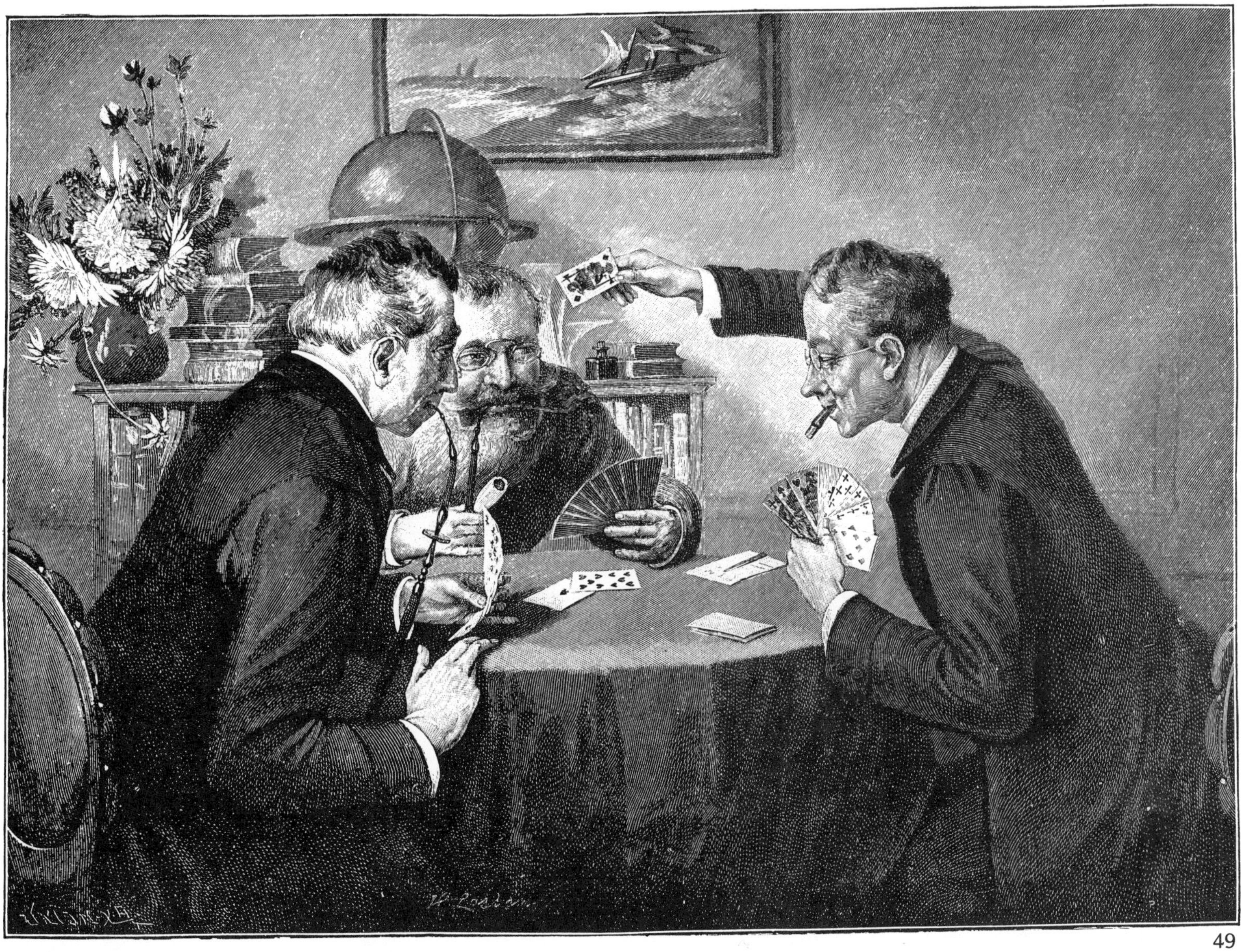

49

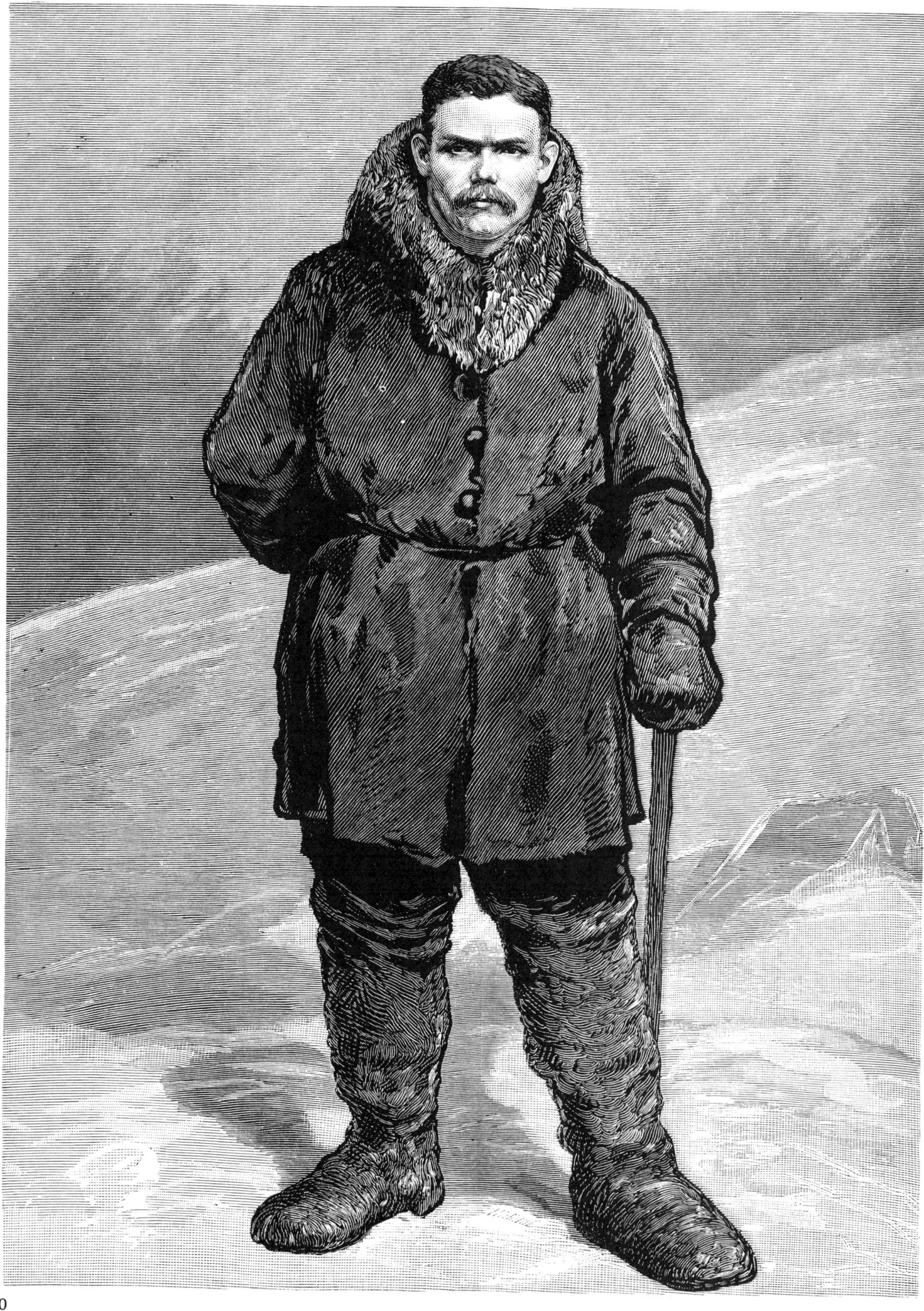

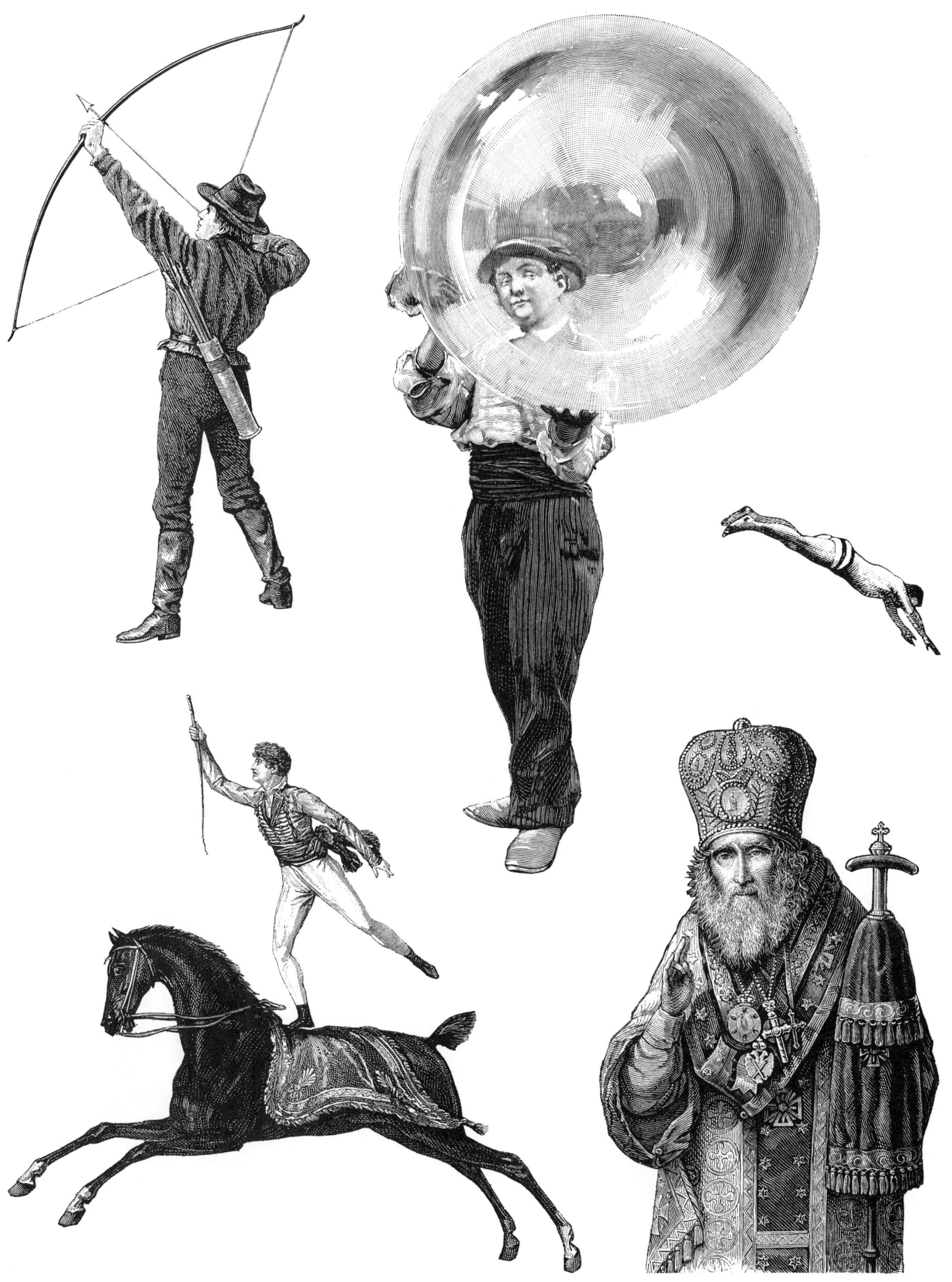

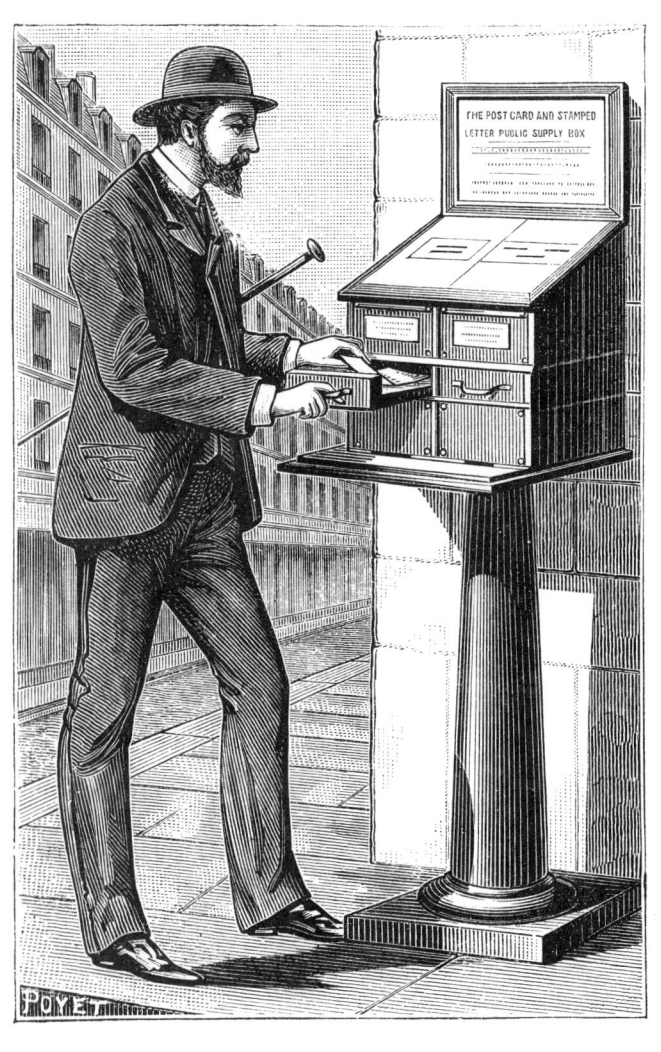
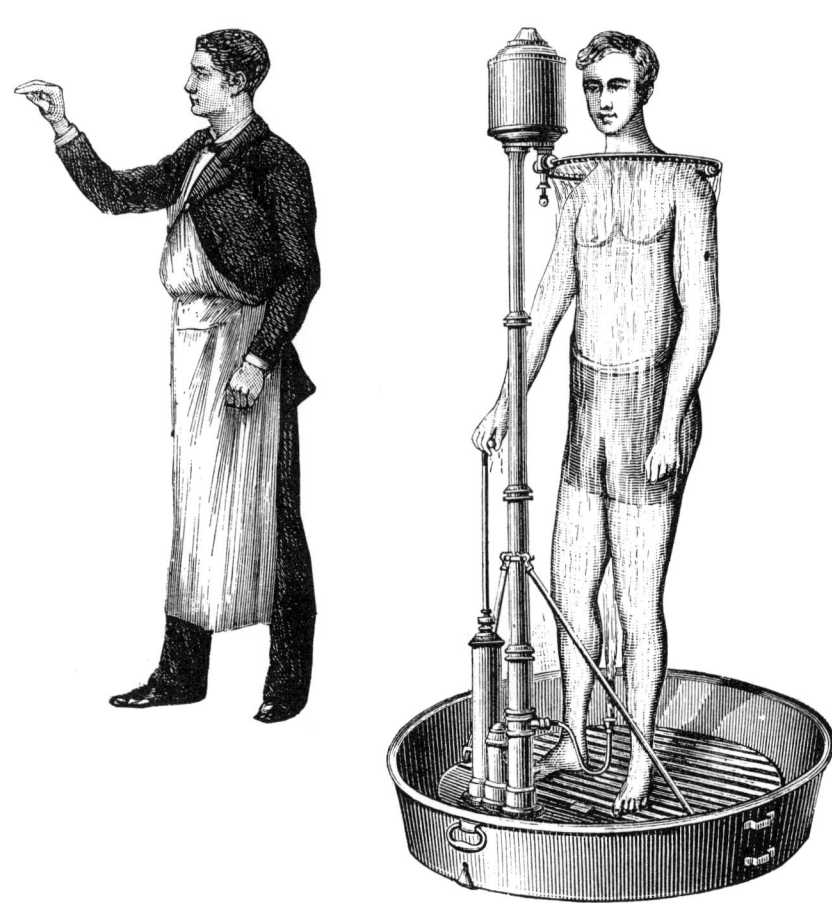
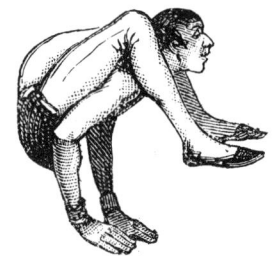
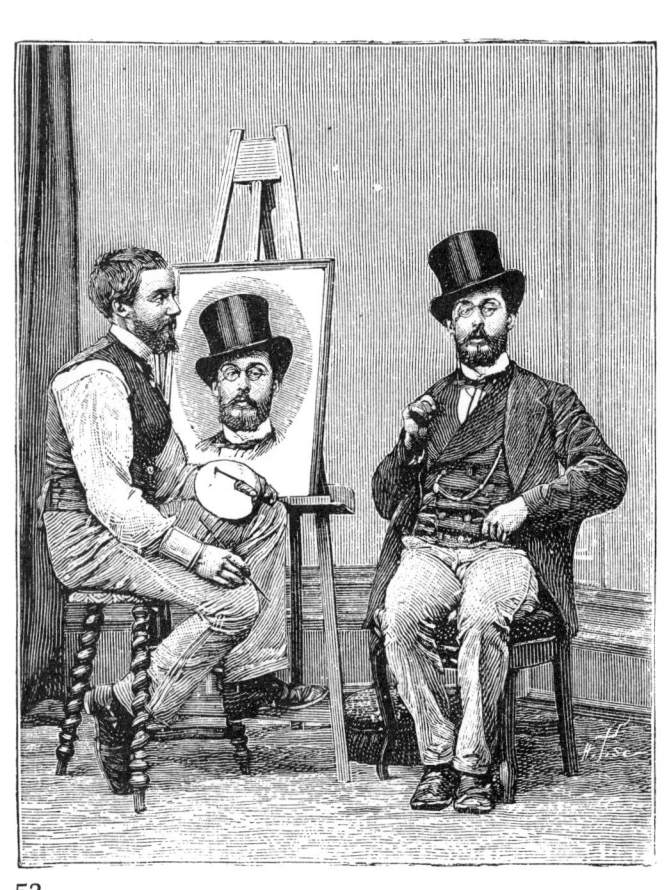
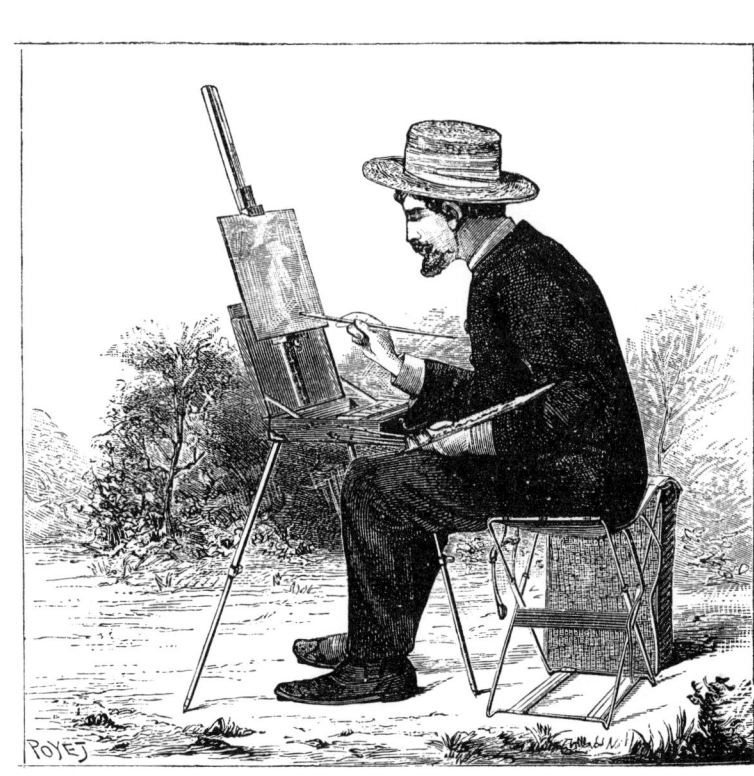

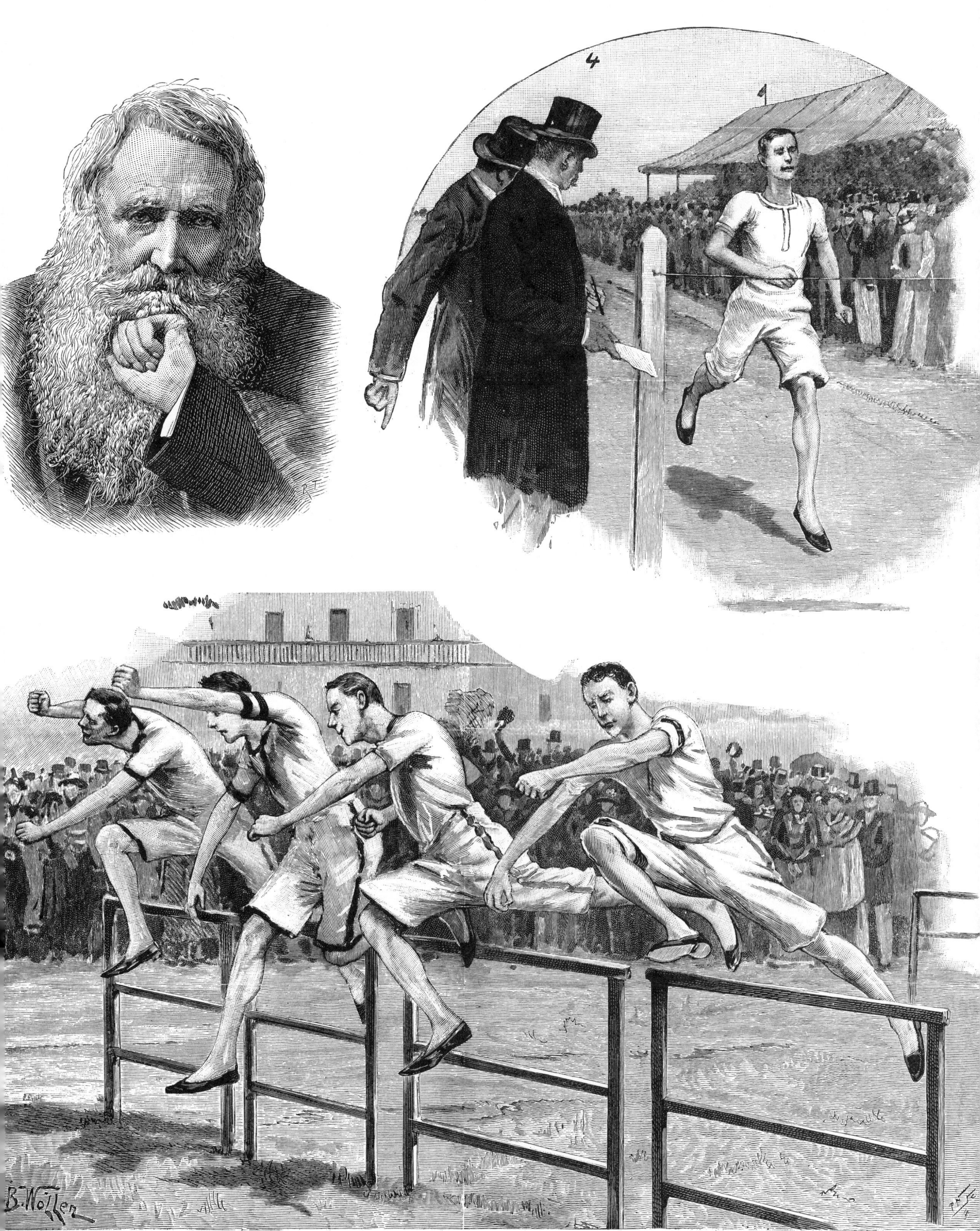

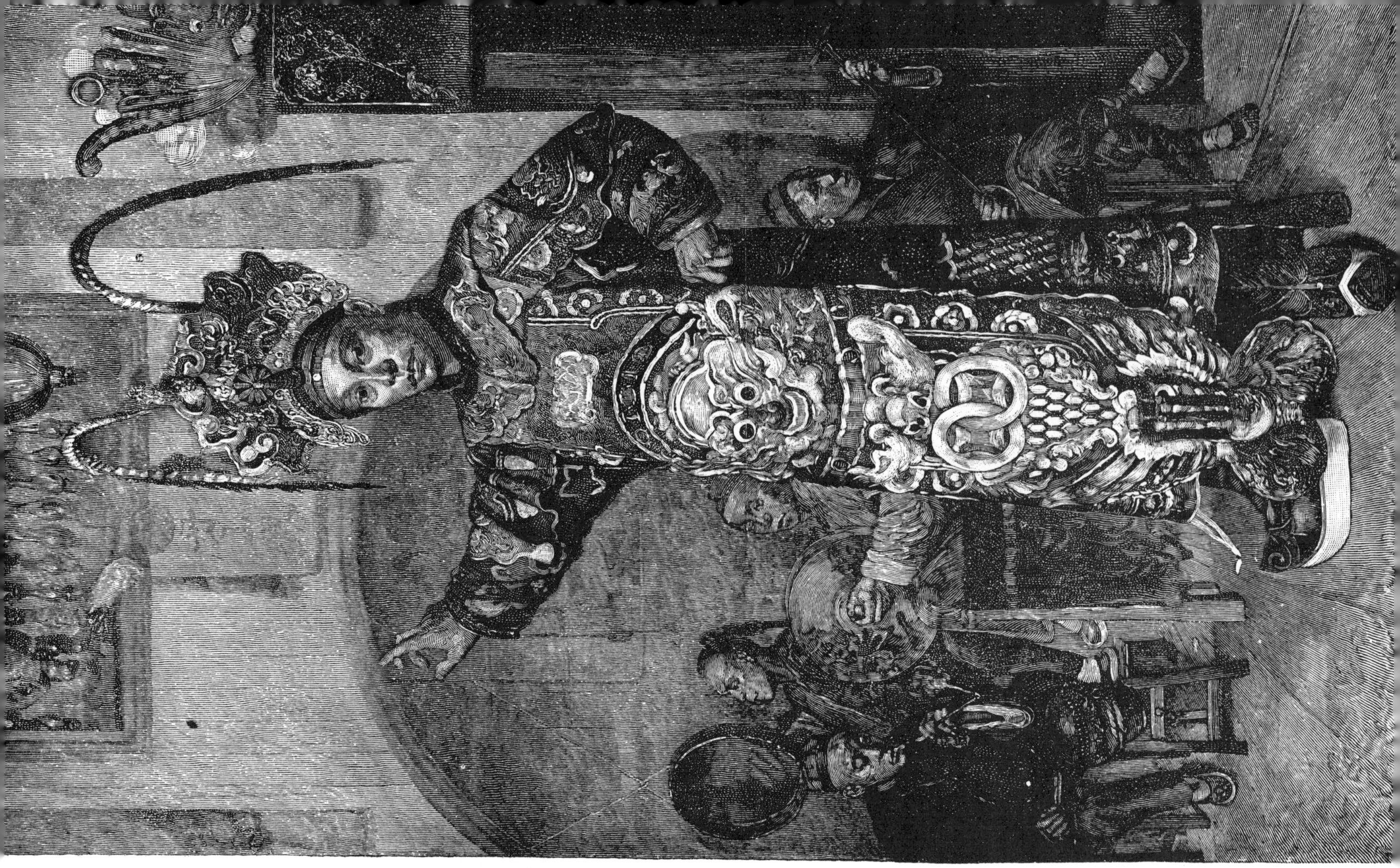

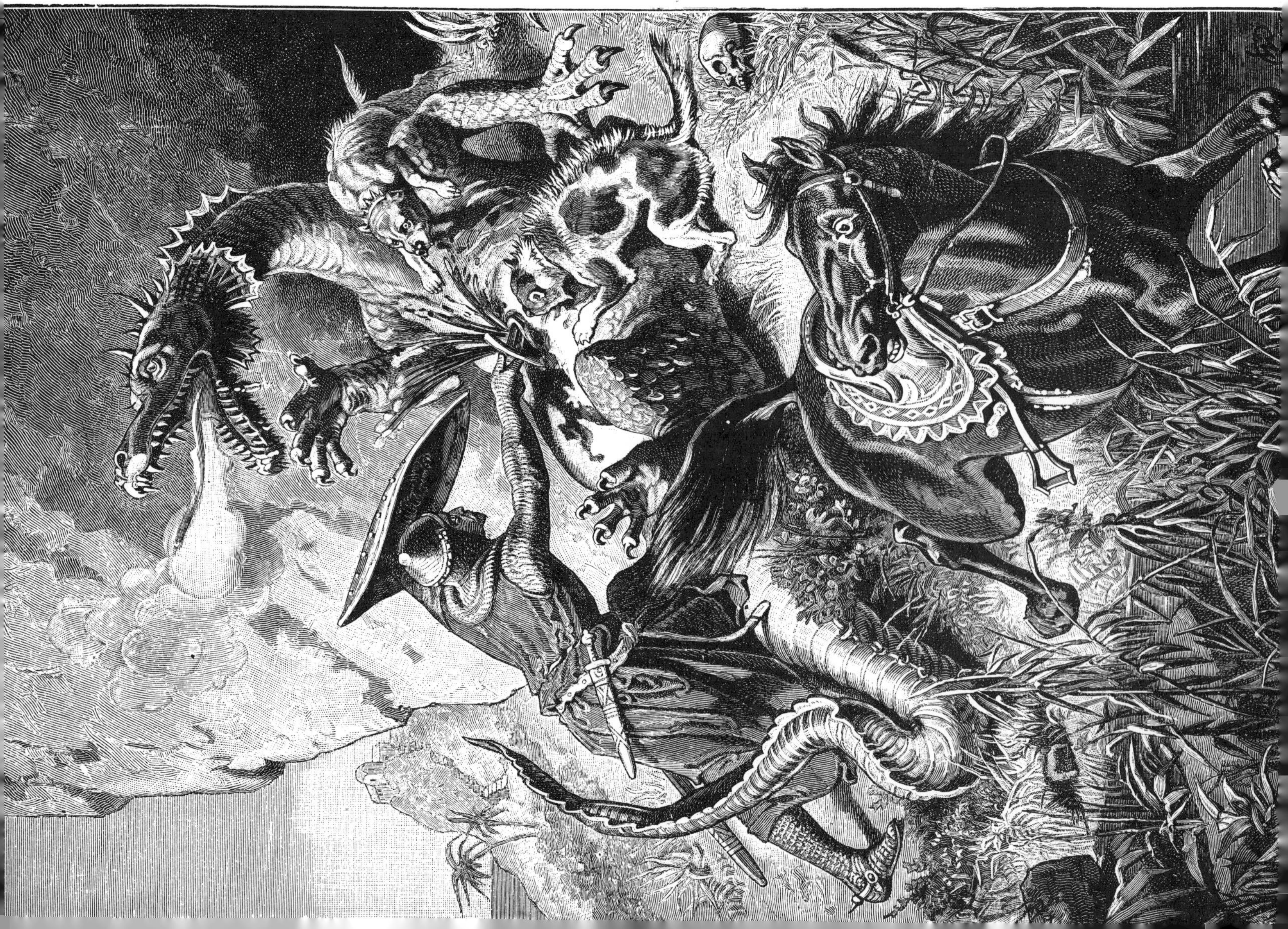

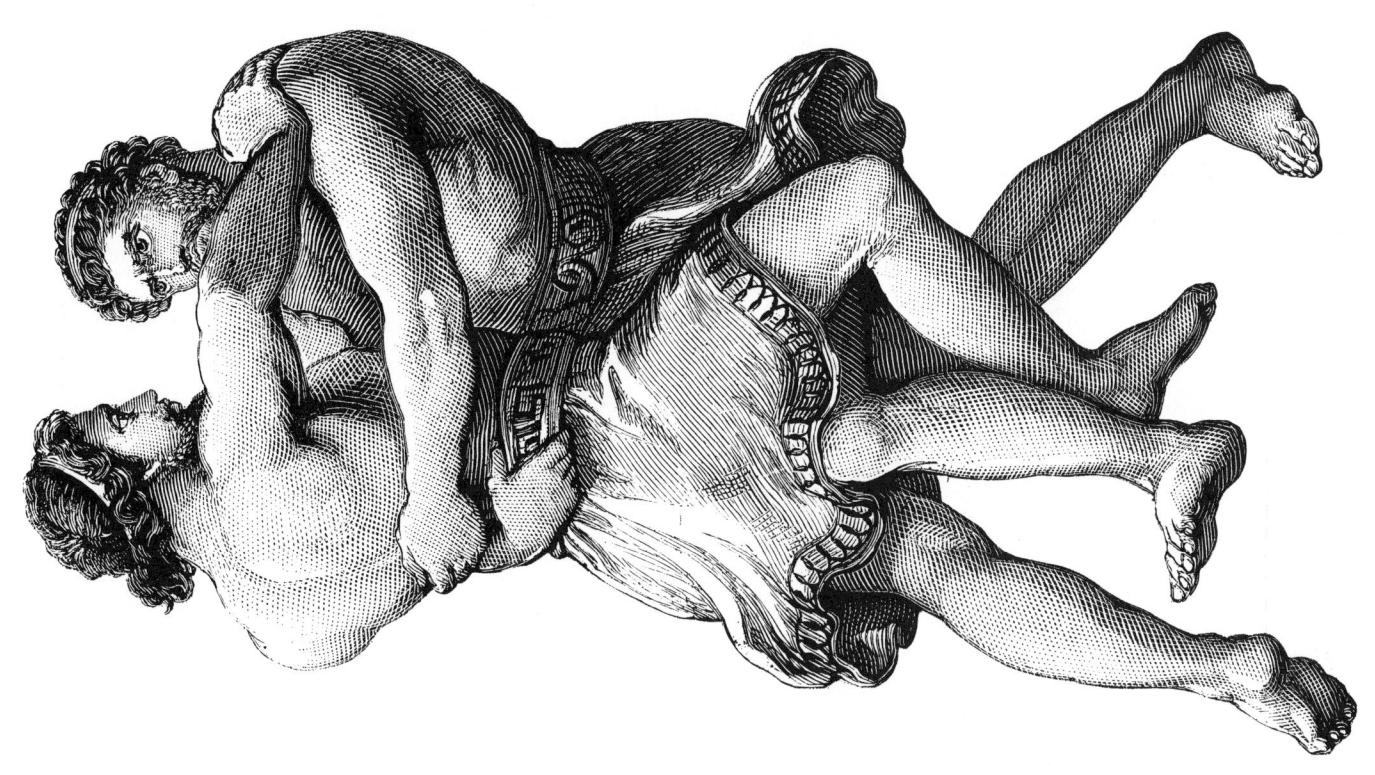

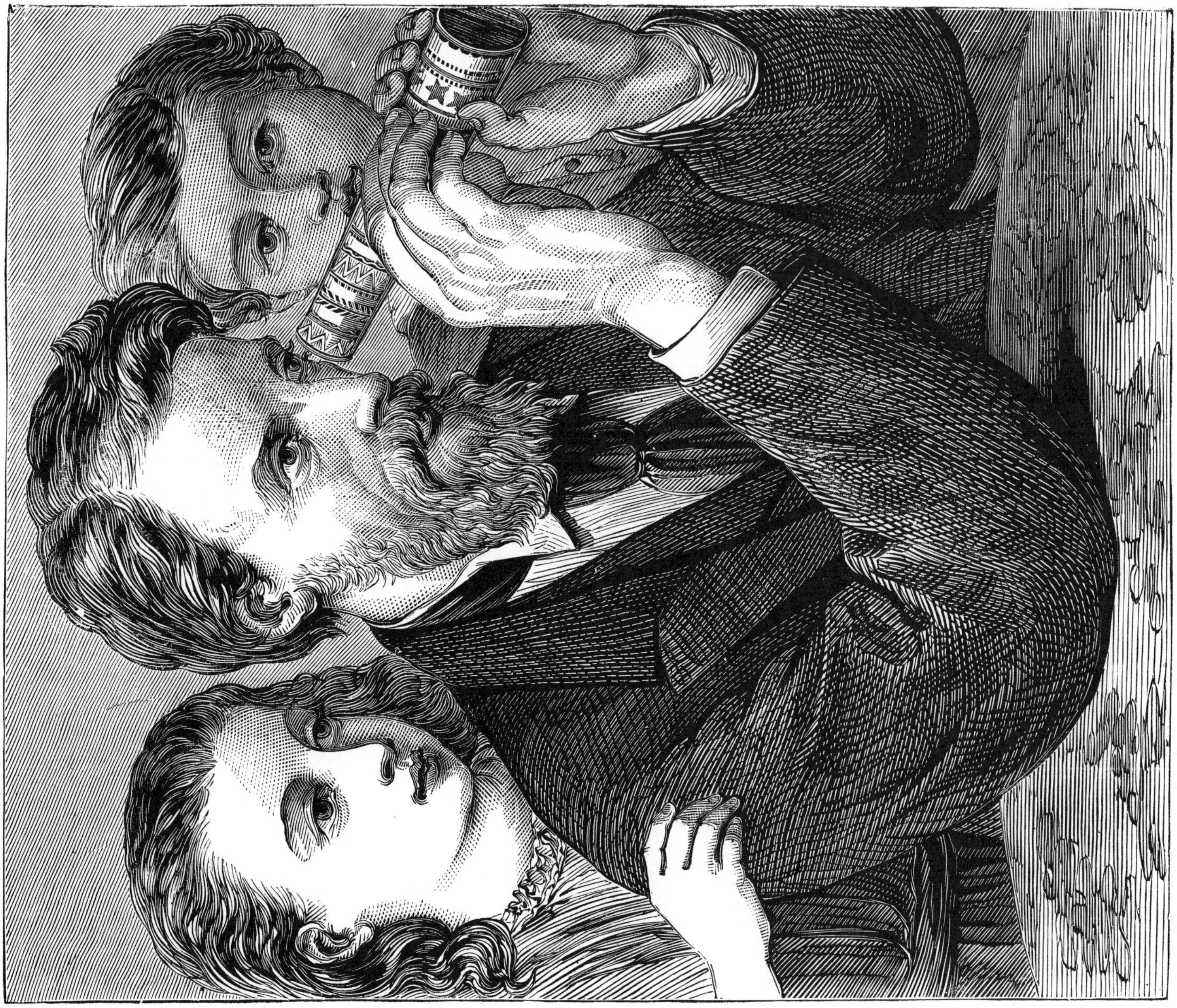

55

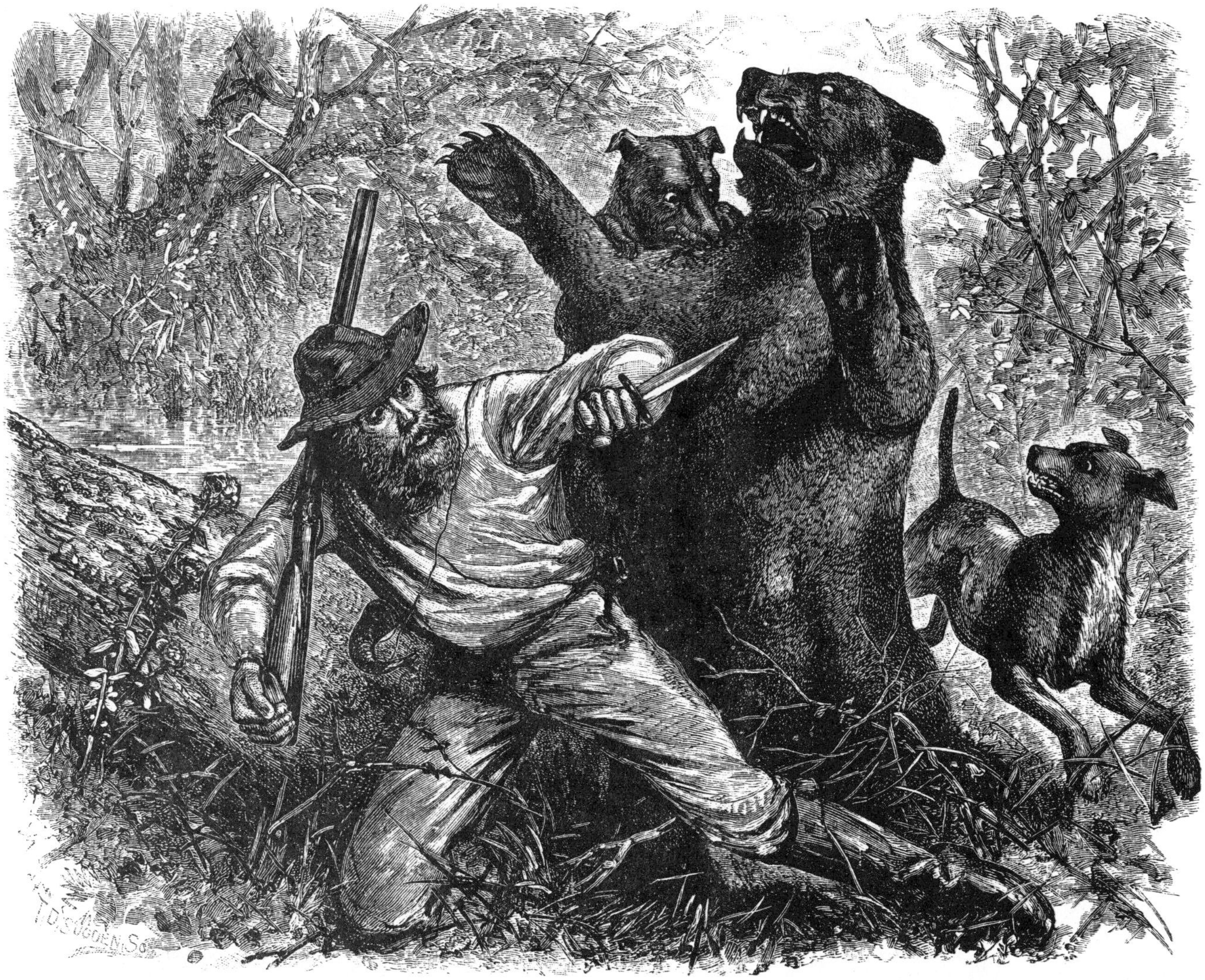

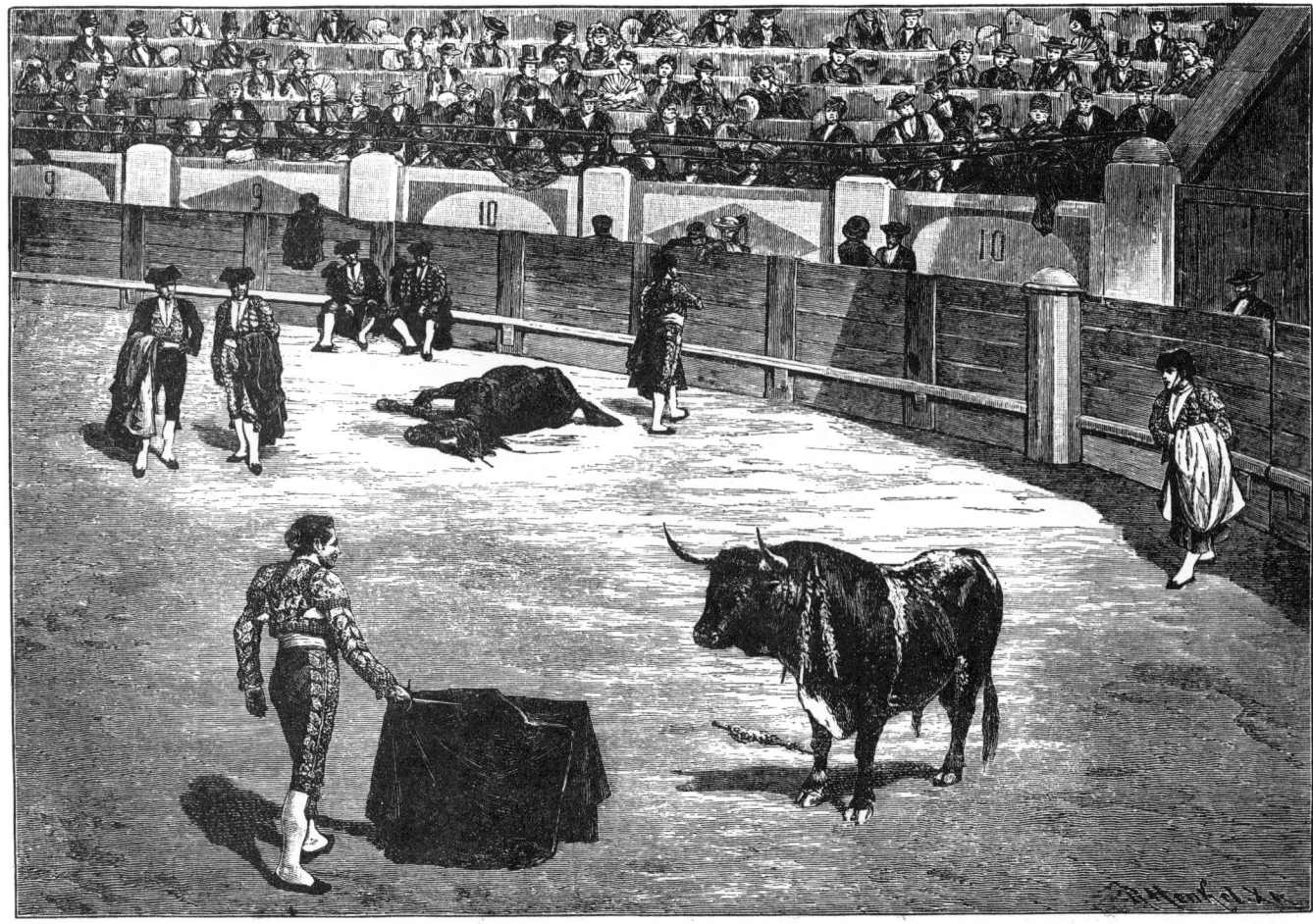

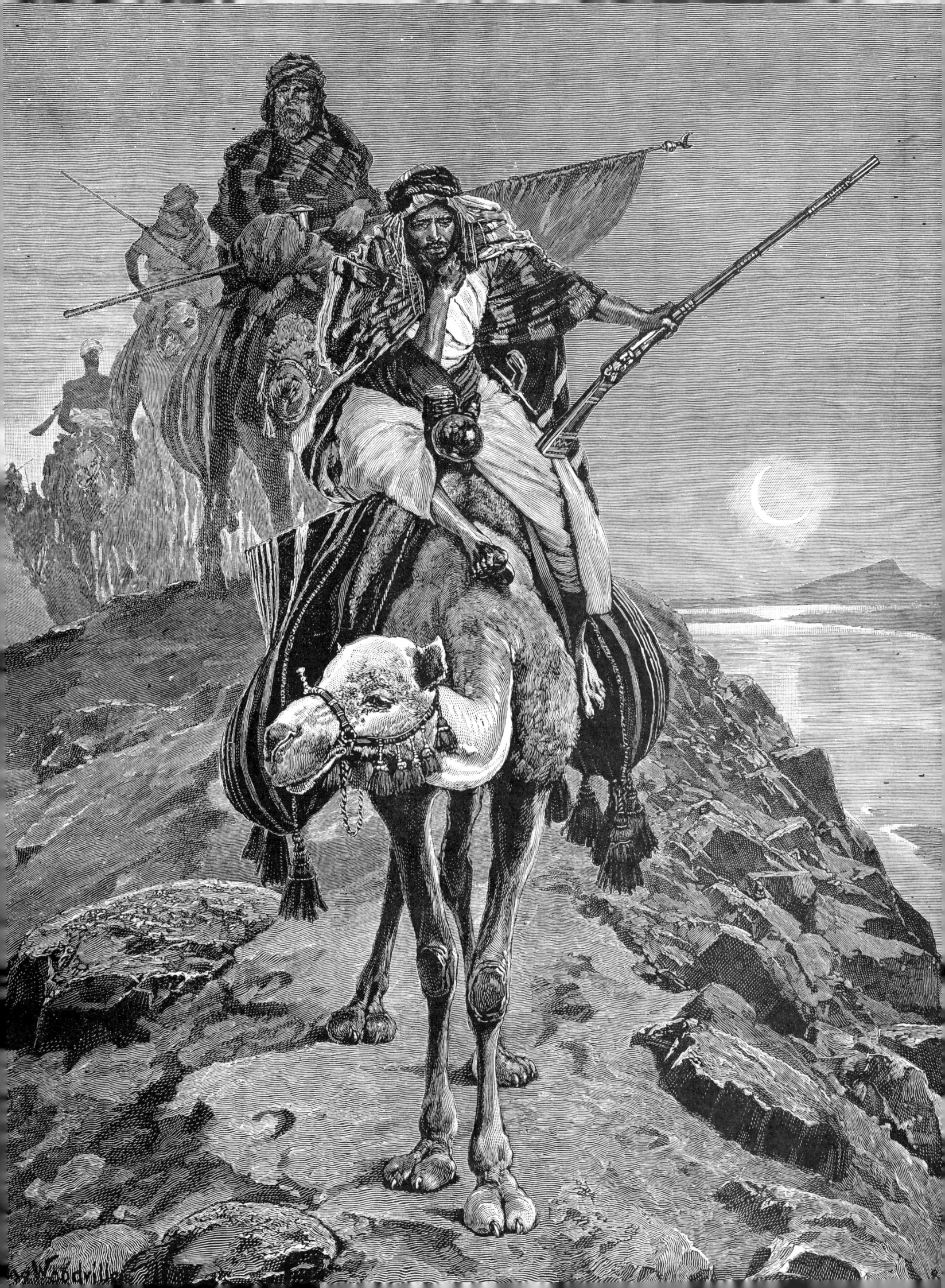

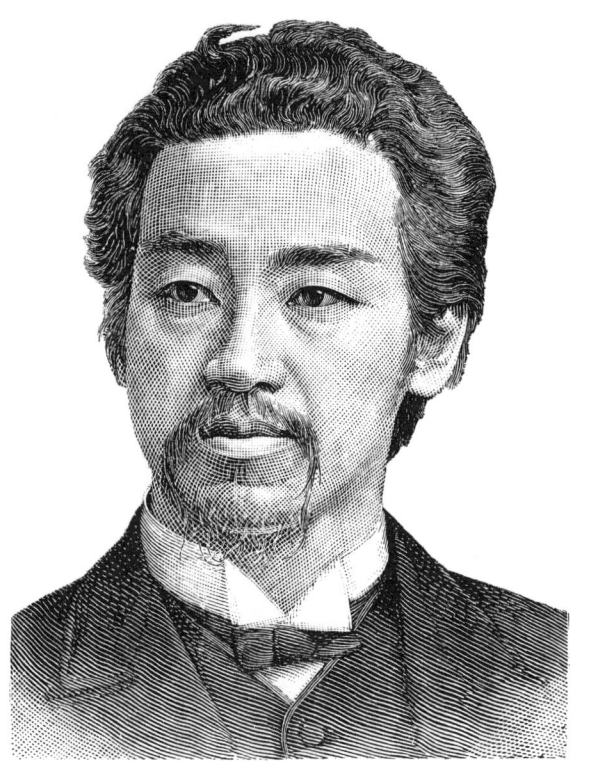
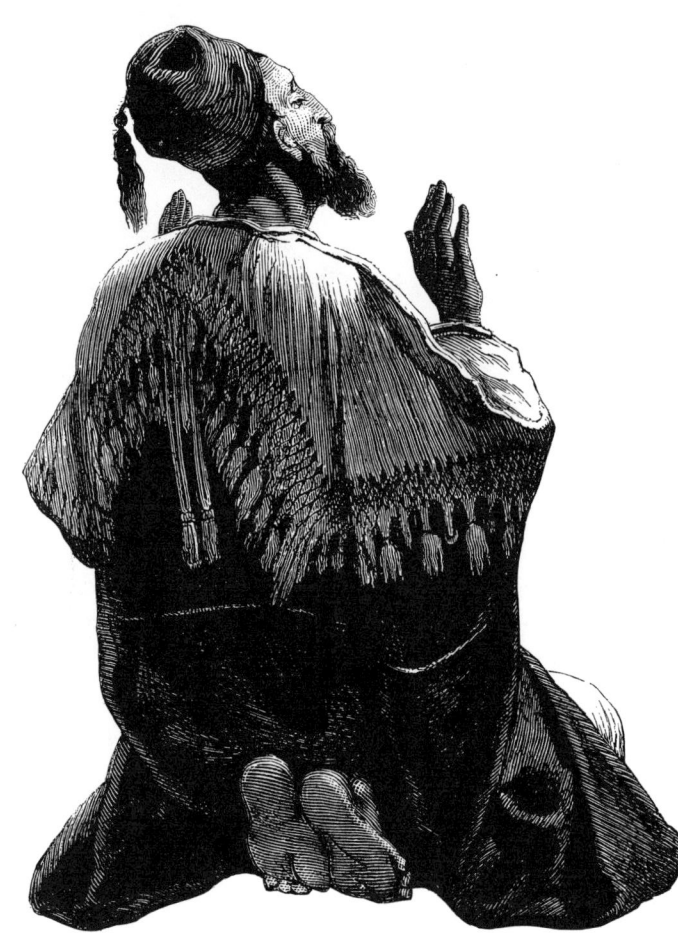
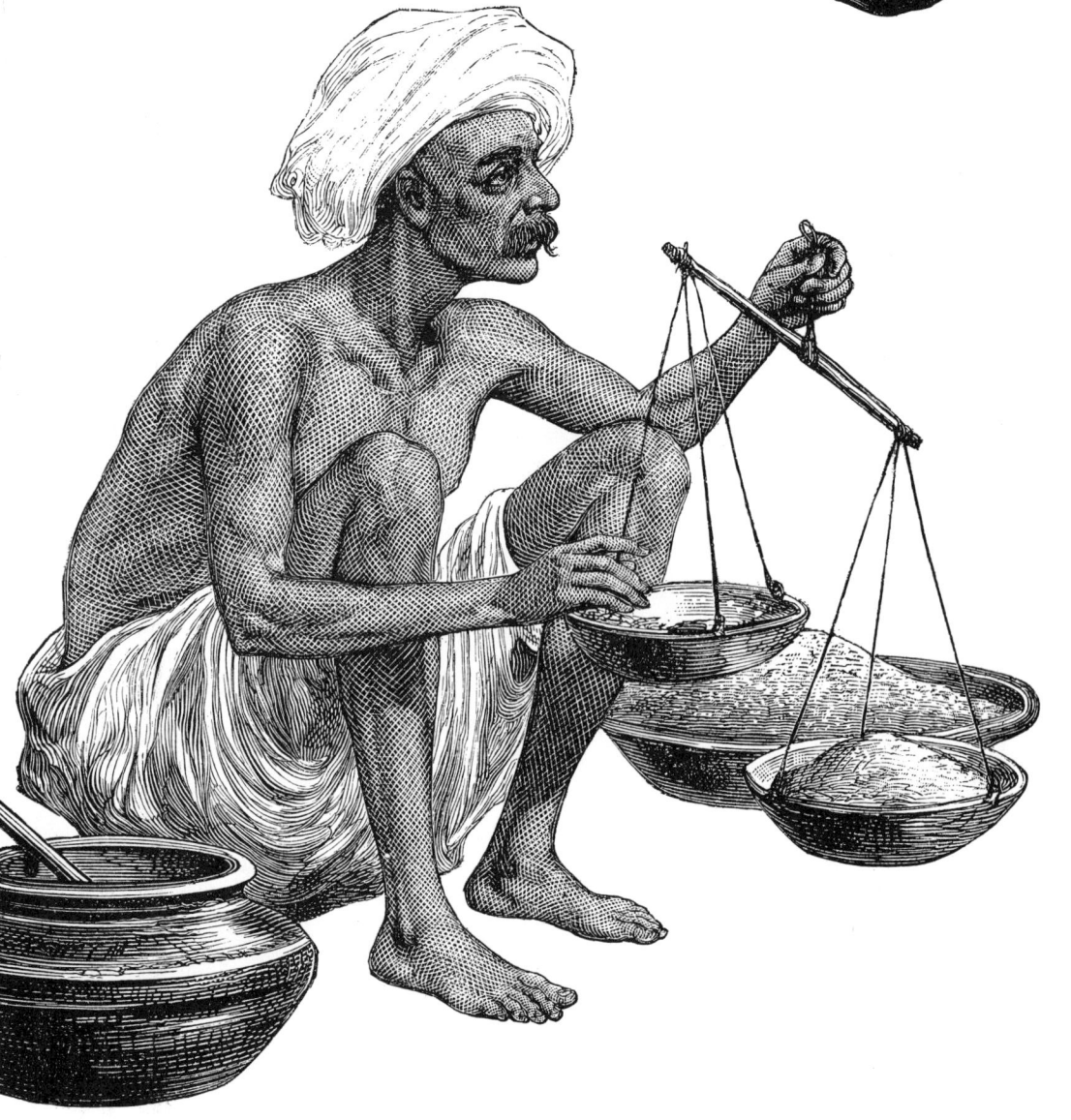
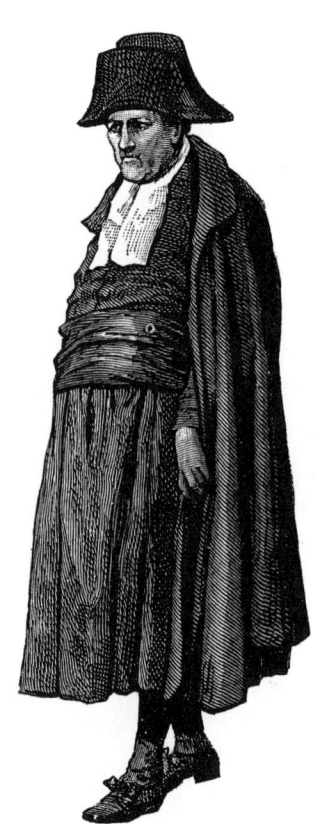

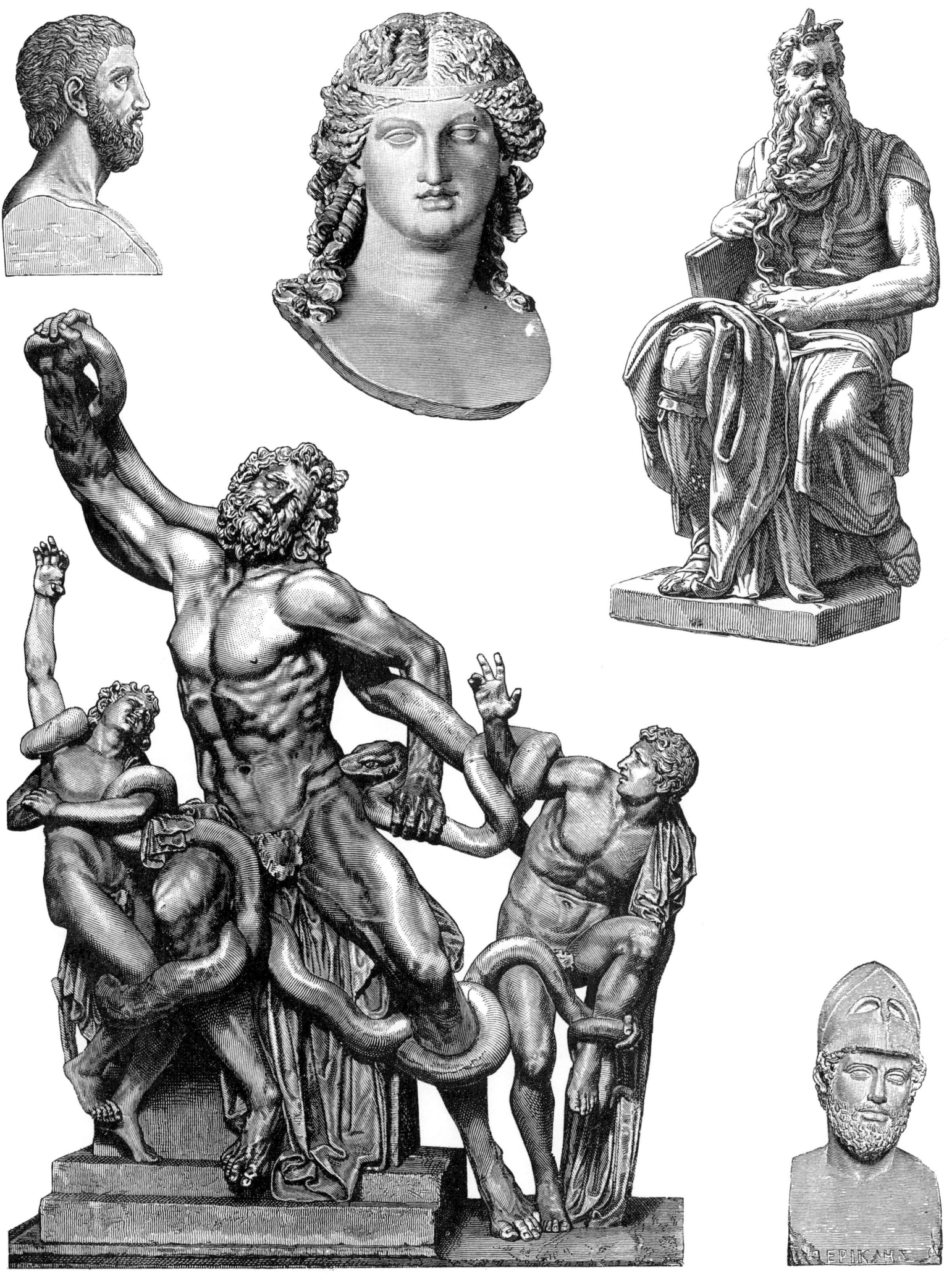

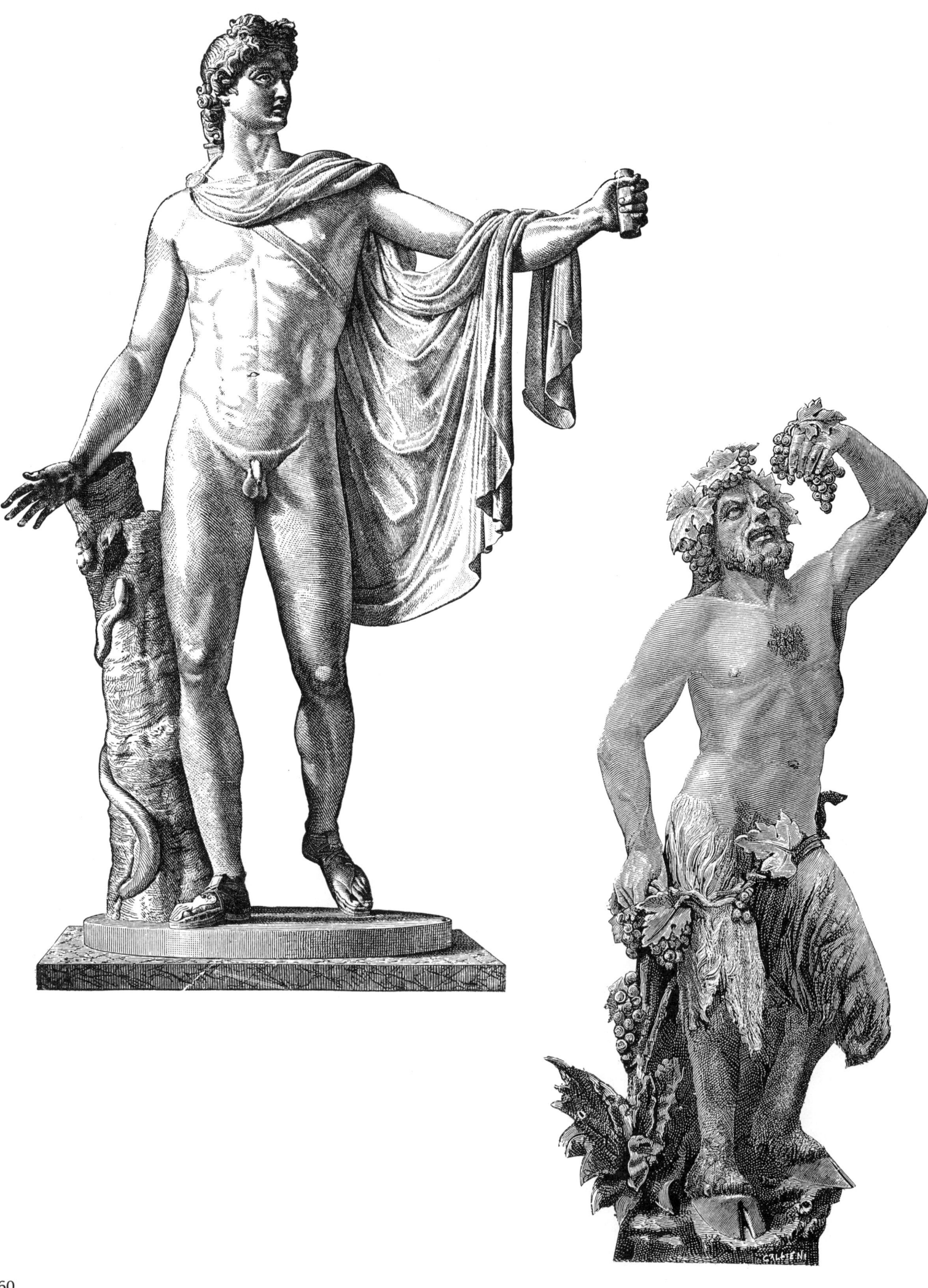

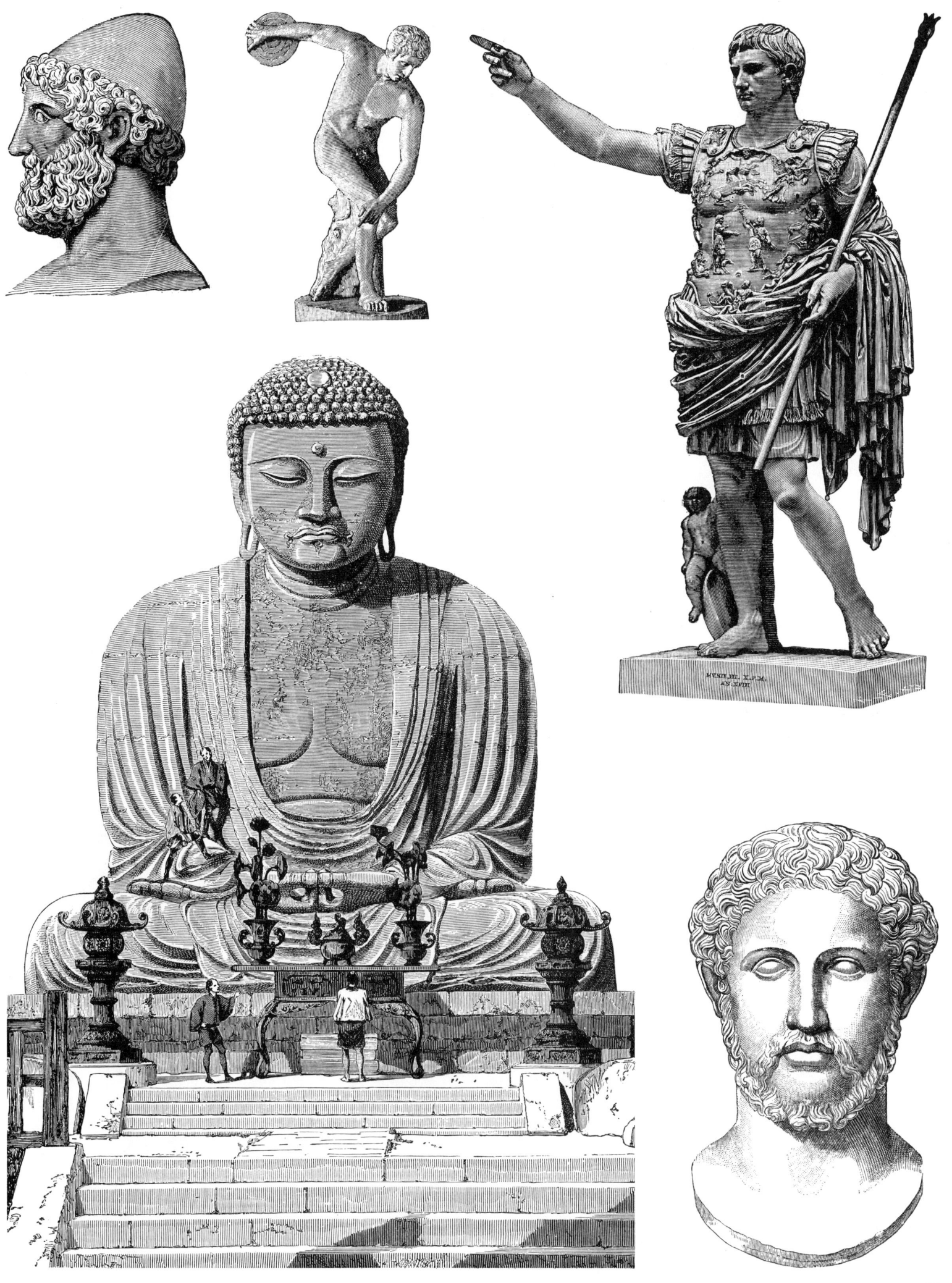

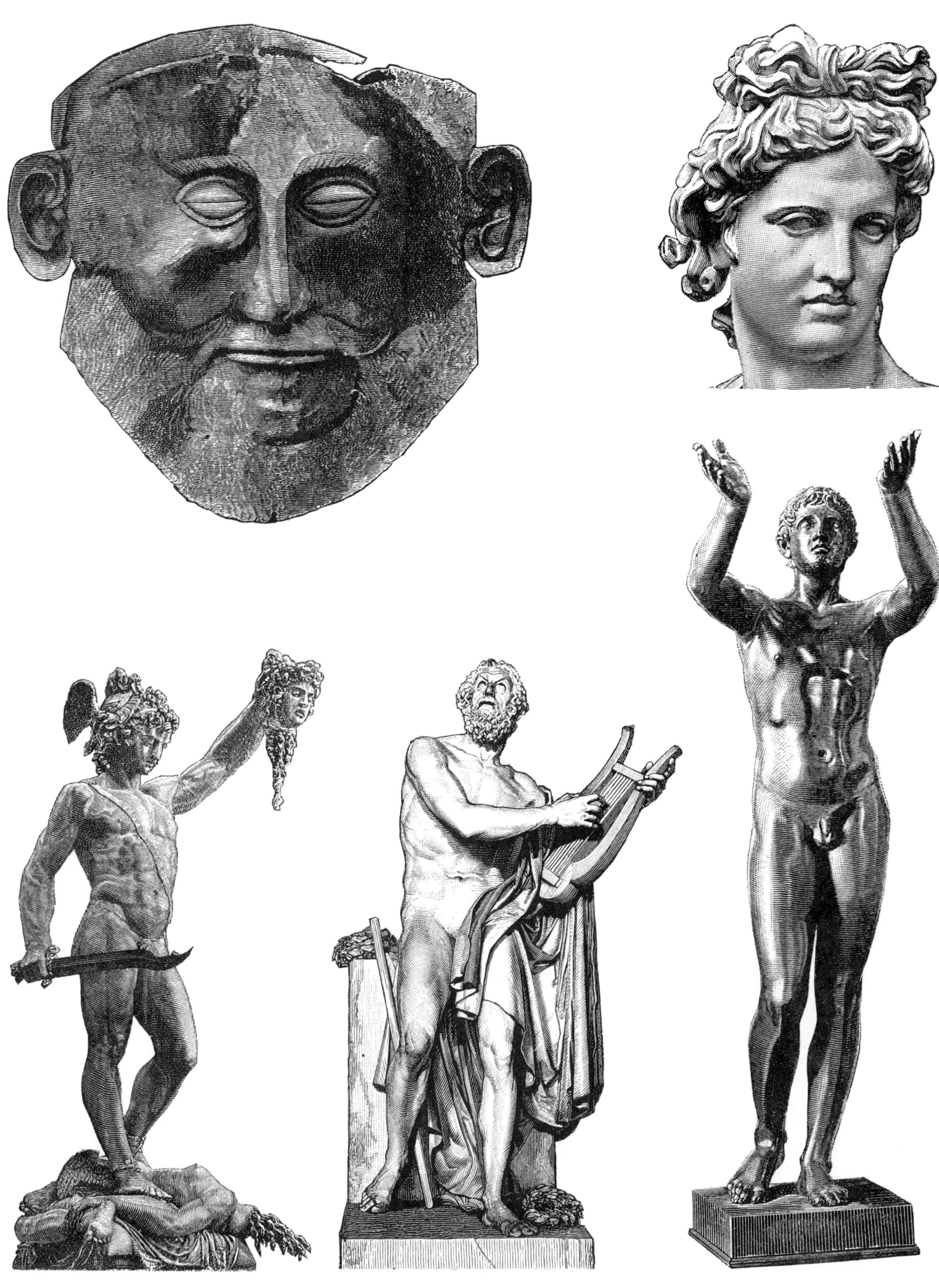

62

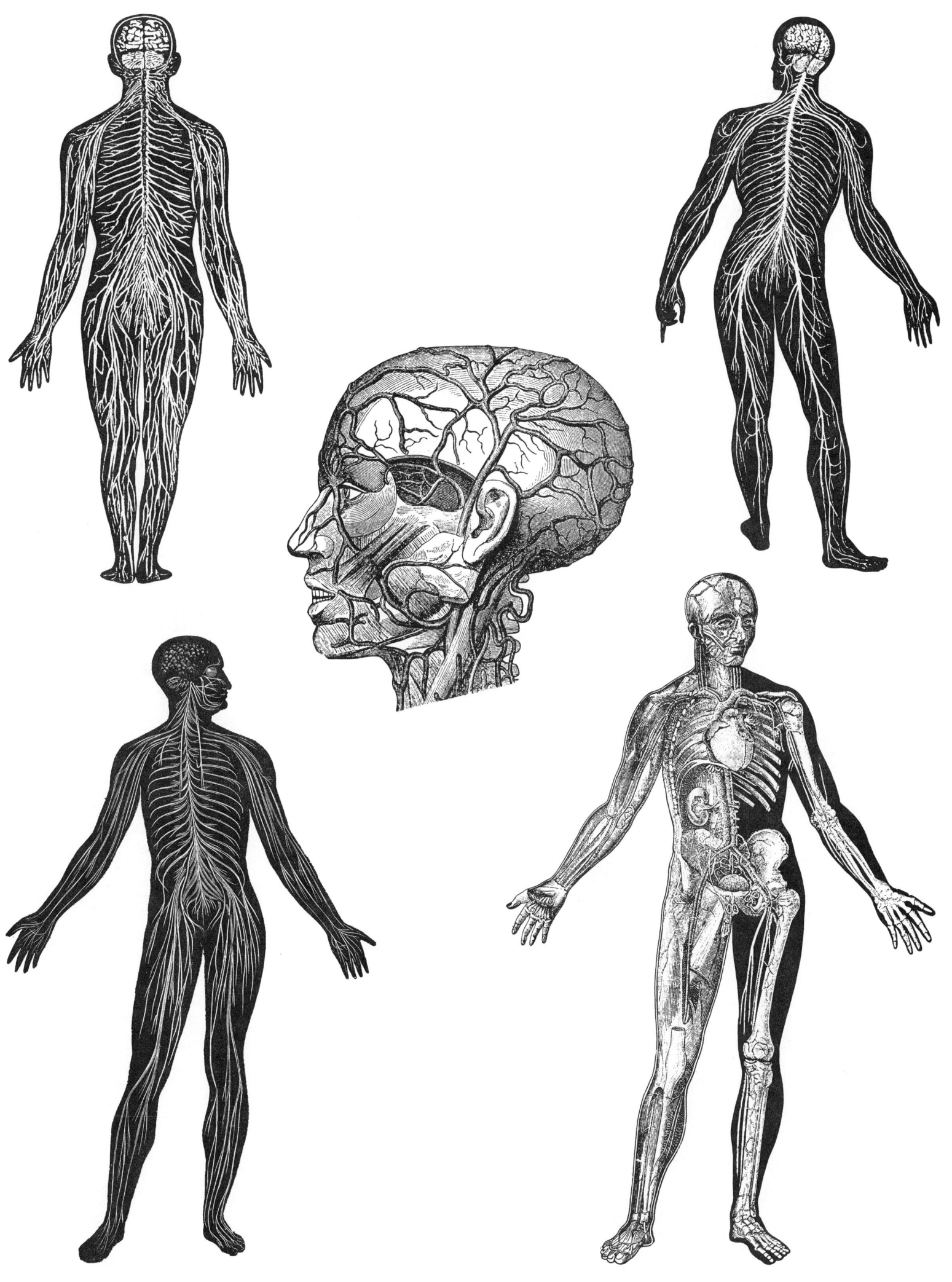

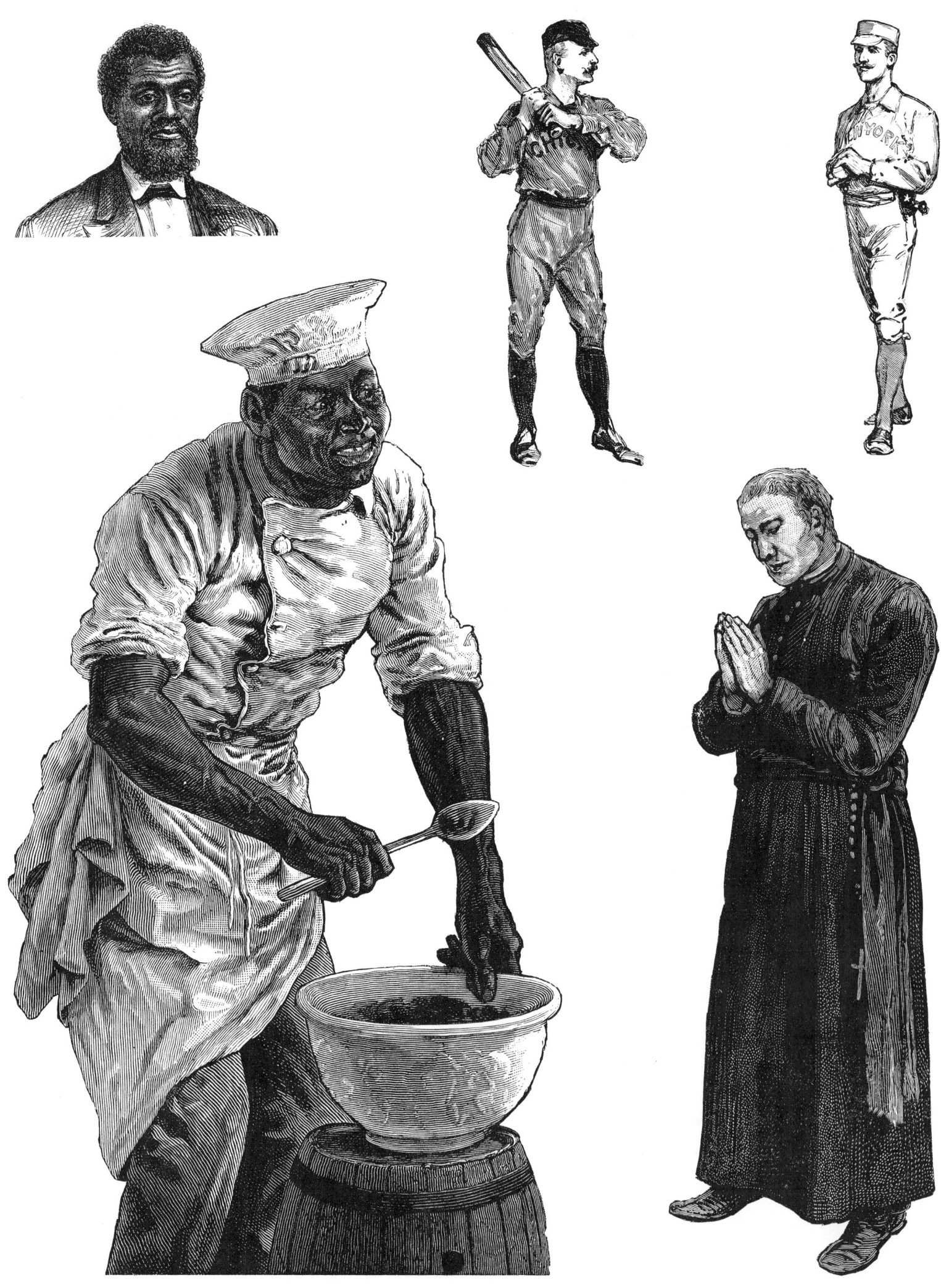

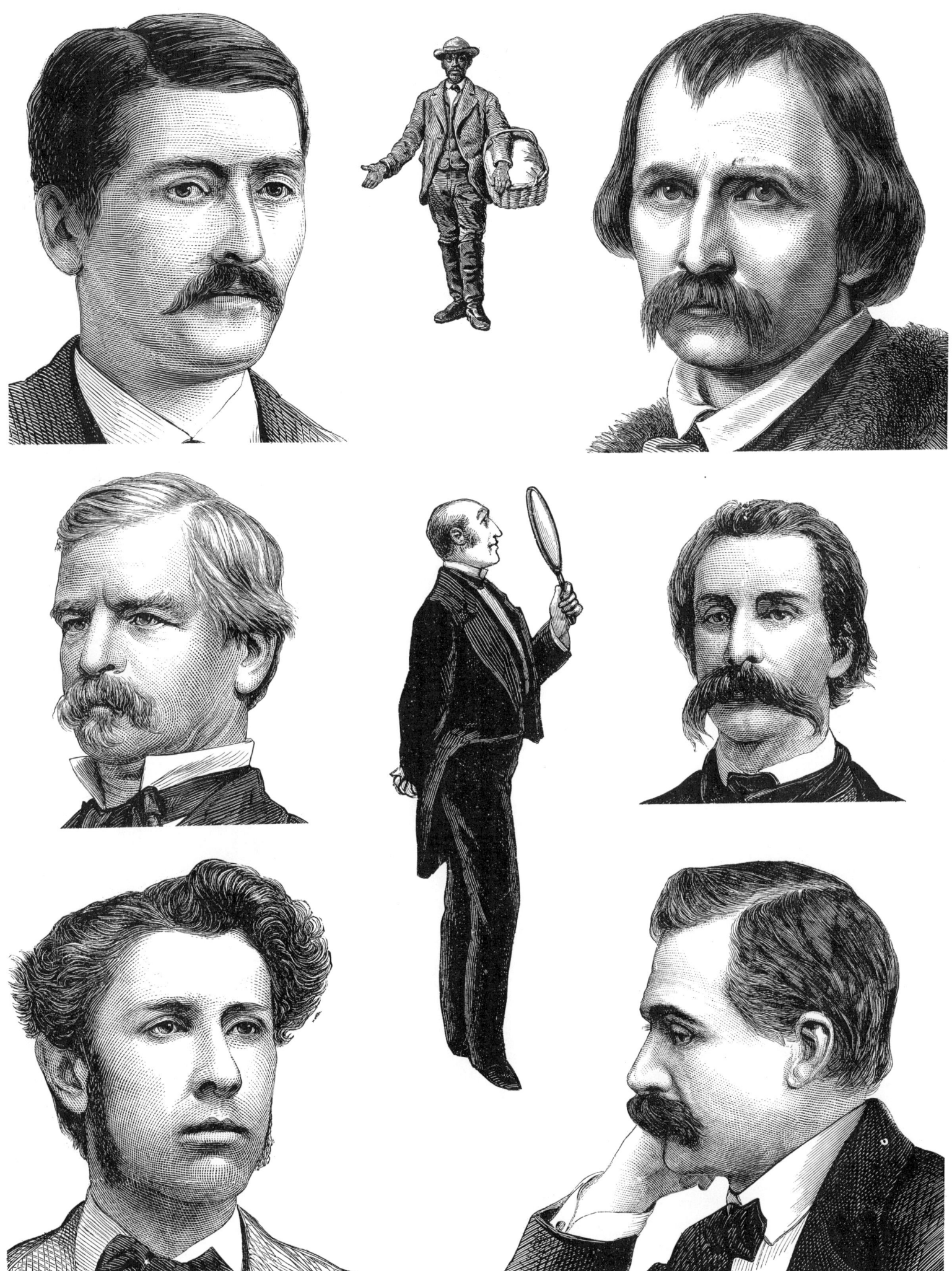

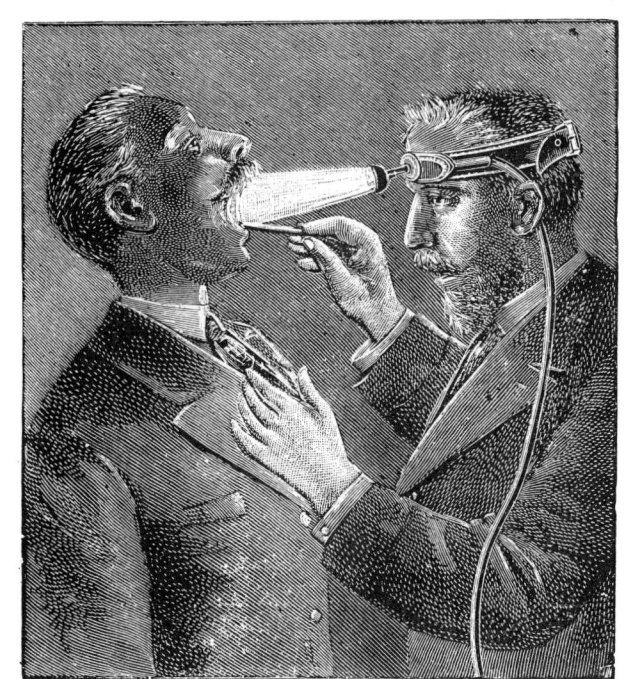
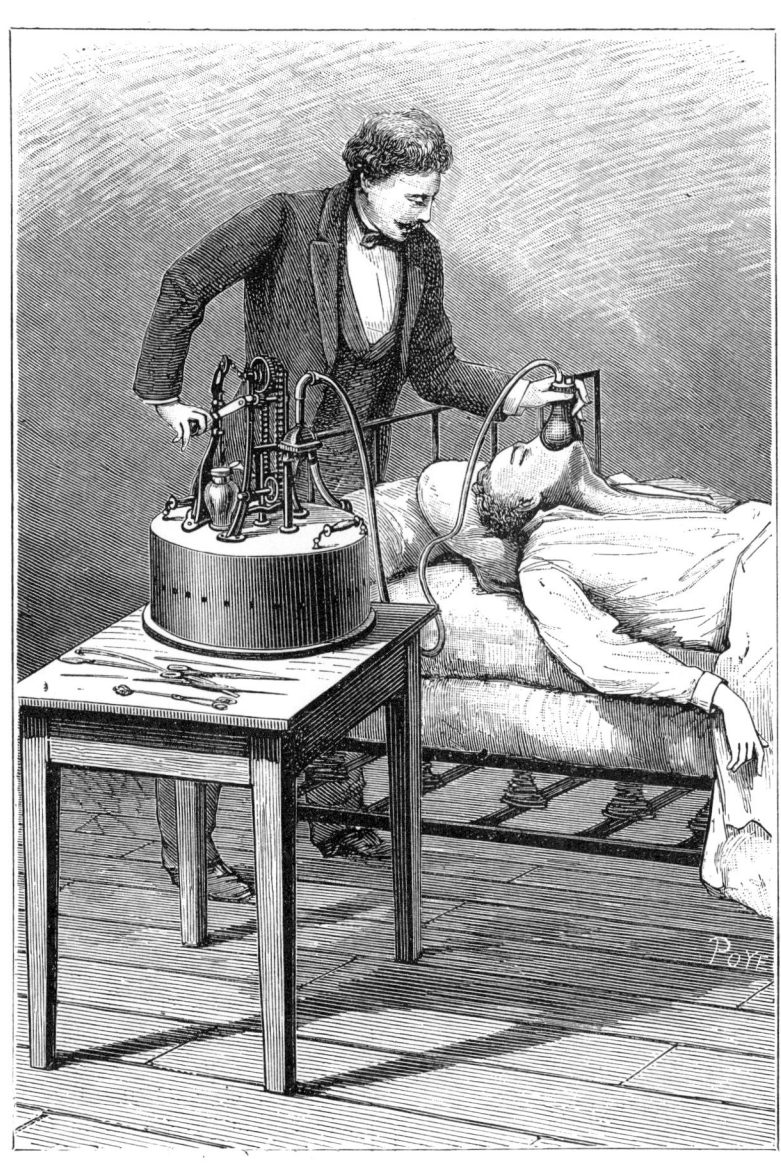
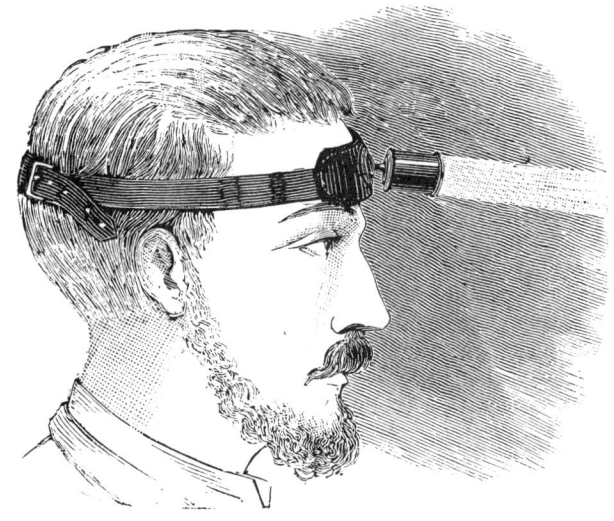
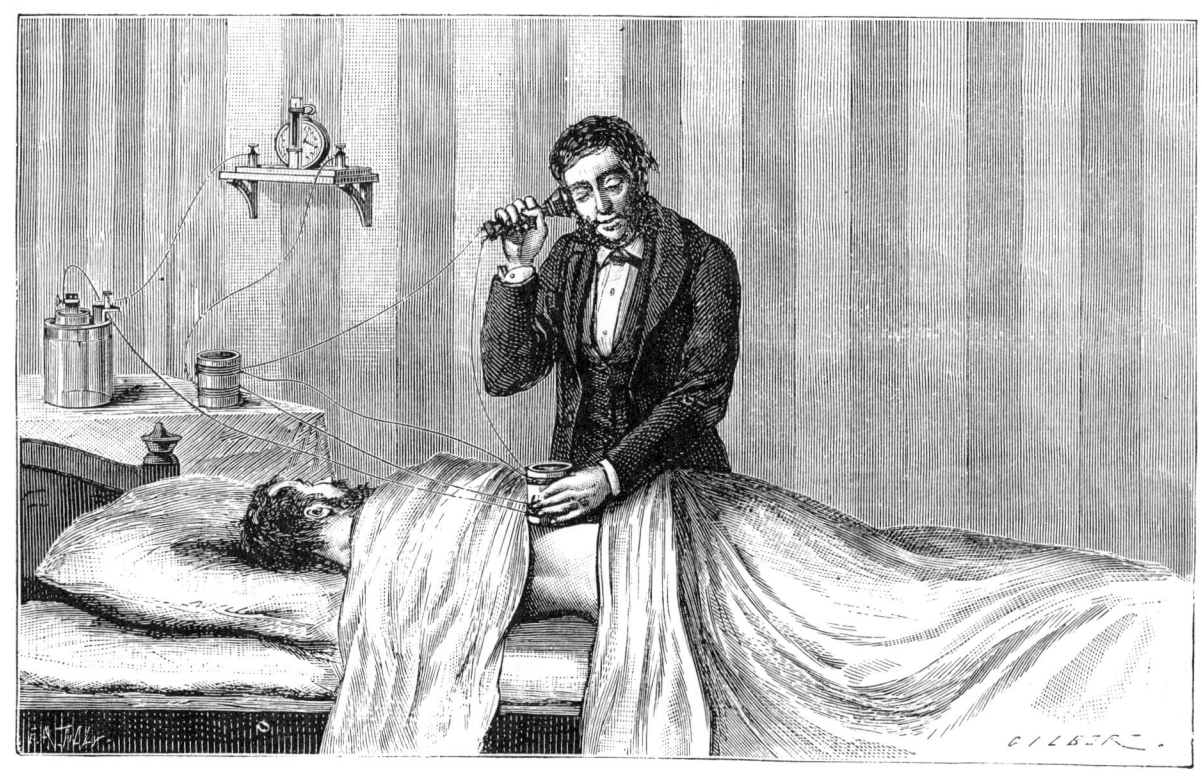

66

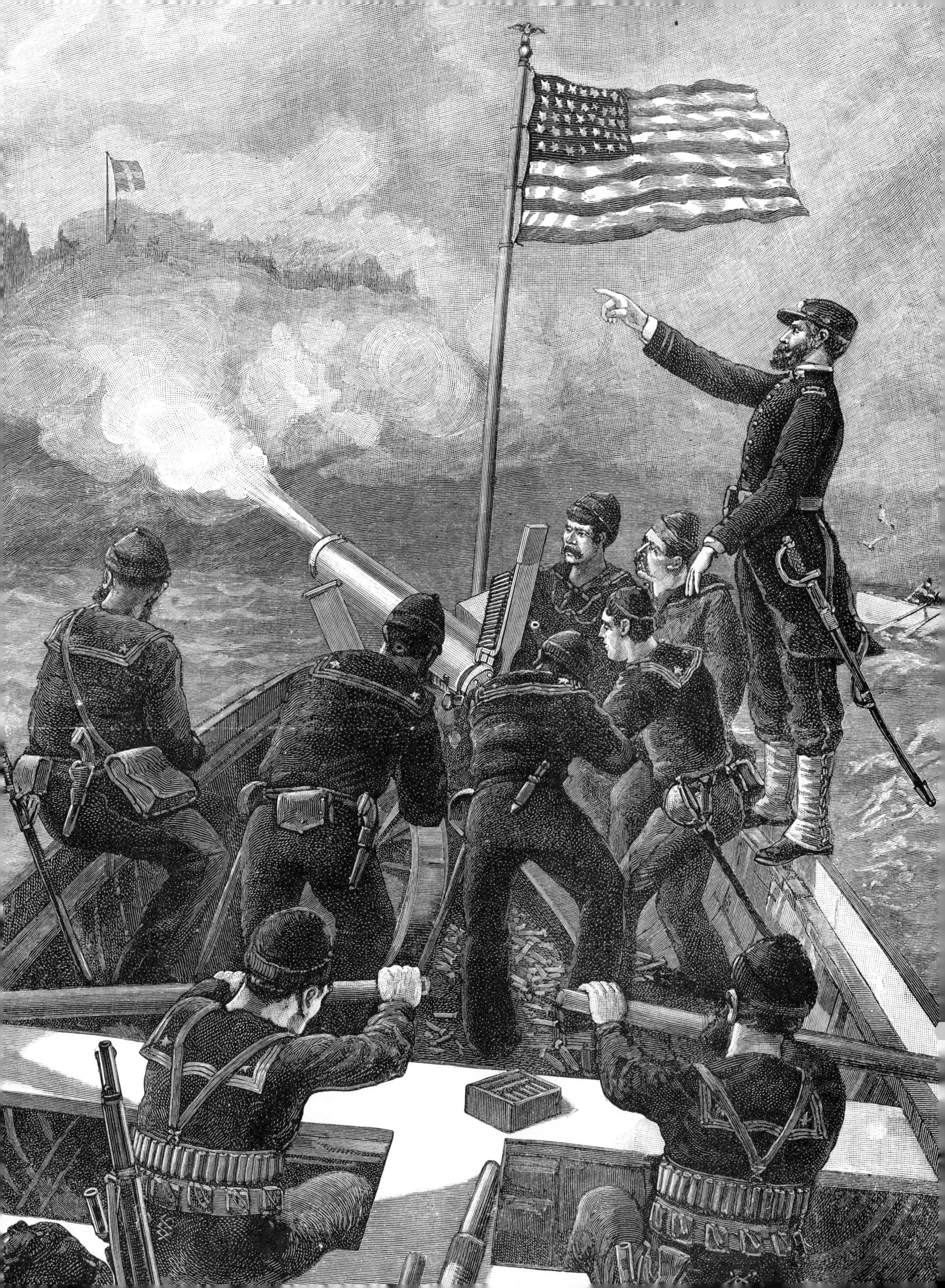

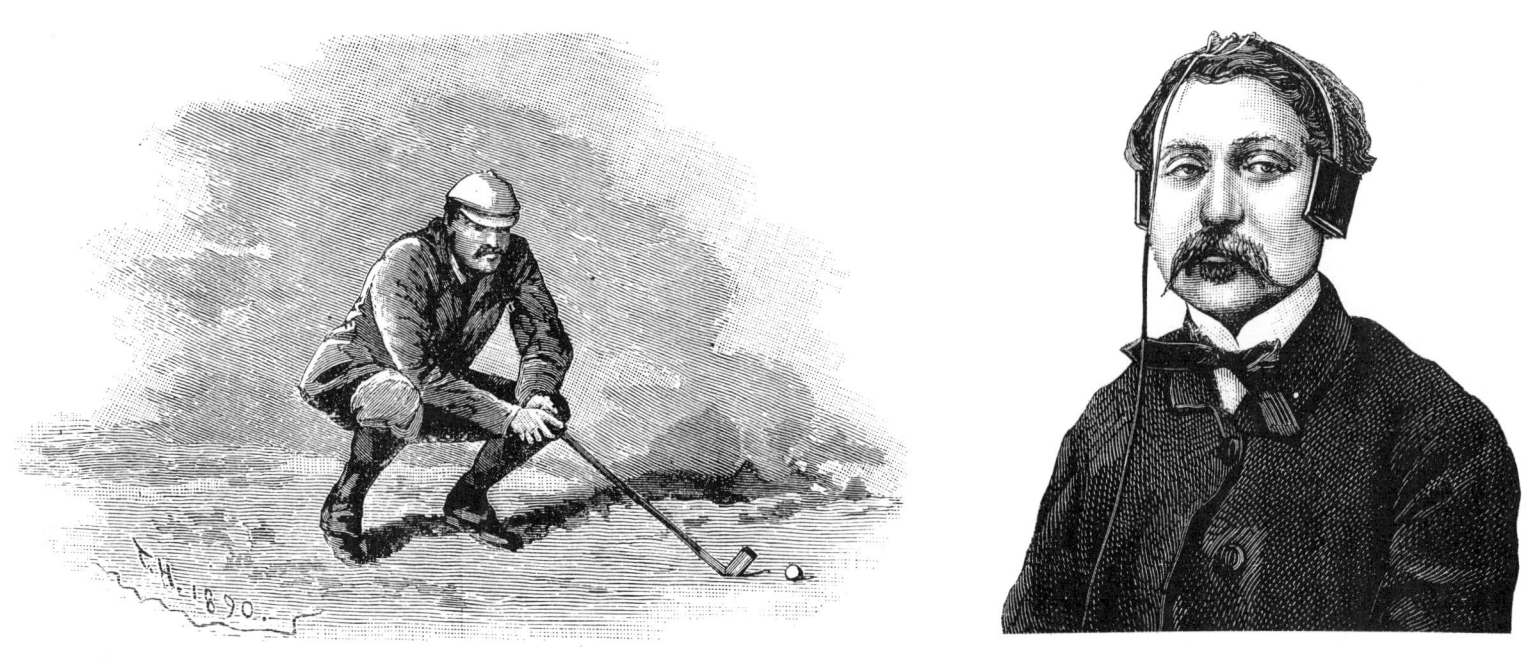

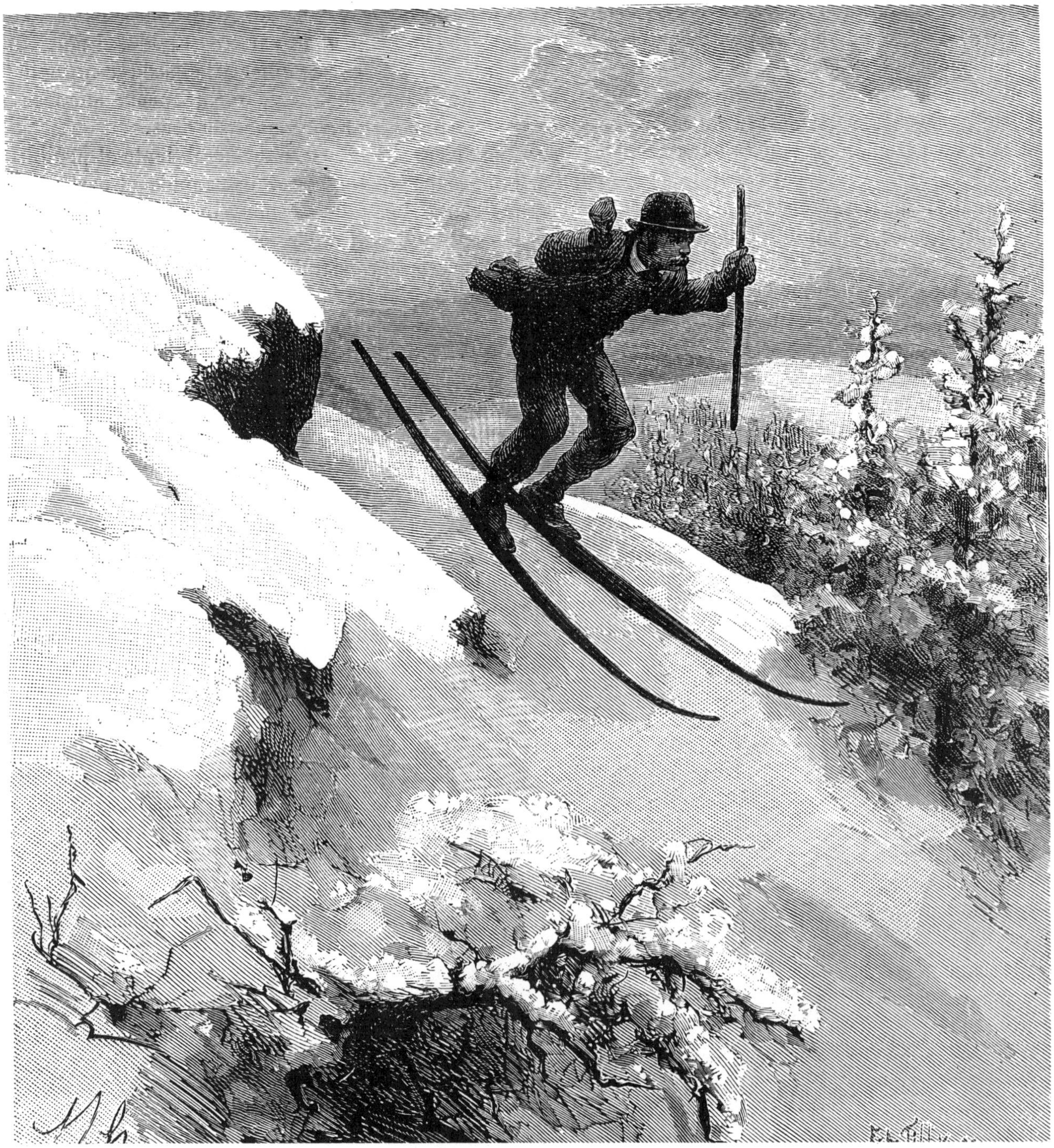

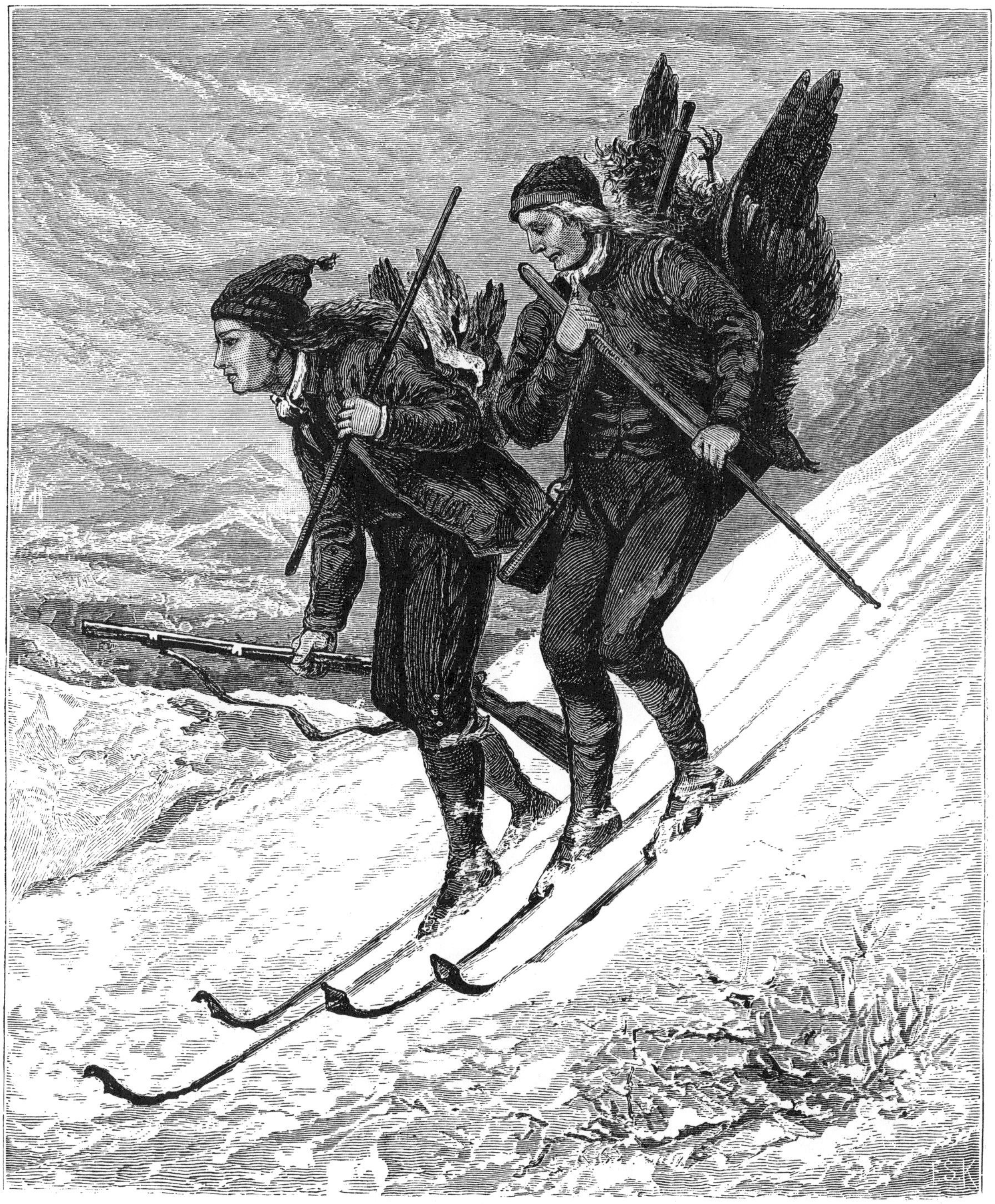

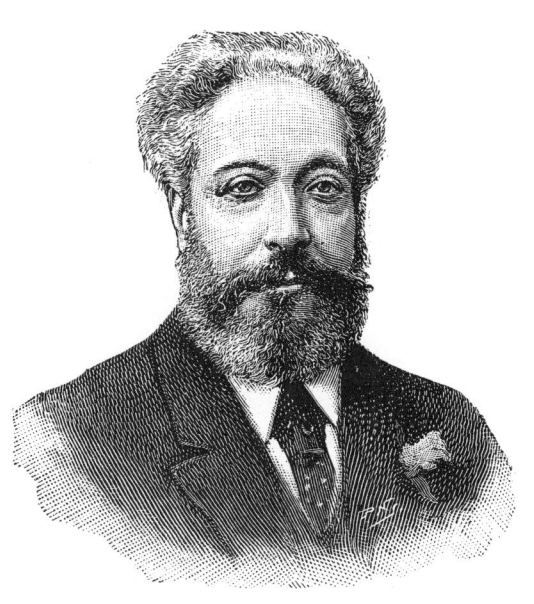
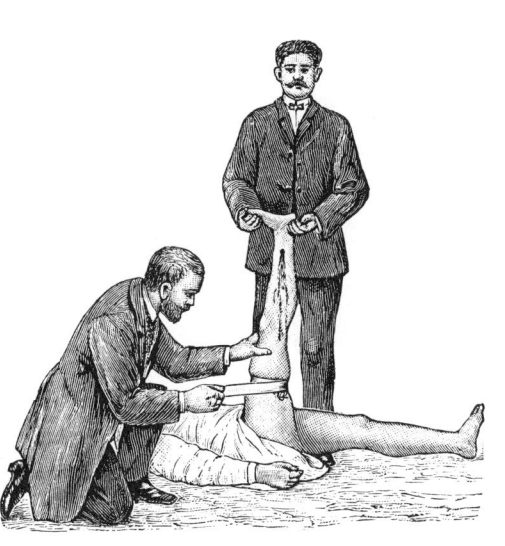
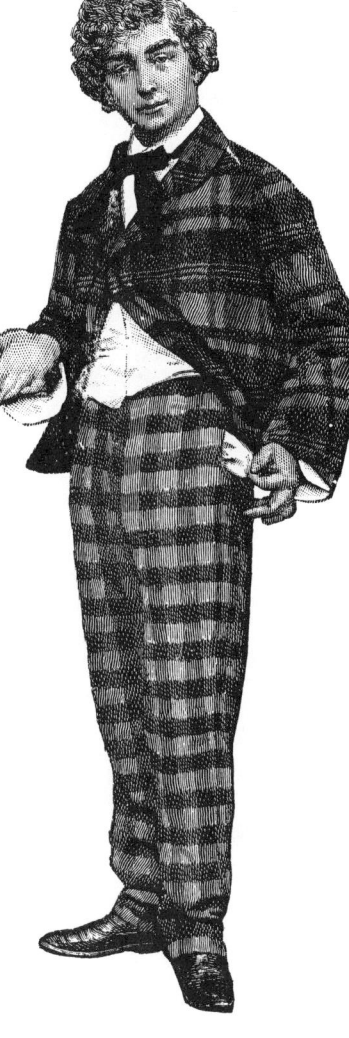
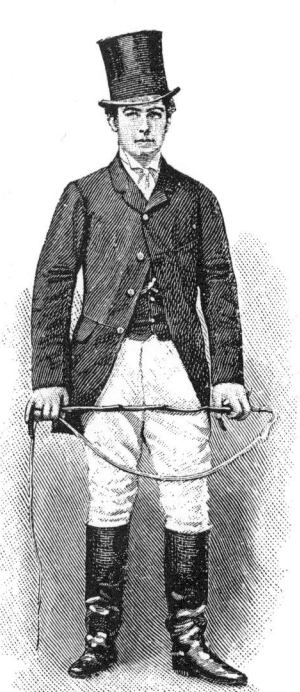

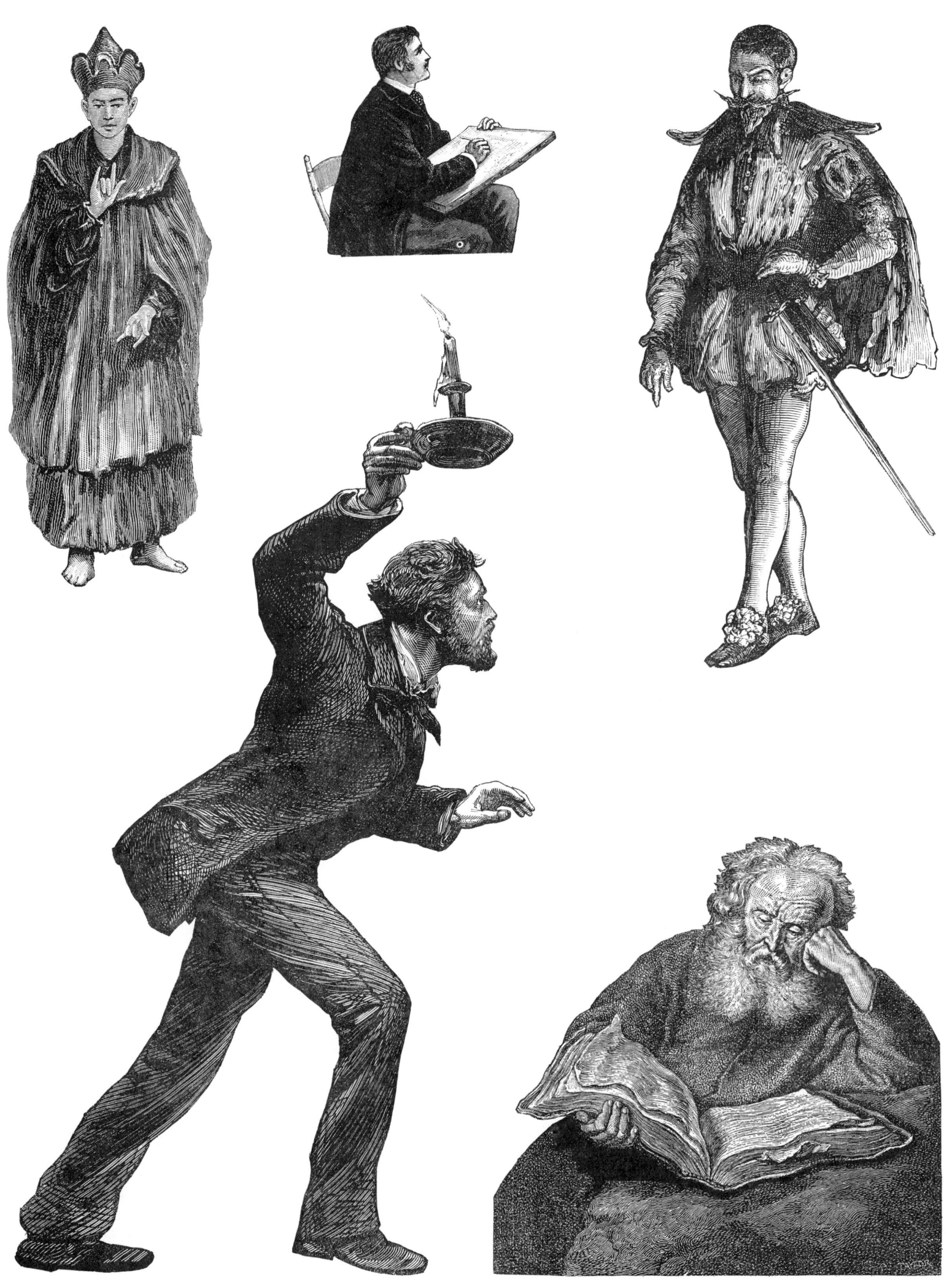

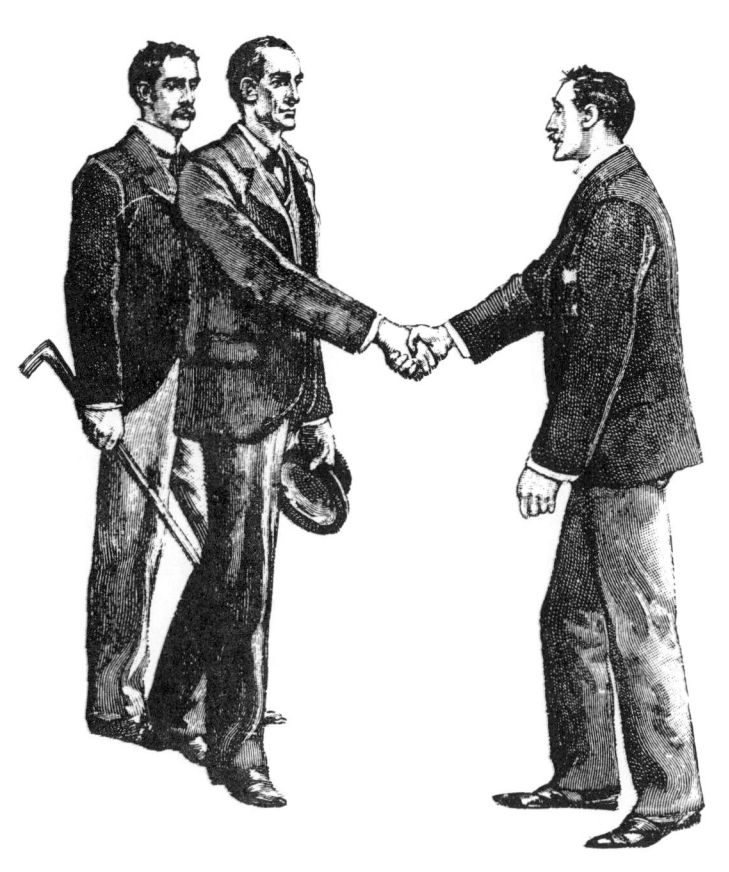
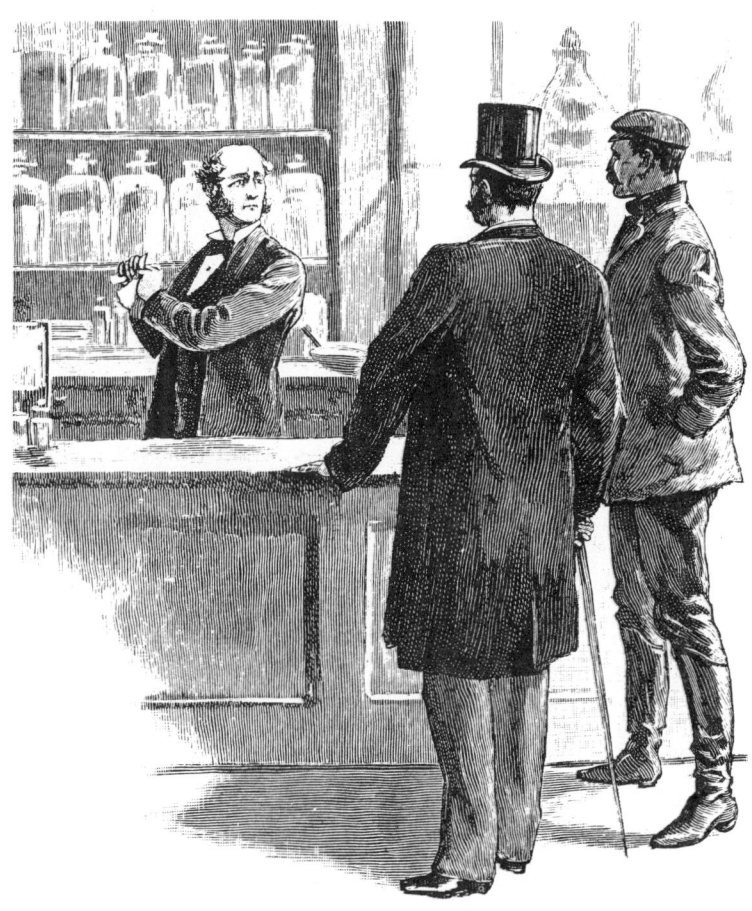

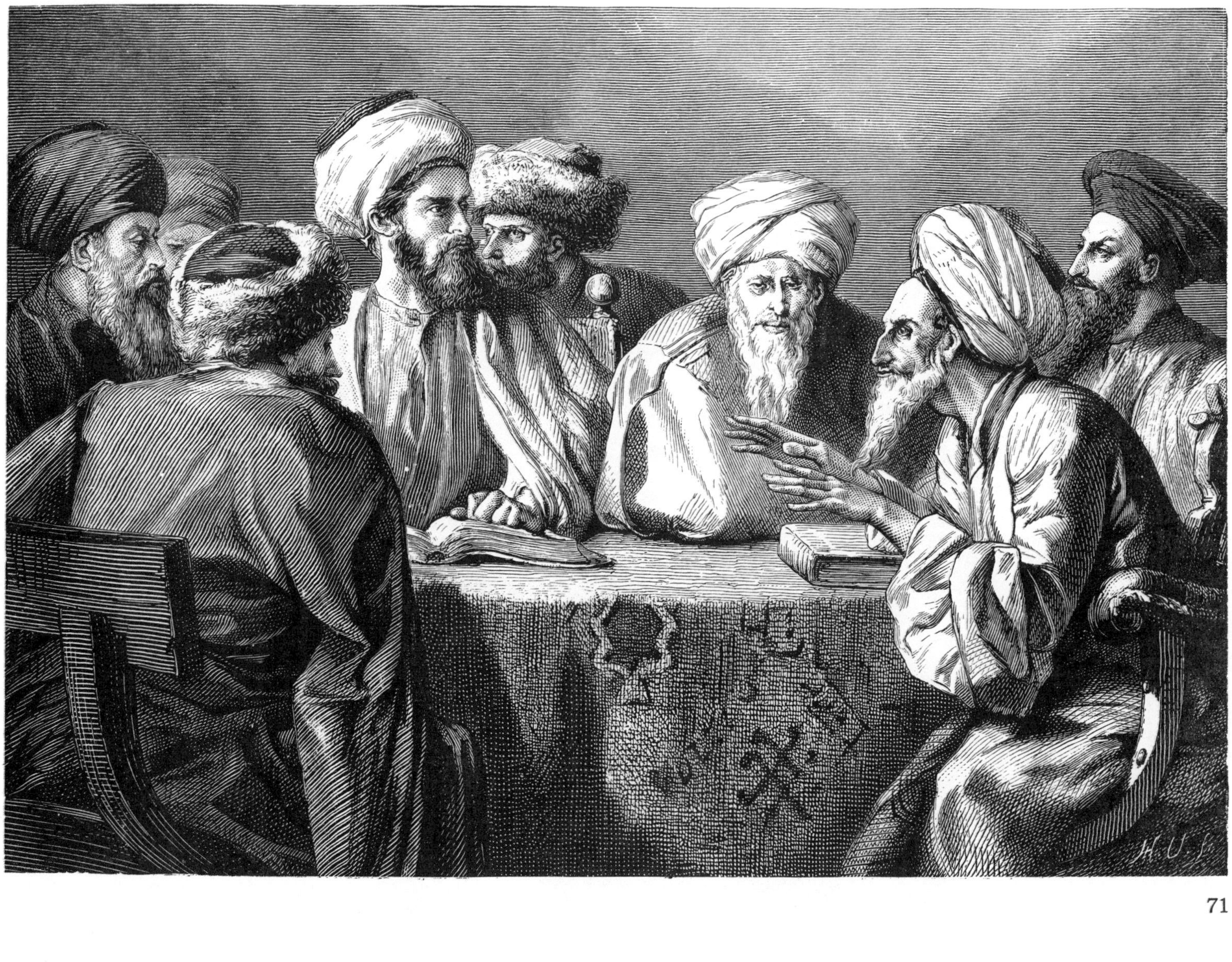

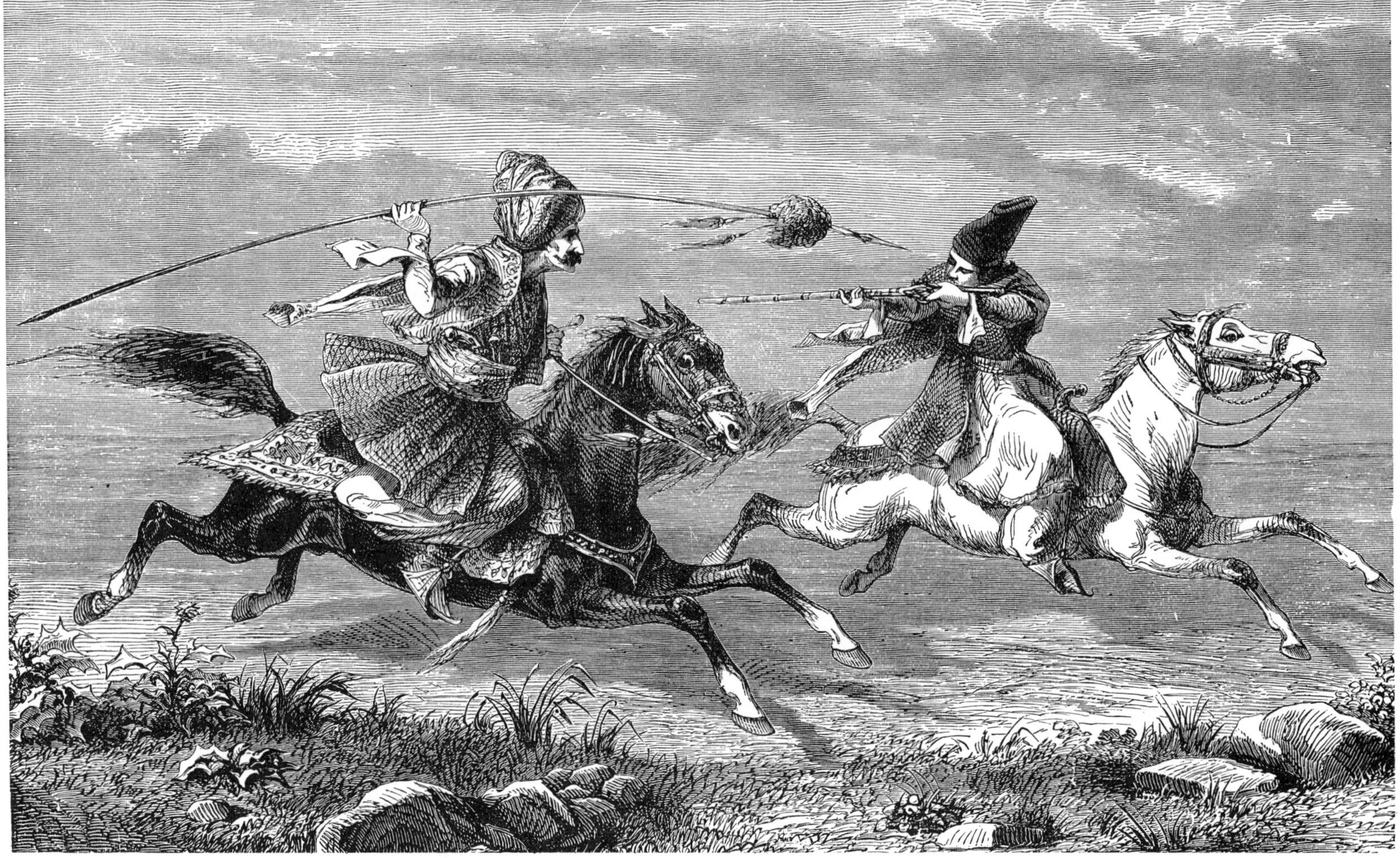

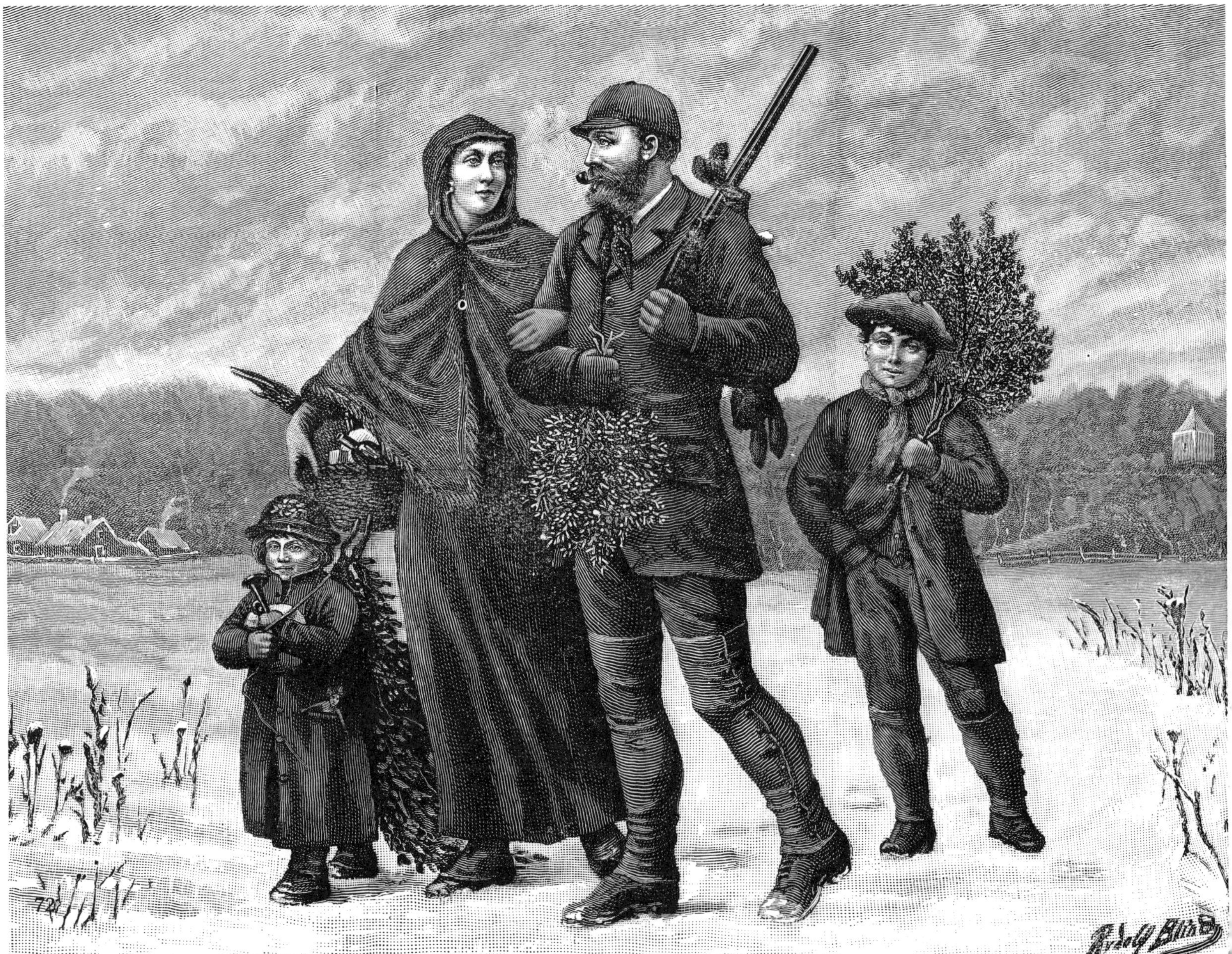

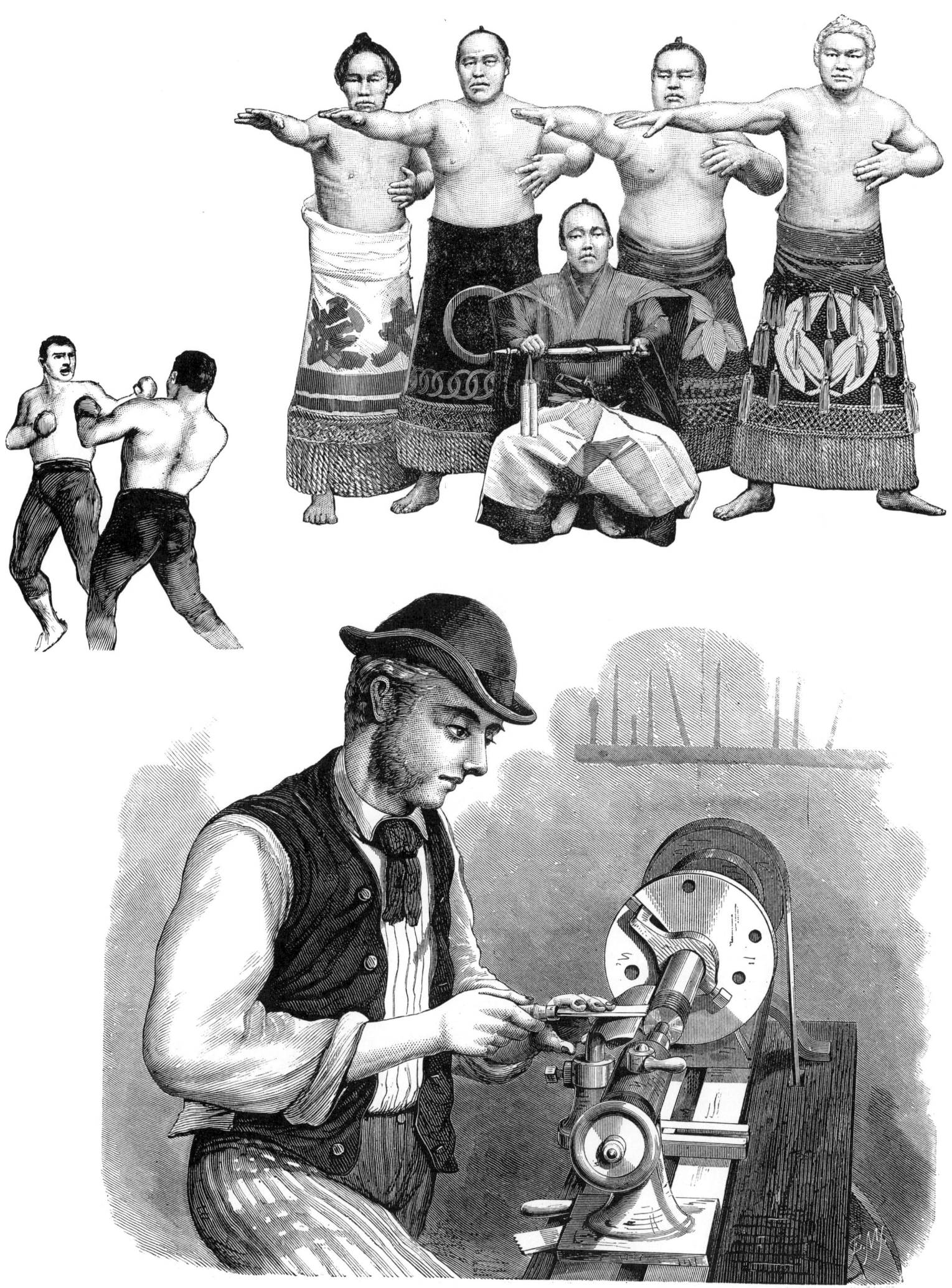

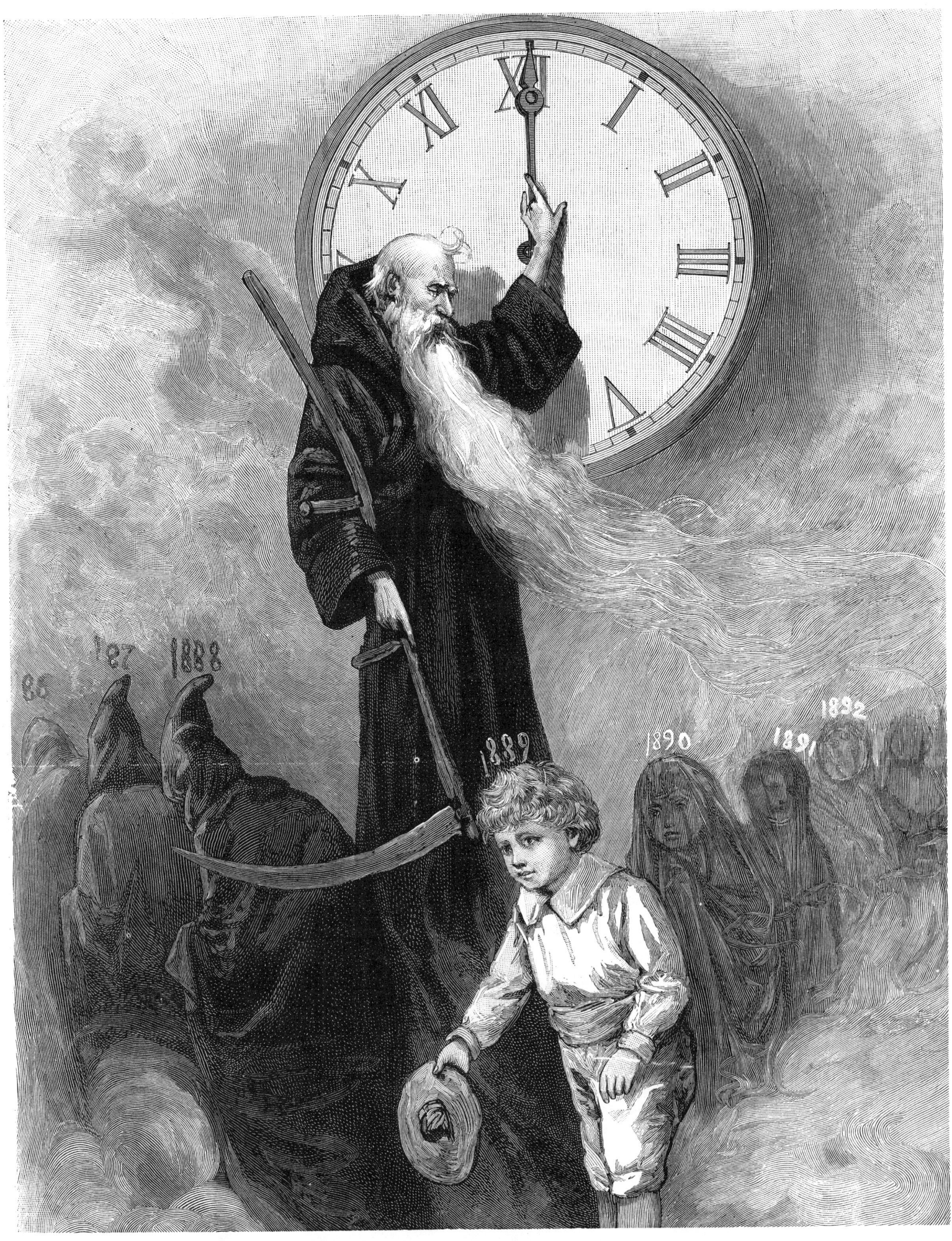

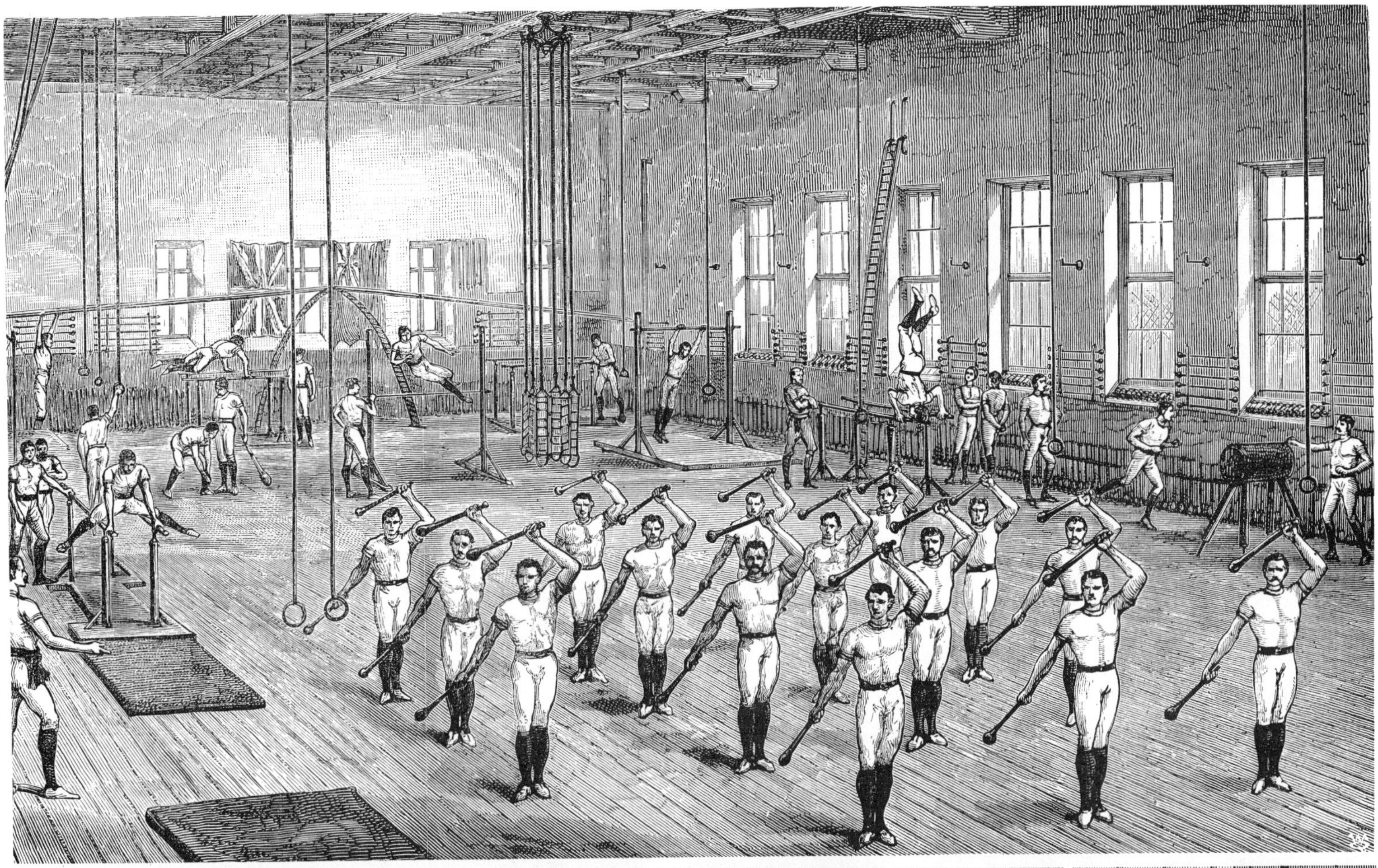

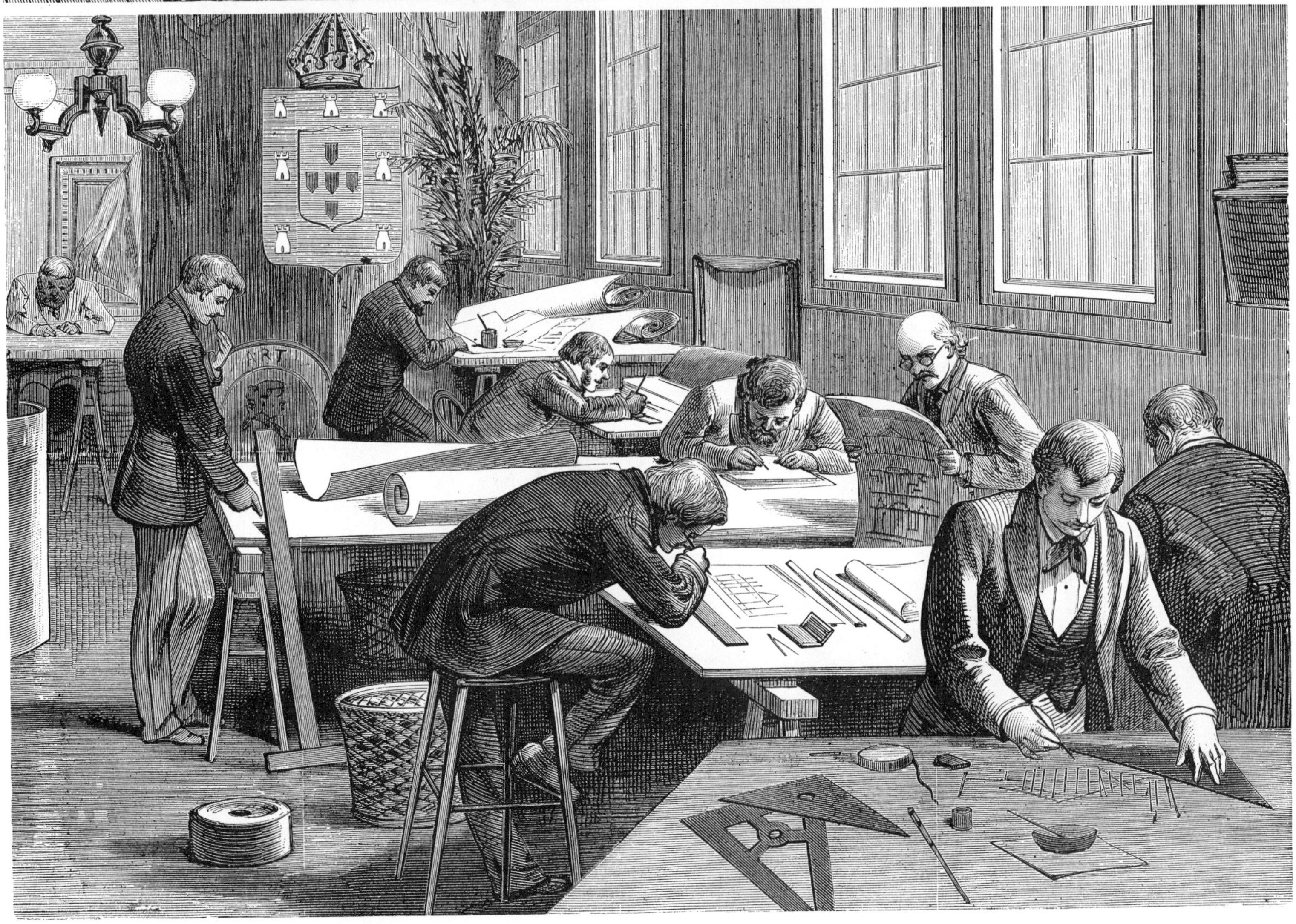

75

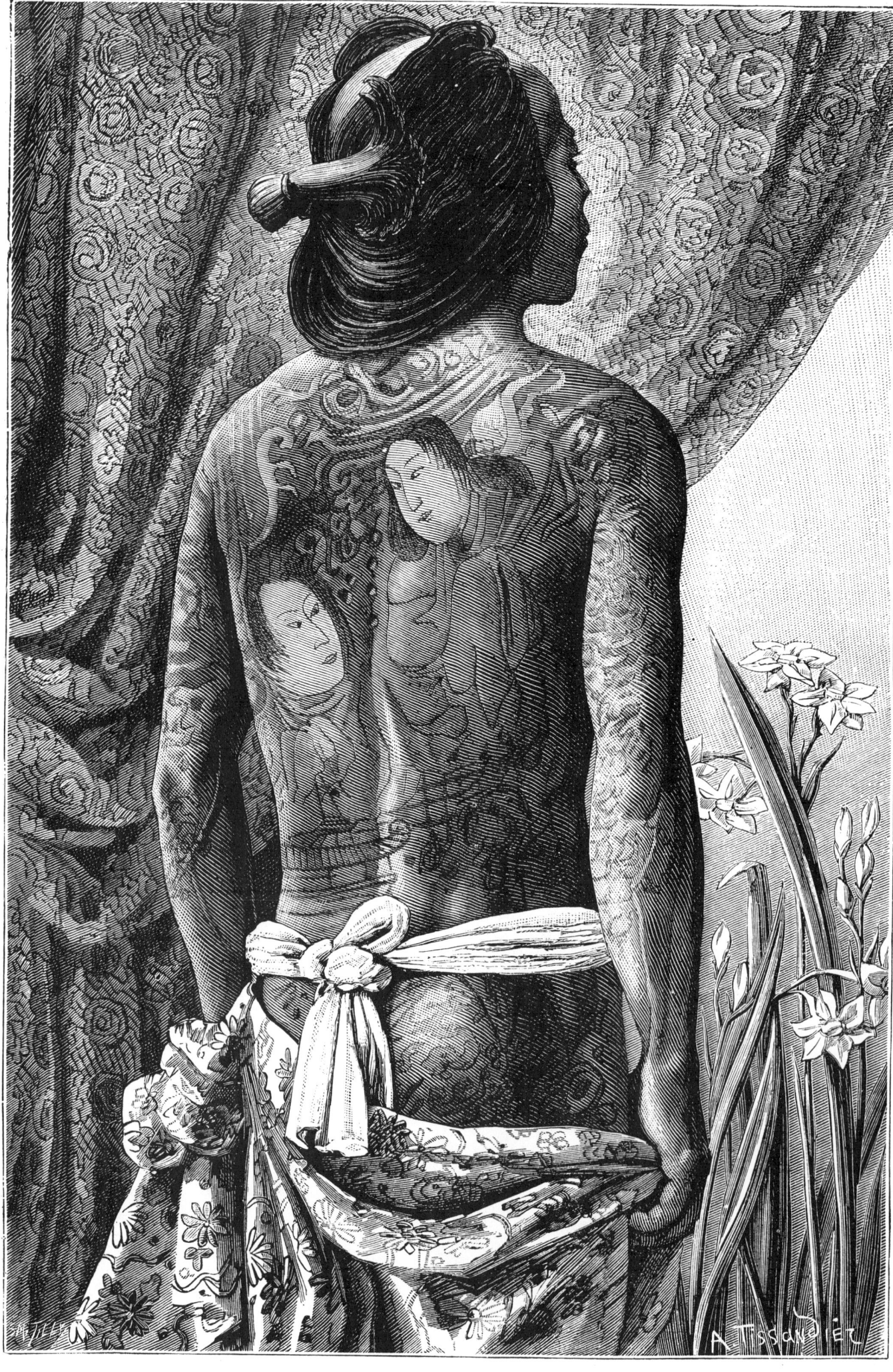

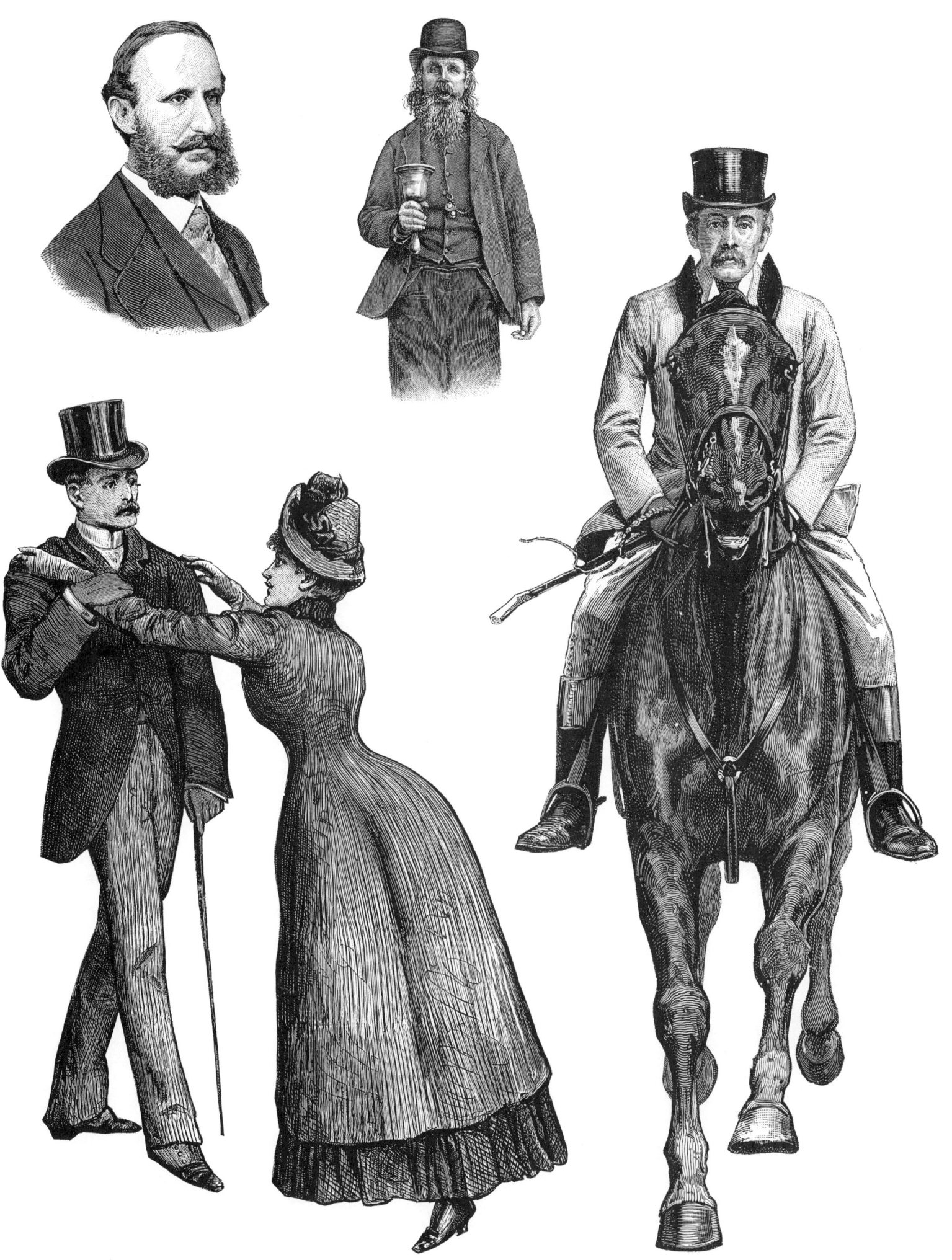

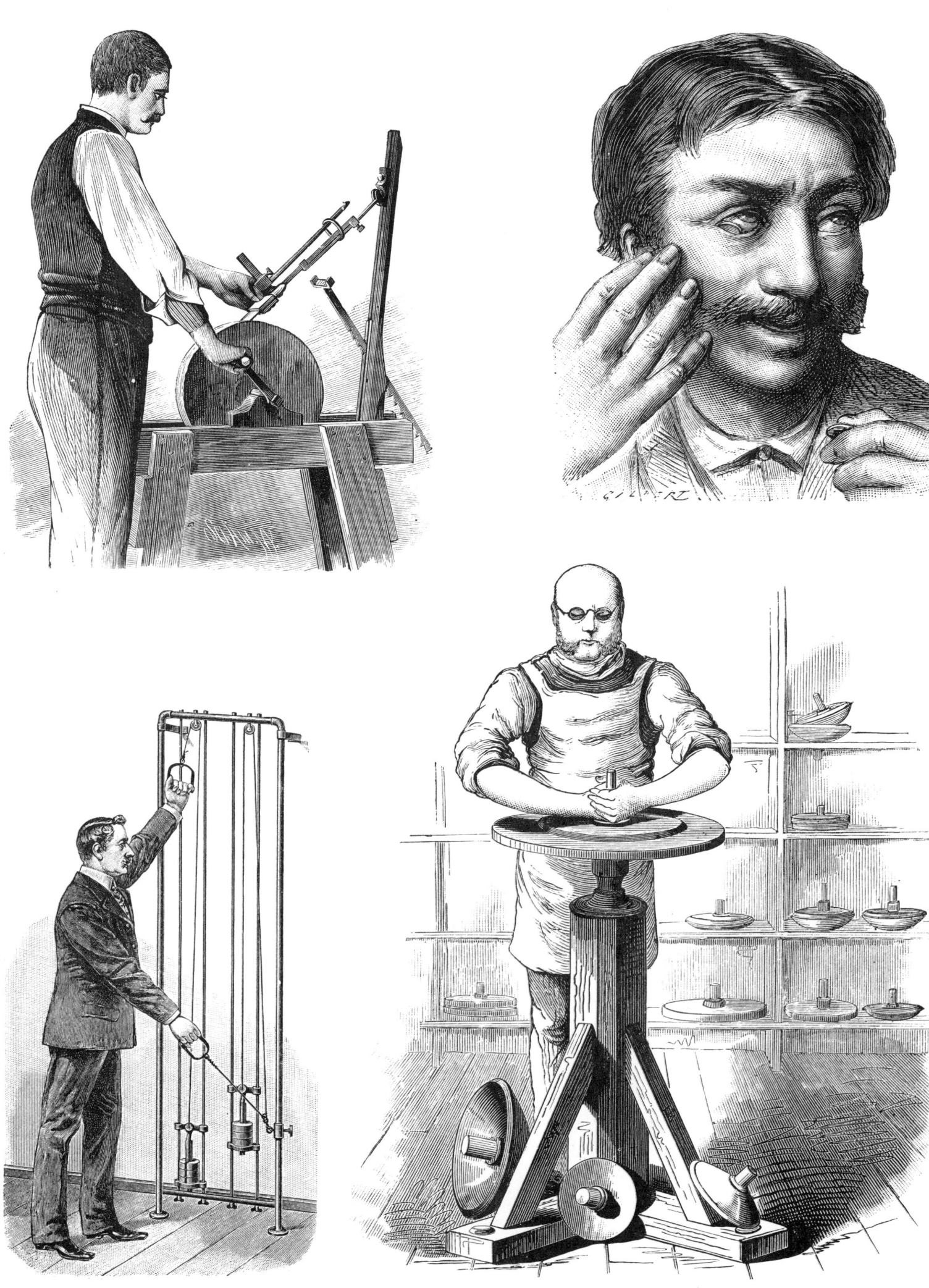

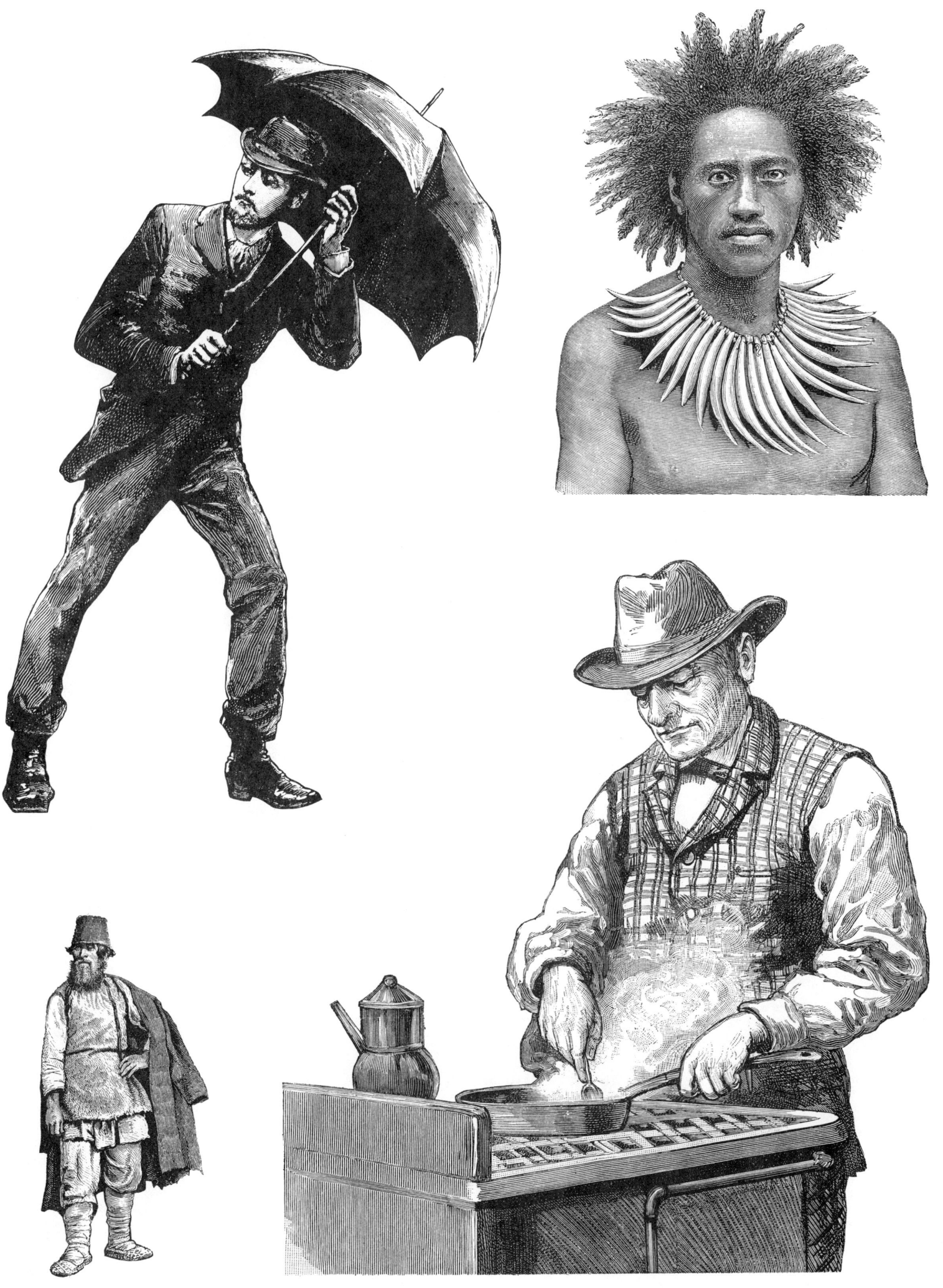

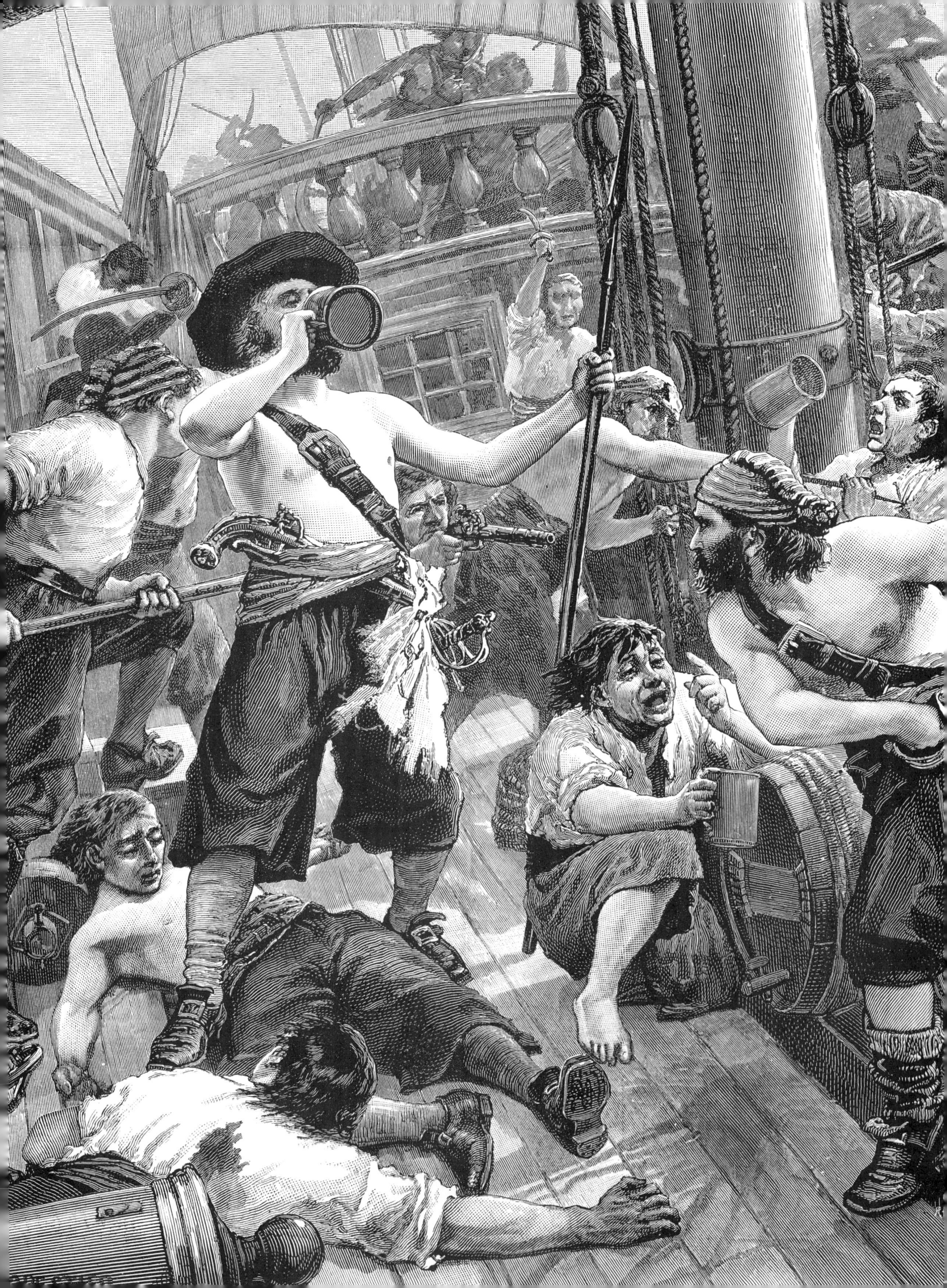

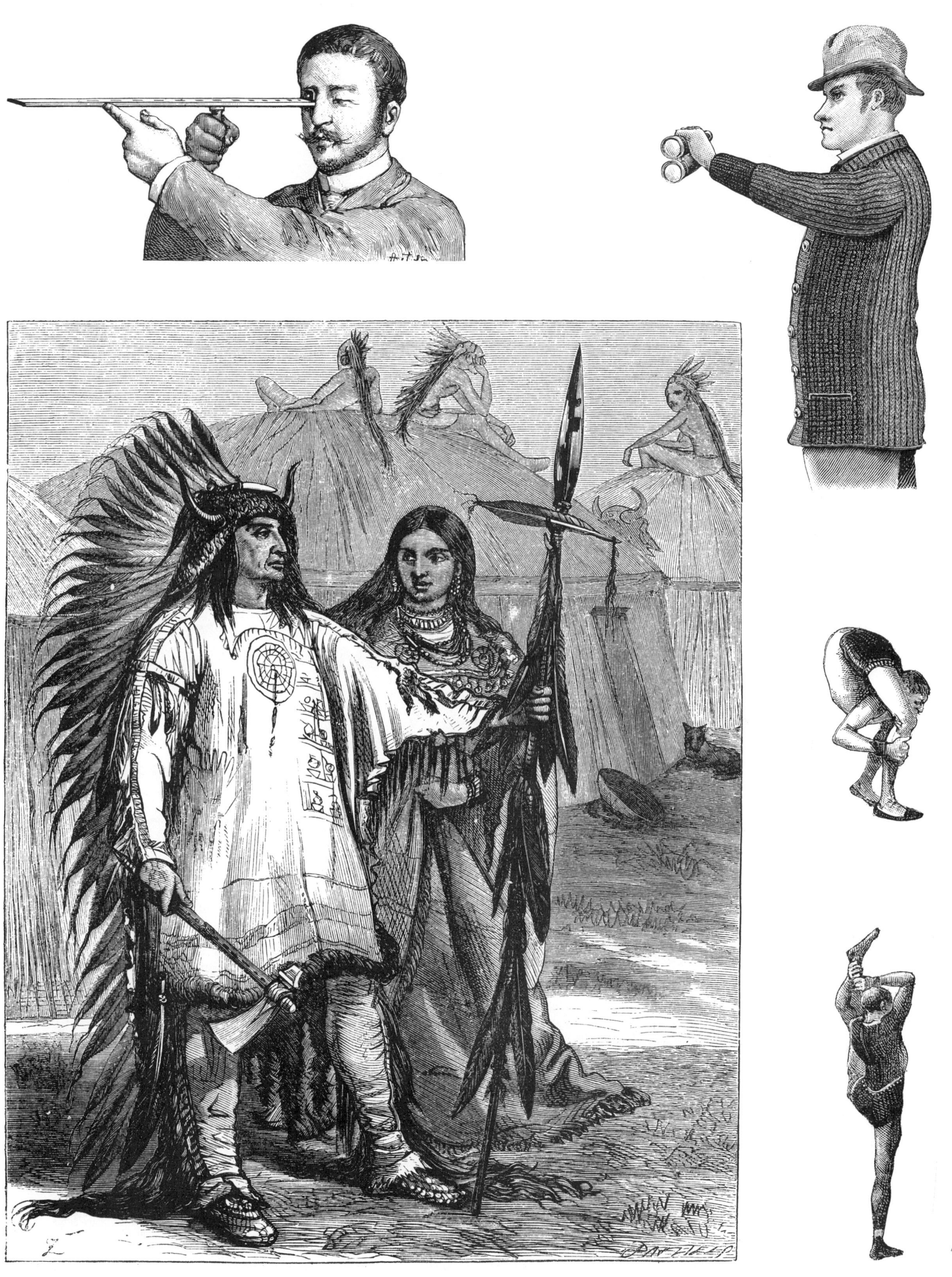

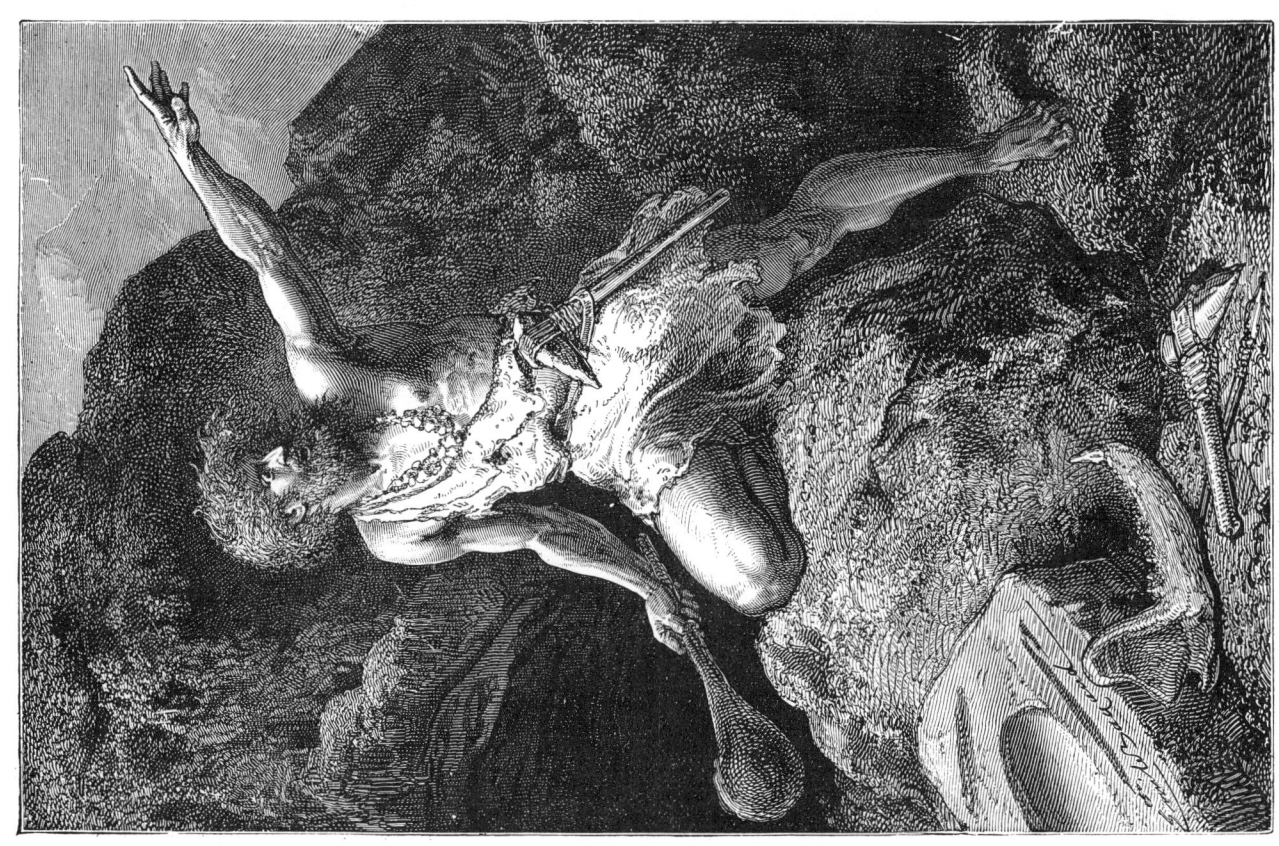

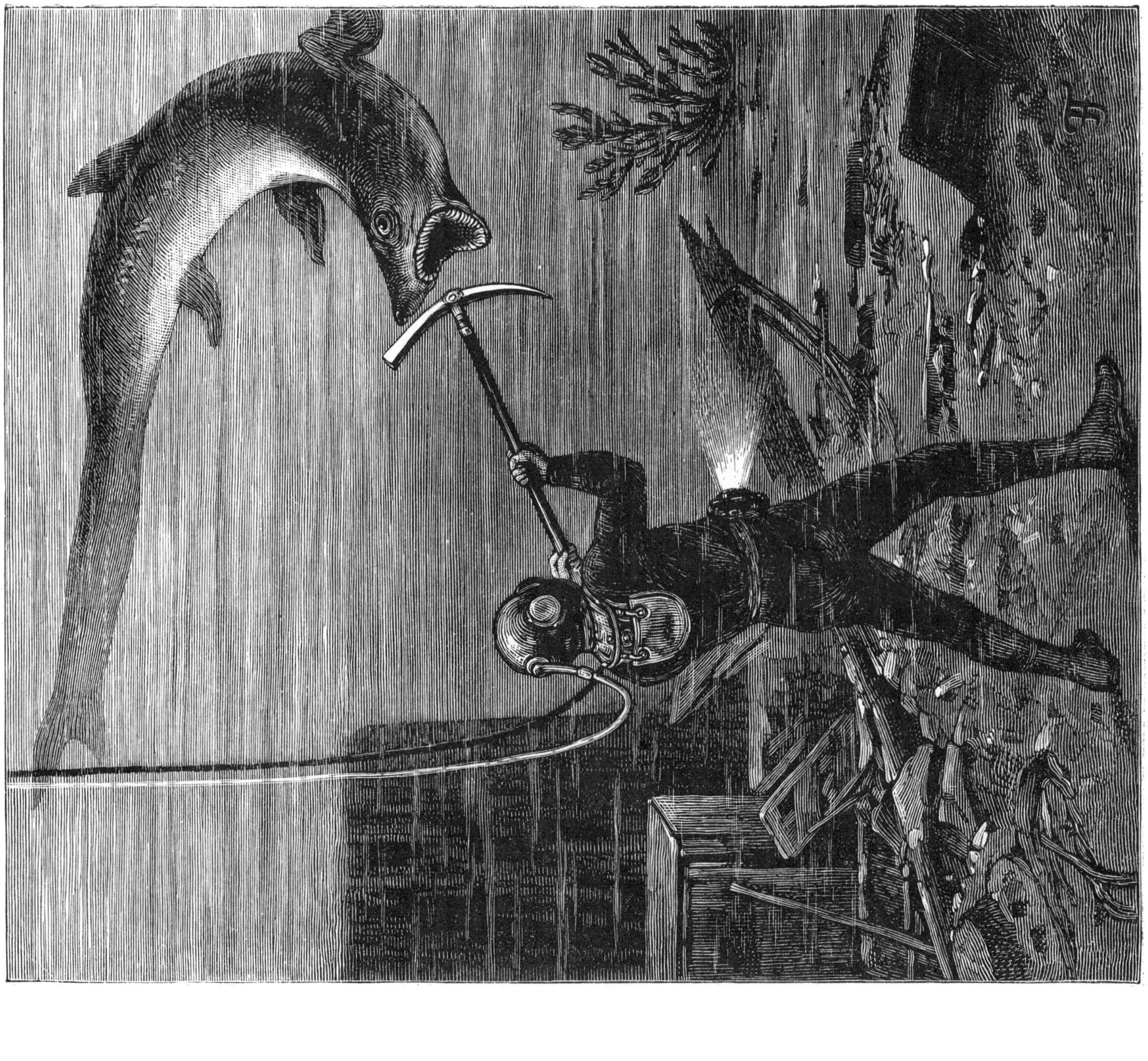

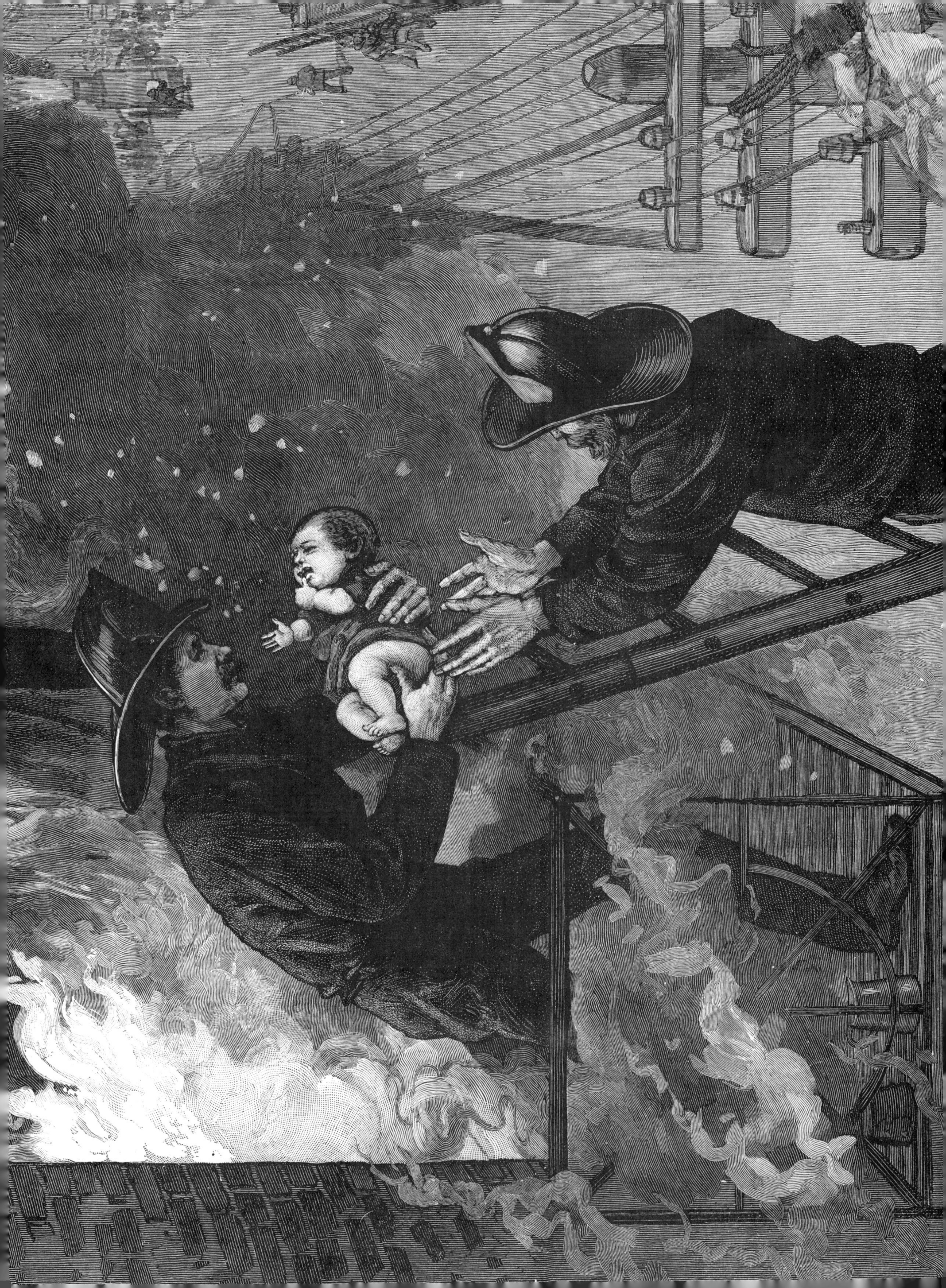

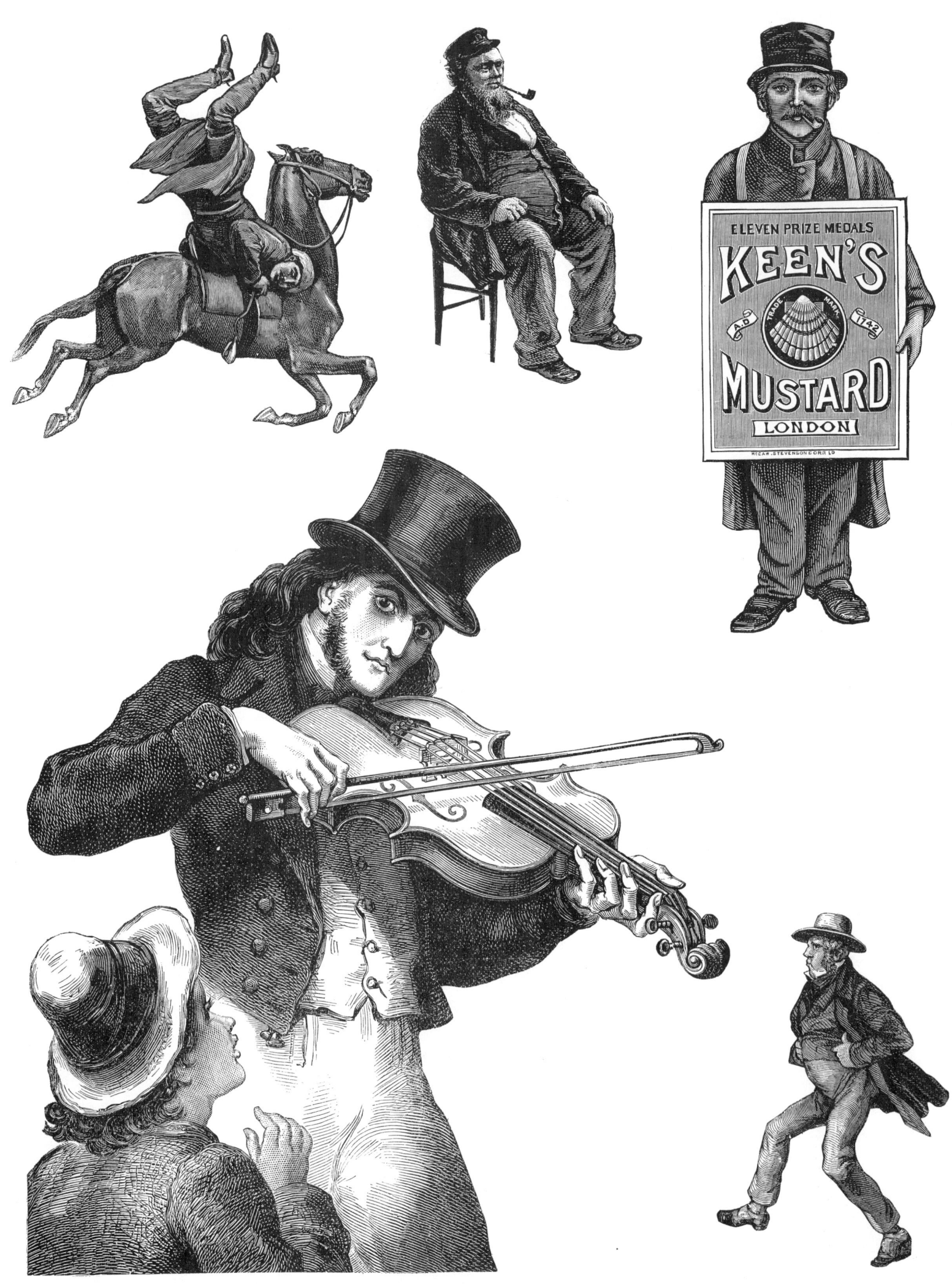

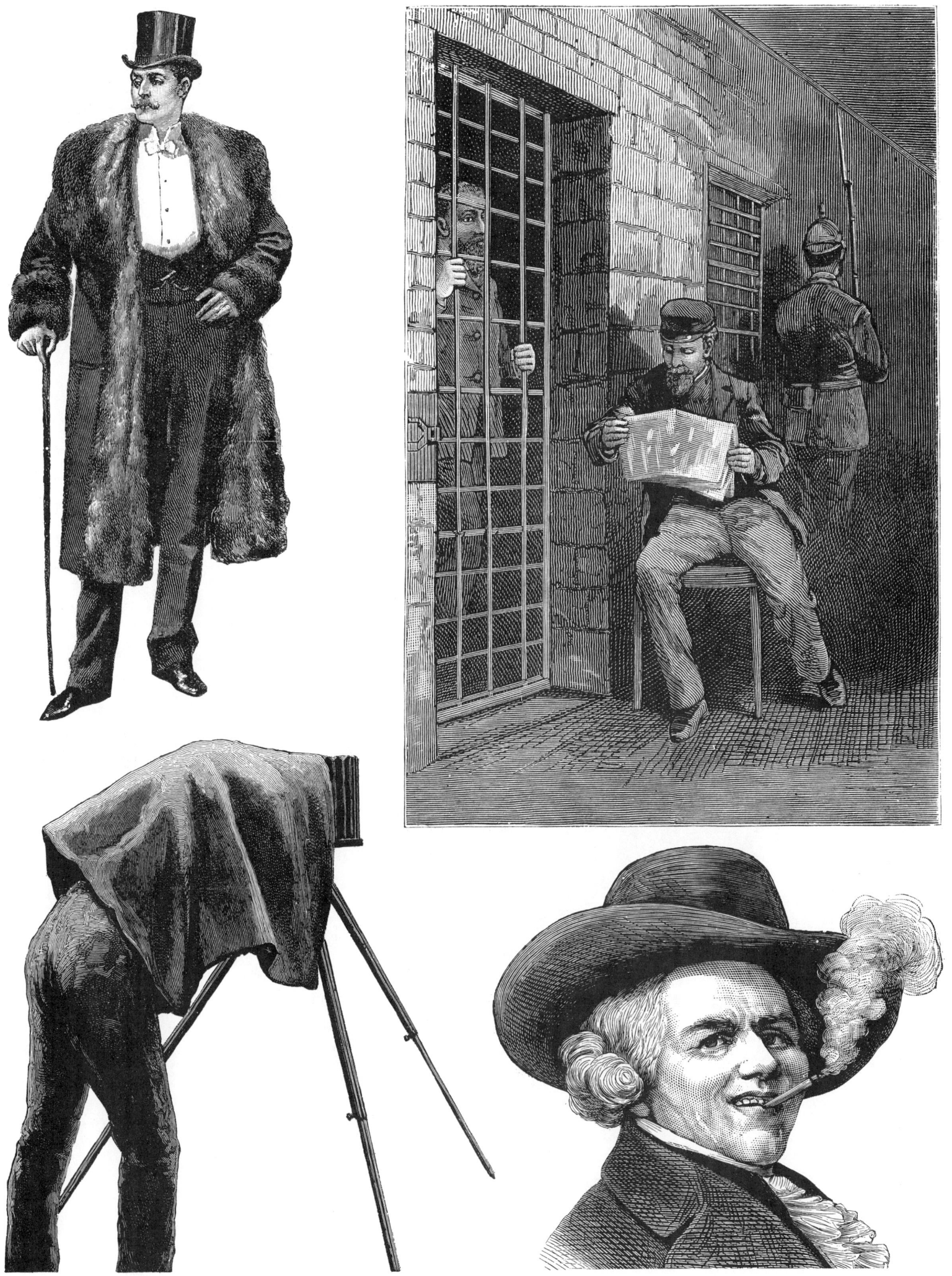

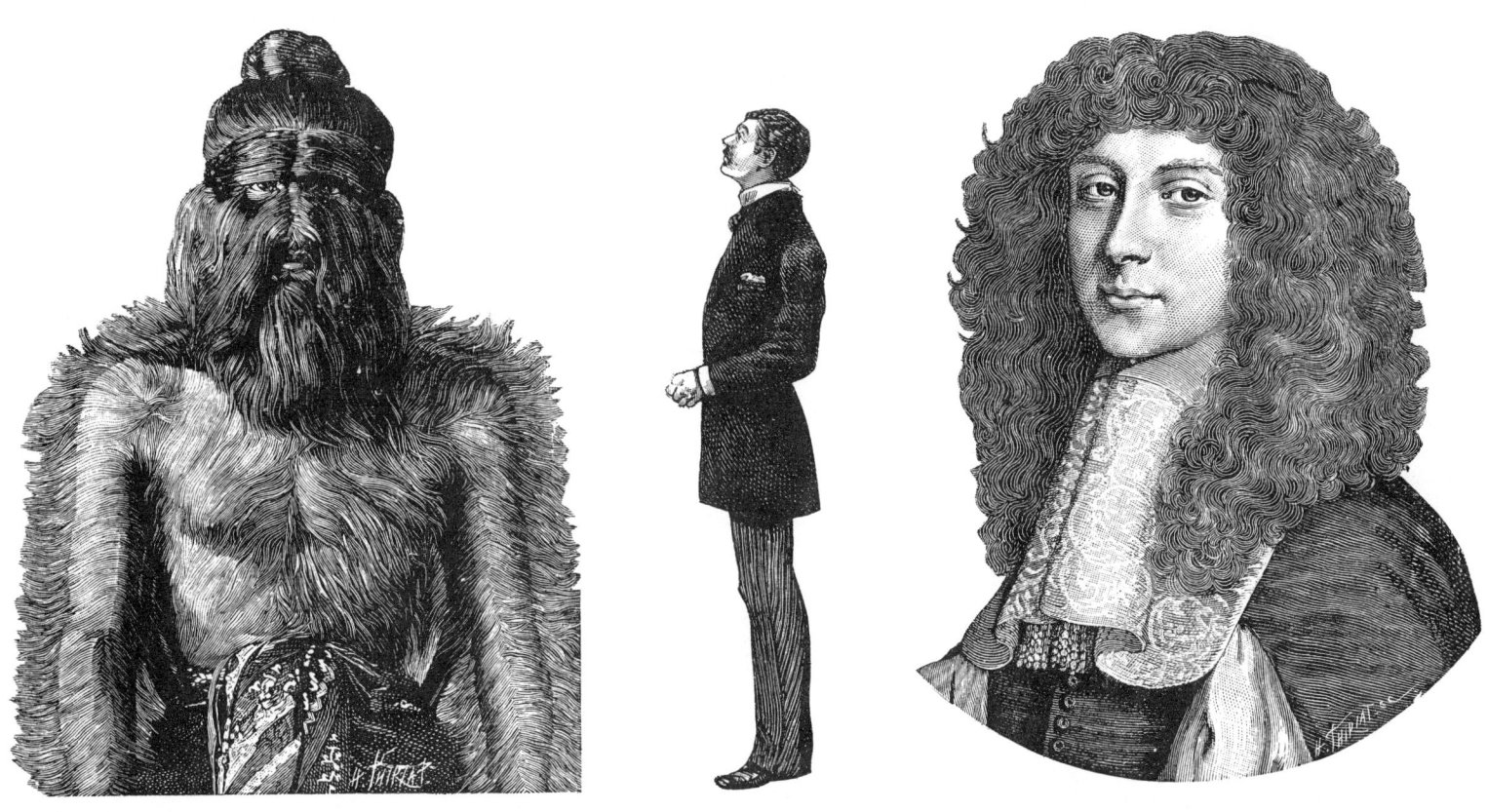

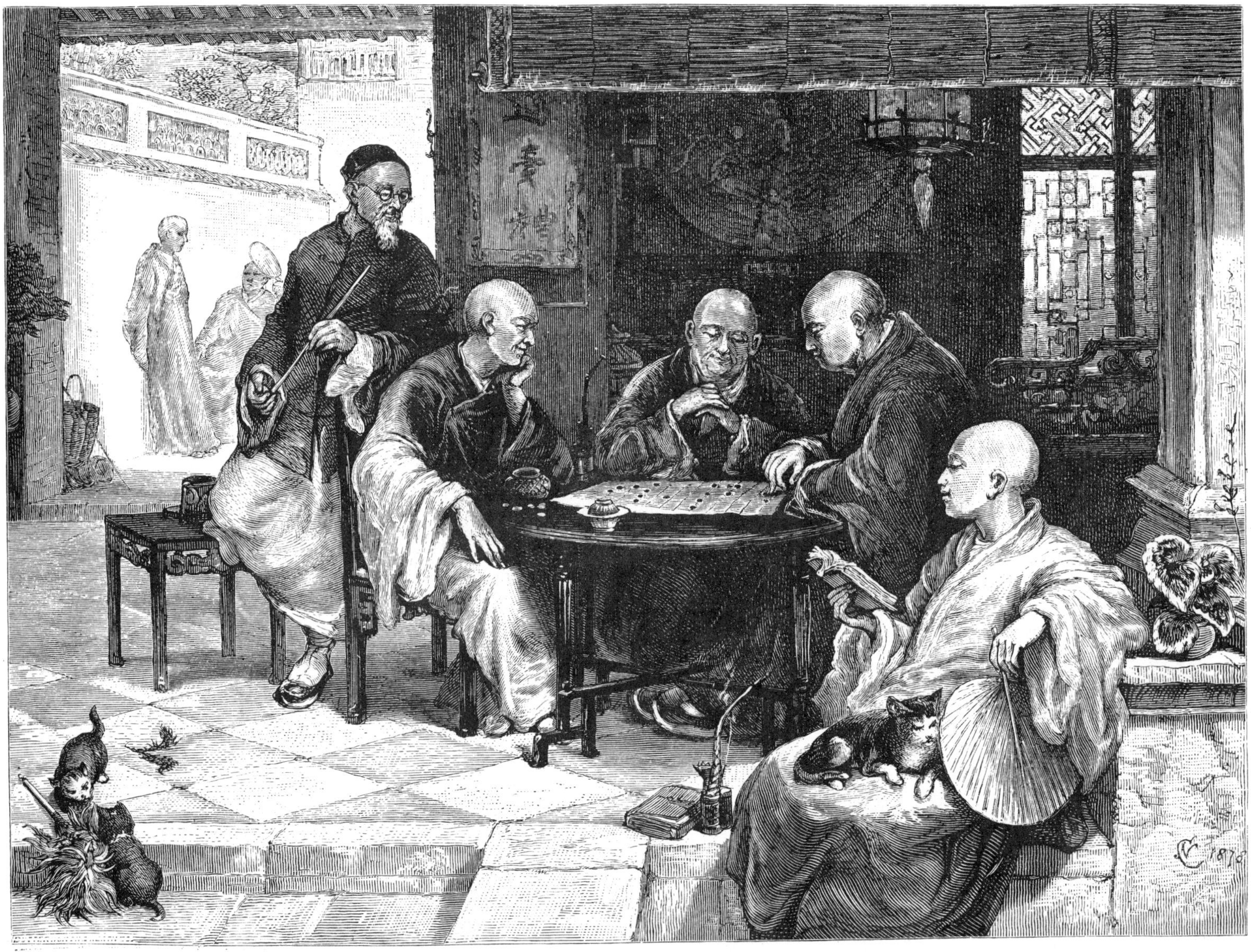

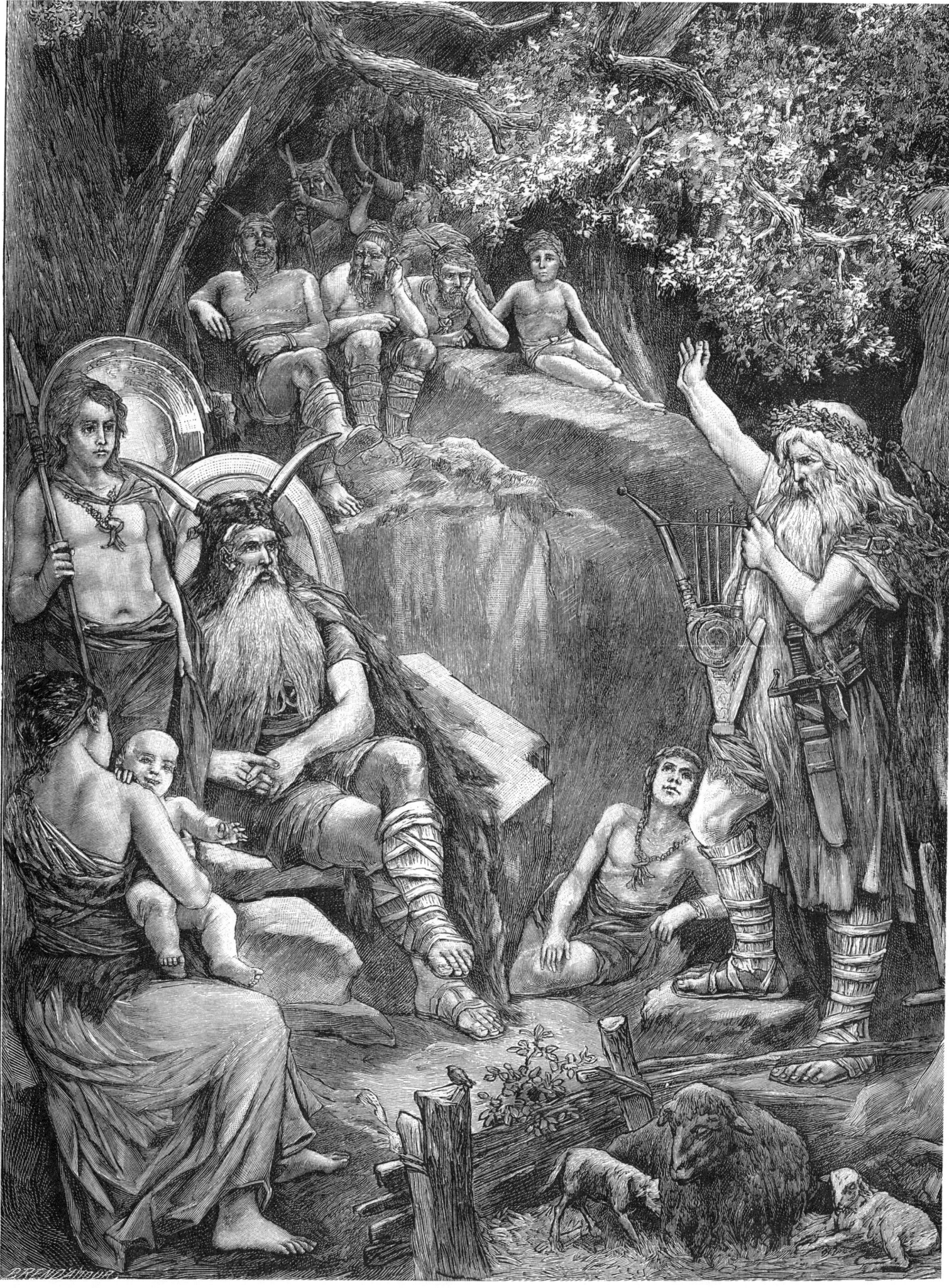

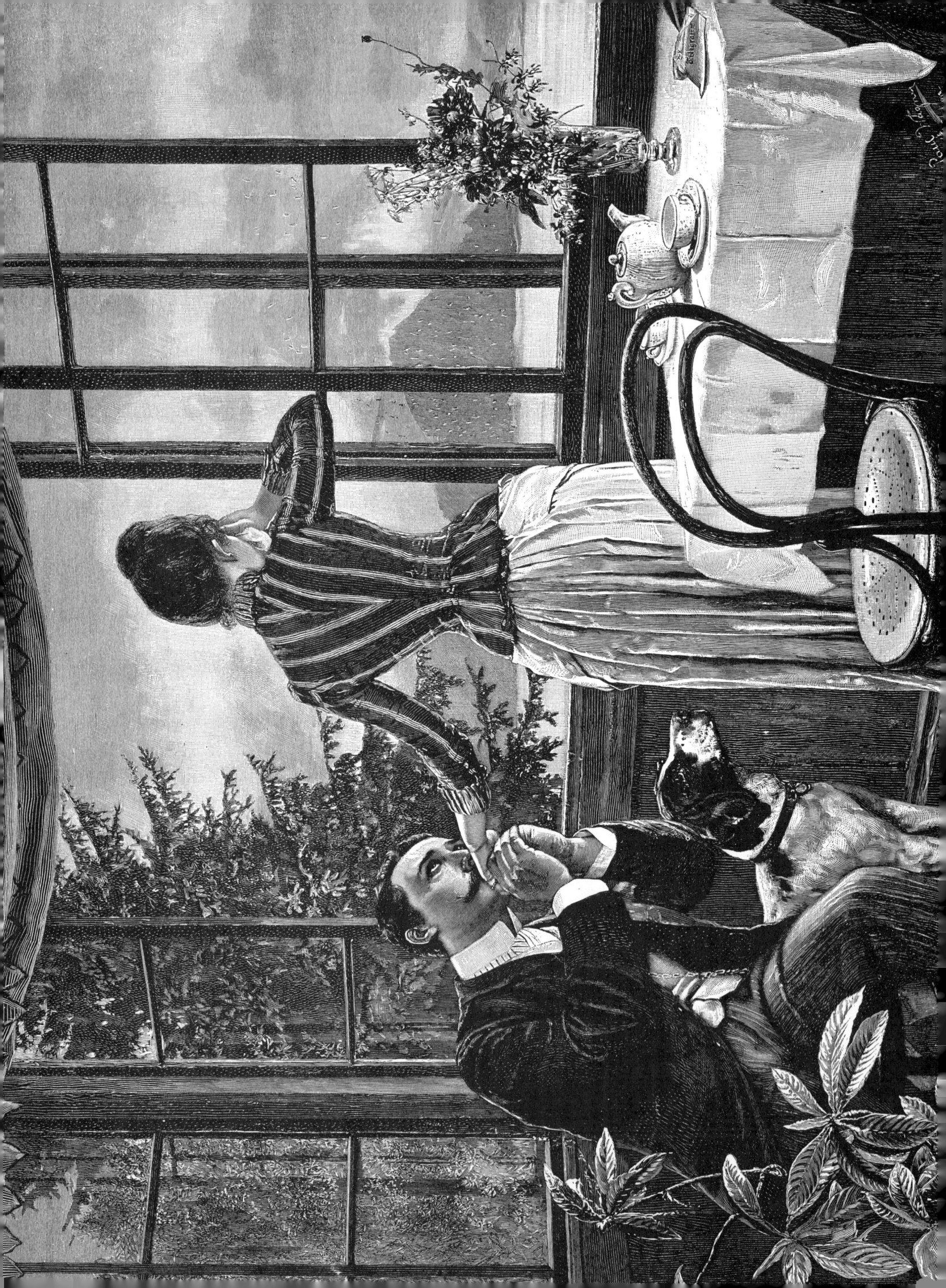

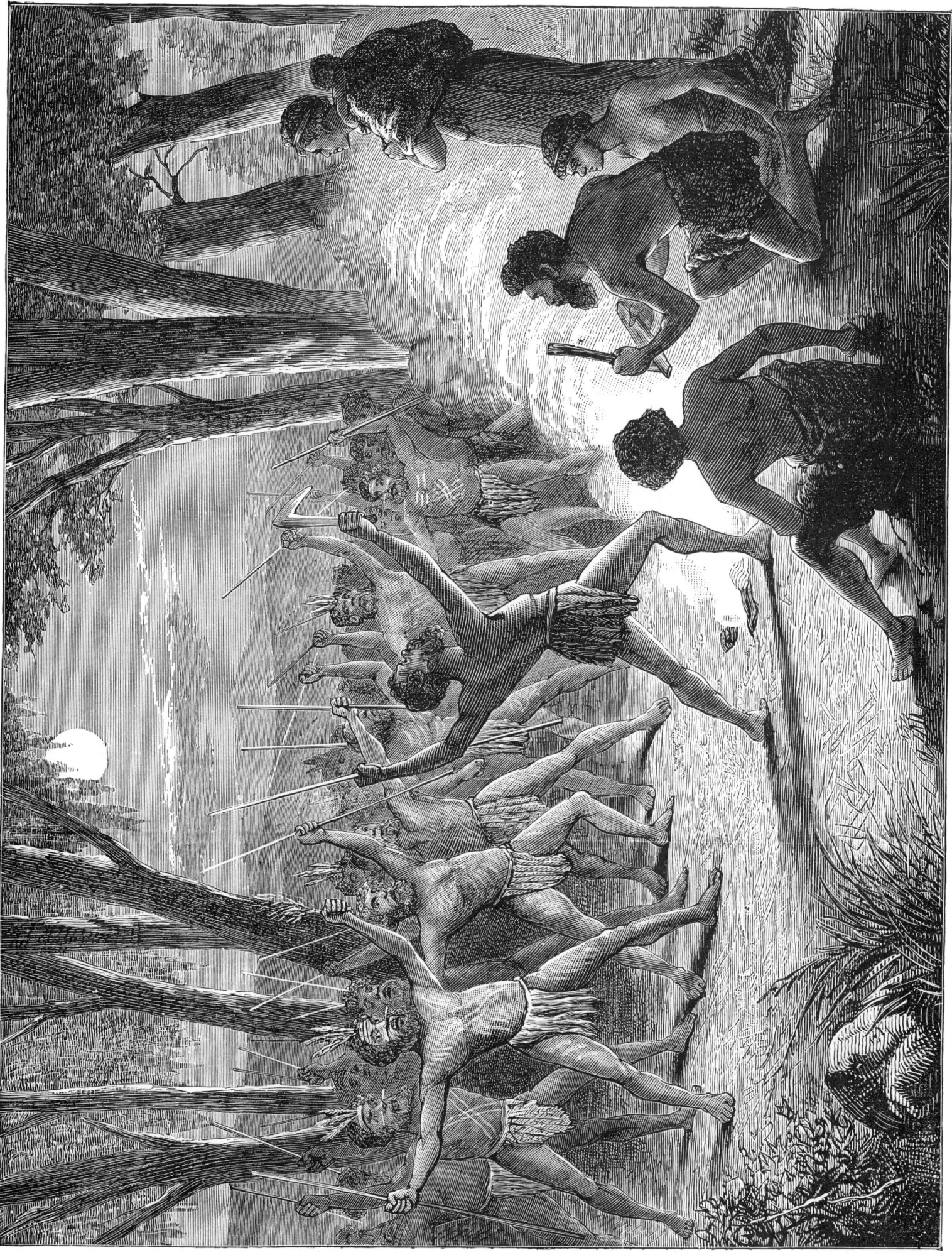

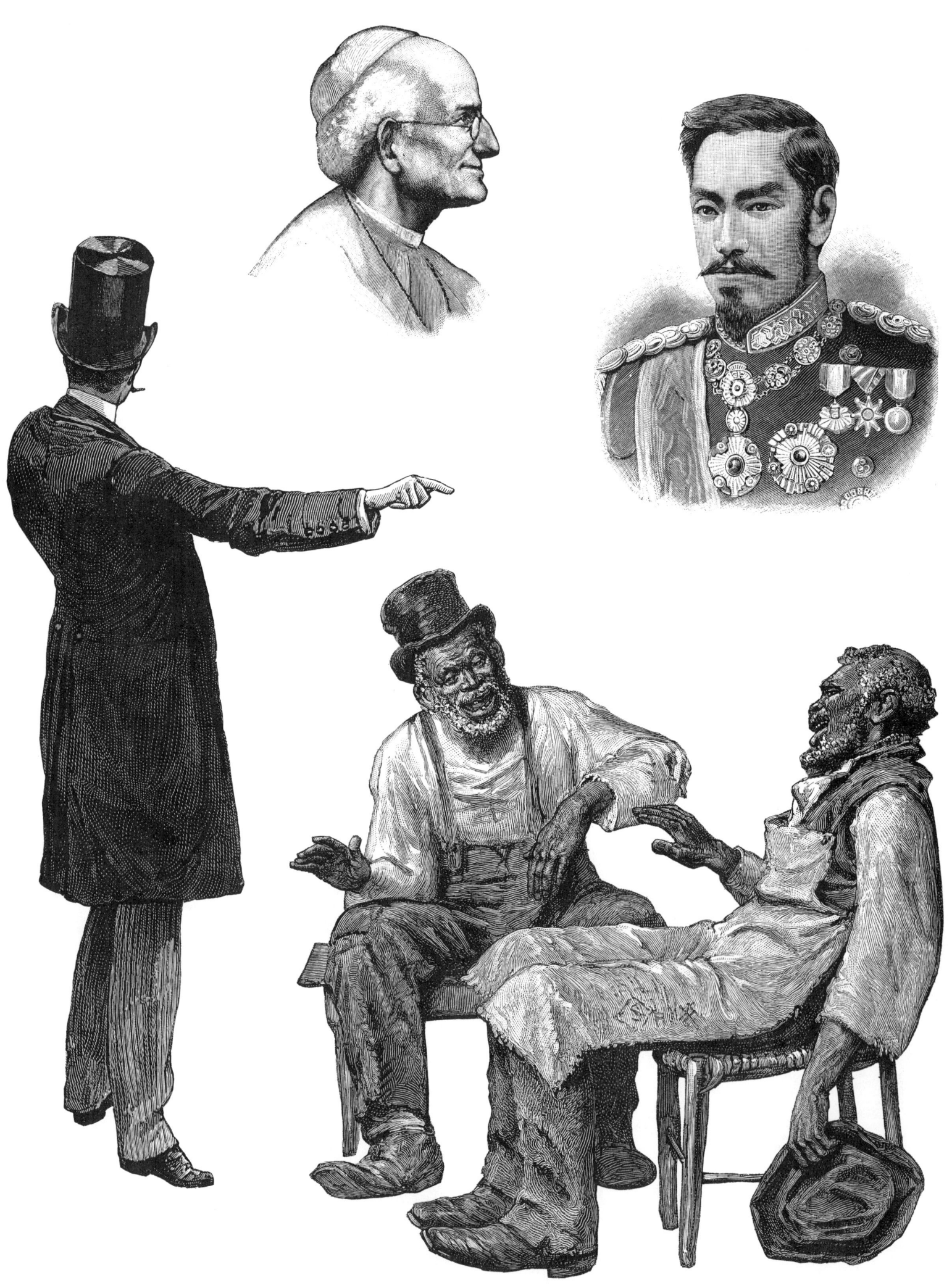

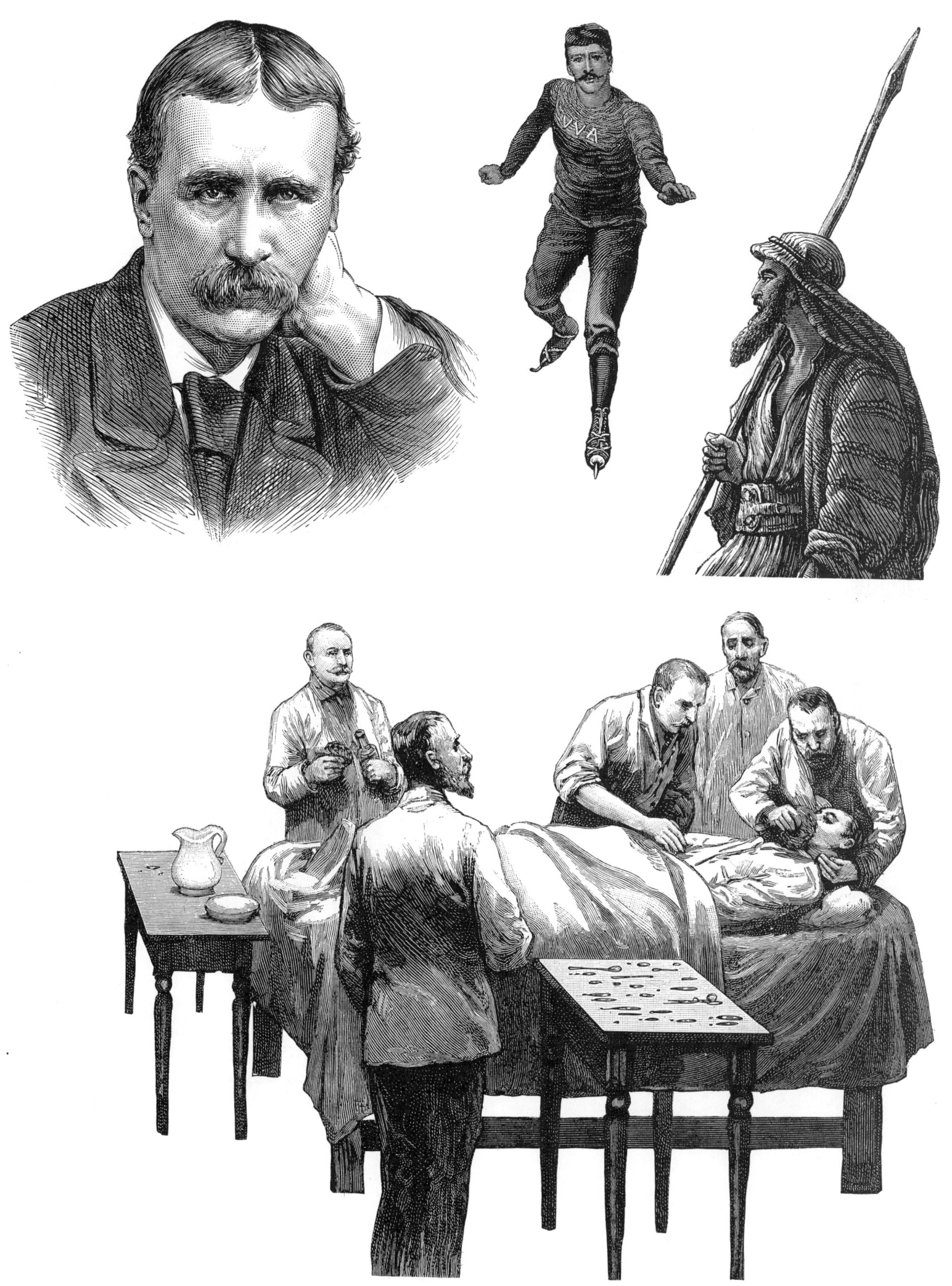

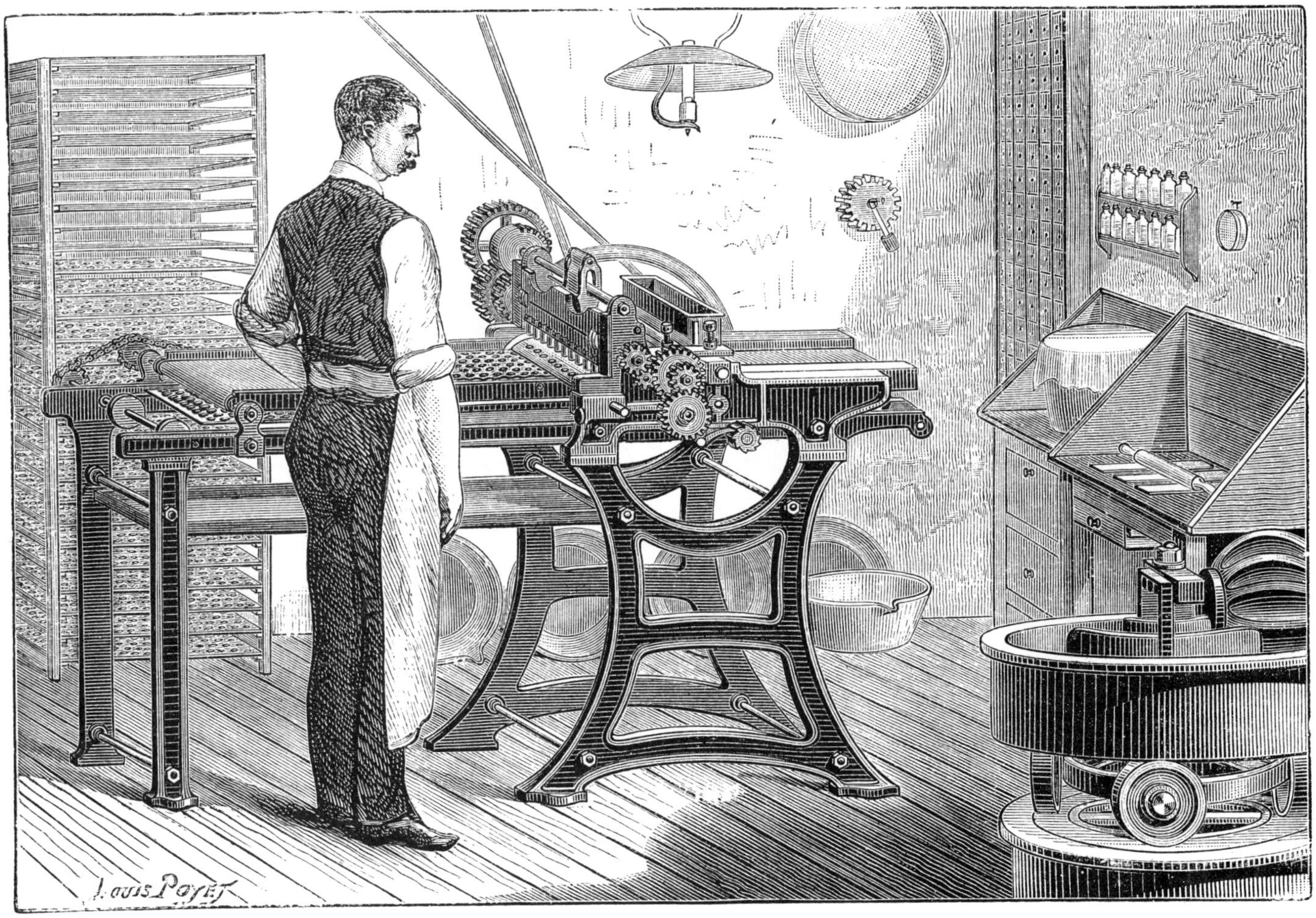

92

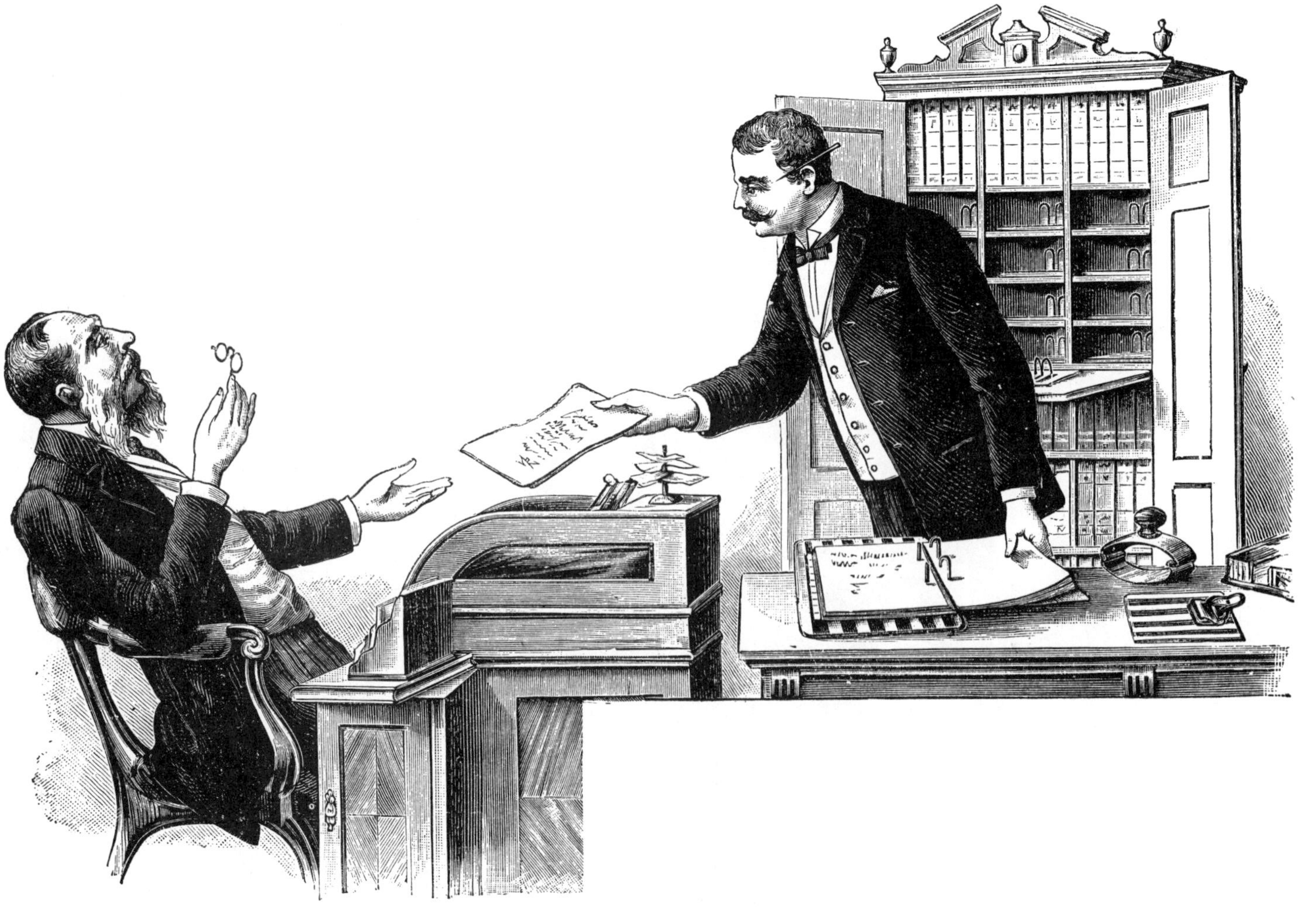

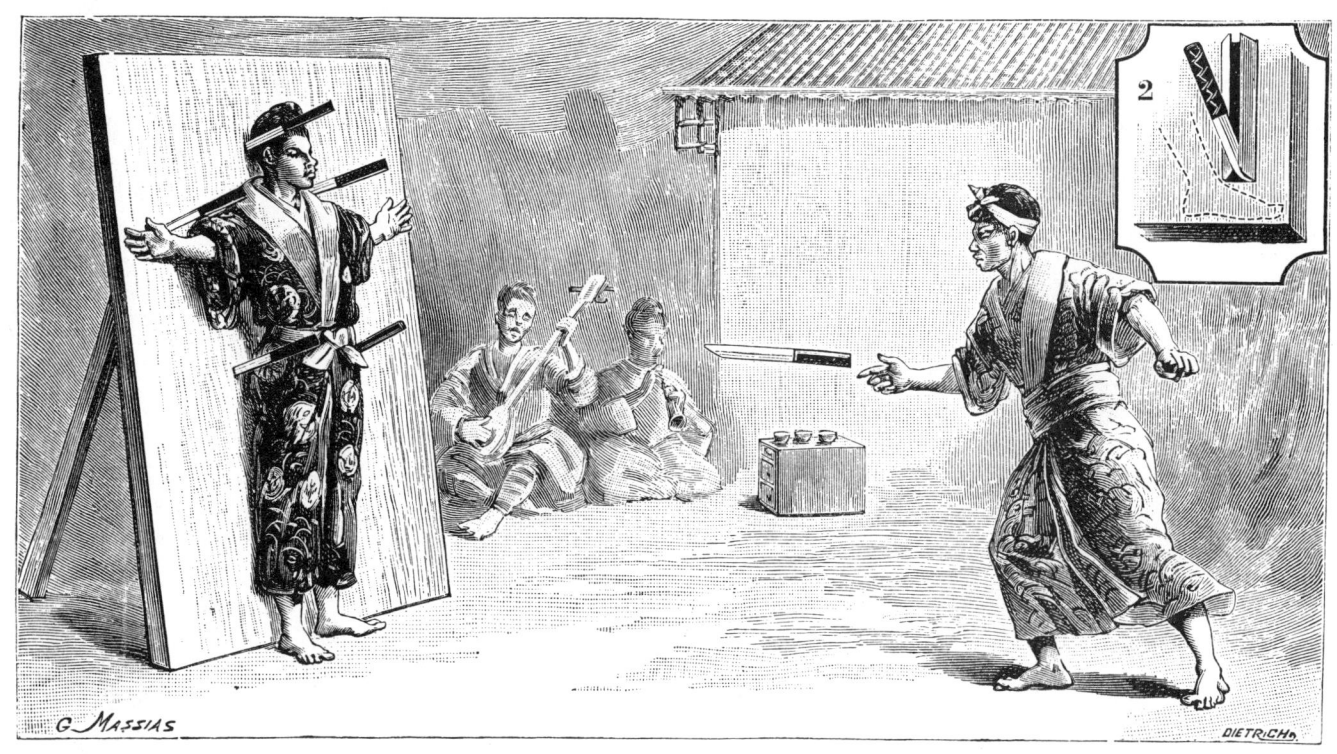

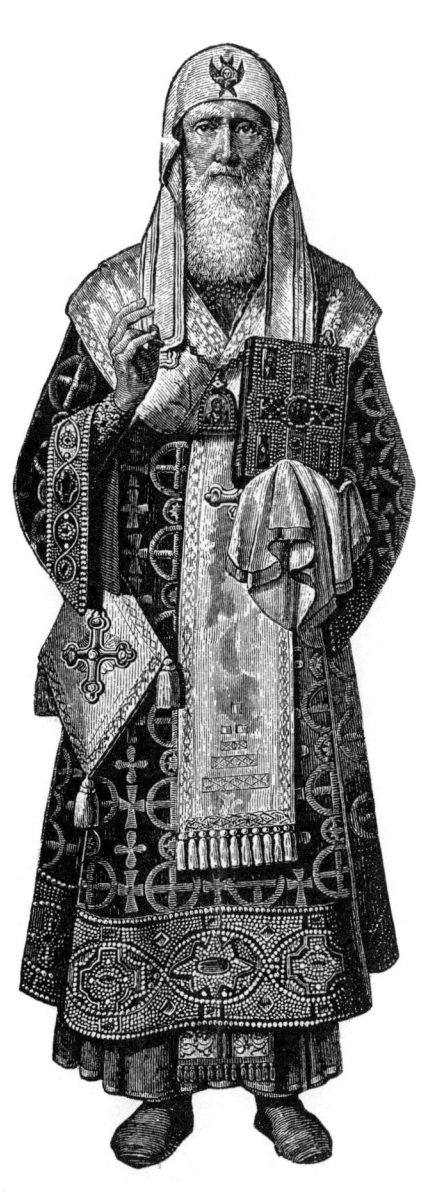

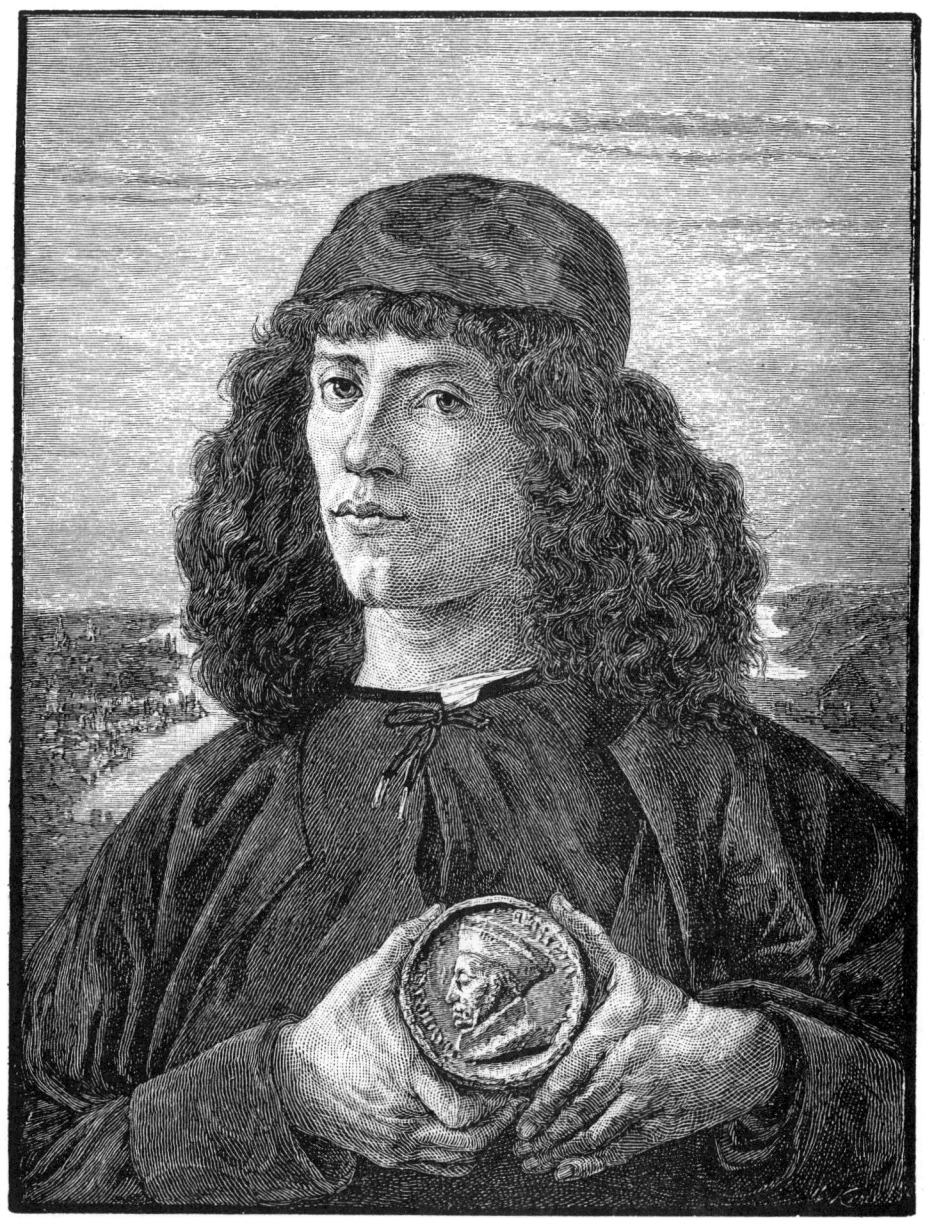

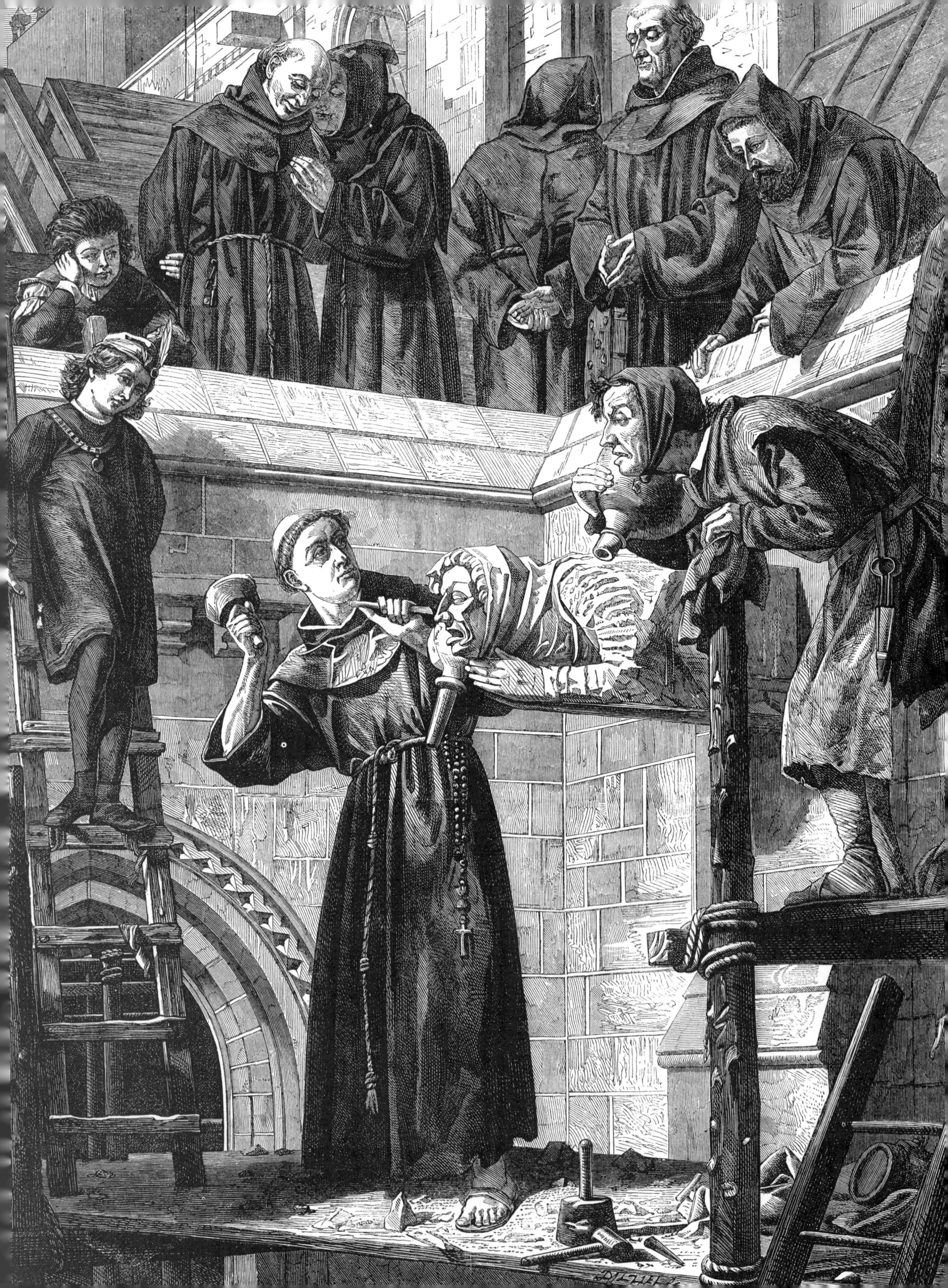

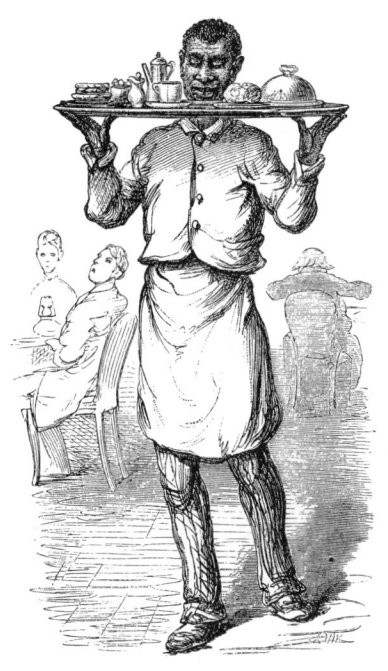
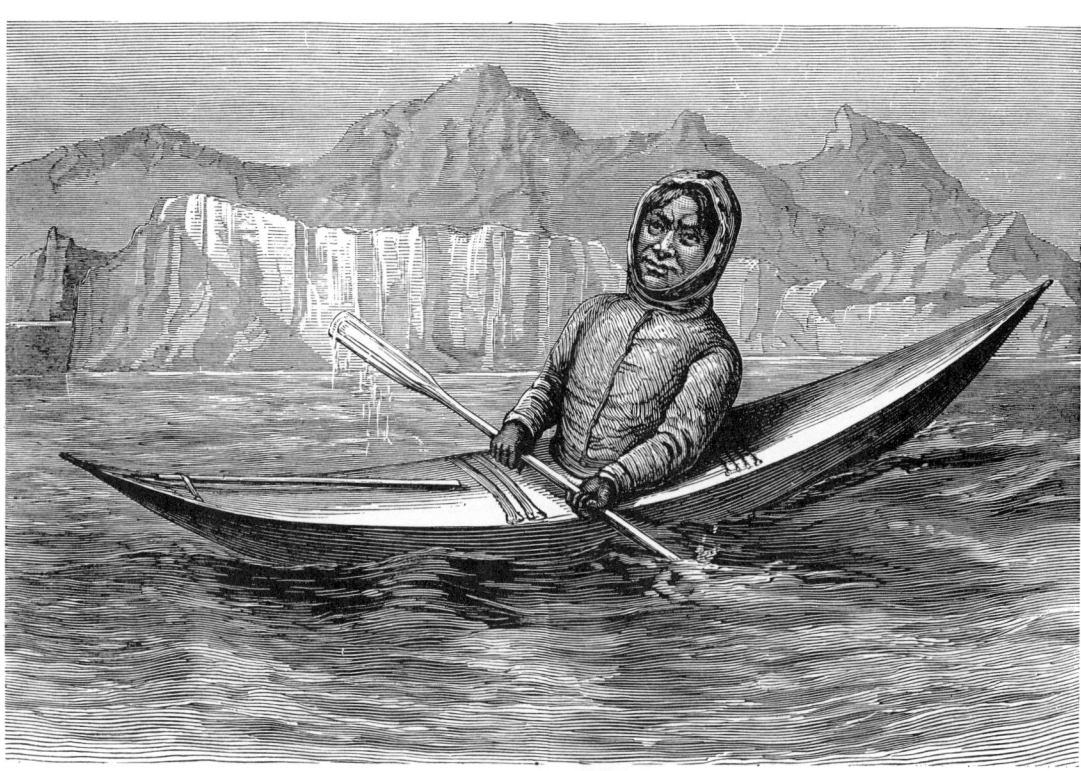

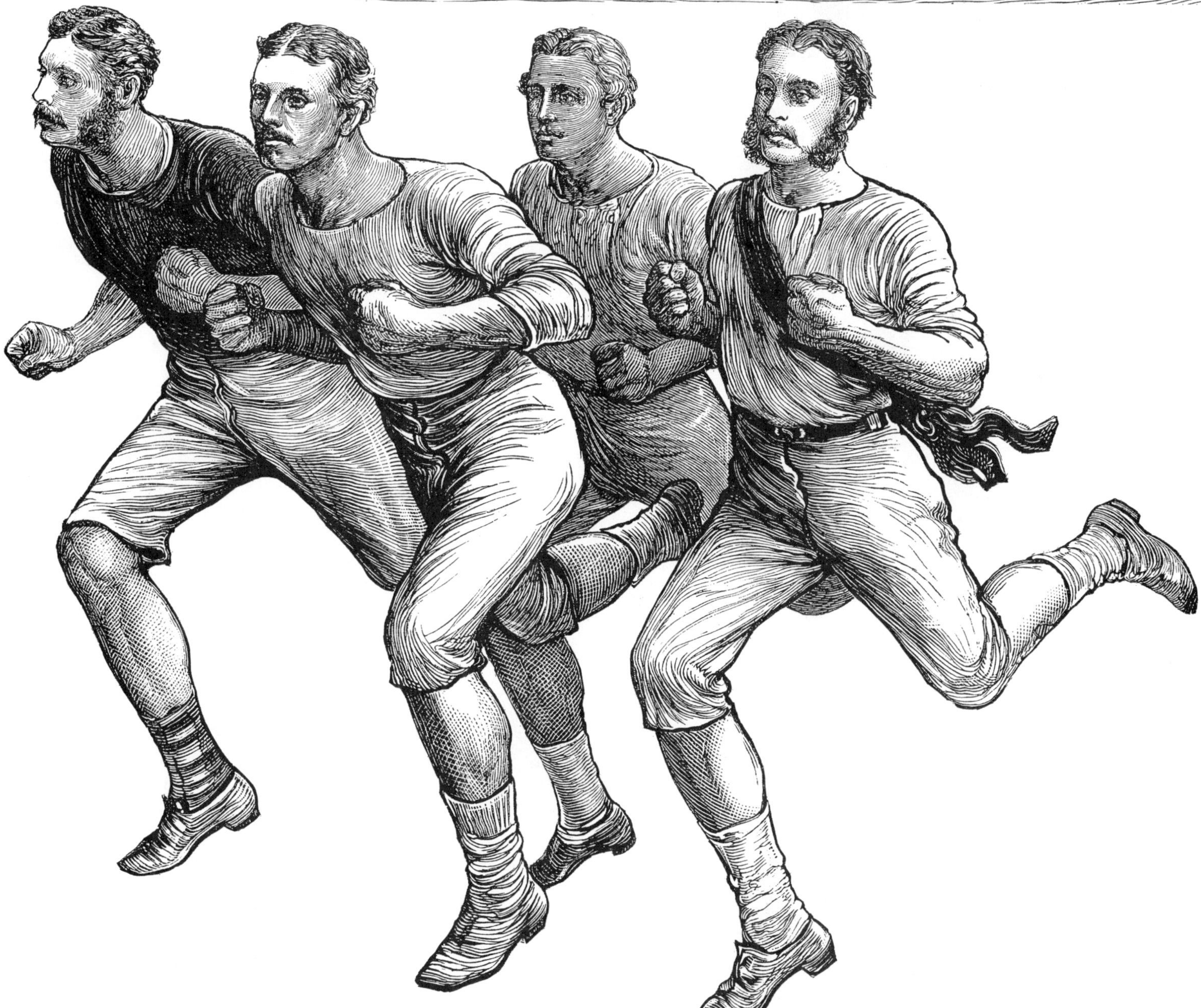

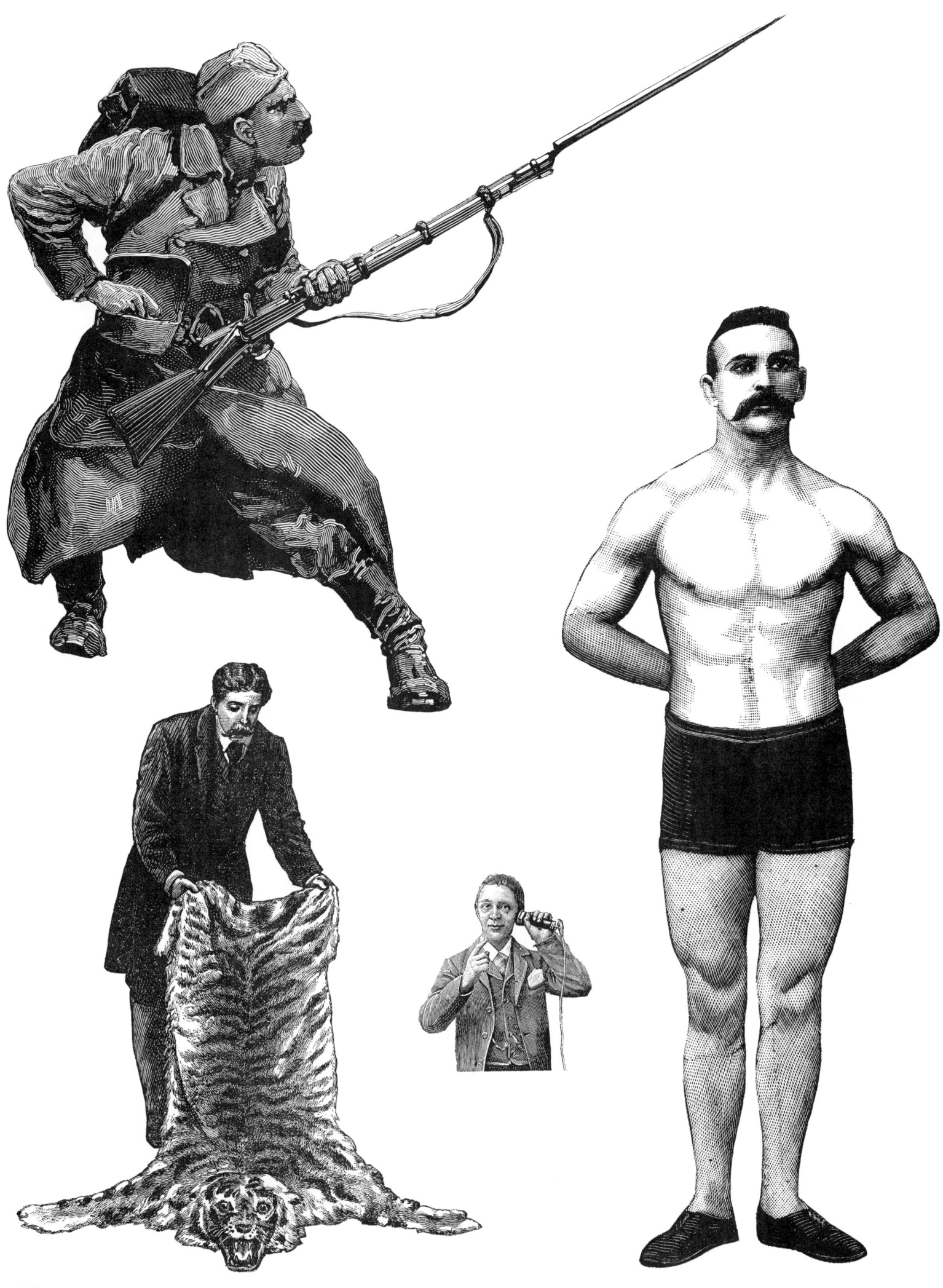

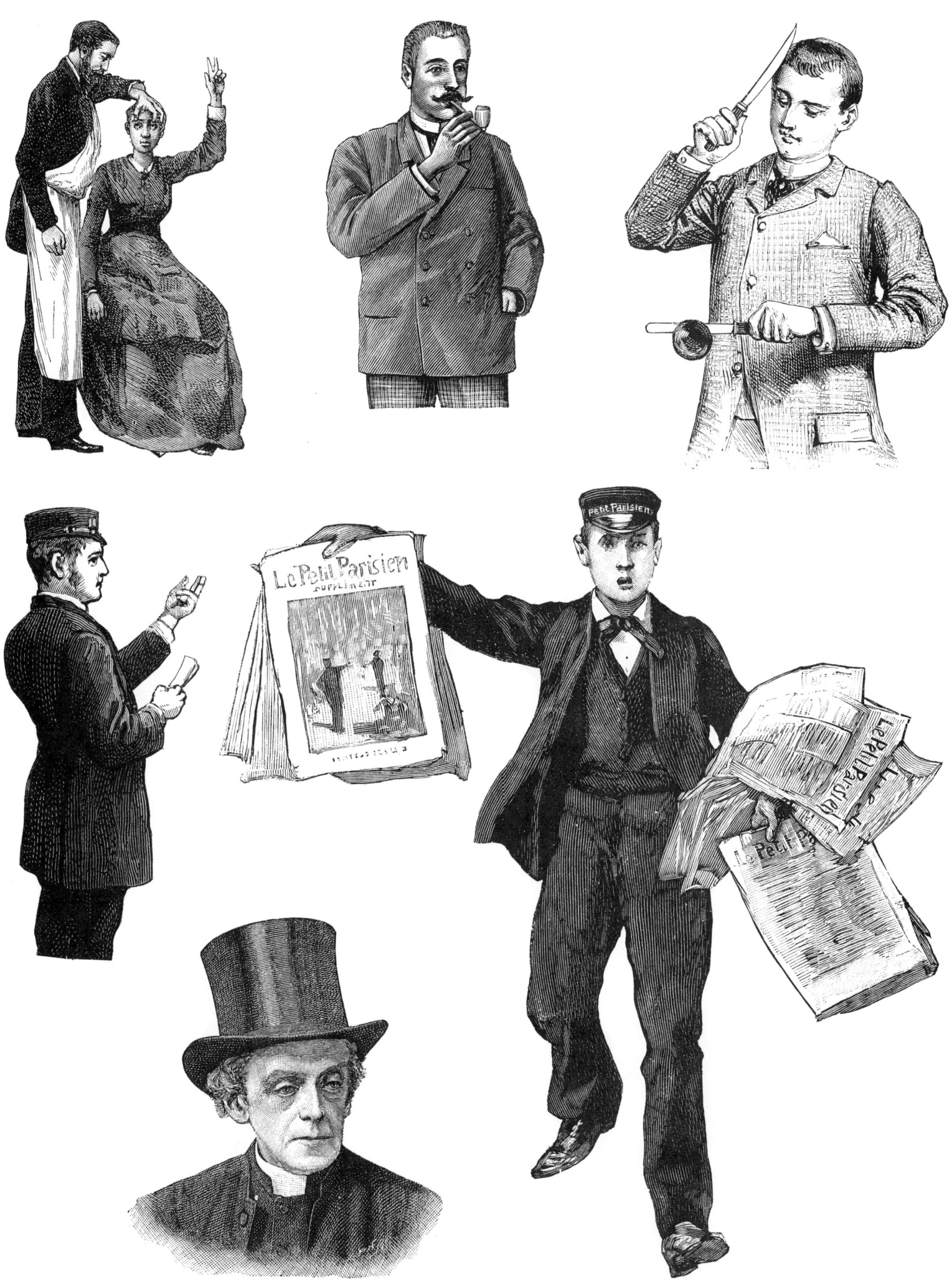

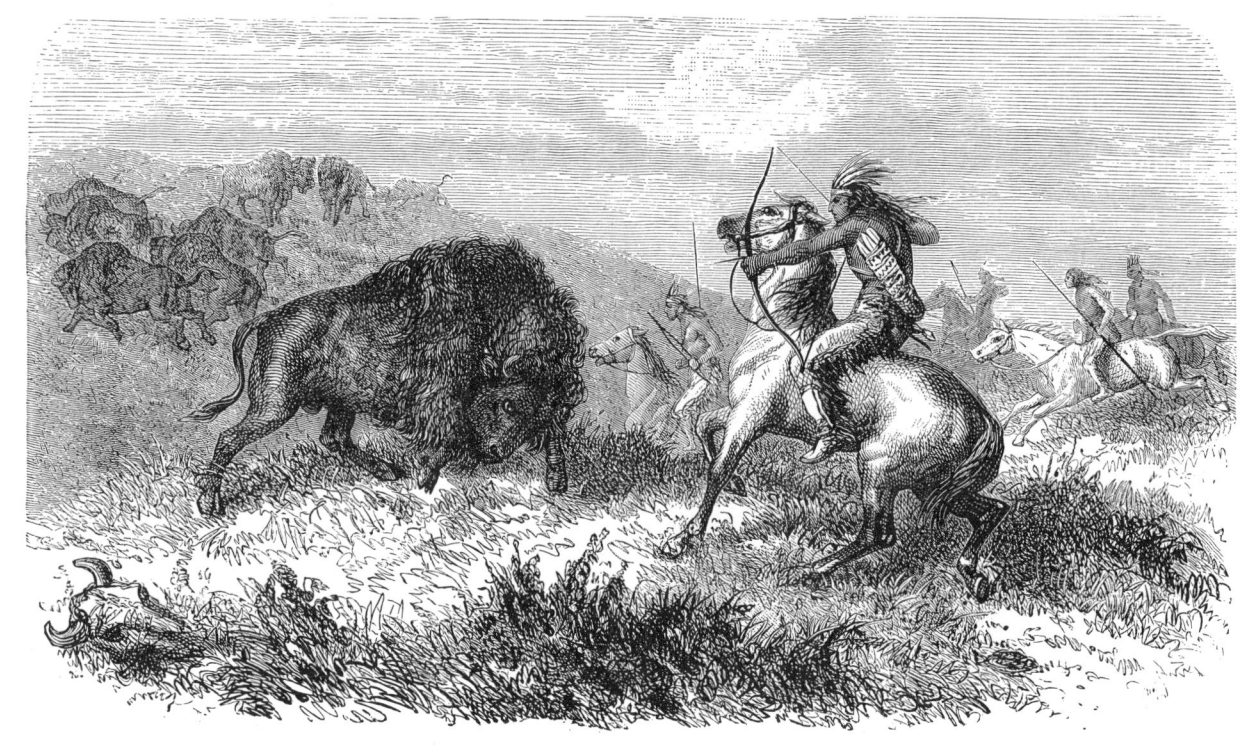
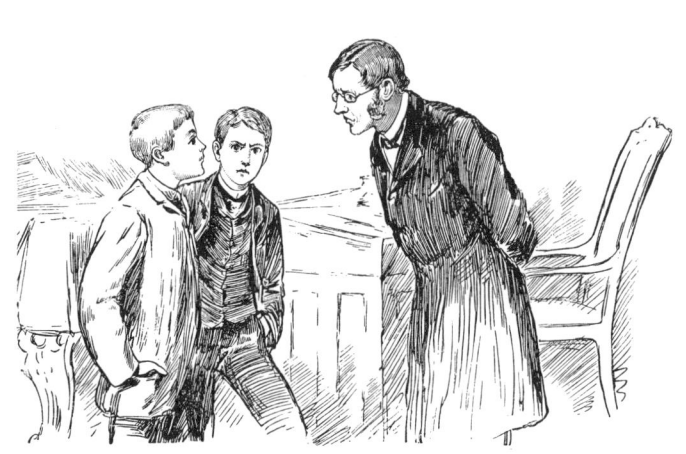
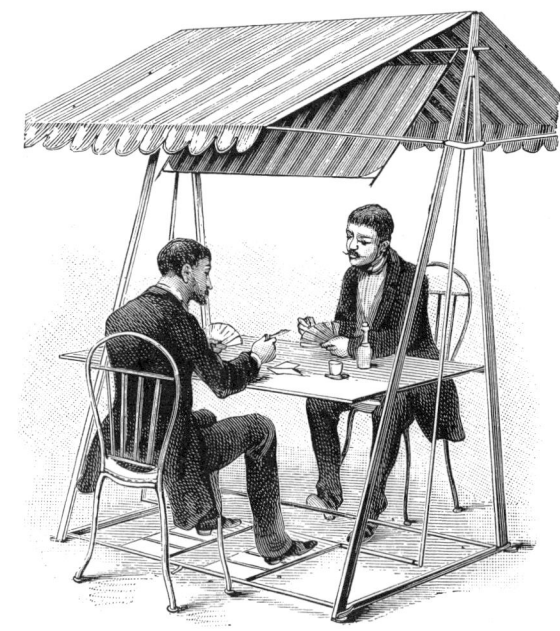
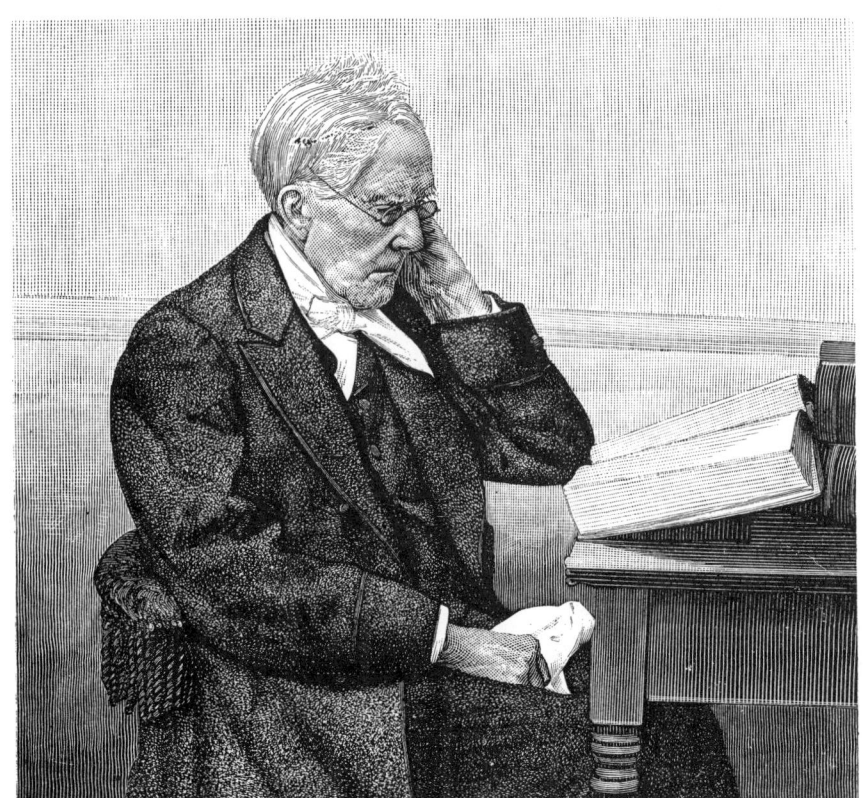
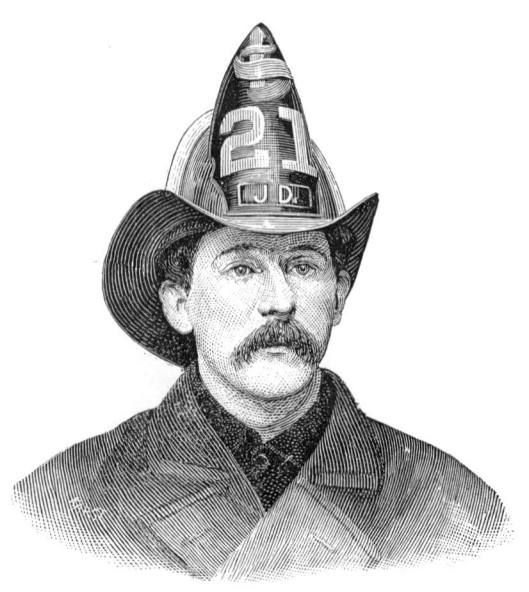

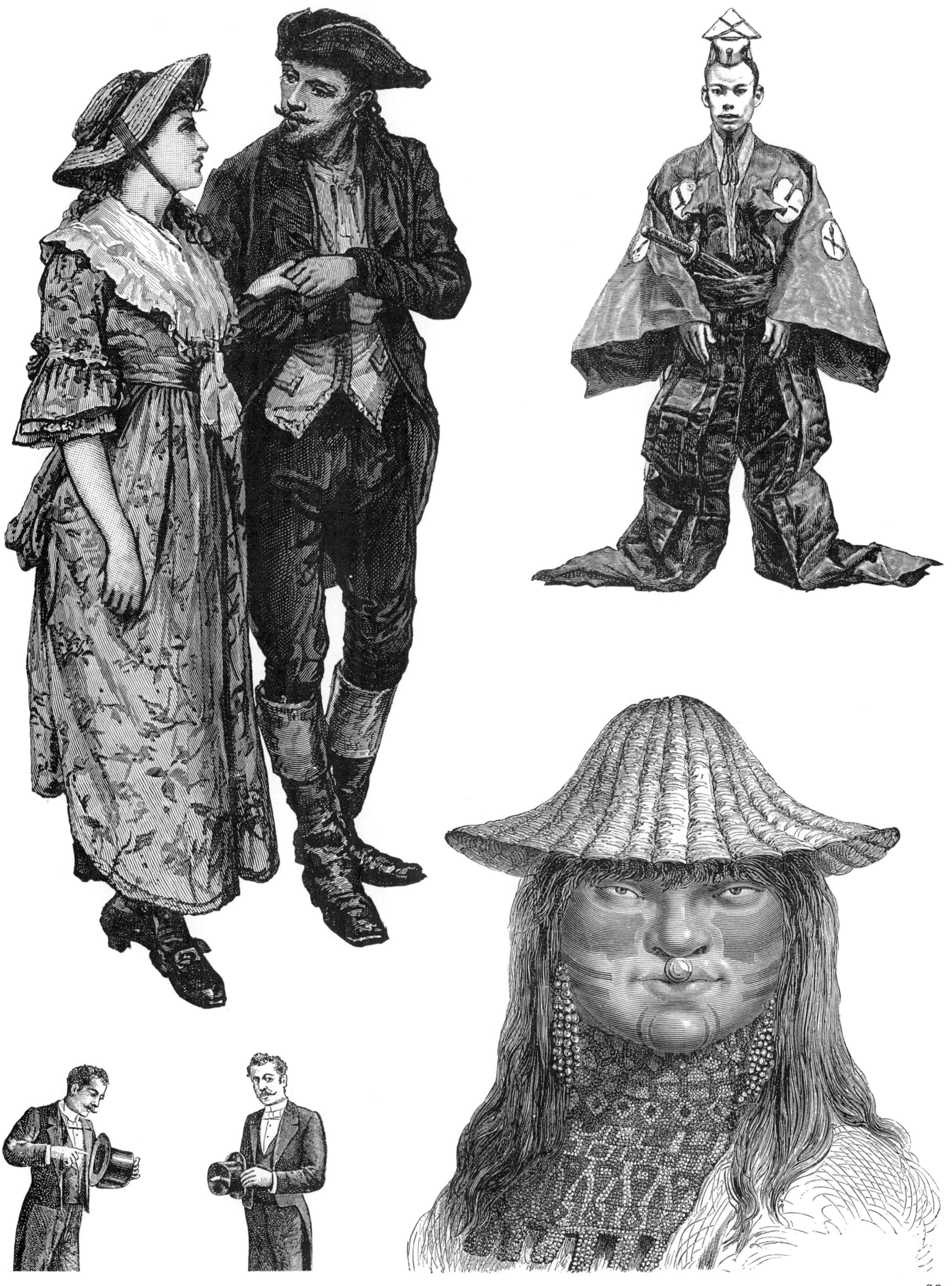

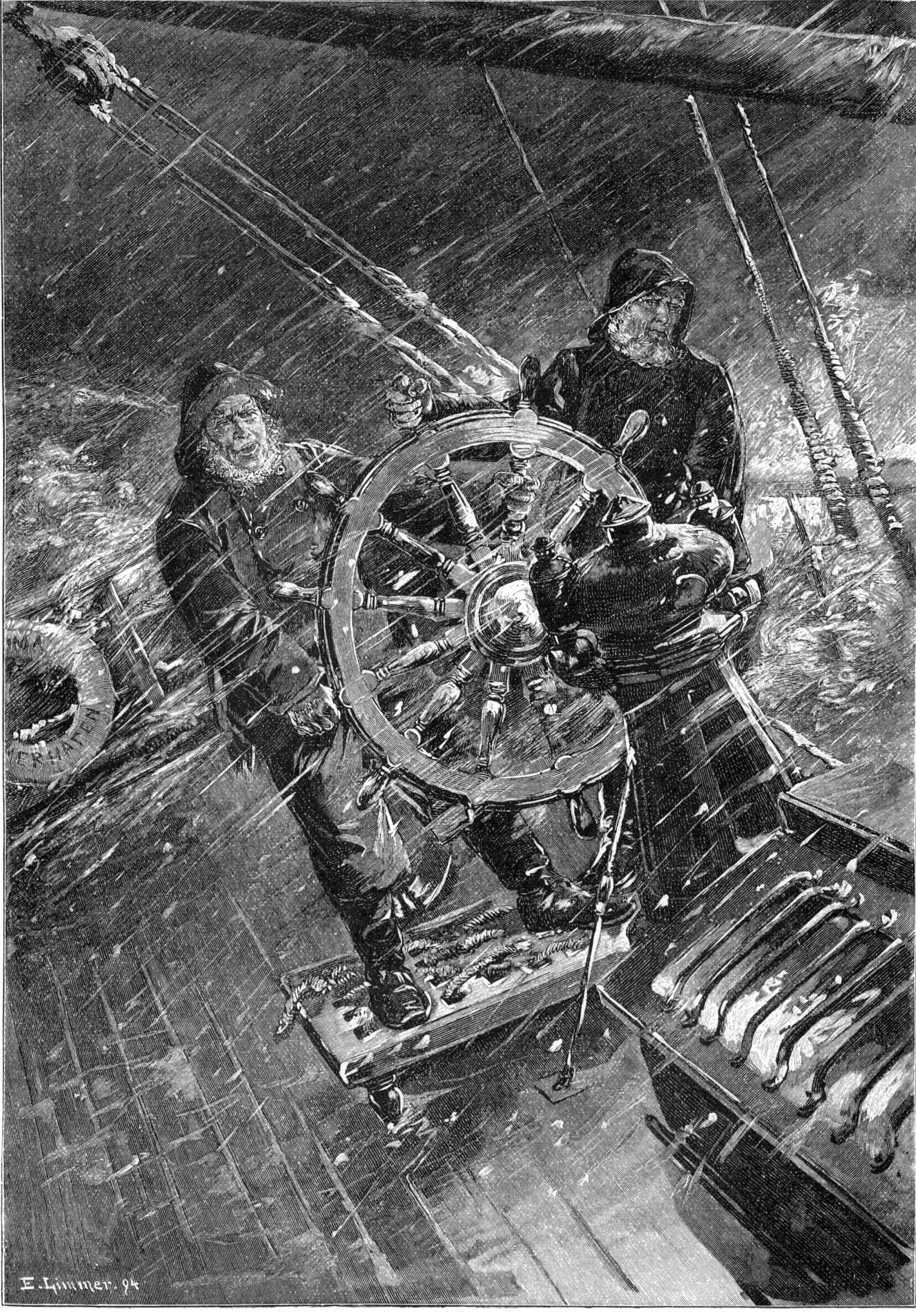

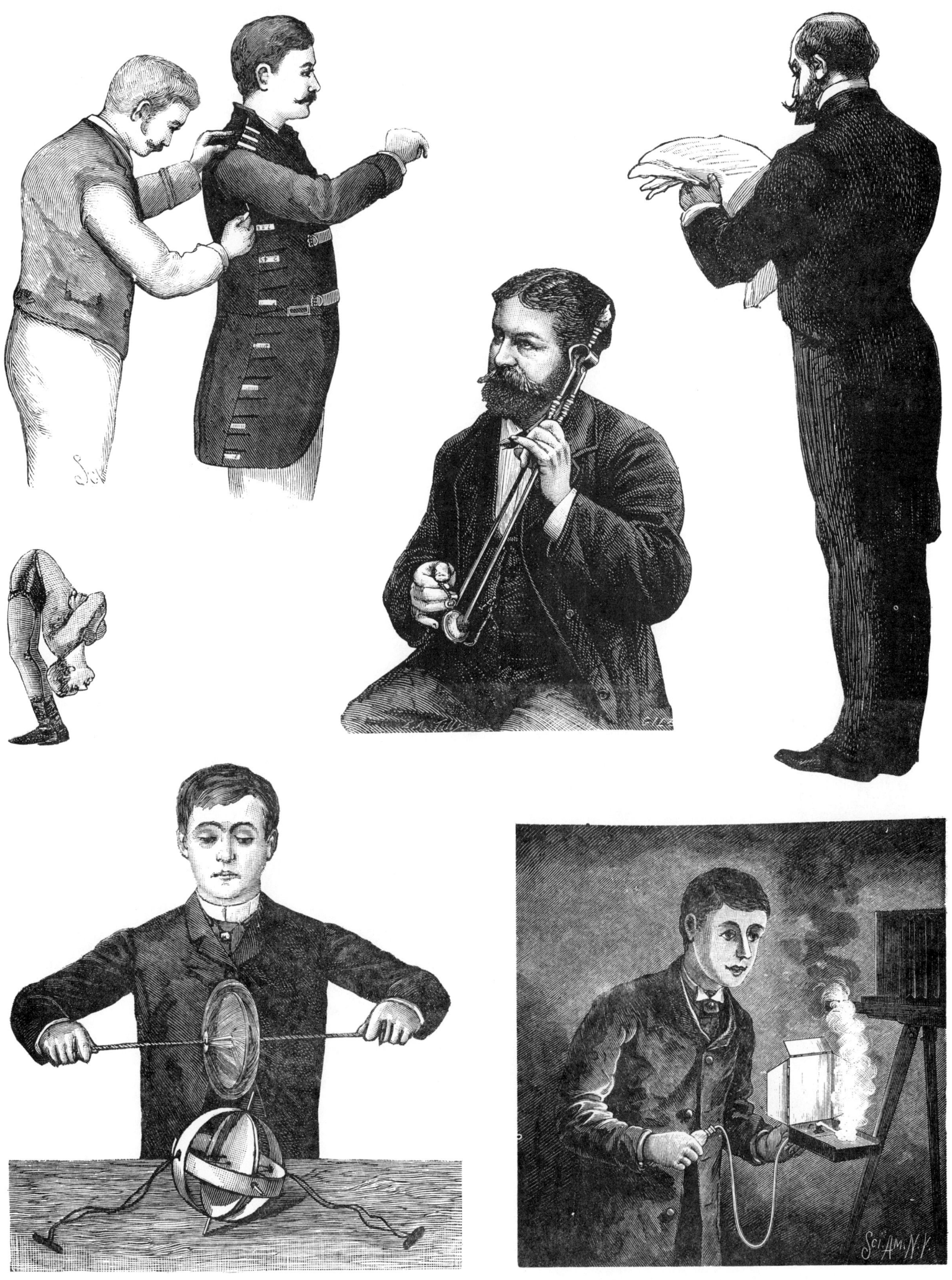

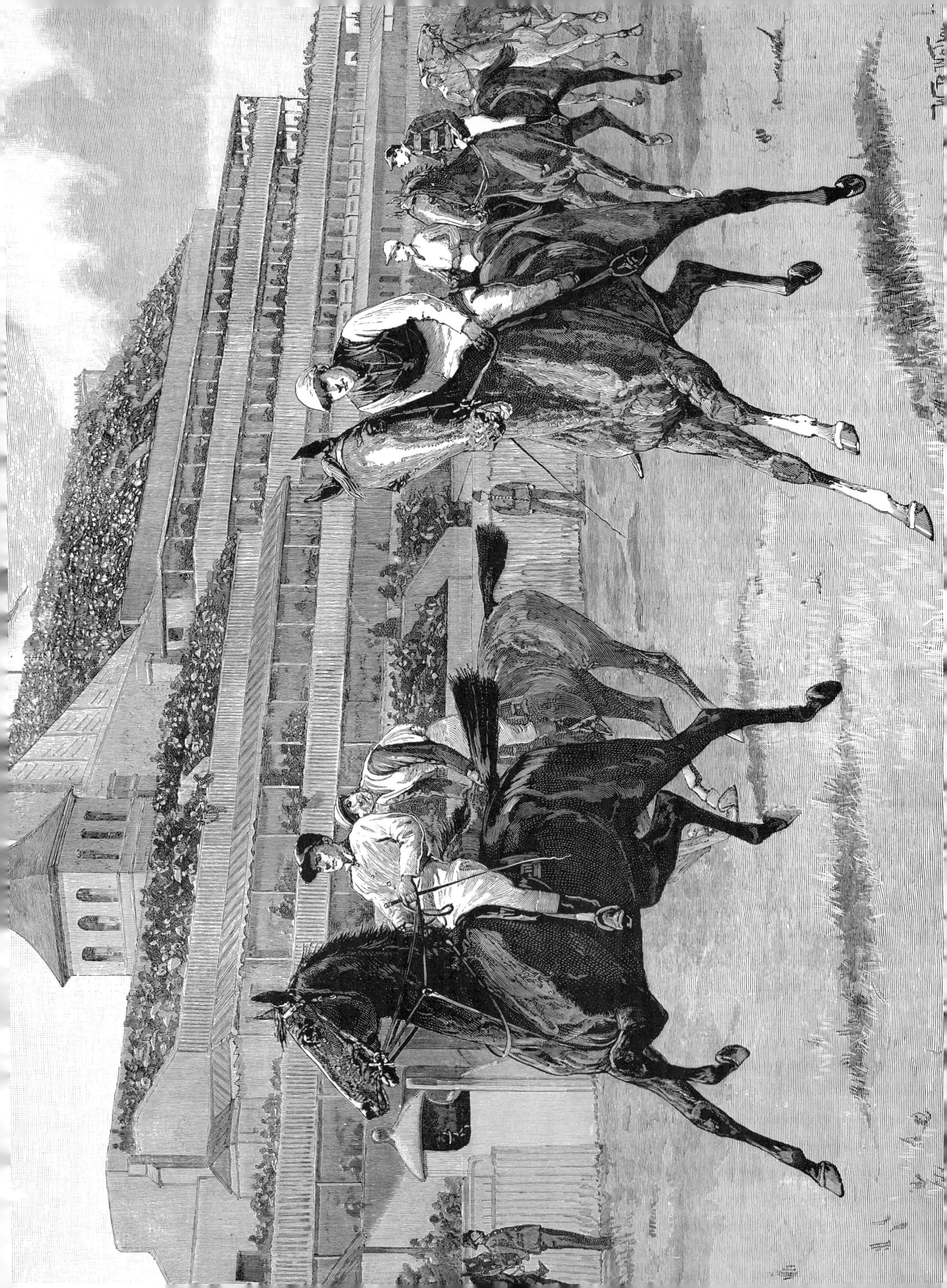

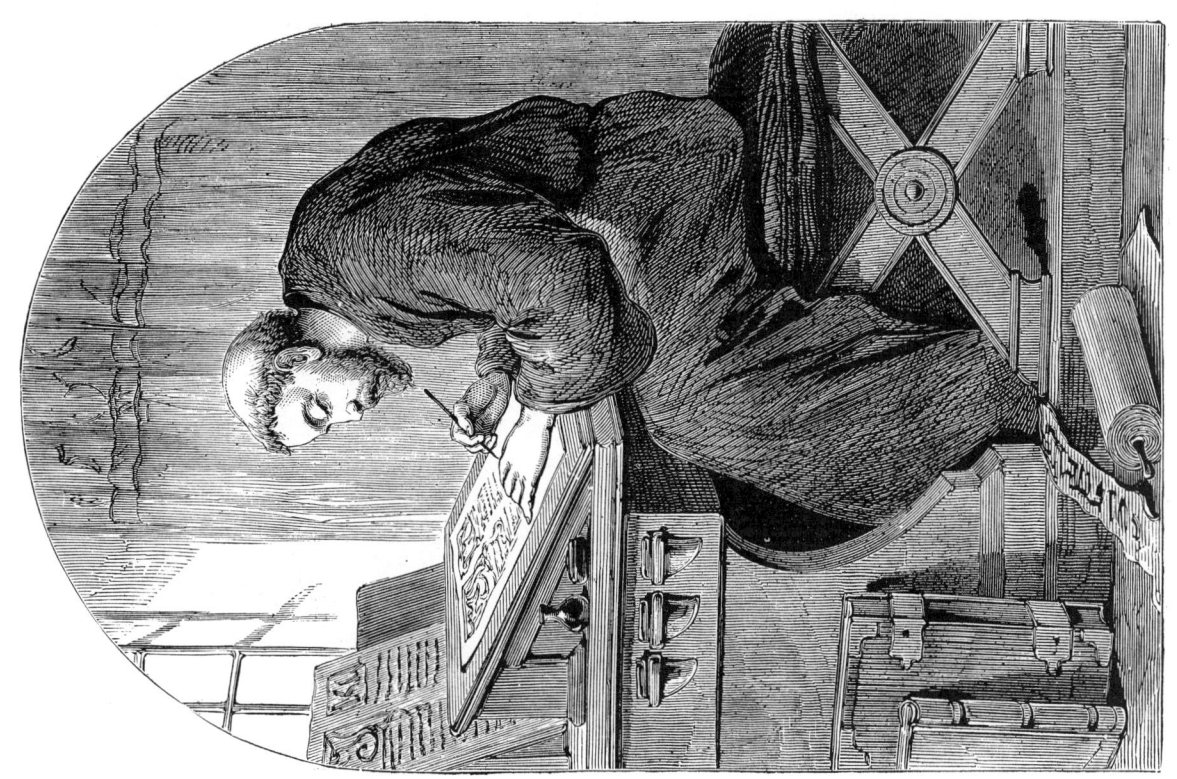
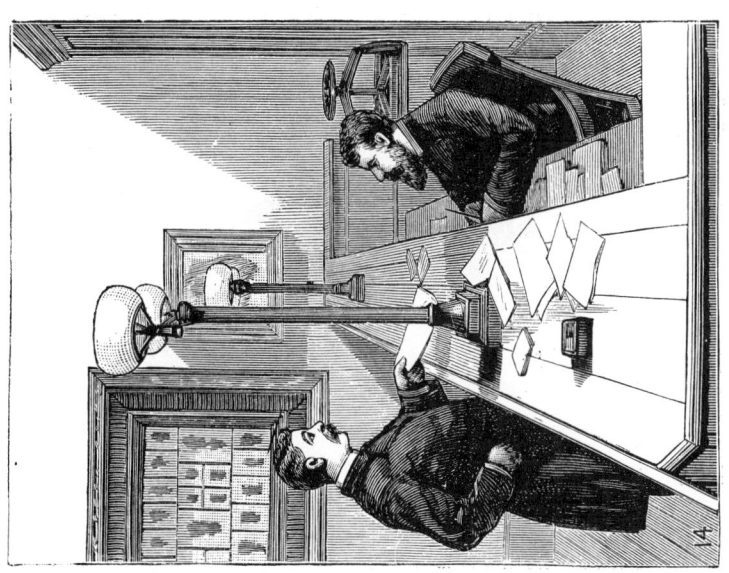
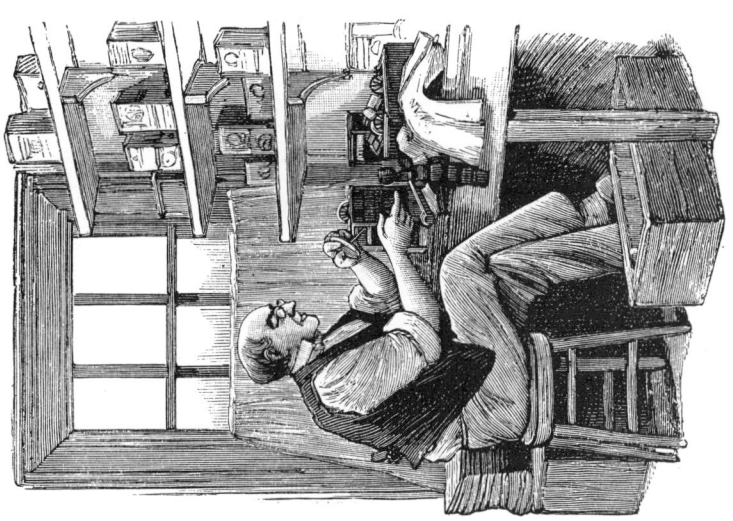
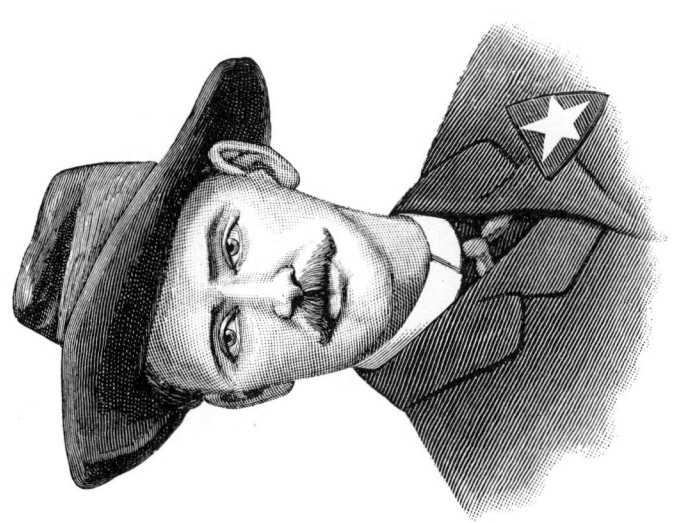
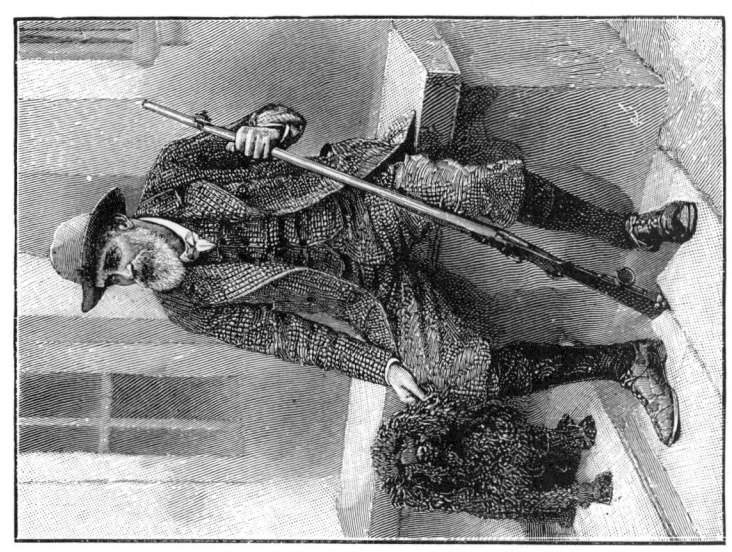

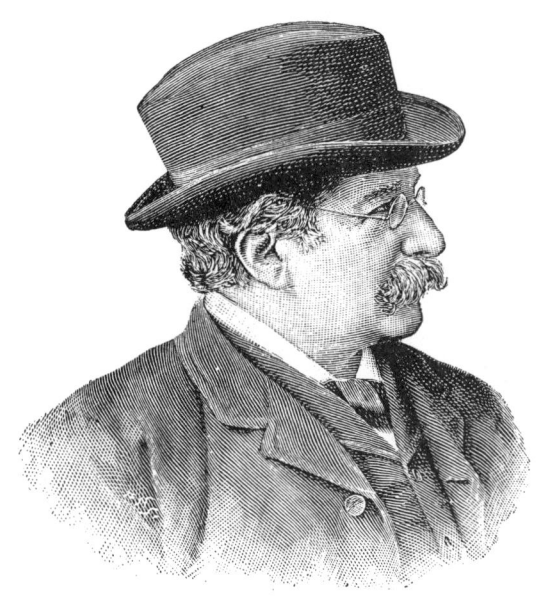
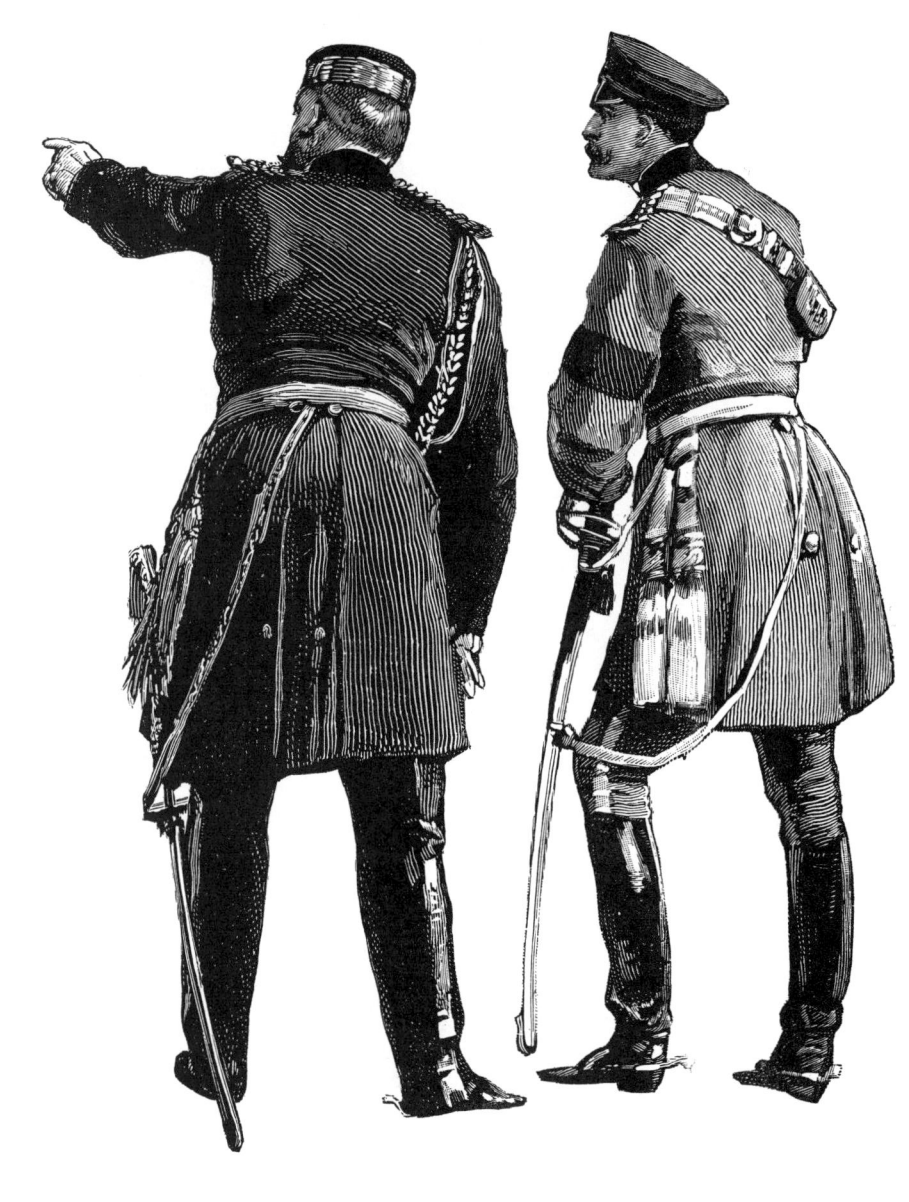
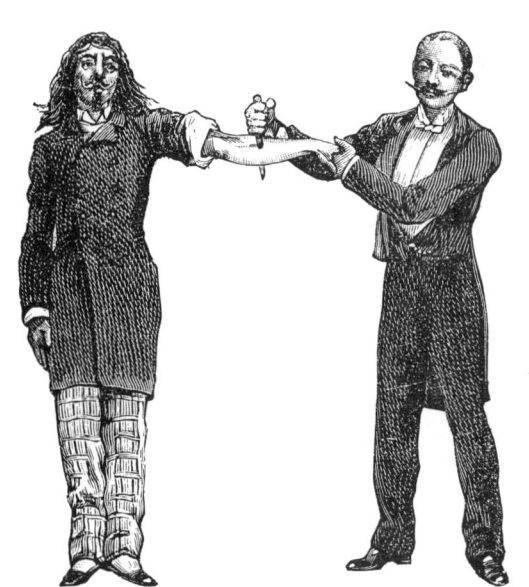
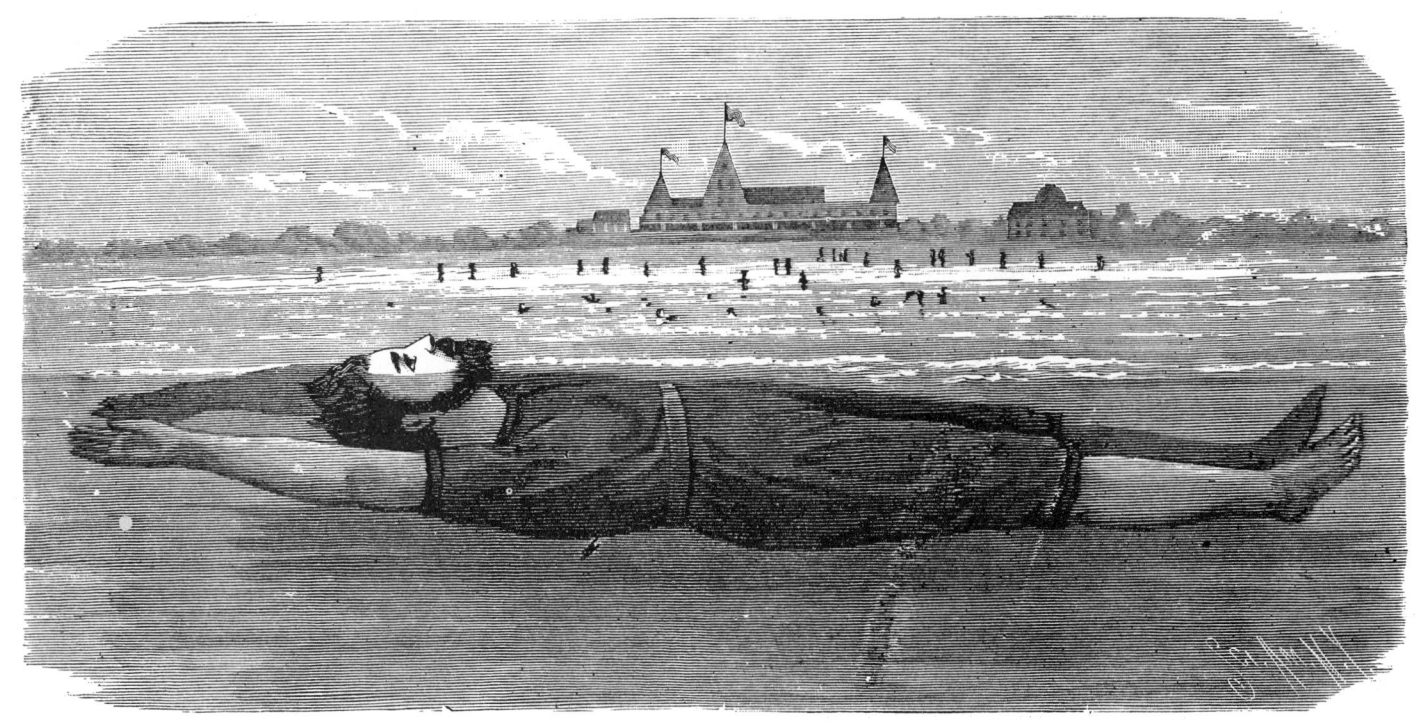

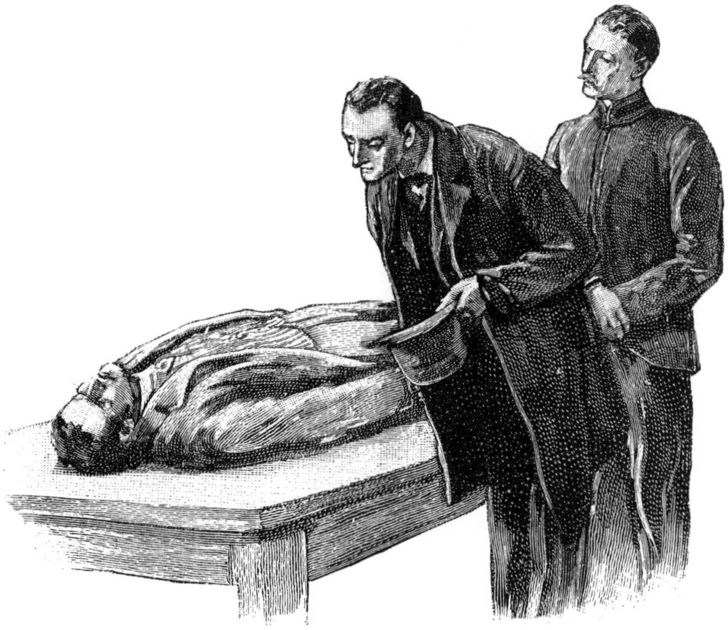

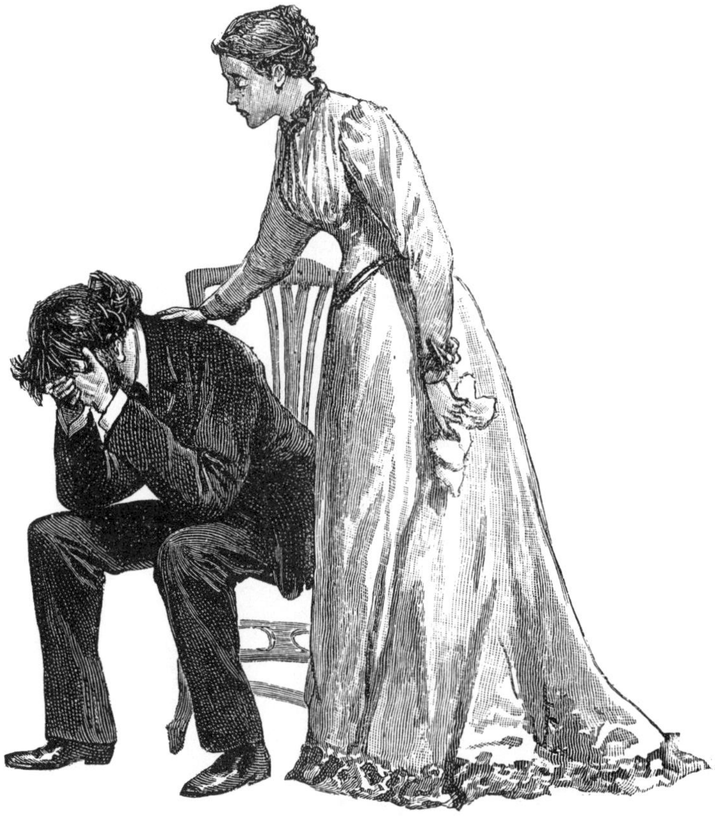

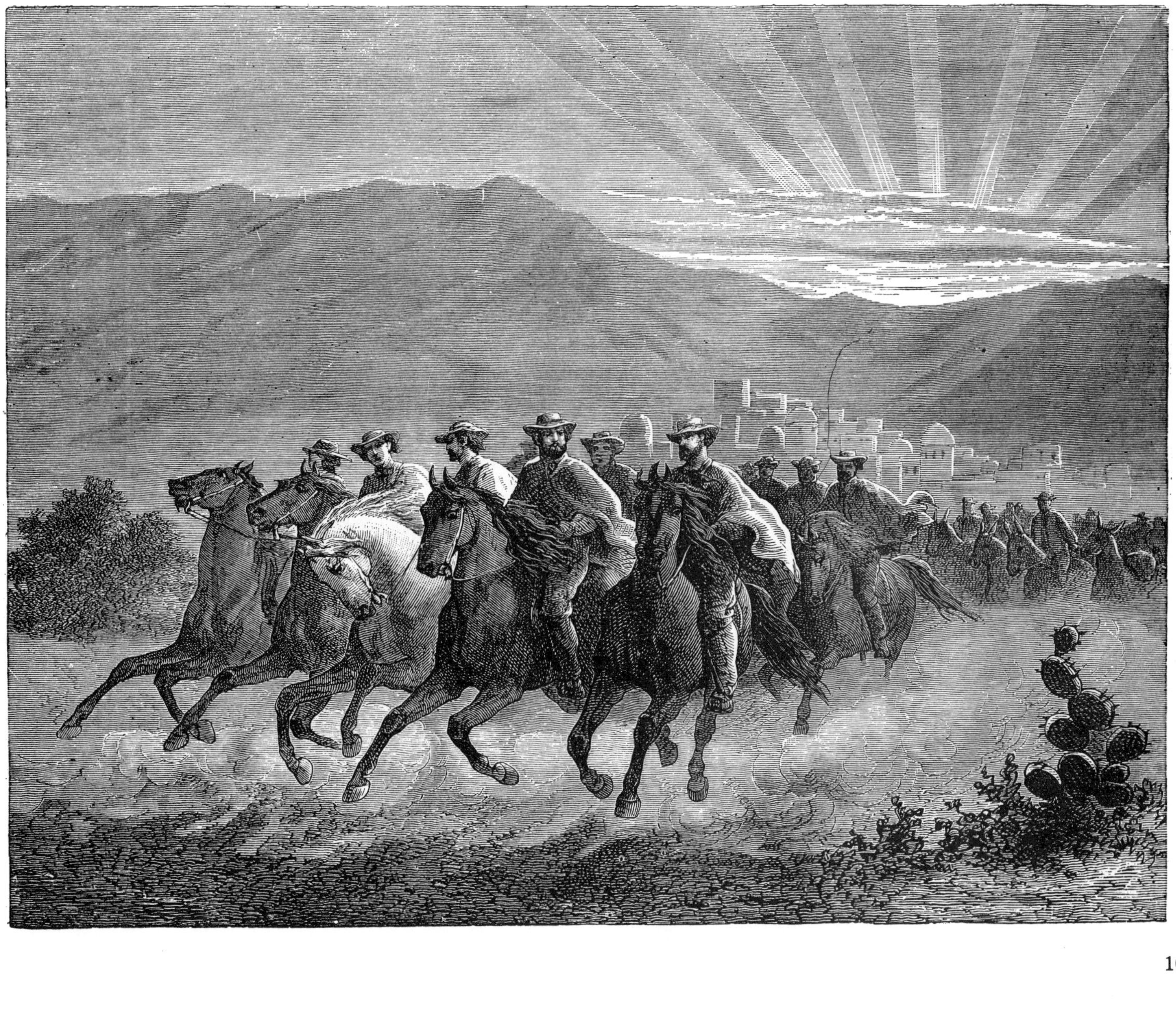

105

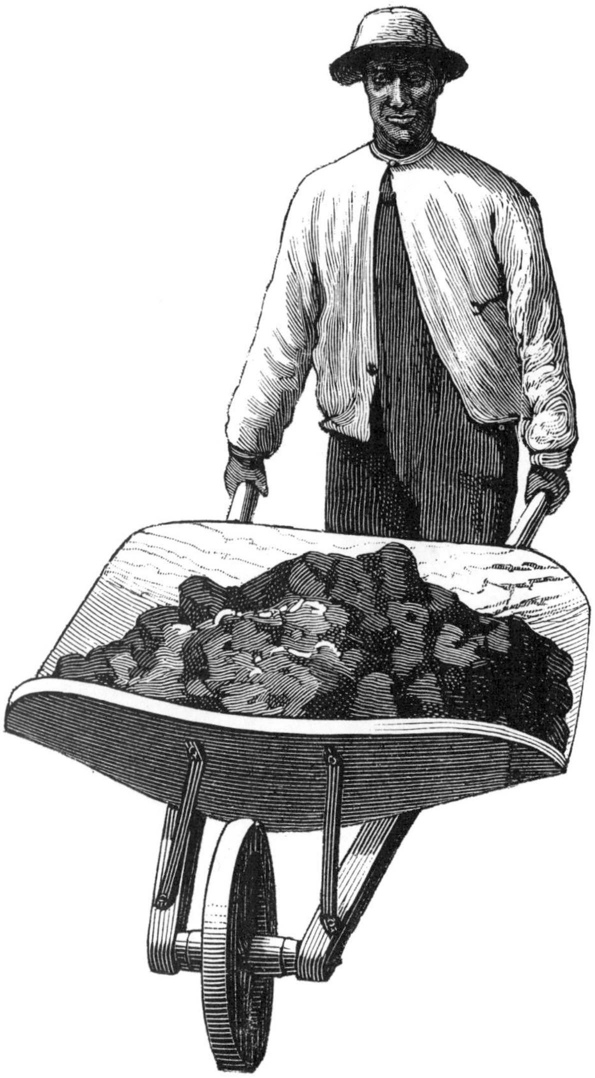

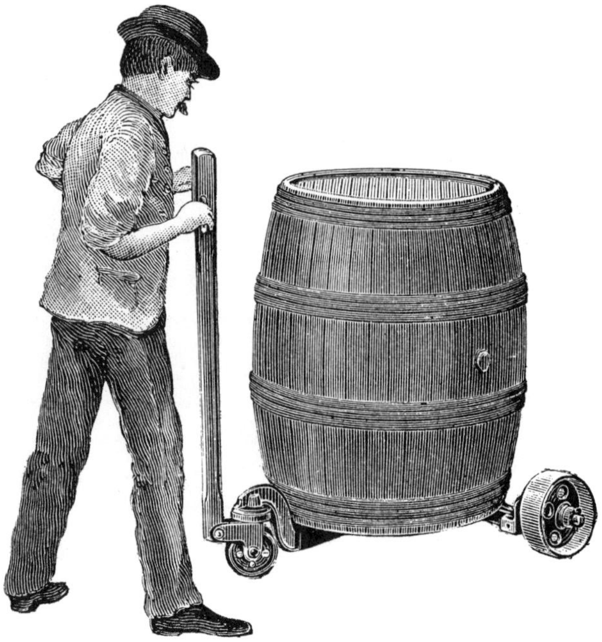

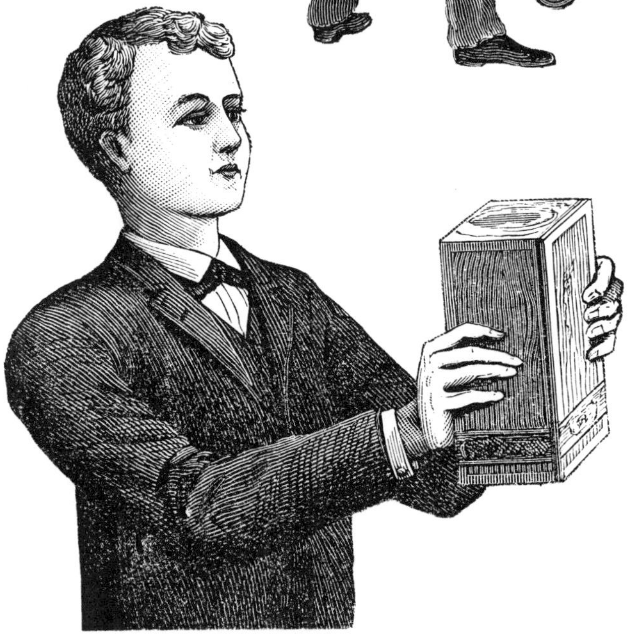

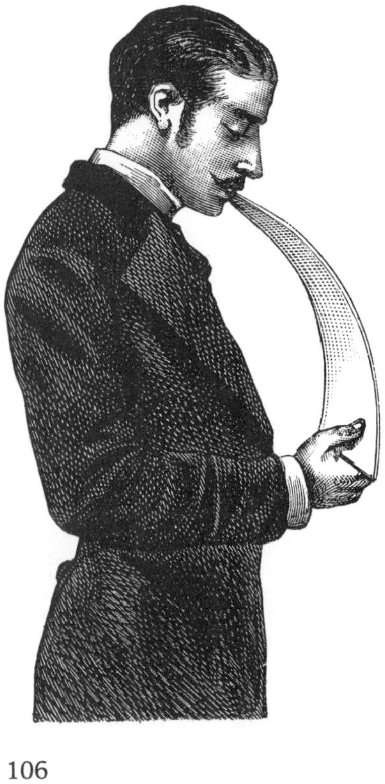

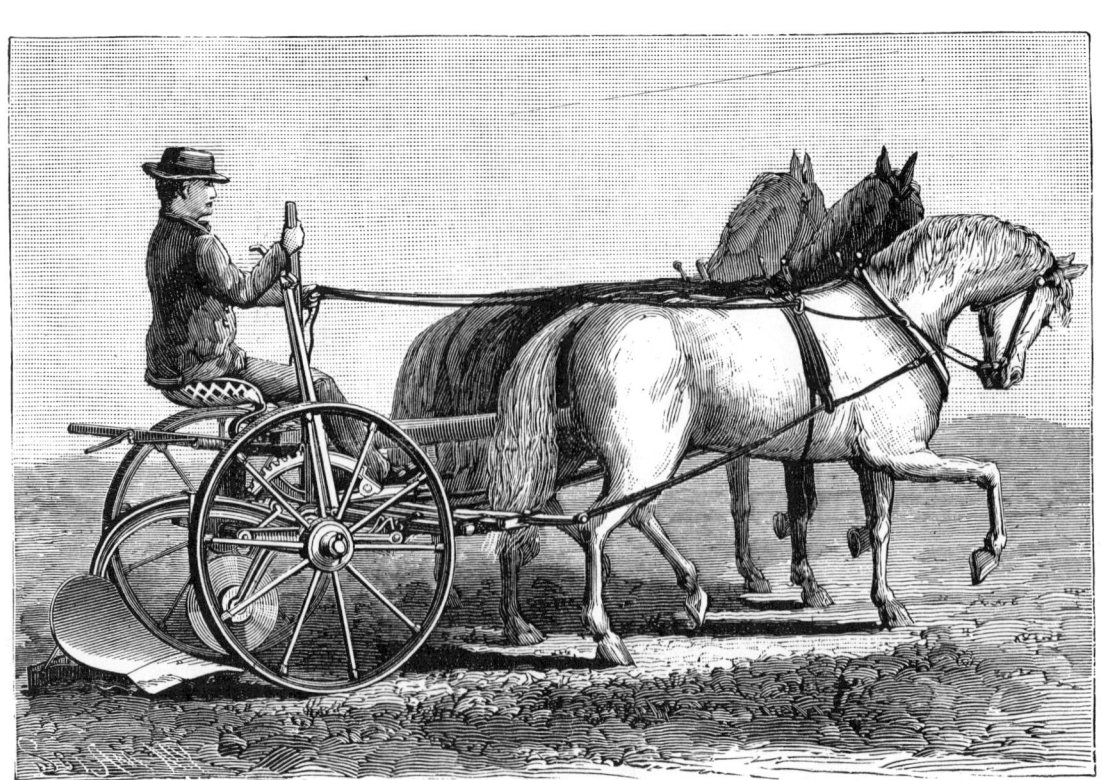

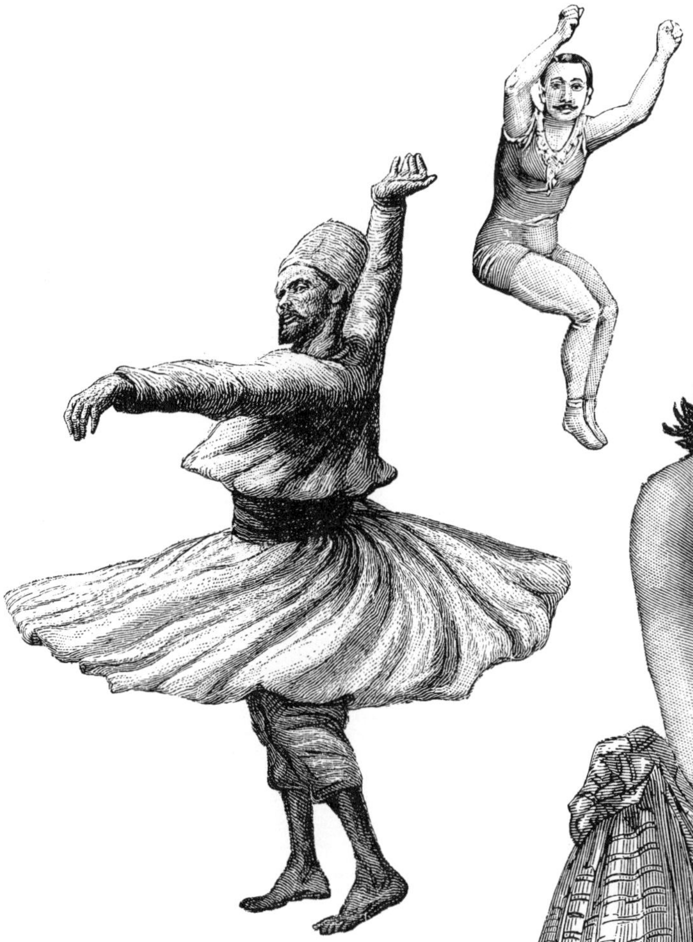

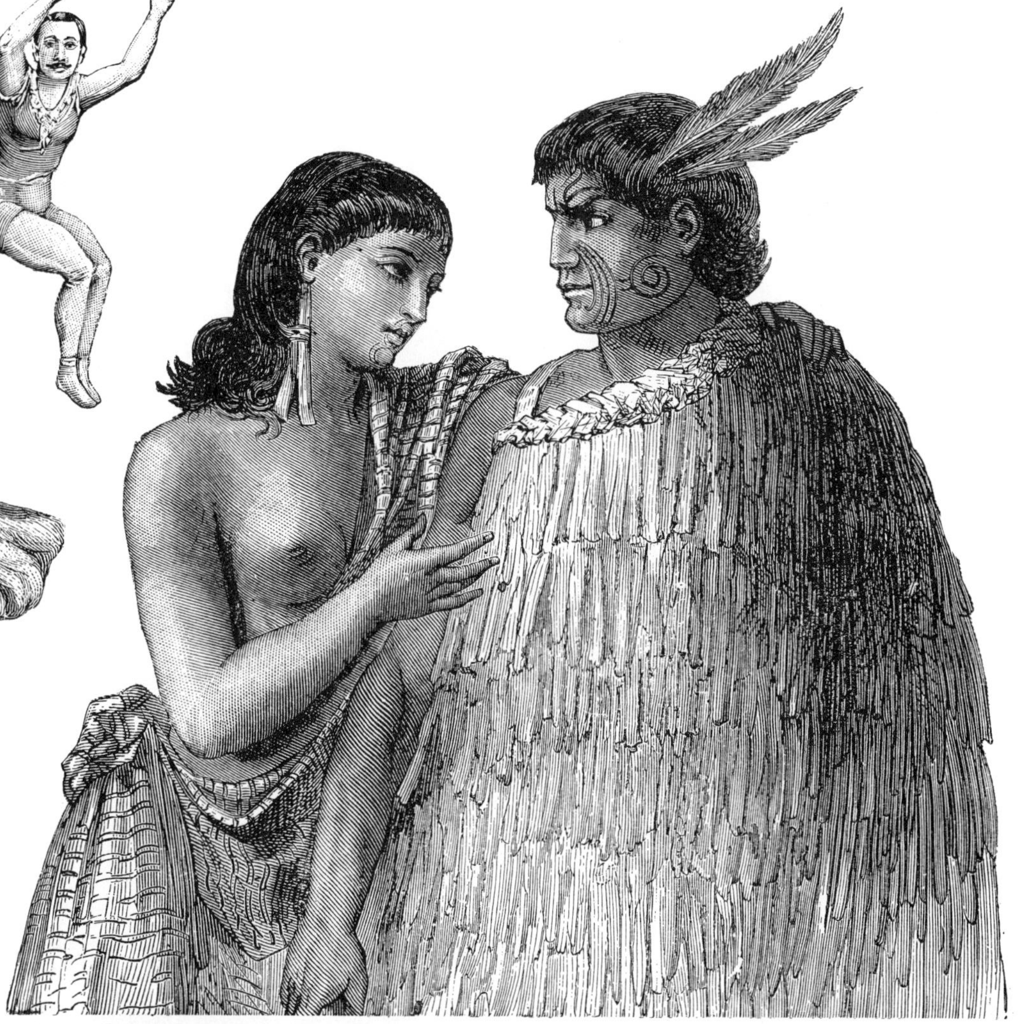

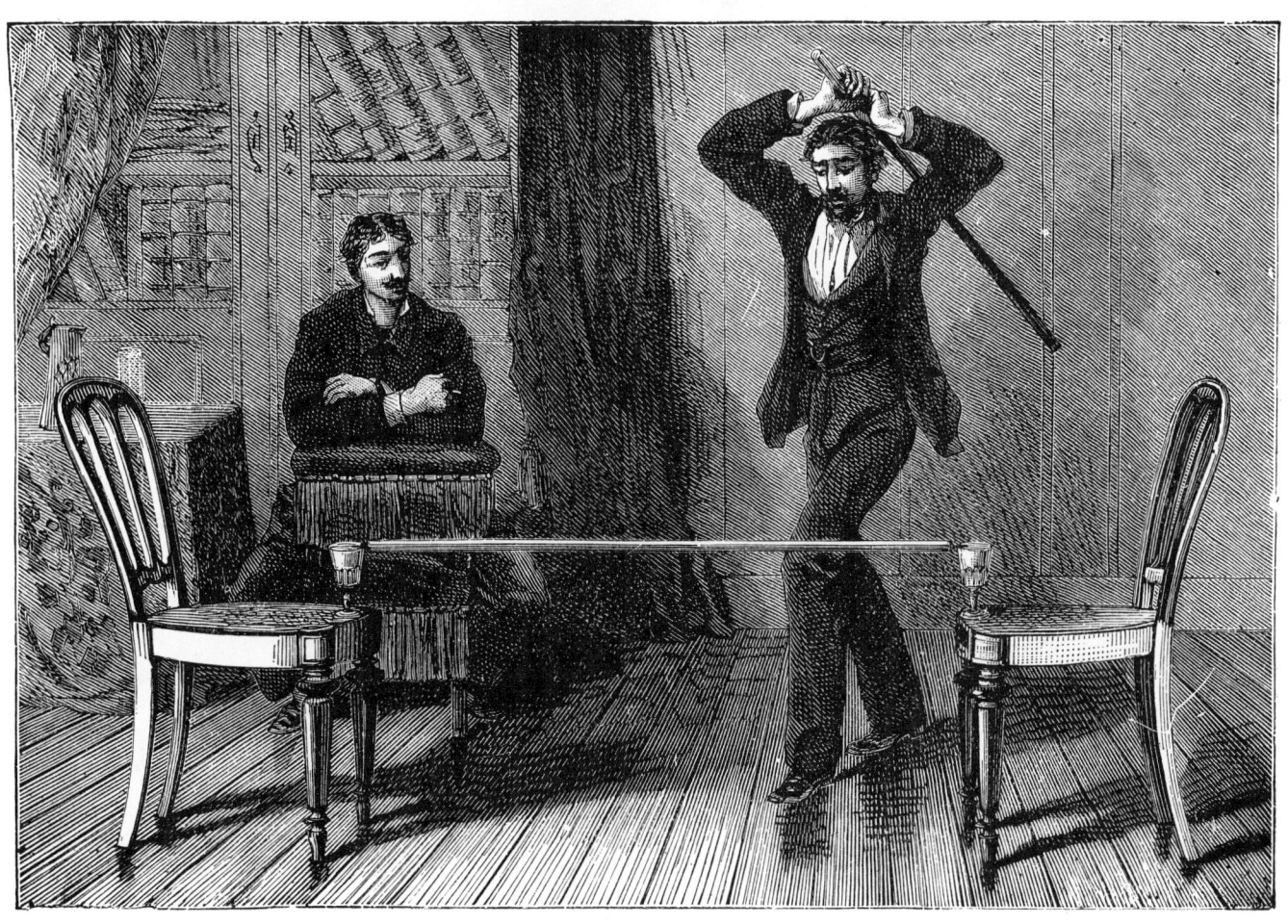

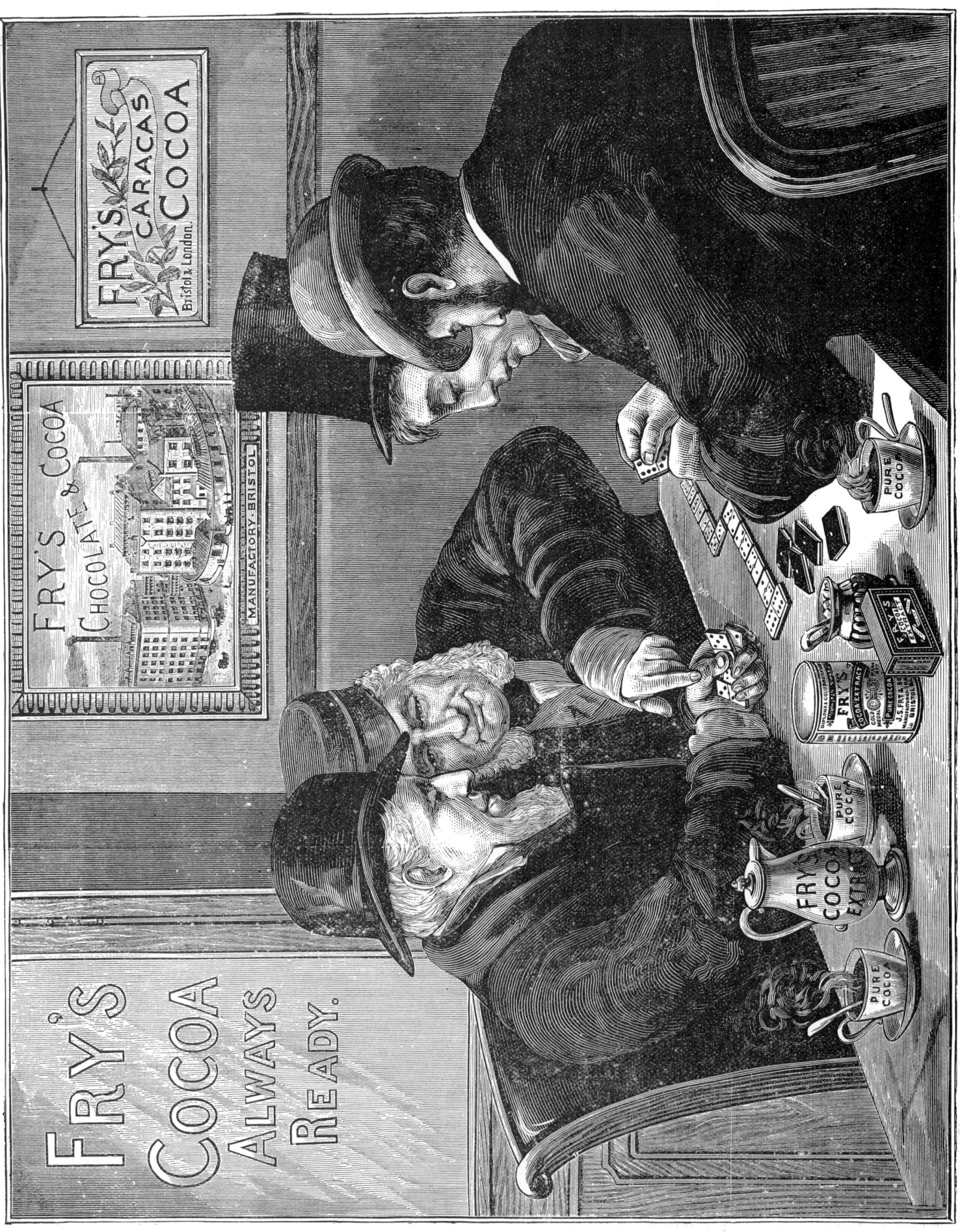

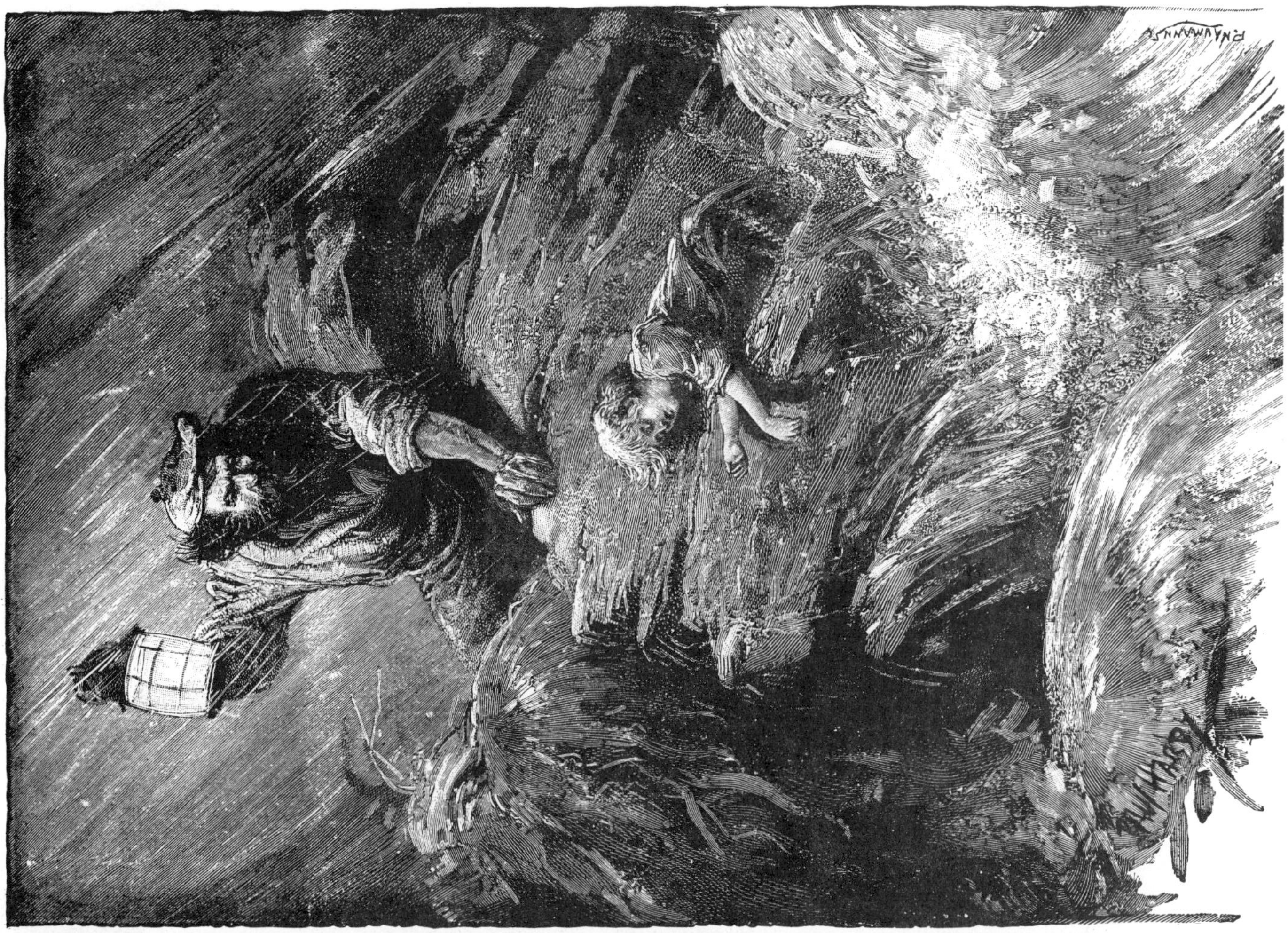

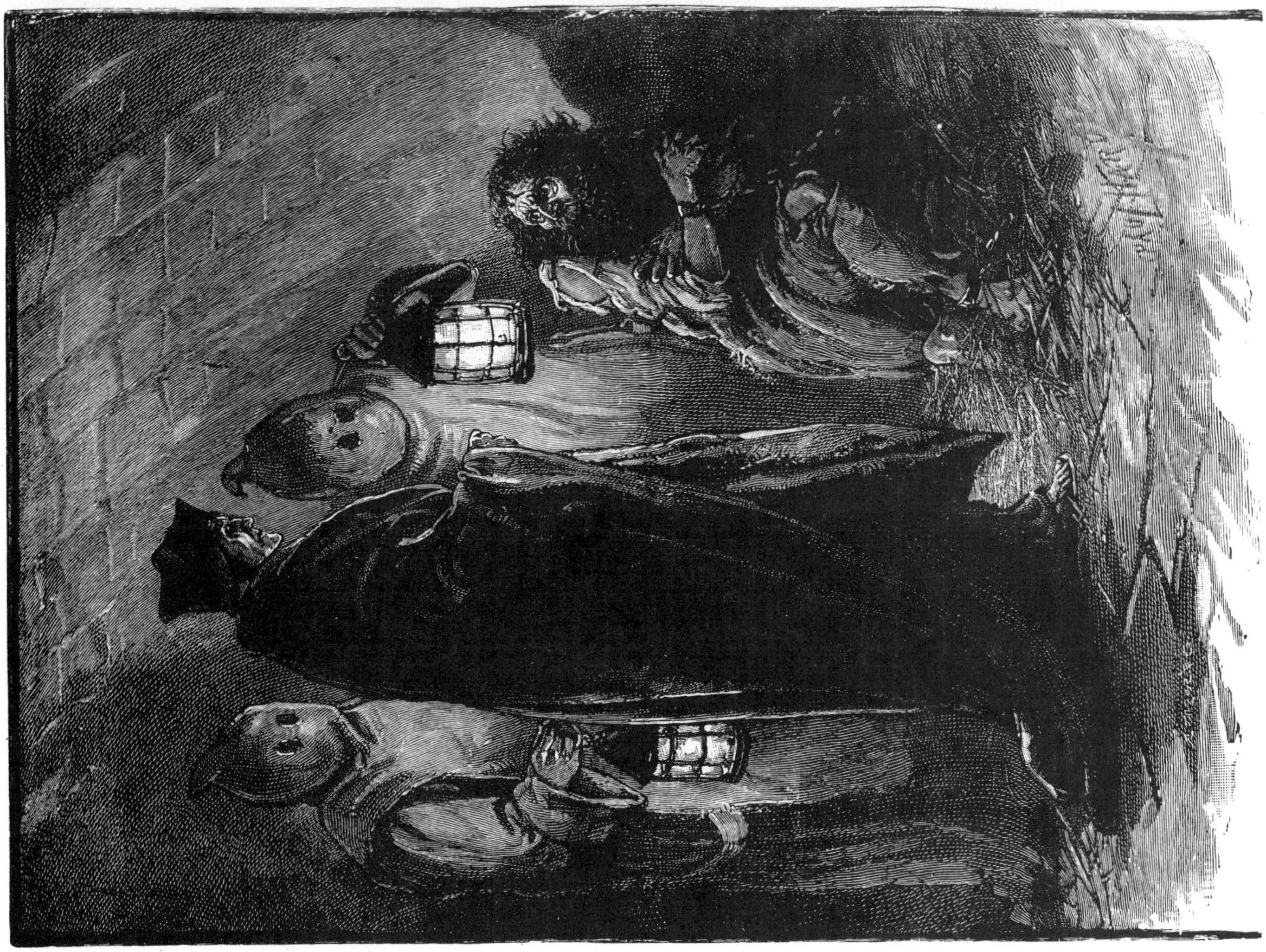

109

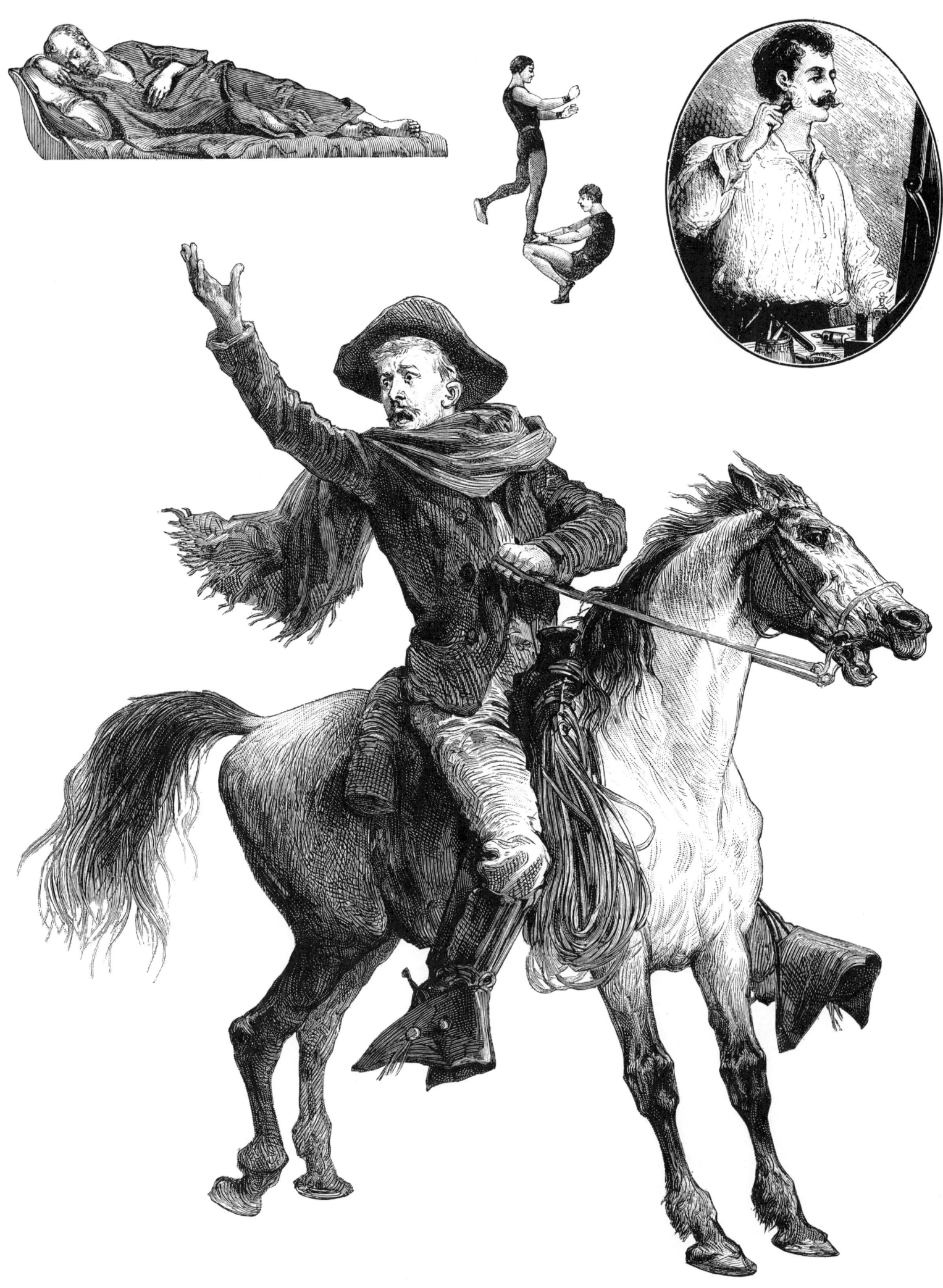

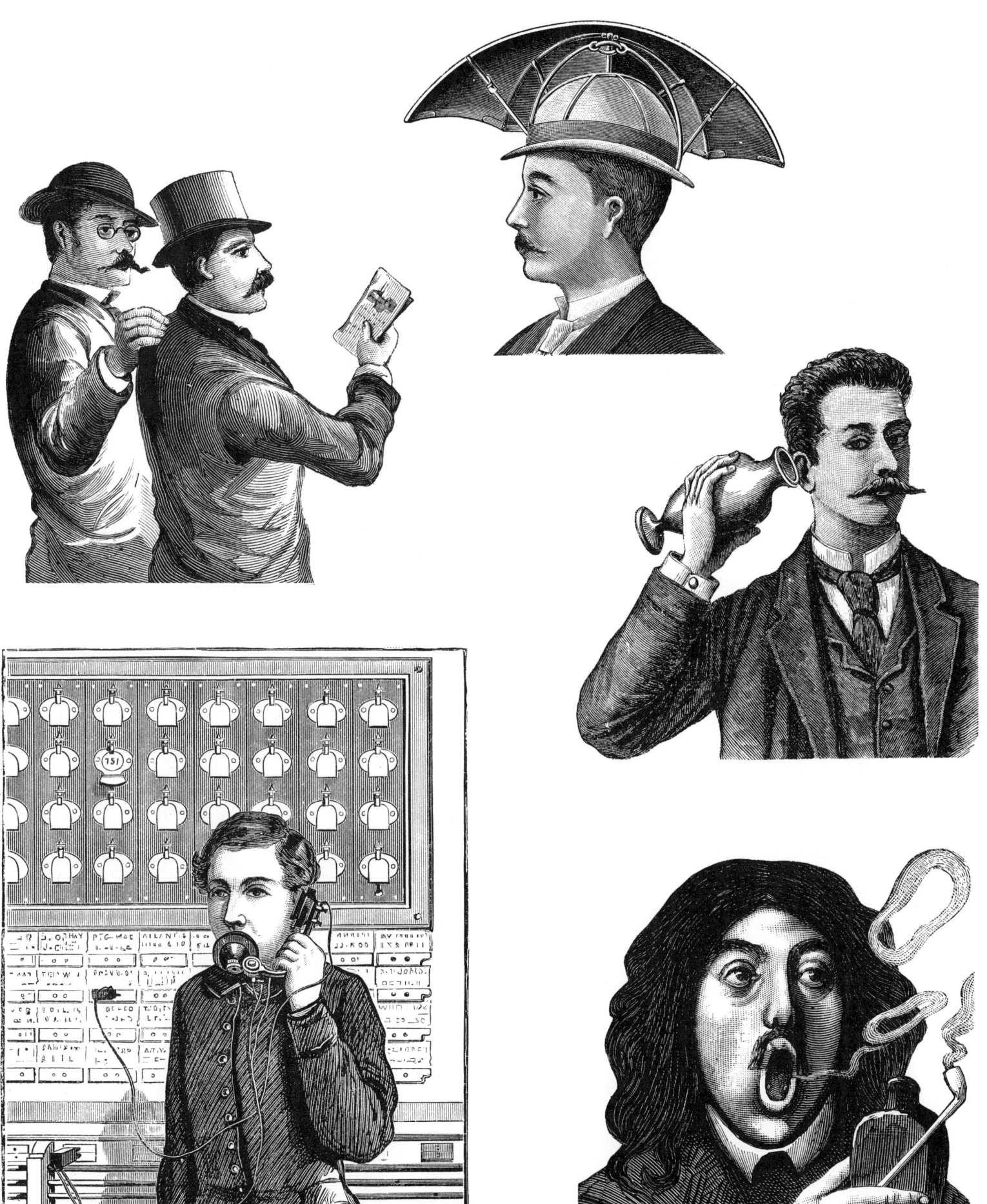

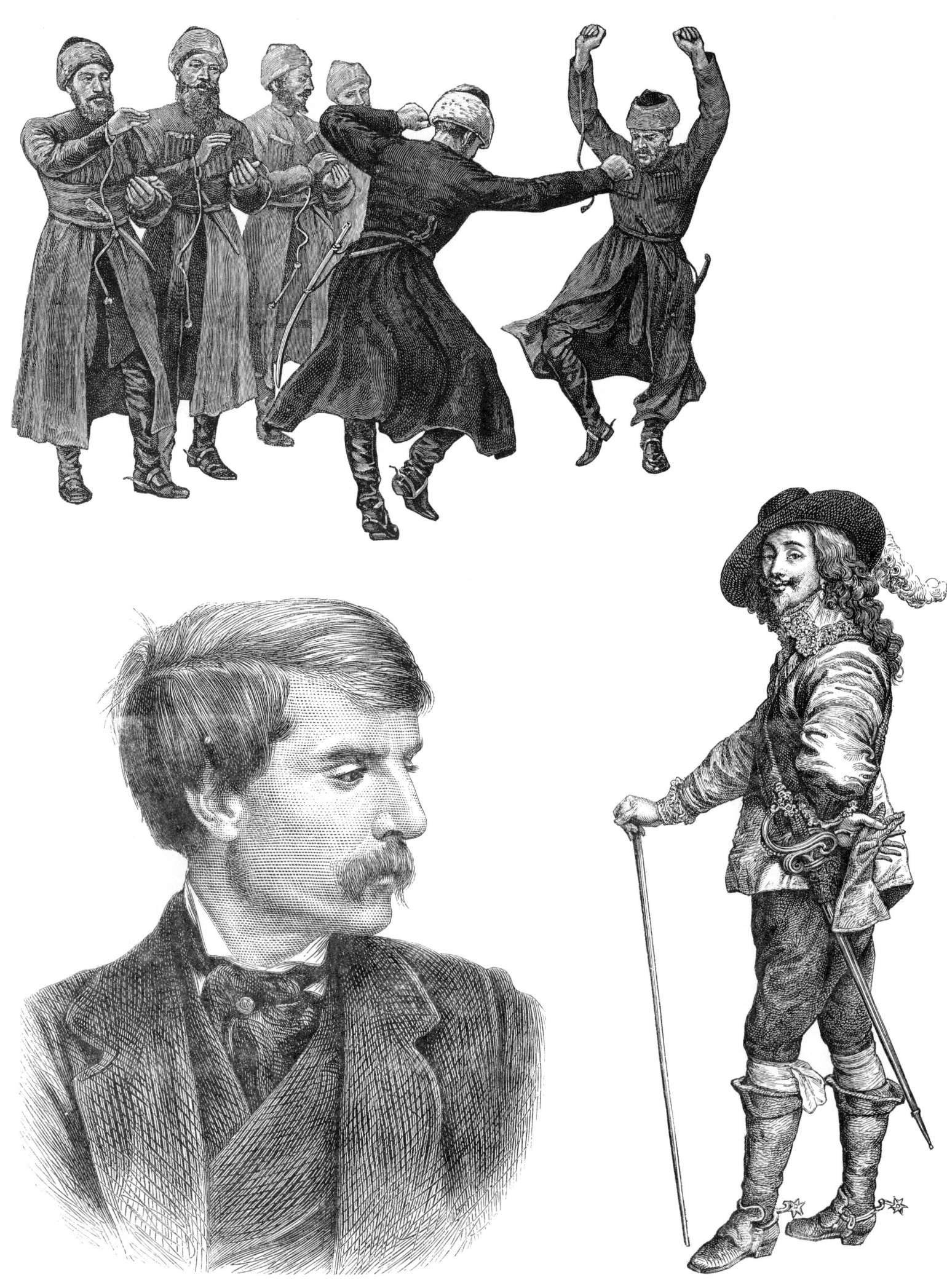

112

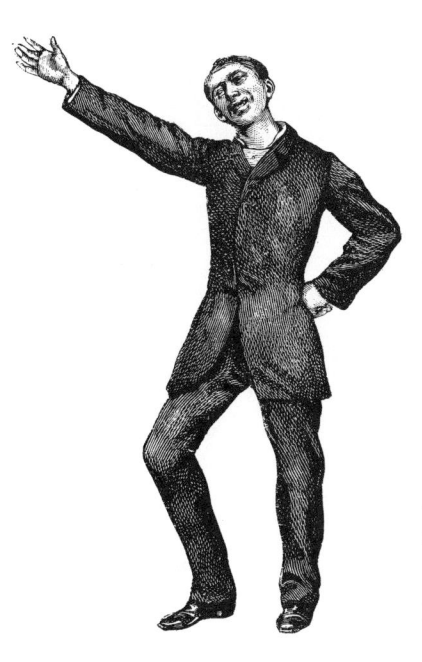
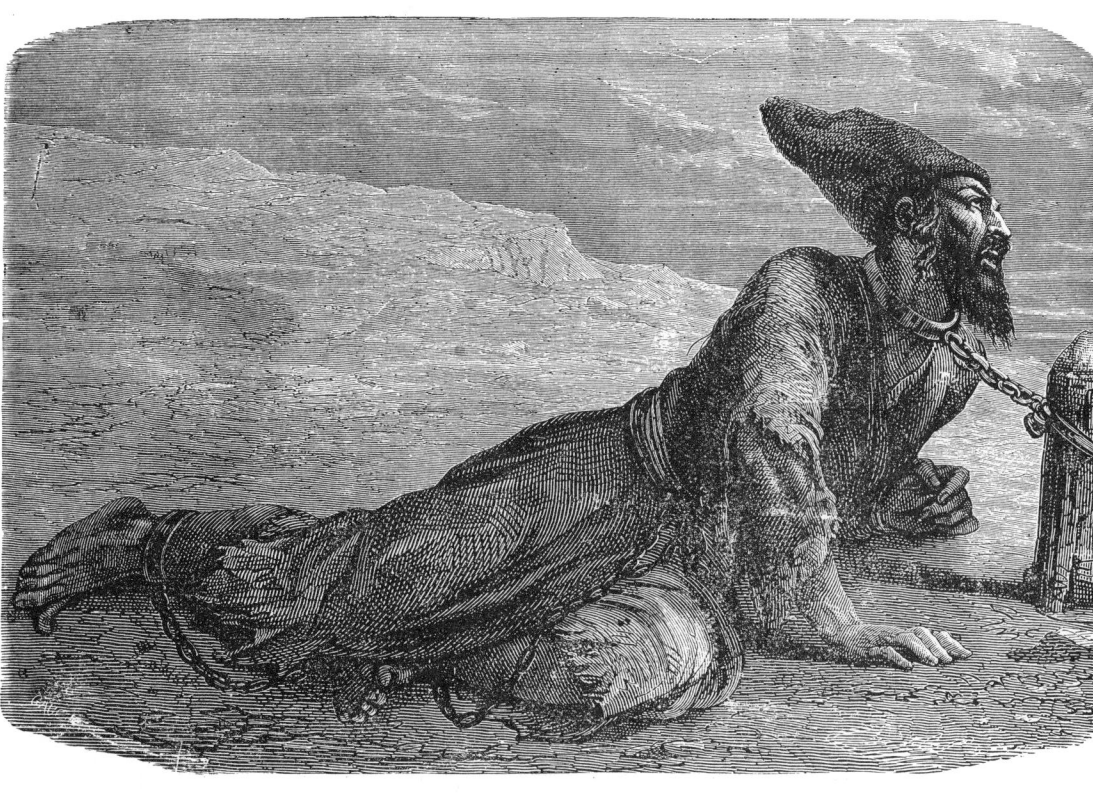
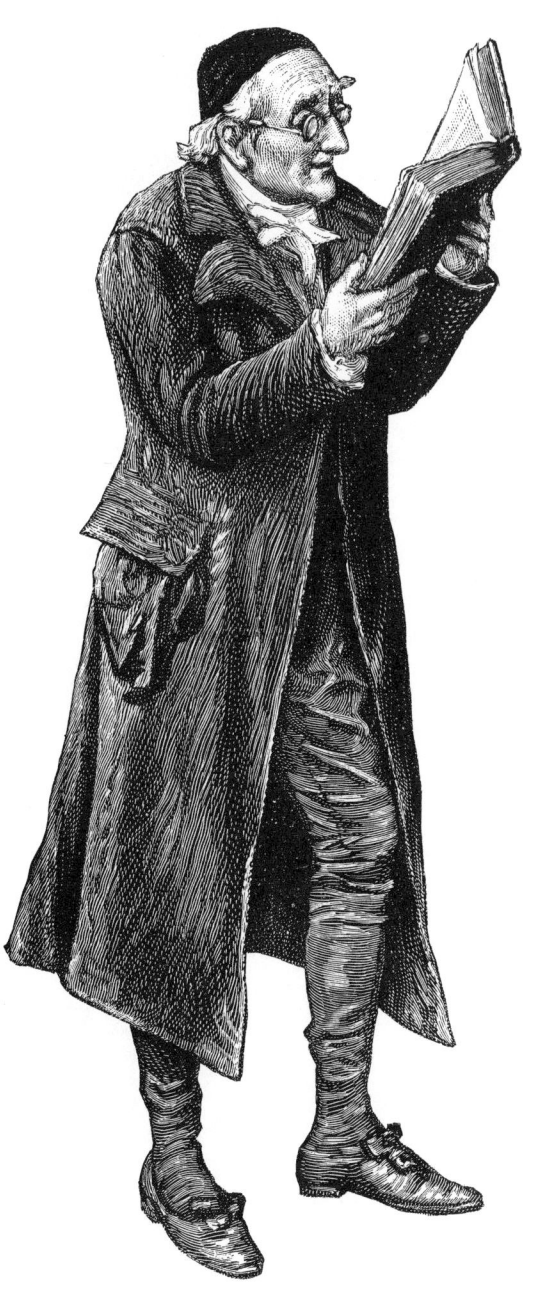
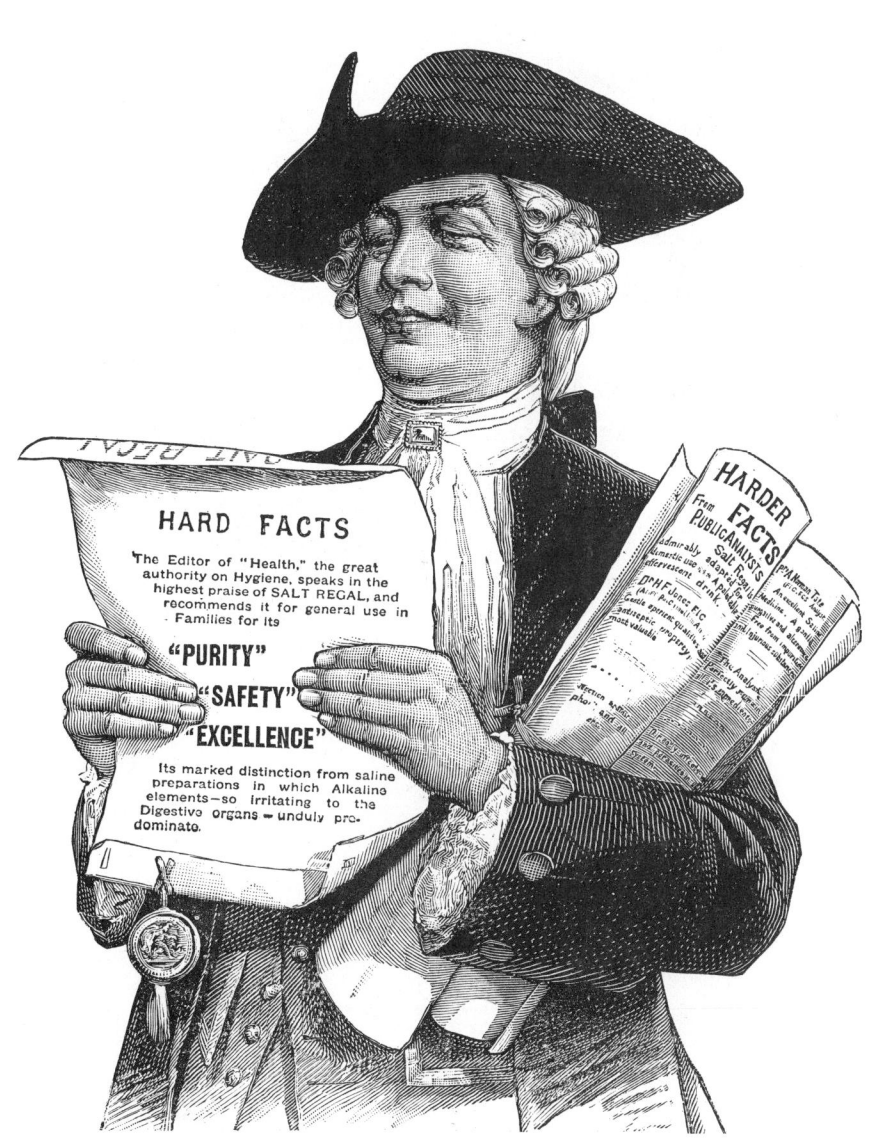

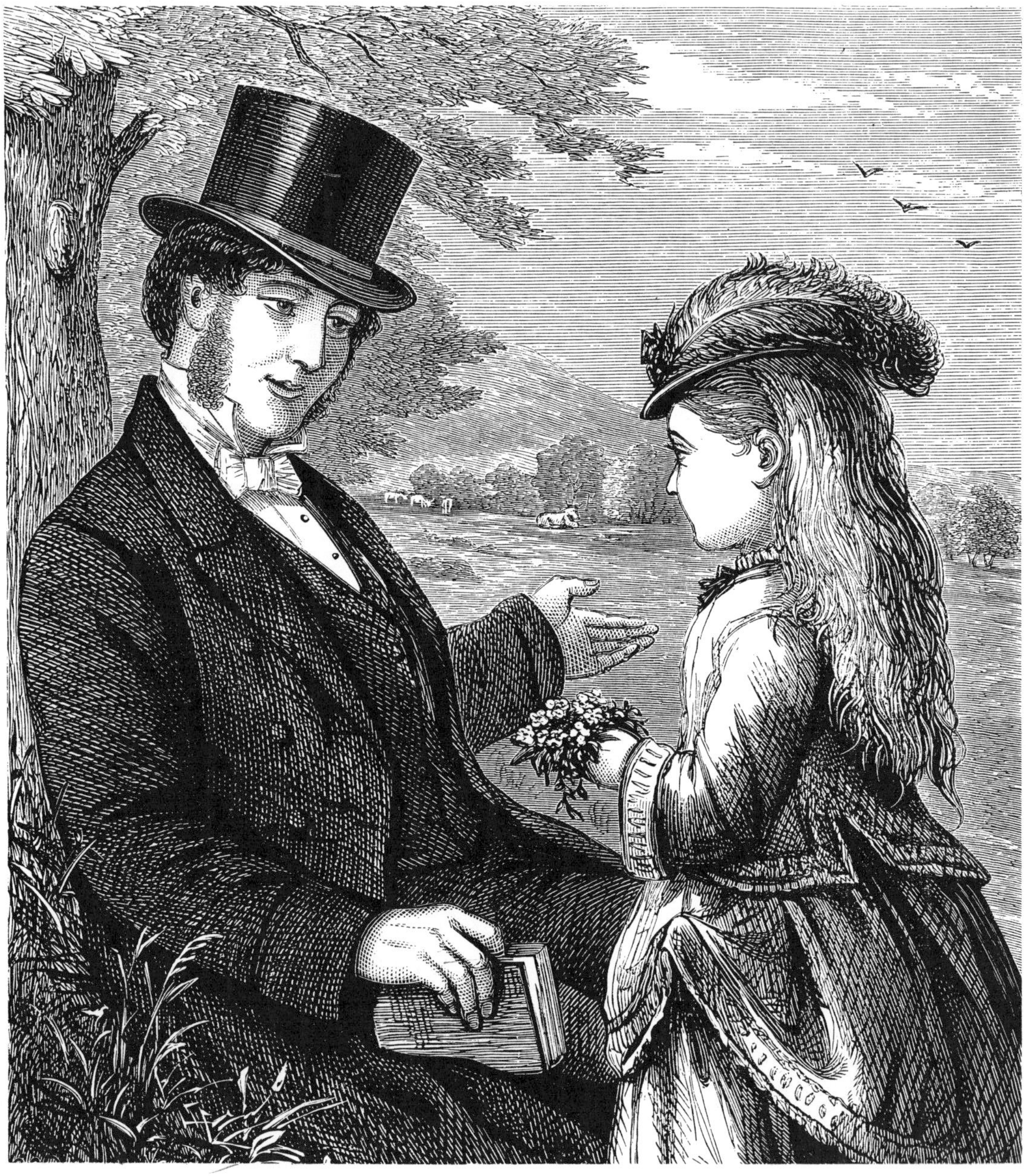

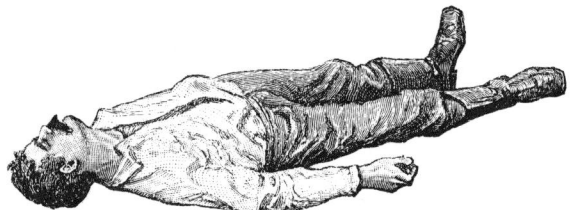
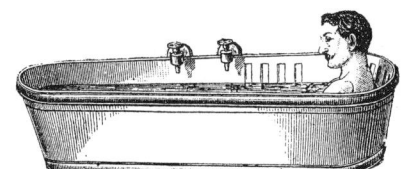
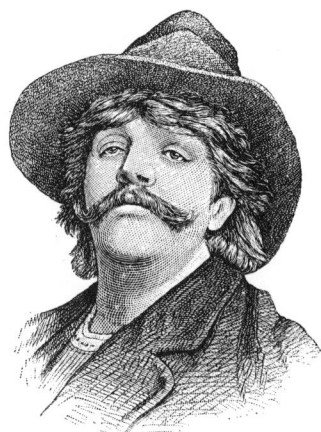
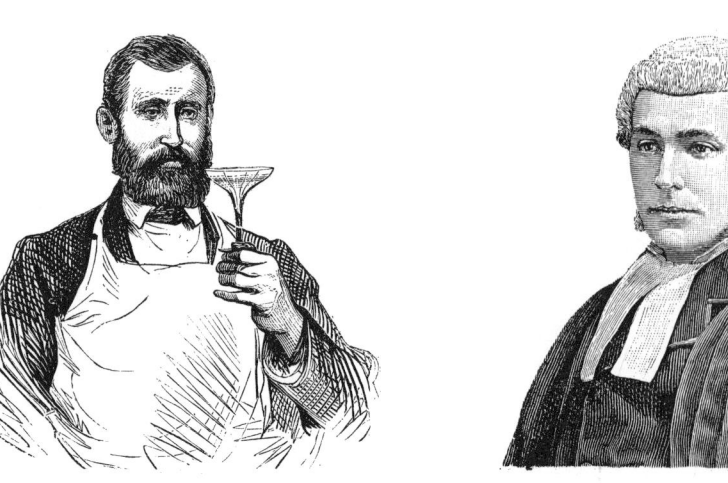
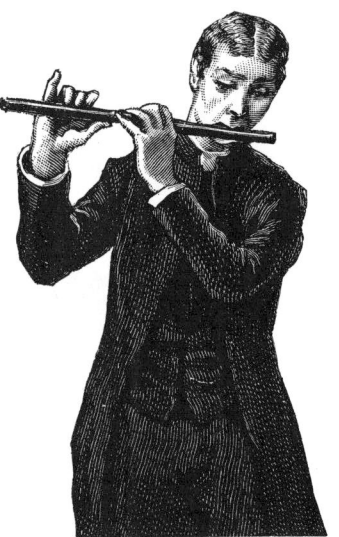
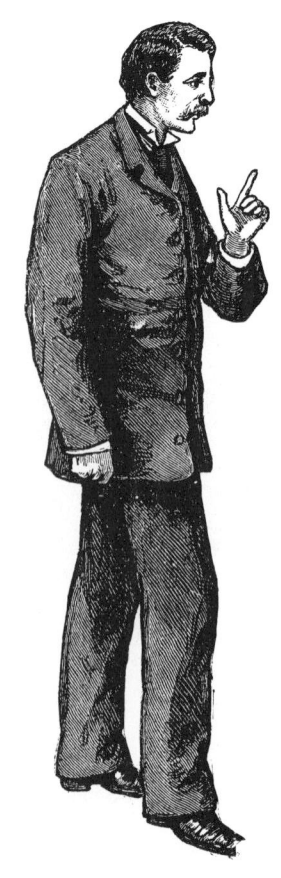

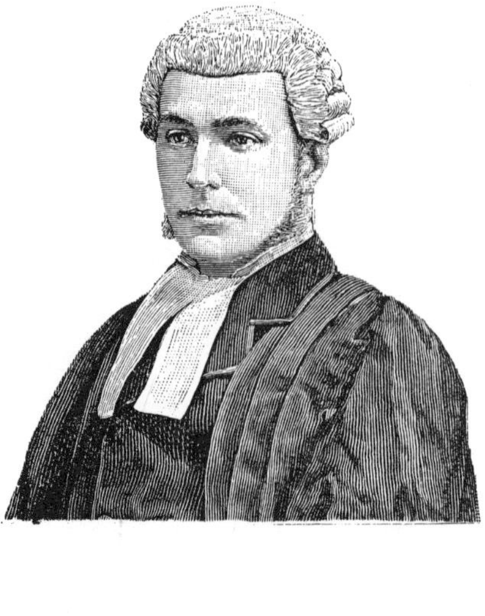

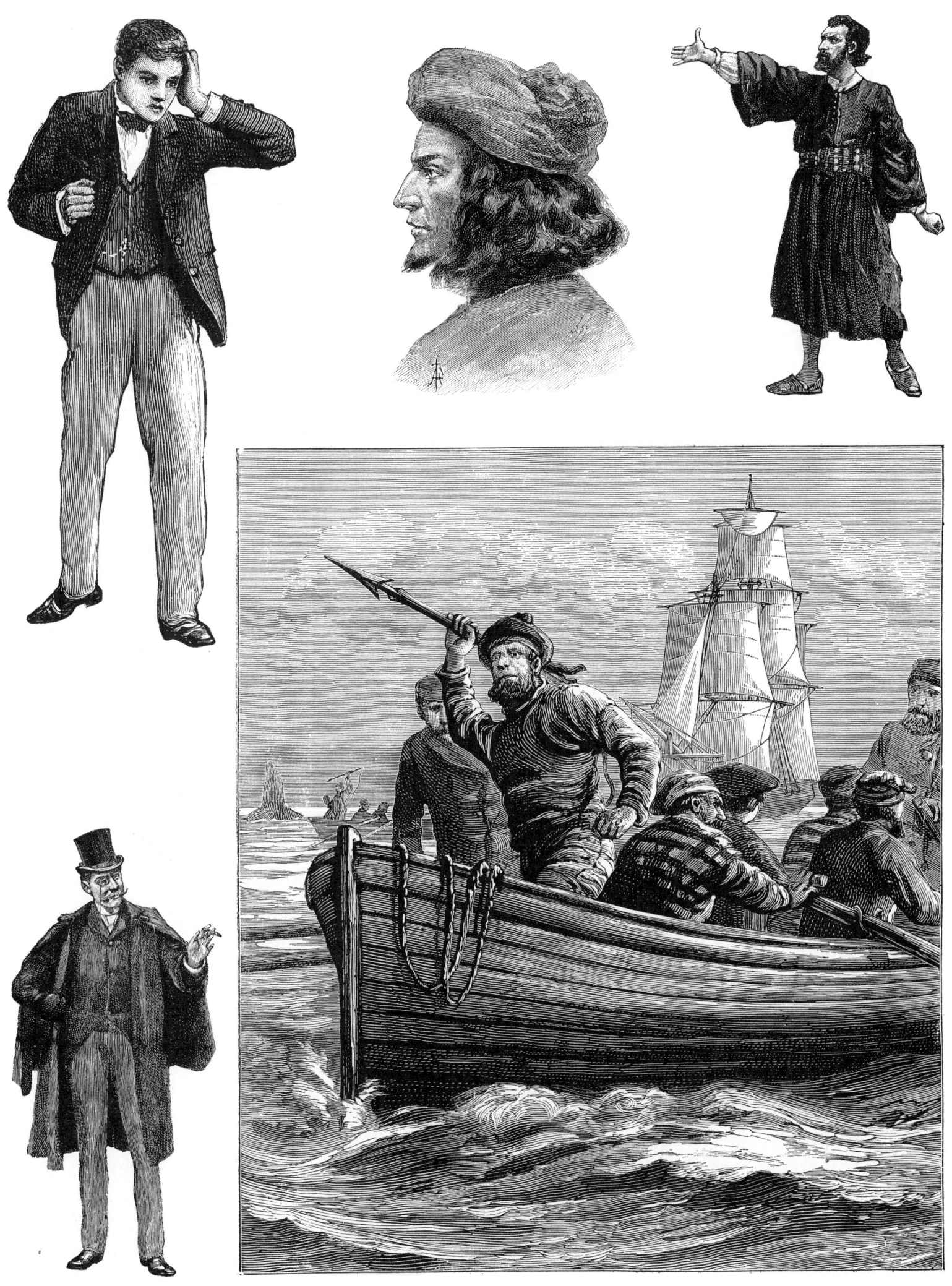

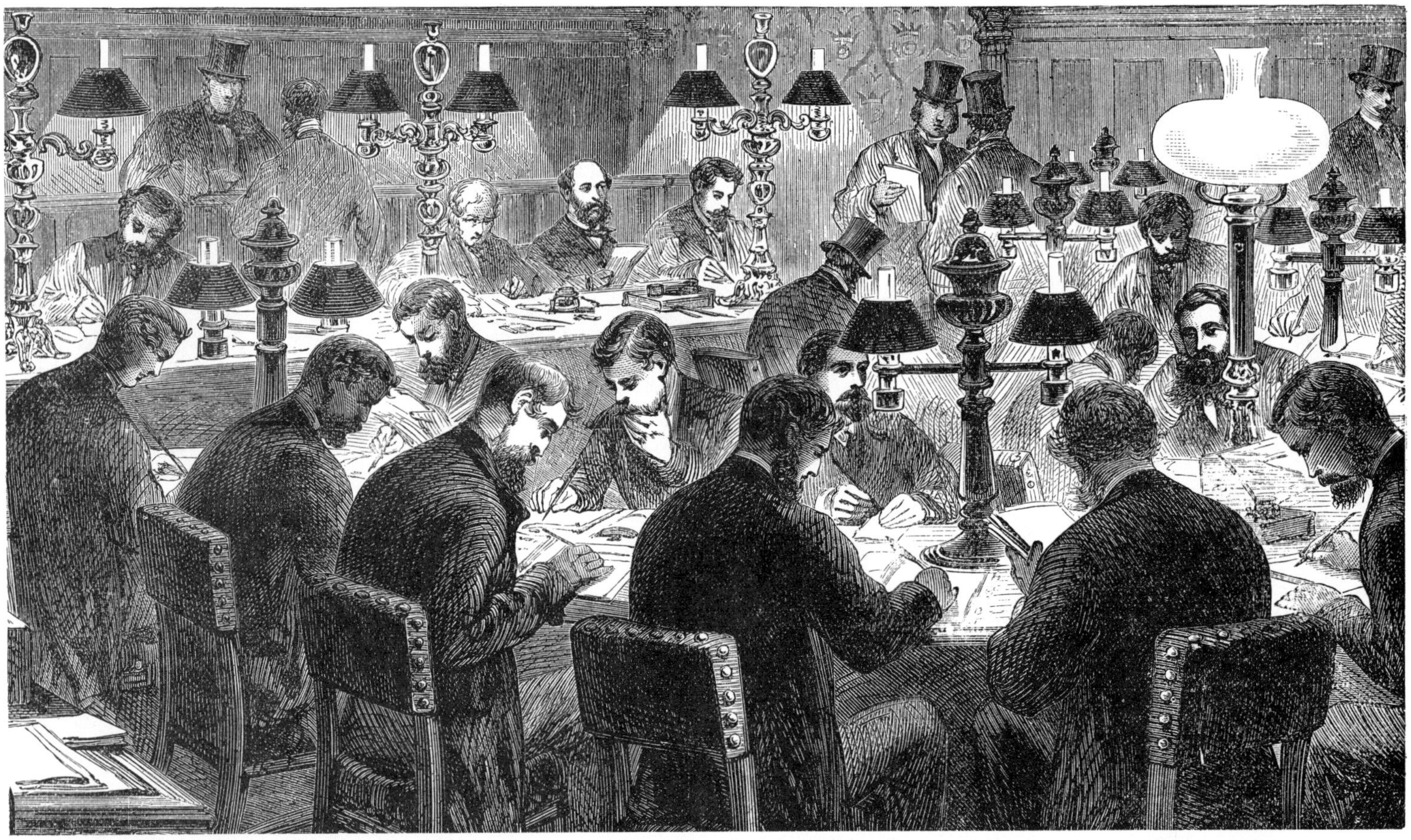

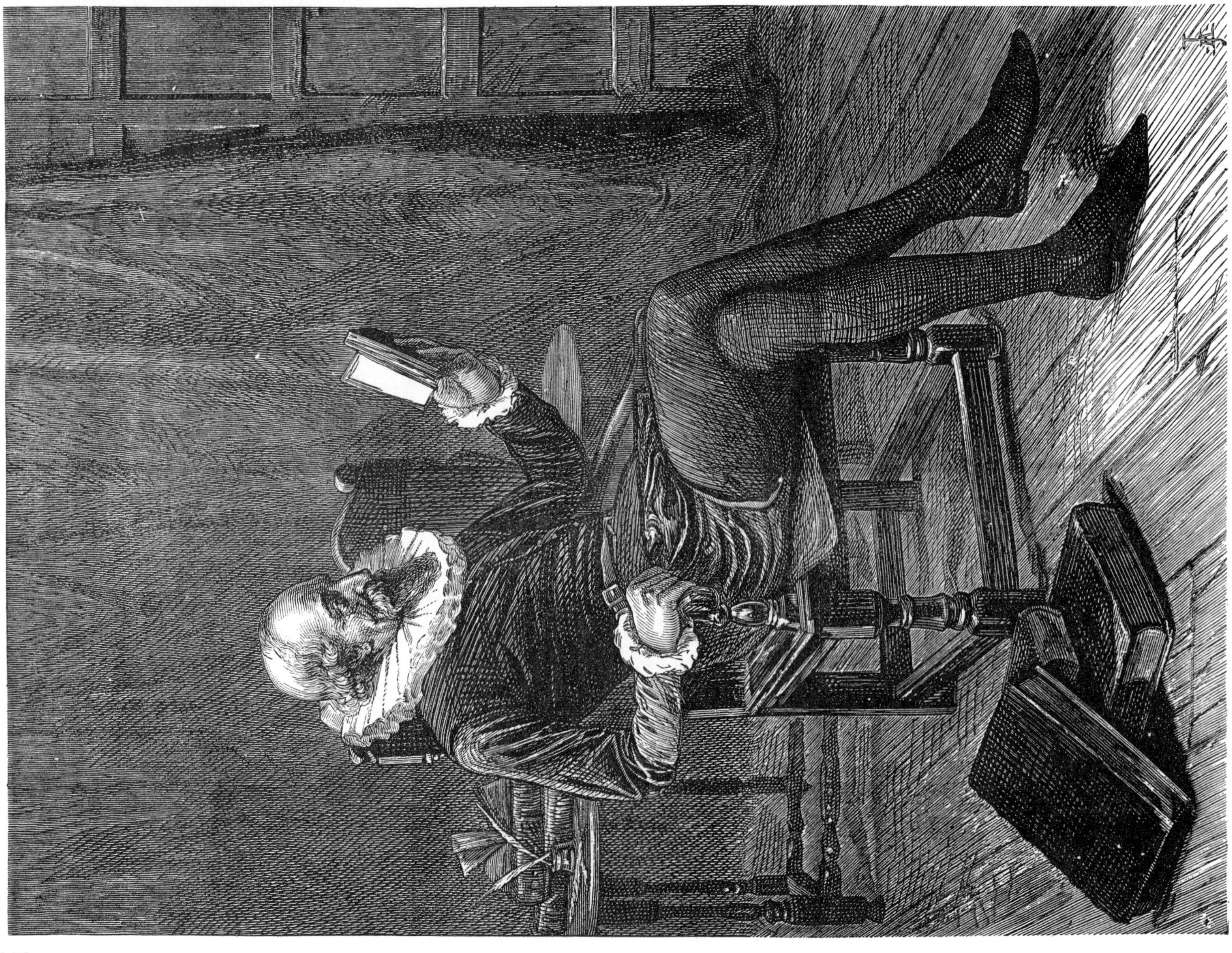

116

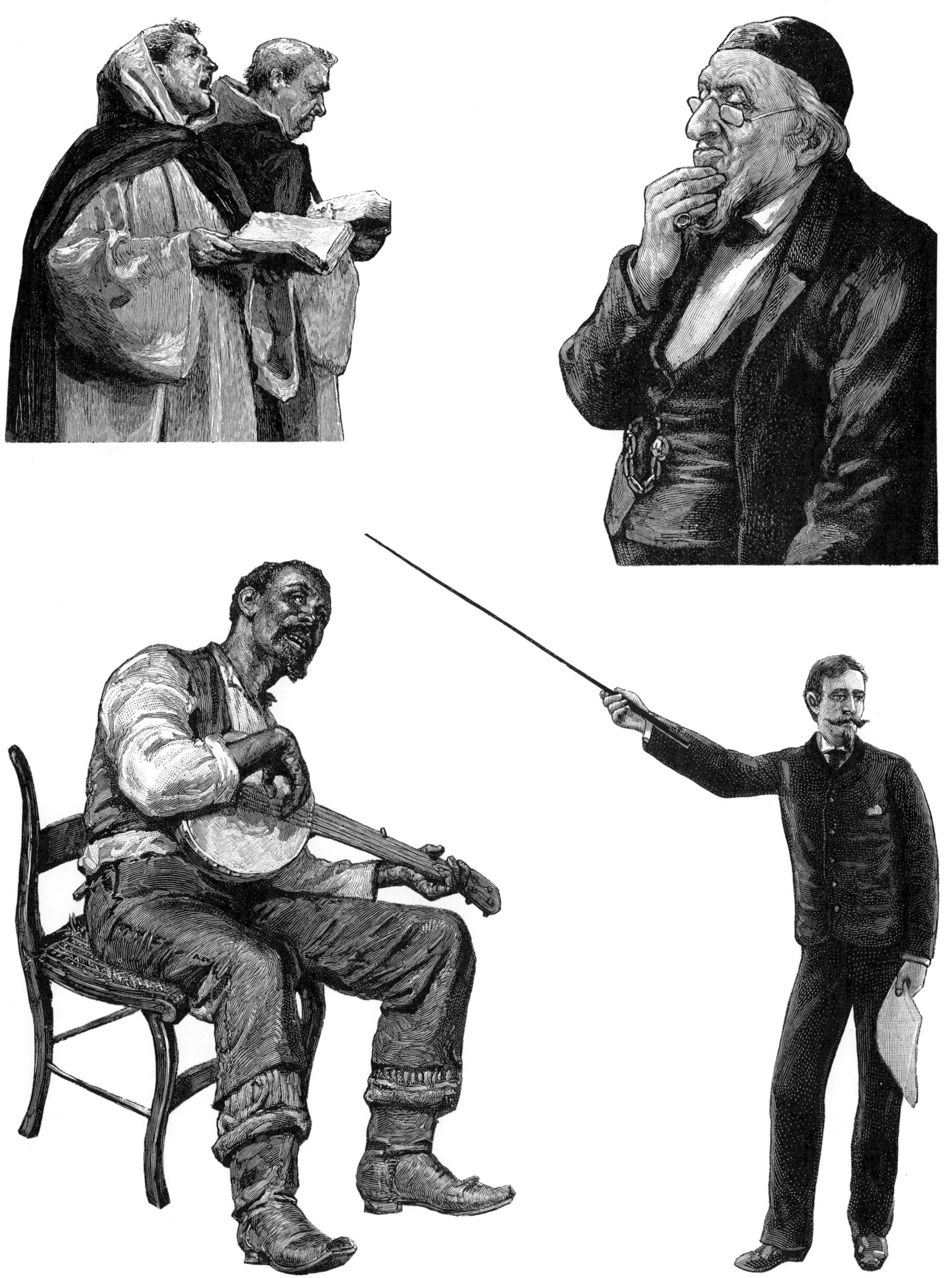

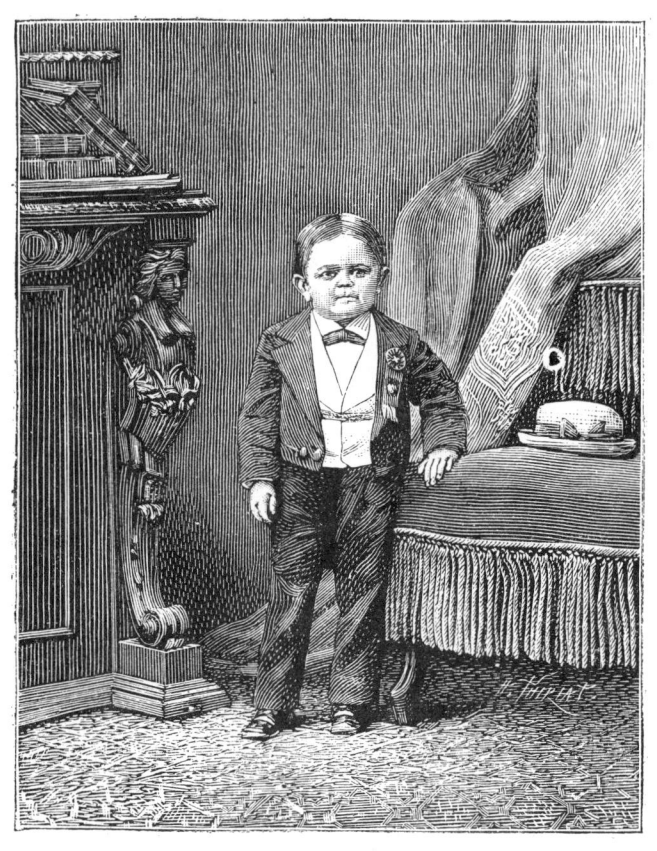
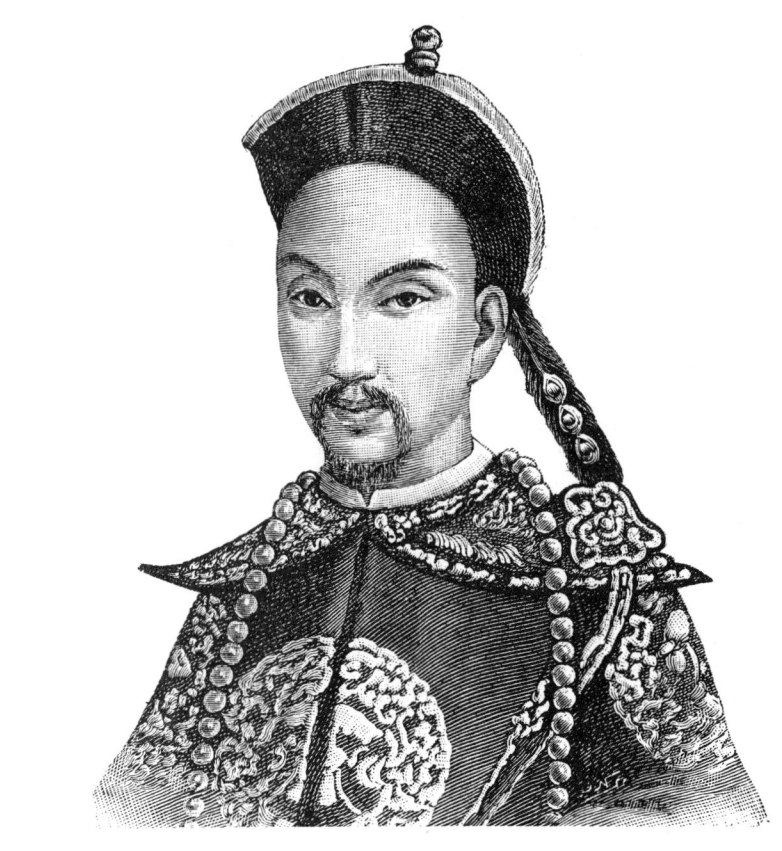
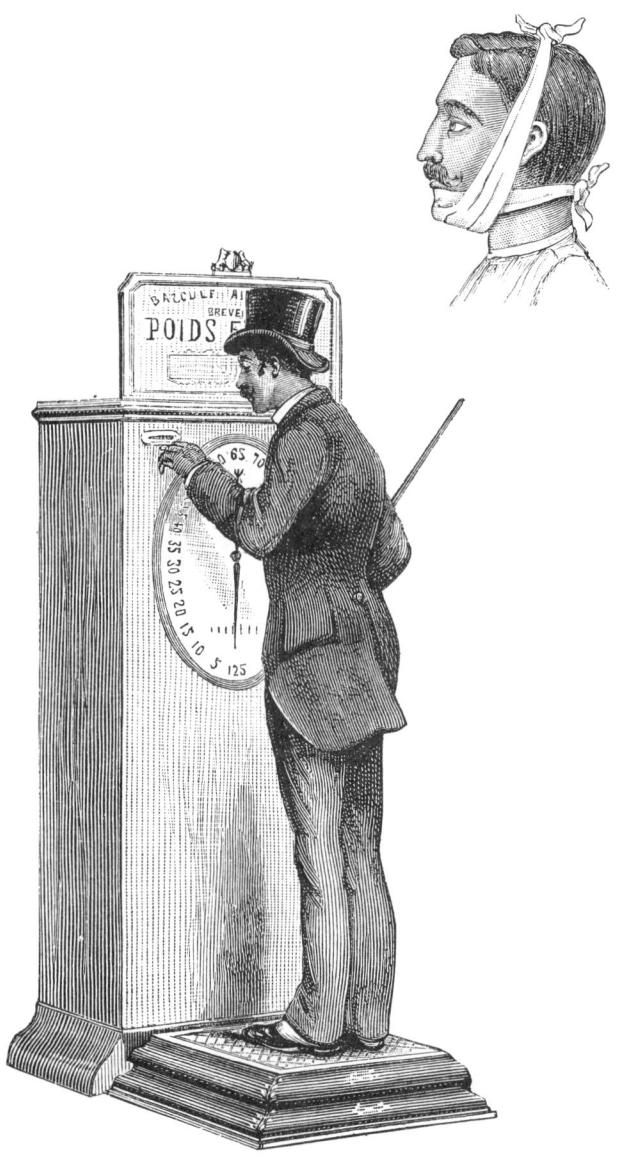
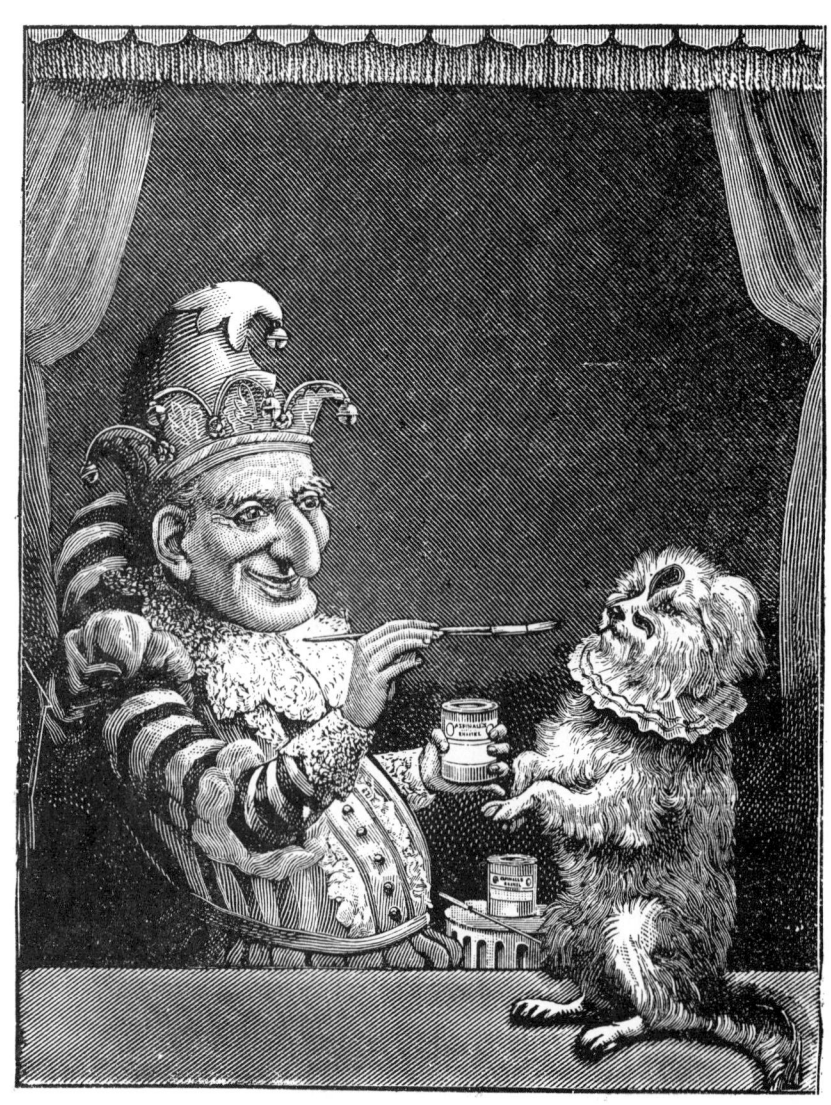

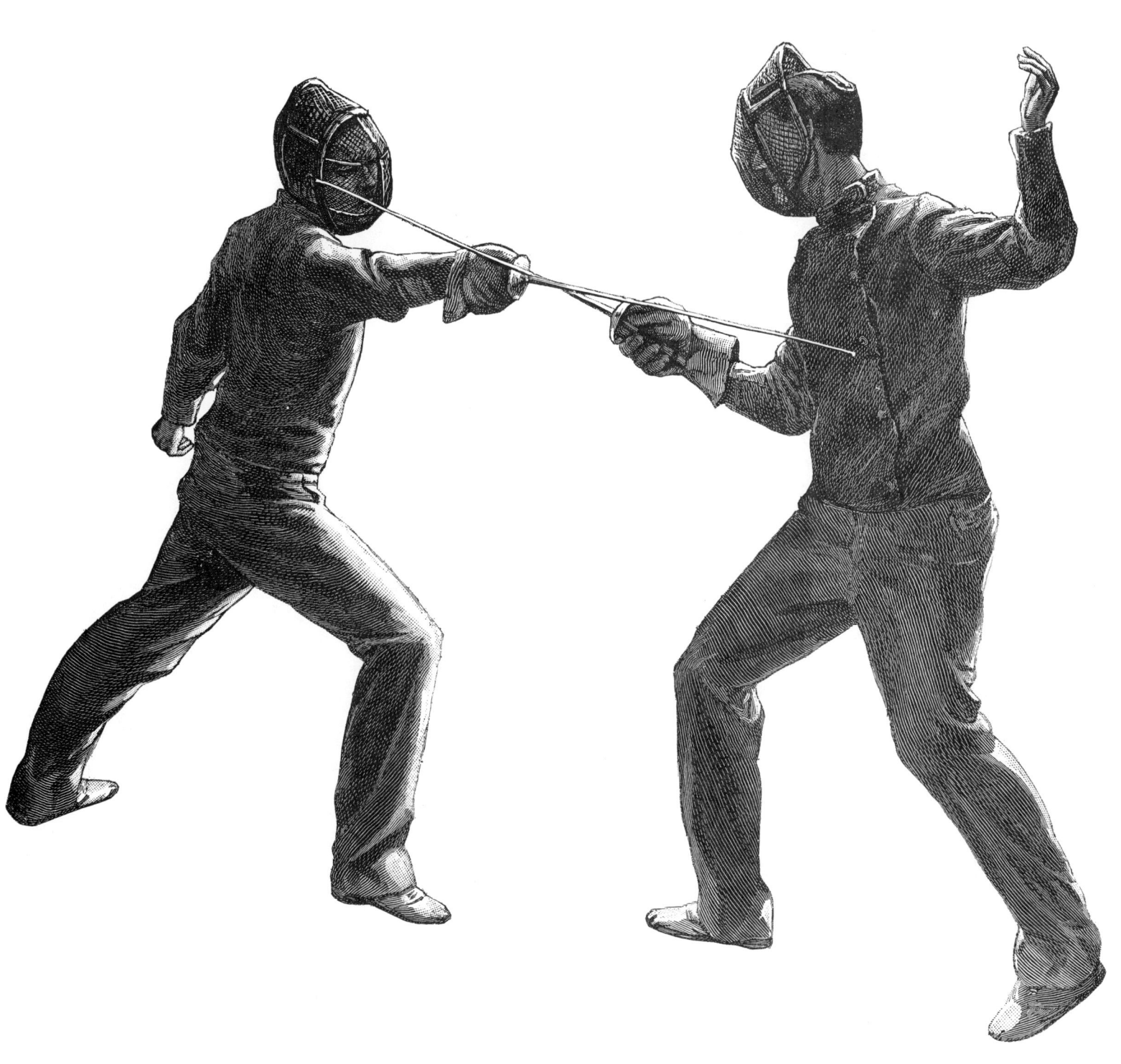